MICHIGAN
Every Day

Patrick Sullivan
Carole Eberly

Cover design by Dawn Paine

To Jessica & Charles

Acknowledgements

Where do we begin? So many people, so few pages.

Thank you to the staff at the Osterlin Library at Northwestern Michigan College, who were eager to lend a hand. All of the folks at the Clarke Historical Library (*CHL*), especially Frank Boles, director, and Samantha, were so helpful as we culled through Clarke's photos and generally cluttered up the place. Thanks to Jerry Morton for his articles, *Muskegon 216, Hastings 0* and *Hudson Hopes to Host Pandas*. Helen Niemiec did a wonderful job with editing. Super-reader, crossword puzzle fan Jessica Sullivan caught all the typos, style errors and convoluted sentences we missed. Our thanks also to Andrew Dost of Frankfort for his early work on the book, the State of Michigan Achives (*SMA*) for their photos and the enthusiastic people at Arcadia Historical Society for hunting up photos of and anecdotes about Harriet Quimby.

Preface

Michigan Every Day is not a narrative history of Michigan. Rather, it is a collection of notable events for every day on the calendar (some days were more eventful than others) and choices were made that enlivened Michigan's past.

The authors, Patrick Sullivan and Carole Eberly, are Michigan journalists.

January

Jan. 1, 1955
G. Mennen "Soapy" Williams
celebrates fourth term as governor

Michigan never before had a governor win four consecutive terms. On Jan. 1, 1955, G. Mennen Williams celebrated this feat at an inaugural ball at Detroit's Masonic Temple Auditorium.

Williams first was elected governor at age 37. Even though he was heir to his family's lucrative soap-producing company, Williams was a progressive Democrat well-known for mingling with regular folks at polkas or square dances. He won his third election for governor despite running in a presidential year that saw hugely popular Dwight D. Eisenhower on the Republican side of the ticket. Eisenhower campaigned for the governor's opponent in 1954. Despite this, Williams swept to a fourth term of office in an overwhelming victory.

Jan. 1, 1947
MSU grad first woman press secretary in Michigan

Governor Kim Sigler took office on Jan. 1, 1947, for a career that would last only two years after losing a re-election bid to G. Mennen Williams. However, the Republican appointed Roberta Applegate as his press secretary. She was possibly the first woman in the country to serve as press secretary to a governor. Born in Idaho in 1919, Applegate wanted to follow her father as a journalist.

She attended Michigan State College (now Michigan State University) and earned her bachelor's degree in journalism. Applegate went on to Northwestern University where she obtained her master's degree in the same subject. Michigan beckoned her back, where she worked at the *Detroit Free Press* in the women's section. In 1943, she took a job with the Associated Press, assigned to the Lansing bureau.

She became the first woman hired to work full-time covering the legislature and the Supreme Court. Working the state capital beat, Applegate caught the attention of Sigler and she was hired as his press secretary. When Sigler's re-election attempt failed, Applegate returned to journalism, working at the *Miami Herald*. From there she went on to teach journalism at the University of Kansas in 1964 until her retirement in 1987.

Applegate was inducted into the Michigan Journalism Hall of Fame in 2008.

Sigler, know as "Hollywood Kim," died at age 55 when the plane he was piloting crashed into a television broadcast tower on a foggy night near Augusta, Michigan. The accident occurred almost five years after Sigler left office.

Jan. 1, 1969
"Mini-Me" Verne Troyer born

Verne Troyer was born in Sturgis and grew up in St. Joseph County's Centreville. He attended community college in Coldwater before moving West to make a living in show business.

At 32 inches tall, Troyer first found work as a stunt man, standing in for babies or children. Later he obtained acting roles in film and television. In his best-known role, he played "Mini-Me" in *Austin Powers: The Spy Who Shagged Me* and *Austin Powers in Goldmember*.

Jan. 2, 1902
Michigan learns results of the First Rose Bowl

The Jan. 2, 1902 edition of the *Evening Record* of Traverse City announced to northern Michigan residents that a football game way out on the West Coast had been played and the boys from the home state were victorious. Although the win only garnered three paragraphs in the second column of the front page, what the article lacked in size, it made up for in unvarnished favoritism to the home team.

"By the decisive score of 49 to 0, the Michigan university football team yesterday defeated Stanford University. The score is quite in proportion to the superiority of the Eastern men at the game of football. It does not, however, tell the story of Stanford's desperate but futile efforts against defeat. Michigan's superior knowledge of the game showed in every play. At kicking, general teamwork, running, tackling and bucking the line, the Michigan men excelled."

Michigan's football program was bolstered by the arrival of Fielding H. "Hurry-Up" Yost, who began coaching the team in 1901. Yost's first squad was known as the "point-a-minute" team and defeated Stanford behind halfback Willie Heston and fullback Neil Snow.

Perhaps it was the lopsided score that prompted organizers of the "Tournament of Roses" not to schedule another football game until 1916.

Jan. 2, 1940
Jim Bakker born

Jim Bakker, a native of Muskegon, admits he had a wild side as a youth, but settled down to become a minister after he attended a revival meeting conducted by Oral Roberts. Bakker had a flair for the show business side of religion and would go on to work with Pat Robertson at the *700 Club*.

He later formed his own television ministry called *PTL*, which first stood for "Praise the Lord" and later stood for "People That

Love."

By the middle of the 1970s, Bakker and his wife Tammy Fae attracted more than 10 million viewers. The couple also ran Heritage USA, a Christian-themed retreat. They preached "prosperity theology," which holds that wealth would come to true believers.

Bakker's downfall began in 1987, when a one-night-stand he had had several years earlier came to light after he attempted to use $279,000 of the ministry's money to buy the woman's silence. He was also charged with embezzling millions from Heritage USA.

Bakker was convicted and sent to prison. The televangelist served several years of an 18-year sentence.

Jan. 3, 1893
U.P. town gets world's biggest pump

As the mining boom of iron and copper in the Upper Peninsula matured, the mines had to go deeper and deeper into the earth to extract the precious metals. This meant miners had great difficulty contending with water seepage. Getting tons of water out of shafts that drove thousands of feet into the ground prompted the production of huge pumps.

On Jan. 3, 1893, the Chapin Iron Mine boasted it had the largest. That day the pump, which was built by the E.P. Allis Company of Milwaukee in 1890 and 1891, began sucking 200 tons of water per minute out of the "D" shaft at the mine. The pump had a flywheel that was 40 feet in diameter and weighed 160 tons and turned 10 revolutions per minute. The pump operated through 1896 when mechanical problems led to its dismantling.

It was purchased by the Ludington Mine and used at its "C" shaft until 1914, when it was replaced by electric pumps. The pump, which is on display at the Cornish Pump Engine and Mining Museum in Iron Mountain, was almost turned to scrap during World War II.

Jan. 4, 1843
Death of Michigan's "Boy Governor"

Stevens T. Mason did not like the nickname "Boy Governor." Even though, he was named secretary of the territory of Michigan at age 19 before he could legally vote. Soon he became acting territorial gvernor and was elected governor of the state at age 24.

Mason never took kindly to the moniker. The name came from a report in the *Ann Arbor Emigrant* calling a candidate who Mason supported "a protégé of the Boy Governor." Mason once encountered the editor of the newspaper on a Detroit street and attacked him, beating him severely with his fists. The fisticuffs didn't help Mason's cause, however. The story of the beating made newspapers across the country, only amplifying the nickname he so despised.

Michigan was still a territory when Stevens T. Mason moved from Kentucky to Detroit with his father, John M. Mason. The elder Mason was brought to Detroit to take the place of Lewis Cass, territorial governor, whom President Andrew Jackson tapped to become his Secretary of War. The young Mason was 19 at the time and worked as a secretary for his father, who had no taste for politics but accepted the position at Jackson's behest because he needed the money. John Mason eventually persuaded Jackson to appoint him to a post in Mexico, leaving the son behind. Stevens T. Mason had shown enough political skill to be appointed secretary of the territory by Jackson. Mason became territorial governor at age 22. He may have been young, but he was capable in overseeing Michigan as it transformed from a territory to a state.

There was opposition in Washington to Michigan becoming a state. Michigan was believed to be mostly swamp, worthless for farming and unfit for settlement. Mason set out to establish a state university, create a public school system, build roads and to change the country's mind about this peninsula way out West. Michigan became a state, in a complicated process involving a war with Ohio over Toledo, a dispute described for the entry for April 16.

Mason was eventually removed as territorial governor by Jackson. Nonetheless, Michigan residents thought the 24-year-old sharp enough to be the state's first elected governor. During Mason's two terms, he established the University of Michigan and proposed the construction of the Soo Locks. But his administration was marred by the Panic of 1837 and an ambitious plan to build two canals across the Lower Peninsula and three railroads. Voters blamed Mason for the economic malaise and he decided against running for a third term. Mason attempted to start a private law practice in Detroit but the disappointment of his governorship left his reputation in tatters.

Mason moved to New York City where he had wealthy relatives. However, he found he could not practice law with a Michigan law license and was forced to spend his first winter in New York studying for the bar exam. Mason passed the exam in 1842 but before he found any success as a lawyer in New York Mason died of pneumonia at the age of 31.

Jan. 5, 1914
Henry Ford institutes astonishing minimum rate

The day after the announcement of a $5 working day, the *New York Times* called Henry Ford's decision "one of the most remarkable business moves of his entire remarkable career." Ford said that every worker in his company would earn at least $5 for an eight-hour day. "Even the boy who sweeps up the floors will get that much," he said.

That was highly unusual in a time when many workers earned a handful of change for a 10 or 12-hour day. Ford believed the people who made his cars should be able to afford to buy them. In a statement to the media, James Cousens, treasurer of the company, said: "It is our belief that social justice begins at home. We want those who have helped us produce this great institution and are helping to maintain it to share our prosperity. Believing as we do, that a division of our earnings between capital and labor is unequal, we have sought a plan of relief suitable for our business."

Ford also announced a profit sharing plan that would see many workers get a stake in the $10 million annual profit. He would run the plants with three eight-hour shifts per day, enabling the company to hire 4,000 more workers. Ford also said that if layoffs were necessary, they would occur during harvest time when farming jobs were plentiful.

Jan. 6, 1994
Figure skating soap opera culminates in Detroit

Detroit found itself to be the stage of a remarkable crime that involved an attractive, beloved figure skating star and her rival.

The whack-heard-around-the-world happened outside Cobo Hall, after a practice session of the U.S. Figure Skating Championship. A large man in a black leather jacket asked a skating coach to point out Nancy Kerrigan. The man ambushed the skater from behind and whacked her in the right knee with a metal truncheon. This put in doubt the skater's bid to compete in the upcoming Olympic Winter Games in Lillehammer, Norway.

Kerrigan fell to the ground and screamed, "God, why me? Why me?"

Could this have been just another example of random street violence in Detroit? Did Kerrigan have some crazed stalker, like the one who had stabbed international tennis star Monica Seles in Germany months earlier?

It turned out, no.

The case quickly unfolded and the conspiracy to prevent Kerrigan from competing led back to Kerrigan's teammate and, it turns out, nemesis, Tonya Harding.

As police looked for the attacker, Kerrigan sat out the national championships and Harding skated to a win.

Within days, the investigation into the attack turned to Harding's ex-husband, Jeff Gillooly, and her bodyguard. Gillooly later

pleaded guilty and attempted to implicate Harding in the plot.
Harding did not admit to being in on the assault but she did
plead guilty to hindering the investigation.

Harding was fined $100,000, sentenced to 500 hours com-
munity service and banned for life from the U.S. Figure Skating
Association.

The incident led to cover stories of Harding on *Time* and *News-
week* magazines.

Kerrigan recovered in time for the Olympics and won a silver
medal.

Harding, who had an assorted career that included a bout as a
professional wrestler, lives quietly in a trailer park.

Jan. 7, 1950
Chevrolet introduces "Powerglide"

Chevy introduced its first afforably-priced automatic transmission engines in 1950, the "Powerglide." Although many
drivers clung to their beloved manual transmissions, much of
the public greeted the new "Powerglide" with enthusiasm. Three
hundred thousand Chevrolets equipped with "Powerglide" were
sold the first year.

The novel transmission had to be explained to consumers
through newspaper reports because for many people it meant
they could afford an automobile that didn't need to be shifted
during operation.

A quadrant mounted on the steering column was marked with
"Park" for parking, "N" for neutral, "D" for drive, "L" for low
and "R" for reverse. A lever below the steering wheel controlled
operations. To start the engine the pointer may be placed at "N"
or "Park" and then the lever is moved to "D." No shifting action
was required once the car was in motion.

The transmission was offered as optional equipment on its "de
luxe" models for an extra $150. That brought the price of a Chev-
rolet two-door sport coupe to $1,765.

Jan. 8, 1856
Dentists say "ahh" to opening professional organization

Before dentists went to school to learn how to fix teeth, they
got organized, forming the first state dental society in the
country. The Michigan Dental Association was organized on Jan.
8, 1856 in Detroit. At the time, dentists received no formal training. To become a member and, thus, one supposes, a dentist, a
person had to be 21 years old, a practicing member of the profession, have earned a good "English education," and be of unques-
tionable moral character.

The association was started by 14 dentists who met in the offices of Hiram Benedict and Lorain Christopher Whitting, according to the Michigan Historical Marker that honors the group.

Soon, the dental society came upon a revelation – that dentists should be trained. In the 1860s and 1870s they advocated the establishment of a dental school in the state. It took more than a decade of effort. In 1875, the state legislature agreed to appropriate money needed for a dental school at the University of Michigan.

Jan. 9, 1933
Men nabbed in northern Michigan's largest manhunt sent to prison

On January 5, 1933, three men appeared at the Kaleva State Bank at 11 a.m., shot and killed cashier Ellsworth Billman, and escaped in a Buick with $3,000 in cash.

Newspapers reported that a farmer who was a customer at the bank was the only witness. He said the shooting of Billman was wanton and cold-blooded. The robbers arrived with guns drawn, announced to the cashier that he should know what they were there for, and shot him when one outlaw thought he was reaching for an alarm.

While the three bandits held up the bank, a fourth held four men at gunpoint in a post office across the street to make sure they didn't interfere with the robbery.

Within minutes, local men grabbed shotguns and rifles, cramming into a car to follow the criminals south on M-55. A Kaleva resident called the state police in Lansing and police across the state soon heard a radio message ordering them to converge on the small Manistee County town.

The brazen robbery and murder set off a manhunt on a scale never seen before in northern Michigan. Hundreds of men were deputized when police from all over the state joined the search.

Soon the men were spotted buying gas and the search focused around Baldwin in Lake County. Police also learned that the Buick used by the desperados had been stolen at gunpoint from an Indianapolis garage. They believed the men would eventually attempt to reach the Michigan-Indiana line.

On the second day, the bandits abandoned the Buick and stole a Chevrolet from a farmer. Later, they got into a gunfight with one of their state police pursuers after a patrolman pursued the Chevrolet. They managed to lose the officer south of Baldwin.

For an entire day, anyone driving a maroon Chevrolet coupe anywhere in much of the Lower Peninsula was chased down by police and checked out.

Across northern Michigan, residents were fascinated by the manhunt. They listened by shortwave radios to police coordinate the 50 cars involved in the chases. Some residents went to the

17

state police post in Traverse City to watch a radio dispatcher in action. The *Traverse City Record-Eagle* noted that residents were so wrapped up in the search that the death of former President Calvin Coolidge went unnoticed. Traverse City took a keen interest in the case because Billman, the victim, grew up and attended high school and college in the city.

On the second night after the robbery, the four men were spotted by a farmer in Newaygo county walking into a swamp. The farmer shot and critically injured one of the men, Wayne Robinson, as they fled. The state police soon arrived in the area and arrested the remaining three, who were too cold, tired and hungry to put up a fight.

Justice was swift in those days in Manistee County. On Jan. 9, 1933, just four days after the crime, three of the bandits were sentenced to spend their lives in prison in Marquette. Each had pleaded guilty to armed robbery and a charge of murder was held in abeyance to be brought in case any of the men managed to secure parole.

Jan. 9, 1886
First-ever article about global warming?

Early in Detroit's history an unnamed writer for the *Detroit Free Press*, or for a wire service used by the paper, considered global warming. Or at least local warming. The writer noticed that winters had become shorter and less severe and wondered what was going on. The conclusion, after consultation with an expert, was not far away from what is believed to be causing climate change today – emissions from industry. But the rationale was different.

The story wasn't much of a big deal, however. It only amounted to two paragraphs. Running on page six, it appeared under the headline "Winters Getting Milder."

"It was nothing strange years ago for snow to fall about Christmas and remain on the ground for weeks and months, often several feet in depth. The mercury dropped below zero and did not cause any wonder. Everything that usually ran on wheels was placed on skis. It is very seldom that the mercury now reaches below zero, and snow rarely packs, even when it is not cleared away by the Street-cleaning Department.

"'One principle cause for this change," said a New York officer of the Signal Service Corps, "can be seen from the windows of this station. Look around you in every direction, east, west, north or south, in this city, Brooklyn, and New Jersey, and what do you see? Clouds of steam rising from almost every housetop. Elevators in offices and apartment houses, factories using steam as a motor, buildings heated by the same hot vapor; all sending forth clouds from the tops of the houses. Do you not suppose this has an effect on the atmosphere, warms the air and half melts the snow before it reaches the ground? Then there are the boilers under the sidewalks and in the cellars; steam-heating pipes along the roadways and thousands of contrivances to generate heat not known a quarter century ago."

Jan. 10, 1964
Ford buys the Lions

For many fans of the Lions, this proved to be a bad day that would linger for decades.

William Clay Ford Sr., son of Edsel Ford and grandson of Henry Ford, paid $4.5 million to become sole owner of the Detroit Lions. The Lions had played in Detroit since 1934, when a team that played in Portsmouth, Ohio was purchased for $7,952.08 and moved to Detroit by a group headed by a radio executive.

The team first played at the University of Detroit's stadium and they won the National Football League Championship in the second year in Detroit. The Lions dominated the NFL in the 1950s, winning four division titles and three league championships, including back-to-back titles in 1952 and 1953. They won their last championship in 1957. Ford took over as president of the team in 1961.

From the moment Ford bought the team, the Lions performed like an Edsel. Since Ford's ownership, the Lions have never played in a Super Bowl and have won only a single playoff game.

In his first season as owner, Ford forced out George Wilson, the coach who had led Detroit to the championship several years earlier.

The Lions' record since has caused frustration in Detroit. But despite miserable years leading up to the 50th anniversary of the team's last championship in 2007, games still sell out.

In later years, Ford's most controversial move was the employment of Matt Millen as team president. Millen's contract was renewed before the 2005 season for five years even though he had the worst record in the league for the 75 games he had been at the helm of the team, 20 and 55. The performance led to a chorus of calls to fire Millen, sell the team, or both.

Hundreds of fans signed a letter at a web site called dearmrford.com that asked Ford to sell the team,

"William Clay Ford Sr., I humbly implore you to consider selling the franchise, even if for no other reason than to try something different. For the sake of the team, the NFL, the city of Detroit, the Ford Motor Company and the fans," wrote Michael Kumm of Redford. "Now it would be an unfair proposition for me to recommend that you act while I sit and do nothing. I therefore make this pledge to you. I have not purchased a Ford product in over twenty years. On the day you announce that the Lions are avail-

able for purchase or have been sold, I will purchase a Ford automobile. Perhaps others will make similar offers...."

Jan. 11, 1945
Senator assassinated

On a rural road near Springport, between Lansing and Albion, a passerby happened upon a burning sedan that
appeared to have come to a screeching halt on a snowy road. It
rested on the opposite side of the highway.

Inside, in the passenger seat, lay state Senator Warren G. Hooper, shot three times in the head by a .38 caliber weapon.

The following day, the story of the slain senator struggled to
find space on the front pages of Michigan newspapers, filled with
closing events of World War II.

But the details of Hooper's murder were titillating. The killer,
or killers, left few clues. And the senator was scheduled the next
day to testify in a corruption case that could unleash turmoil
among his fellow legislators in Lansing.

Hooper was to appear before a one-man grand jury investigating bribery and corruption.

The 41-year-old Republican from Albion was the key witness
against Frank D. McKay, former national Republican committee
member, and two other men, Floyd Fitzsimmons, a Benton Harbor sports promoter, and William Green, of Hillman, a former Republican state representative. Hooper had been granted immunity
from prosecution in exchange for his testimony against the three.

The case involved only a fraction of the grand jury investigation into corruption in the legislature. Fifty-three people had
previously been indicted and 20 convicted.

McKay and the others were under indictment for allegedly
bribing other legislators to influence the outcome of a horse rac-
ing bill.

McKay, a Grand Rapids multi-millionaire, expressed "great
shock" upon learning of the slaying, according to a United Press
report. McKay had arrived home in Grand Rapids the day of the
killing from a vacation in Florida. "I sincerely hope that the authorities find and punish the person (who is) guilty," McKay told
a reporter.

McKay said he didn't know Hooper was the state's witness
against him.

State police said they had few clues in Hooper's murder and
they appealed to newspapers and radio stations to find a motorist who may have seen a hitch-hiker in the area where the murder
took place. A $15,000 reward was offered for the assassin.

Police struggled to put together what clues they had in the case.
Footprints that trailed through the snow away from the car were
small enough to have belonged to a woman. A mysterious caller

had telephoned the Hooper residence hours before his death, asking for the senator's whereabouts.

Hooper was known never to pick up strangers and apparently was seen in his car shortly before his death with three other men, leading police to believe he knew his attackers. A rip in Hooper's hat indicated he had been taken by surprise and struggled as his hat was pulled down over his face.

Hooper's death signaled a serious blow to the corruption investigation and brought the grand jury to its end. His killer, or killers, never were discovered.

Jan. 12 1959
Launch of Motown

Berry Gordy, Jr. probably didn't realize he was about to spark a musical revolution on Jan. 12, 1959. He put down $800 borrowed from his family and launched Tamla Records, the precursor to Motown Records, home to a unique Detroit sound.

Gordy is credited with coining the term Motown and the following year that became his label name.

It was the first well-known label to be owned by an African-American and feature primarily black artists. It was revolutionary by successfully breaking those artists into mainstream pop music.

Tamla's first single in August, 1959 was titled "Money (That's What I Want)" by Barrett Brown. The first gold record for Motown came in 1960 with the single "Shop Around" by Smokey Robinson.

In a decade, Motown became the largest independent manufacturer of 45 rpm records in the world. By 1968, the company had transformed from a family-run outfit to an international business and moved its headquarters to 2457 Woodward Avenue.

Eventually, Motown labels included Tamla, Motown, Gordy, Soul, VIP, Rare Earth, Black Forum, Workshop, Jazz, Divinity and others. Motown left Detroit for Los Angeles in 1972. There, the company branched into film and produced *Lady Sings the Blues*. In 1980, the Motown Historical Museum was established at Hitsville U.S.A. on West Grand Boulevard.

Jan. 13, 1854
The rich get richer; the poor get poorer

Jim Paul was a man caught in Michigan's rapid transformation from a pioneer outpost to a settled and relatively civilized state in the mid-1800s. Paul arrived at the mouth of the Ontonagon River in 1843, becoming the first white man to settle in that remote region of the Upper Peninsula.

He came from Virginia, a pioneer looking to strike it rich by discovering copper and making a claim. He laid out the plat of Ontonagon and had it registered on Jan. 13, 1854.

When Paul arrived, there was good reason to believe the location on the southern shore of Lake Superior promised a prosperous future. Paul heard of stories by Alexander Henry, who had written of looking for copper in the region in 1809, and Douglass Houghton, about his expedition through the U.P.

Paul's plat for Ontonagon, included a town square, with the county seat located on the side of the river he believed belonged to him. However, he failed to get title to the land registered properly in his name. Part of the problem could have been that Paul was illiterate.

Making a fortune in copper required investors and a keen sense of where to stake a claim. Paul assisted others in finding fortunes but wealth passed him by, as did any claim he had to the land he settled.

Paul died in 1881 after 40 years in Ontonagon. He watched fortunes rise and fall in the copper boom, witnessed the discovery of silver and saw the arrival and departure of lumbermen. His wife, Amanda Paul, died 20 years later, living in poverty and surviving through the charity of others who remembered that her husband had founded a city that was at one time the largest on Lake Superior.

Jan. 14, 1920
From poverty to wealth to an early grave: death of the Dodge brothers

The brothers were as close in life as they were in death. John Dodge died of influenza on Jan. 14, 1920. His brother, despondent over the death of his closest companion, followed months later, on Dec. 10, 1920. In some accounts, Horace also died of influenza. In others, he is said to have drunk himself to death.

John and Horace Dodge grew up impoverished in Niles, sometimes unable to afford a pair of shoes. In Niles, the brothers spent their free time tinkering in their father's and grandfather's machine shop. Eventually they built their first vehicle – a high-wheeled bicycle.

The family moved to Windsor in 1882 when John and Horace were teenagers. The boys used their experience to take jobs at machine shops in Detroit and Windsor and started a bicycle company that they sold at the end of the century. They opened a machine shop across the river in Detroit in 1900, determined to make auto parts for a fledgling and uncertain new industry.

The business got off to a quick success because they established reputations for being excellent mechanics. Their company, called "Dodge Brothers" sold engines and transmissions to a company owned by Ransom E. Olds. In 1903, the brothers signed a contract with Henry Ford to build 650 chassis in exchange for 50 shares of Ford stock. The stock was worth $10,000 when they built the chassis. When they sold the stock back to Ford in 1919, it was worth $32 million. By the mid-teens, having seen the profits made by Olds and Ford in products that they largely produced, the Dodges decided to build their own cars. In 18 months, they came up with plans for a new automobile.

When asked why he wanted to stop making parts for Ford and build his own car, John Dodge reportedly said: "Think of all the Ford owners who will someday want an automobile."

The first car, called the "Old Betsy," rolled off the production line in Hamtramck on Nov. 14, 1914. The brothers produced a car that emphasized quality and sold for more than a Ford, which was produced with economy in mind. Their factory complex, built on a 30-acre site, employed 20,000 workers at the time of their deaths and produced 145,000 cars.

The Dodge widows sold the Dodge Brothers Motors Car Company for $146 million to a group of New York investors. By the late 1920s, ownership of the company returned to Michigan when it was purchased by Walter P. Chrysler, who dropped the "Brothers" from the brand.

Jan. 15, 1878
Barnes "Castle" opens in Lansing

L ansing was nothing but a swampy wilderness when it was named the state capital in 1847. All the state's records were moved from Detroit in a single wagon-load to the capitol building constructed that year.

So 30 years later, when a mansion that could be described as a castle was constructed by one of Lansing's leading citizens, the local newspaper buzzed about the residence.

The *Lansing Journal* called a gala at the castle the "leading social event of the season," where attendees danced far into the night in the third floor ballroom.

Then-mayor Orlando Mack Barnes opened his home to the elite of Lansing – state Supreme Court justices, state officials, leaders of industry and commerce. Some in attendance could remember what their city was like just three decades earlier when they arrived at a bend in the river to a swamp and struggled to survive life on the frontier.

Barnes made his money in banking and railroads, and built his mansion on four acres at the corner of Main Street and Washington Avenue. The Victorian-style home had 17,357 square feet, 26 rooms, 11 halls and landings, six stairways and nine fireplaces. It cost $40,000 to construct.

The building stood vacant for decades after Barnes died in 1899 and his widow could not afford to maintain the house. There was a proposal in 1948 to renovate the house for the official governor's residence. An architect selected the building as a suitable home for the governor due to the structure's opulence and it location away from "undesirable neighbors." But the $200,000 price tag was considered too high, according to state of Michigan records.

The building was demolished in 1957.

Jan. 16, 1938
First ski resort in Midwest opens

Caberfae, a ski resort near Cadillac, was one of the benefits to the state born out of public works projects spurred by the Great Depression.

The land around Caberfae had been a ranch owned by three Chicago businessmen in 1919 and obtained its name from the Gaelic word for stag's head, because of the large number of deer in the area.

When the Civilian Conservation Corps was looking for ways to put men to work in the 1930s, one of the projects selected was the large hill at Caberfae. Working with the U.S. Forest Service, CCC workers surveyed the land, cleared runs, built roads and constructed a shelter for skiers.

The formal opening of the ski hill, on Jan. 16, 1938, was celebrated in the pages of the *Cadillac Evening News*. Among those who attended the formal opening were "expert skiers, some of whom had skied the mountains of Europe. In addition, skiers from Grand Rapids, Kalamazoo and Lansing tried out the slopes with great enthusiasm."

A tow rope was added in 1940, constructed with $5 donations collected from skiers.

Over the years, groups formed to make improvements.

By the 1950s, the first ski resort in the Midwest and the third to open in the nation (behind Sun Valley, Idaho, and Stowe, Vermont) was one of the largest and most popular ski resorts in the Midwest.

Today the resort offers 34 runs, four chair lifts and two surface tows.

Jan. 17, 1899
First military funeral in Michigan for a woman

Although Michigan women served in the Civil War, including one who gained particular fame for passing herself off as a man to get into the army, the *Owosso Evening Argus* determined that the first military funeral for a woman occurred on Jan. 17, 1899. Ellen May Tower, a veteran of the Spanish-American War, received that military funeral.

The daughter of a Civil War captain, Tower was born in 1868 in Byron, a small town between Flint and Lansing. She attended a nurses' training program at Detroit's Grace Hospital and worked for several years at the Michigan School for the Blind until it was apparent that war would soon break out with Spain.

Tower volunteered as an army nurse and within months was sent to Camp Wikoff, in New York, where she cared for soldiers who returned from the war with injuries or disease. Shortly, she volunteered to be closer to the action and was sent to Puerto Rico, where she died within three months.

As was the case in 90 percent of American casualties in that war, Tower died of disease – in her case, typhoid fever. Her remains were shipped to Detroit and her funeral took place in Byron, where it was attended by thousands of soldiers, villagers and visitors. There is a Michigan historical marker in honor of Tower in Byron. A town near Onaway, where her family had moved, was named Tower soon after her death.

Jan. 18, 1802
Detroit incorporated as an American city
(Maybe free drinks do buy an election!)

Michigan and Detroit were precariously located, politically-speaking. As part of the Northwest Territory, huge chunks of Michigan could have wound up as Ohio or Indiana. The first representative to formally represent Michigan on a national scale was elected in Detroit, in balloting that took place over three days in December, 1798, at a bar called John Dodemead's Tavern.

Solomon Sibley prevailed over his opponent, James May, and became the Wayne County representative for the Northwest Territory. May had once been a British subject and was supported by the Brits, who remained in Detroit. Sibley was supported by the Americans and the French. May didn't believe Sibley truly won the election, however. He charged that Sibley used free liquor to influence voters and stationed soldiers outside the tavern, armed with clubs, to intimidate anyone who thought of voting for May.

As the first elected representative from Michigan to take part in an American legislature, Sibley headed on horseback to Cincinnati, where the lawmakers met. In 1802, Sibley managed to pass legislation incorporating Detroit as a city.

When Sibley returned to Detroit, a public celebration was held. However, some residents were upset that Detroit was not included in the region that had just become the State of Ohio. They wanted to be part of Ohio because residents of states were able to elect representatives to Congress while residents of territories were second-class citizens.

Eventually, the northern boundary of Ohio was drawn on a line extending east from the southern tip of Lake Michigan. This set the stage for the formation of the Michigan Territory and, finally, for Michigan to become a state.

Sibley went on, in 1806, to become the first mayor of Detroit, was appointed attorney general of the United States and served on the Michigan Territorial Supreme Court.

Jan. 18, 1922
Bob Bell, aka Bozo the Clown, born

Bob Bell, a native of Flint, became the first portrayer of Bozo the Clown to be inducted into the International Clown Hall of Fame in Wisconsin. Bell began in show business when he returned to Flint after a stint in the navy at the end of World War II. He joined a community theater group, which led to a job as an announcer at a Flint radio station.

Bell bounced around several televisions stations and honed his improv skills before he landed at Chicago's WGN in 1960, where he hosted a show as Bozo the Clown, a character that had been created in the mid-1940s in California. Bell's version of Bozo was a smash success and the show was broadcast nationwide beginning in 1978, when there was a waiting list of 10 years to get a ticket to be a part of the studio audience. The show featured comedy sketches, an orchestra, cartoons, and games and prizes for children.

Bell retired in 1984 and moved to California. He died in 1997.

Jan. 19, 1868
"Snowshoe Priest" dies in Marquette

On the road from Baraga to L'Anse, at the very base of the Keweenaw Peninsula, just as the road corners west around Keweenaw Bay, an enormous statue rises from the wilderness – the likeness of a Catholic bishop, peering down, clutching a cross and snowshoes, and apparently standing atop a five-legged spider that stands on five teepees.

The statue, which is 60 feet above the Red Rocks Cliffs, was erected in the 1960s to honor Bishop Frederick Baraga, a missionary who spent decades devoted to the people of northern Michigan until his death on Jan. 19, 1868.

The spider legs represent Baraga's five major missions dotted along the south shore of Lake Superior. And the snowshoes are a reflection of his nickname – the "Snowshoe Priest" – earned because Baraga tirelessly spent his years trudging around the unforgiving terrain of the Upper Great Lakes to save the souls of Indians and European settlers.

Baraga was born on June 29, 1797 in a town in modern-day

Slovenia. Baraga attended law school in Vienna before entering the seminary, a decision which in those days could lead to some adventurous travel. In 1830, Baraga found himself in the United States as a missionary. A little more than a year later, he was among the Ottawa settlement of L'Arbre Croche, where Cross Village stands today.

In America, Baraga studied Indian languages. He went on to write *Otawa Anamie-Misinaigan*, a prayer book that was the first published in the Ottawa language. Baraga also published a book of Ojibway grammar and an Ojibway dictionary. Baraga spent time ministering in Grand Rapids and Wisconsin until the 1840s when he founded a mission at L'Anse. There he worked against a movement to have Indians relocated to Western territories.

Baraga was elevated to bishop in 1853, just as the Upper Peninsula's population exploded with European immigrants and settlers drawn to the north by copper. In his 60s, Baraga continued to trek around the U.P. on snowshoes in the winter, using his fluency in eight languages to minister to the newcomers.

Baraga died in Marquette, where he was buried beneath the Cathedral of Saint Peter.

Jan. 20, 1960
Disastrous fire at Dow Chemical averted

When morning dawned over Bay City on Jan. 20, 1960, the bright sky had turned red.

Some 60 firefighters scurried to a new Bay City Dow Chemical Company petroleum refining plant just in time to prevent a catastrophic fire.

The fire began when some high-octane ethylene exploded in a medium-sized storage tank. Witnesses said what followed sounded like a string of firecrackers as a network of petroleum lines exploded in quick succession.

The flare-up may have been a minor incident, but it was another indication of how the tinkering of Herbert Dow transformed this part of the state. Though Dow had been dead for 30 years, his experiments and breakthroughs in chemical research changed mid-eastern Michigan from a swampy, cut-over forest to an industrial center.

Dow attended school in Cleveland, where he loved chemistry and problem-solving.

He proved he was a talented inventor even as a child. At a farm in Cleveland, he developed an incubator for chicken eggs that worked well enough to be sold around the country. Dow became discouraged, however, as people bought his product, copied his design and competed with his small business.

During his senior year at Cleveland's Case School of Applied Science, now Case Western Reserve University, he visited an Ohio oil well to seek a sample of natural gas. There he took a sample of the brine bubbling from the earth with crude oil and gas, sparking a fascination with the seemingly worthless by-product from oil drilling.

Once out of school, Dow convinced investors in Cleveland to fund a company that would pump brine and separate bromine from salt water. Dow believed he could compete profitably with other manufacturers of bromine, a chemical compound similar to chlorine.

His first company failed, primarily because he picked a poorly performing brine well in Ohio. But during his venture, Dow developed an efficient process to separate bromine from brine with an electrical current.

Dow was determined to carry on. In his studies at Case, he discovered that brine deposits around Midland, Michigan, were of extremely high quality.

He moved there in 1890 when it was a bawdy lumber town that had seen better days and appeared destined for the sawdust heap of history.

Using a generator hooked up to a flour mill, Dow set out to perfect his electrolytic process in Midland as local residents looked on, thinking a crazy man had moved to their town. He struggled to get a company running, eventually forming the Midland Chemical Company, which was majority-owned by a group of Cleveland investors. Dow put up his patents to get a small stake in the company.

This caused Dow to lose control of the company. For years Dow attempted to develop a method for producing chloride from brine, only to be stymied by his bosses in Cleveland. Finally his experiments in Midland caused a costly explosion that further diminished Dow's influence in the company, leading to a break from his investors. He then set off to develop a chlorine production process on his own.

Dow raised money through a larger group of Cleveland investors and Dow Chemical Company was formed in 1897. Although it struggled in its first years with explosions in the electric cells used to extract chloride from the brine, Dow eventually perfected the production of bleach and the company spread into other chemical products.

Jan. 21 1895
Steamer *Chicora* sinks in Lake Michigan; 26 dead

A turbulent storm in early 1895 led to tragedy for those traveling aboard the *Chicora*, which was headed from Milwaukee to St. Joseph in a month unfriendly to vessels in the Upper Great Lakes. News that the ship had gone down was disturbing because she was thought to be well constructed – it was nearly

200 feet long and built to break through ice.

A few oddities about the *Chicora*'s final voyage made its loss resonate more than other shipwrecks of the day.

First, the ship already had been tied up for winter but was put back into the lake when its owners received a request to deliver a shipment of late-winter flour from Milwaukee. Also, the captain enlisted his 23-year-old son into the crew after a second mate was unable to sail due to illness. Finally, despite great weather for the journey to Milwaukee the previous day, early in the morning of Jan. 21, the owner in St. Joseph telegraphed Milwaukee with an order to delay the voyage home because low pressure indicated perilous weather ahead. The message reached the docks minutes after the *Chicora* departed.

None of the 26 bodies were ever found. The fate of the *Chicora* remained mysterious for more than a century.

In September, 2001, a shipwreck was discovered that matched the description of the ill-fated steamer. Shipwreck hunters found the remains of a boat sitting upright on the bed of Lake Michigan 300 feet below the surface. The ship was found off Michigan's coast near Holland.

Jan. 22, 1813
"Remember the River Raisin"

The first months of the War of 1812 did not go well for the Americans. Detroit had surrendered to the British. The fort on Mackinac Island had been captured by surprise. The British could depend on the loyalty of the Indian warrior Tecumseh, who mustered armies of men from Great Lakes tribes to fight alongside the British and Canadians.

It may have been the fall of Detroit that galvanized people across the Ohio valley to organize an army. Raising troops had been difficult work prior to the fall of Detroit. In the weeks after, thousands joined.

But if the fall of Detroit motivated Americans to take the war seriously, an event occurred on the way to recapturing Detroit that would send the scrappy settlers into a frenzy.

American General James Winchester, who commanded a section of the army determined to retake Detroit, learned that the British planned to send an expedition to Frenchtown, or present-day Monroe, to block the army's march into Detroit. In January 1813, Winchester ordered about 650 men into Frenchtown to secure its inhabitants and supplies against the British. The soldiers marched to the village, starting their fight with the British in the afternoon of Jan. 18, 1813. The Americans took Frenchtown by nightfall. Winchester ordered in 300 more troops to secure the town.

But the British troops and Indians were preparing a large-scale attack to retake Frenchtown. On Jan. 22, 1813, the British attacked in numbers that overwhelmed the Americans. Groups of American soldiers who attempted to retreat were tracked down and massacred. Winchester saw the American troops were losing the fight and he ordered an all-out retreat of soldiers on one side of the River Raisin. However, the British were unsatisfied with merely winning back Frenchtown. As the American soldiers retreated into the woods, an army of Indian warriors fell upon them, killing 100 of the Americans in a matter of minutes. Winchester was taken prisoner.

As a group of soldiers hunkered down by the river, Winchester finally agreed to an all-out surrender. He attempted to negotiate terms of surrender that would protect wounded Americans.

However, the British marched the American prisoners out of Frenchtown, leaving behind the American wounded. The Indians, wanting to avenge losses they had suffered in the fighting, entered the village, killing the wounded soldiers.

In all, the British took some 500 American prisoners and left about 80 men to be massacred. The result made "Remember the River Raisin" a popular battle cry for the rest of the war.

Jan. 23, 1837
Michigan's second oldest newspaper hits the streets

The state's first newspaper was published in Detroit, but the second oldest began in western Michigan. The *Kalamazoo Gazette* actually began life as the *Michigan Statesman and St. Joseph Chronicle* and was published in White Pigeon beginning in 1833, where there was a United States land office.

When the land office moved to Kalamazoo several years later, so did the paper. The *Gazette* is the second oldest newspaper in the state to be published under the same name, behind only the *Detroit Free Press*. The paper first appeared as the Kalamazoo Gazette on Jan. 23, 1837. The paper was a weekly until March, 1872, when it became a daily publication.

Jan. 24, 1938
Upper Peninsula's "Storm of the Century"

People who live in the Upper Peninsula are accustomed to harsh winters. That doesn't mean something cannot come along to give them a jolt.

They took in stride a forecast one morning that predicted a so-so winter storm. But by the time the Weather Bureau better understood the situation and issued an update, it was too late for many schools, which had opened for the day. School buses were snowbound by a blizzard of historic proportions.

In Ironwood, students were trapped in a school for four days, sleeping on exercise mats in the gym as 12-foot drifts blocked the streets around the school. Two people died in the storm – one, a road commission employee who was asphyxiated in his truck while attempting to clear a road and, the second, a lumberjack who died of exposure. Workers were stranded at their jobs for days, while neighbors rescued neighbors from their homes. Rescuers braved the fierce, gale force winds and snowdrifts up to 18 feet to deliver food to the stranded.

On top of that mayhem, a fire broke out in Marquette that threatened the city's downtown. The Opera House and the Masonic Temple burned, along with two other structures. But despite the cold, winds and snow, firefighters were able to contain the fire the following day.

Karl Bohnak, a meteorologist at WLUC in Marquette, described the day in his book *So Cold a Sky: Upper Michigan Weather Stories:*

"The residents of Upper Michigan were enduring the midwinter doldrums quite well as they began a new week on January 24, 1938. The day dawned cloudy with a stiff northeasterly wind and a Weather Bureau forecast of rain or snow with much colder weather and flurries the next day. A storm followed by a cold wave; it was all part of the time-honored sequence of events during a normal winter. But this storm was to be different. Somehow, the atmosphere delivered up just the right combination of energy, moisture and cold air in just the right spot to unleash a blizzard of historic proportions from Ironwood to Newberry and from Houghton to Menominee."

Bohnak said the storm developed when a low pressure system over Texas collided with a cold front crashing in from Canada, sucking moisture from the Gulf of Mexico and pulling it north into the frosty Canadian air. The dynamic created a snow-making machine. The 30-hour snow and gale force winds left 32 inches on the ground at Ironwood.

A report from Marquette of 18 inches is probably low, Bohnak said, because the wind blew the snow around it was difficult to measure accurately. The snow was also heavy because the temperature was in the low 30s. Traffic around the city of Marquette ceased for three days.

Jan. 25, 1979
Robot kills worker

A robot, programmed to remove casting from shelves, fatally struck Robert Williams of Dearborn Heights with a mechanical arm when he climbed up to a rack to search for parts stored there. The robot smashed Williams in the head, killing him instantly. He worked at a Ford Motor Company casting plant in Flat Rock.

A jury awarded $10 million to his family. The family's lawyer, Paul Rosen, said: "The question, I guess is, 'Who serves who?'...I think we have to be very careful that we don't go backwards to the kind of notions we had during the industrial revolution that people are expendable."

Jan. 26, 1837
Michigan becomes a state

On this day in 1837, President Andrew Jackson signed legislation making Michigan the 26th state in the union. The act "to admit the State of Michigan into the Union, upon an equal footing with the original states" also was signed by two future presidents, James K. Polk and Martin Van Buren.

Many in Michigan were anxious to become part of the union and gain the benefits that came along with statehood, such as representation in the federal government.

Two years before statehood, acting territorial Governor Stevens T. Mason helped organize a convention to draft a state constitution. By June 1835, Michigan had a constitution, even if it wasn't yet a state. It was approved by popular vote that October.

But Michigan's efforts to become recognized by the federal government were delayed because of its dispute with Ohio over the land that contained Toledo. Ohio already was a state and therefore had more influence in Washington. Michigan's statehood was delayed until the territory agreed to give up Toledo for the Upper Peninsula. The story of that dispute is told in the entry for April 16.

Because Michigan had been behaving like a state since the fall of 1835 by operating an elected state government, the exact date on which to celebrate statehood was a matter of contention 100 and 150 years later. The solution was to stretch the celebration over three years.

Jan. 27, 1899
Death of Potawatomi Chief Simon Pokagon

Simon Pokagon, born near the St. Joseph River in 1830, authored many books and was considered the best-educated full-blooded Indian of his day.

The *Literary Digest* said of him: "He was a man of great moral strength. His appetites and passions were always under the control of an awakened conscience. There was something of the woman's tenderness and sweetness in a nature that could be stern when wrongs were to be denounced. He was a poet, orator, and philosopher.... With his death there passed from view one of the noblest children of the red race – a man whose life, thoughts and deeds proved how closely akin are the noble natures of all races, ages, and times."

Although he distributed a pamphlet, *The Red Man's Greeting*, at the 1893 Chicago World's Fair labeling the discovery of America as the Indians funeral, there is evidence that at other times Pokagon sought to strike a more conciliatory tone. In July 1897, the *New York Times* noted that Pokagon was ill and in a short front page article remarked about his achievements: "He is nearly eighty years old. For years he bent every energy to secure from Congress money which the United States owed the Potawatomis for lands. The old man's persistency finally won."

Pokagon wrote books about Indian history and Indian wars. He became a celebrity and a popular speaker.

He died a poor farmer on Jan. 27, 1899, in southeast Michigan.

Pokagon's tribe now owns and operates the Four Winds Casino in New Buffalo.

Jan. 28, 1898
Newspaper opposes very slow speed limit

Even before the state's roads and highways were clogged with cars and trucks, there was a lively debate about how fast was too fast to travel.

The Sault Ste. Marie city council passed an ordinance that set a 6 mile-per-hour speed limit, a little slower than a brisk jog.

The *Soo Times* said: "It is violated every day in the year by every man who by any means navigates in a wheeled or 'runnered' vehicle. A second-class ox team will go 6 miles an hour. A horse with every leg spavined and suffering in the last stages of the heaves will travel 6 miles an hour over a corduroy road. The average man will walk at the rate of 6 miles an hour – that is, when he is going to supper.

"If this council had made it 10 or 12 miles an hour, there would be some sense to it. There should be some law to regulate the speed of vehicles on the principal streets but any person with sense knows that it is a preposterous idea to think of limiting the speed to 6 miles an hour. It would be a wonder if a funeral procession wouldn't violate such a law as that."

Jan. 29, 1966
Nation's ice box warmest place in Michigan

Pellston, long known as the "nation's icebox" because the town at the tip of the mitt consistently records lower temperatures than the rest of the state, weathered a cold snap on this date in January, 1966 better than anywhere else around Michigan.

"The nation's icebox, Pellston, Mich., pulled the switch today,"

United Press International reported.

The temperature in Pellston was balmy compared with the rest of the state at 4 degrees Fahrenheit. It was the only weather station in Michigan to report a temperature above zero.

That day Grand Rapids and Lansing reported the lowest temps at 16 below zero, setting a new state record for Jan. 26.

Not far from Pellston, the deep freeze caused trouble for residents of Sugar Island. Three hundred people were stranded on the island after St. Mary's River froze and cut off the residents' only connection to the outside world, a ferry.

According to *USA Today*, several towns have vied for the title of "Icebox of the Nation," including three in Minnesota – International Falls, Tower, and Embarrass. The newspaper determined that based on its archive of daily temperatures going back to the mid-1990s, Stanley, Idaho is the nation's coldest town, in the contiguous 48 states.

According to the Village of Pellston, it claimed the icebox title in 1933 when residents endured the coldest temperature on record in the state of Michigan at -53 degrees Fahrenheit.

Jan. 29, 1945
Tom Selleck born

Tom Selleck was born in Detroit and the actor would maintain ties to his home state even after he found success in television as the star of Hawaii-set *Magnum PI*, in which he often donned a Detroit Tigers baseball cap. The mustachioed Selleck won fans by portraying an affable private eye with a good sense of humor.

He went on to star in the hit film *Three Men and a Baby* and he had a recurring role in the hit sitcom *Friends*. Early in his career Selleck was forced to pass on the role of Indiana Jones in *Raiders of the Lost Ark* because he had committed to *Magnum PI*.

Jan. 30, 1962
Acrobats killed in performance; panic averted by clown

Eight thousand people showed up at Detroit's Michigan State Fairgrounds Coliseum to watch a legendary high wire act.

While performing their famous seven-member chair pyramid, two members of the famous "Flying Wallendas" were killed and two seriously injured after one of the performers who was supporting the pyramid faltered.

Richard Faughan, 29, and Dieter Schoep, 33, were killed in the performance.

"For a moment there was a threat of panic in the crowd. But a circus clown calmed the spectators," the Associated Press reported.

A teenage girl, who was in a chair on top of the pyramid, was saved by two men in the group. They held onto her while circus attendants improvised a net she could be dropped into. Three of the performers managed to hold on to the wire.

The "Flying Wallendas" were an international sensation for decades. The was formed in Germany in 1923 by Karl Wallenda.

The performers were not sidelined by the Detroit tragedy, however. They went on to perform the following night.

"I feel like a dead man on the ground," Karl was heard to tell his wife about performing after the tragedy, according to the Flying Wallenda's web site. "I can handle the grief better from up there. The wire is my life. We owe it to those who died to keep going."

Karl Wallenda died after falling from a high wire in 1978 but his descendants continue to perform their circus act today.

Jan. 31, 1800
First Native American writer inspired by Ojibwa lore

Jane Johnston Schoolcraft was born Bamewawagezhikaquay in Sault Ste. Marie on Jan. 31, 1800 to Ozhaguscodaywayquay and Ireland-native John Johnson.

Not much is known about her early years, but as a young woman she married the famous anthropologist Henry Rowe Schoolcraft. It is known that her father loved to read and encouraged her and her seven other siblings to adopt that passion. Her mother was skilled at telling stories of her tribe. The combination of pursuits lead young Jane to begin writing poetry and prose at a young age.

While working as an Indian agent, Schoolcraft met Jane in 1822 and they married a year later. Both worked at collecting local histories and stories, preparing them for publications. The publications were the main source for Henry Wadsworth Longfellow's "The Song of Hiawatha," published in 1855.

Jane wrote a number of essays, stories and poems using Ojibwa legend and heritage as their base. She became the first known American Indian literary writer, first to write in a Native American language and to write out traditional Indian stories.

Jane died in 1842 while visiting her sister in Ancaster, Ontario. Even though she spent her life in Michigan, she was buried in Canada. Despite her mother's requests to Schoolcraft that he have her remains reburied in Sault Ste. Marie, he refused.

Jan. 31, 1945
Private Eddie Slovik executed for desertion

Private Eddie Slovik, a drafted soldier from Detroit, became the only solider executed for desertion during World War II on Jan. 31, 1945. The young man thought he would be excused from the draft because, as a teen, he acquired a prison record. However, with the manpower shortage, he was drafted in spite of that record.

He served in France and when he was ordered out for his final mission on Oct. 8, he refused. A military judge gave him the option of returning to his unit to fight rather than face court martial but Slovik refused to return. He was sentenced to death. Slovik petitioned Dwight D. Eisenhower, commander for the European front, for clemency but that request was denied because of the high desertion rates.

The 24-year-old Slovik was killed by a firing squad at 10 a.m. on Jan. 31, 1945, near Saint-Marie-aux-Mines. He was buried in the Oise-Aisne American Cemetery, along with 96 other American soldiers executed for crimes such as murder and rape.

John Tankey, a Dearborn Heights man who served with Slovik, said he wasn't surprised that Slovik chose a military arrest rather than fighting. "He told me once that he would gladly shoot at targets but if he had to kill an animal or a person, he wouldn't do it," Tankey recalled in 1974, the same year a television movie about the private aired bringing attention to the case and also to Slovik's widow, Antoinette. Slovik met his wife when both worked at Montella Plumbing in Dearborn.

After Slovik's execution, Antoinette and a group of Slovik's friends, including Tankey, lobbied politicians and even President Jimmy Carter to get a pension for Slovik's widow and to have Slovik's body returned from France for burial in Detroit.

In 1987 Slovik's remains were returned to Michigan and buried at Woodmere Cemetery in Detroit. He is buried next to his wife, Antoinette, who died in 1979. Despite the petitions, Slovik never has been offered a presidential pardon for his crime.

Jan. 31, 1849
Construction of Fort Wayne

Americans determined in the mid-19th Century that they needed yet again to build a fort in Detroit to prepare for war with Canada.

In January 1849, construction of Fort Wayne was completed.

But before a cannon could be delivered to the fort, differences between America and Britain were resolved and there was no need for another fort on the Detroit River after all. Instead of housing soldiers preparing for war, the fort sat unused for a decade, manned by a single watchman.

Then came the Civil War, when Americans in the North worried about Britain's support of the Confederacy. Suddenly Fort Wayne didn't seem so useless. The fort's walls were reconstructed and reinforced. In the first weeks of the war, Michigan's 1st Volunteer Regiment gathered at Fort Wayne to prepare for the war farther south. Throughout the war, the fort served as a place to organize troops for battle and as a war-time hospital for returning veterans. It served a similar purpose during the Spanish-American War.

After the war, Fort Wayne remained in service. It was a place of rest for troops rotated out of stations on the Western frontier.

During World War I and World War II, Fort Wayne served as an intermediary post between the army and the Michigan industrialists who furnished vehicles and airplanes for the war. Soldiers gathered at Fort Wayne before heading off for service in the Korean Conflict and the Vietnam War.

The fort also was used to house the homeless during the Great Depression and after the Detroit riots of 1967 it housed displaced families.

In the 1990s, a county-wide millage was adopted to fund the renovation of Fort Wayne so it could become a historical attraction. The renovation work never has been completed.

February

Feb. 1, 1937
The Flint sit-down strike

A labor dispute between workers and General Motors had been brewing for months. It boiled over when striking workers made a stand and escalated their sit-down strike to an all-out takeover of a Chevrolet plant in Flint. The workers stockpiled food and clubs in anticipation of the effort to stop cars from rolling off the assembly lines.

The United Auto Workers seized Chevrolet Plant No. 4 while staging a diversionary strike at nearby Plant No. 9 to draw company guards away from the true target of the strike. Plant No. 4 was of strategic importance to the strikers because it produced engines. Its closure meant the shut-down of Chevrolet's worldwide production.

The "Women's Emergency Brigade" played a critical role in the takeover. A group of 30 to 40 women, donned red berets along with red and white armbands and armed themselves with clubs. They took part in disturbances in both plants, breaking windows in the No. 9 Plant so the strikers inside could see what was coming at them as National Guard troops were called in.

During the takeover at No. 4, the women gathered before the plant and locked arms. When Flint police arrived to remove the strikers, they were met by the line of women. In one newspaper account, a girl in her teens spoke out to the police: "You can't get into this plant. Nobody can get in except our men. We are only protecting our husbands. Your wives would protect you just the same way if they had to. We are peaceful and law-abiding citizens but we are not going to let you into the plant."

The *New York Times* described the policemen's reaction: "The police, only a small detail commanded by a sergeant, stood around for a while with sheepish expressions on their faces."

Meanwhile, the 126th Infantry had been called in, including a machine gun detachment. The National Guard troops surrounded plants where strikes were taking place and cut off the food supply. Governor Frank Murphy, sympathetic with the strikers, never ordered the Guard into action.

The strike ended 10 days later when General Motors agreed to recognize the UAW as the bargaining agent for its members.

Feb. 2, 1784
Hatchet remains unburied

Taking Detroit and Michigan from the English after the Revolutionary War turned out to be more complicated than planned. Even though the Treaty of Paris put Michigan squarely in the hands of the Americans, in the frontier, treaties hashed out on another continent meant very little.

Michigan Every Day

Whoever controlled Detroit and Mackinac Island controlled the fur trade, so Britain was not eager to hand over Michigan. Wealthy fur merchants in Montreal used their influence with British authorities to block attempts to cede Detroit. The British maintained control of important forts and encouraged Indians to make life difficult for American settlers.

The first effort to take the region for the Union was in July, 1783 when General George Washington ordered Baron Steuben to Canada in an unsuccessful attempt to work out an agreement to obtain Detroit for the Americans.

Meanwhile, Major Ephraim Douglas was sent to Detroit to claim it for the Americans but he also was rebuffed. First he attempted to set up a council with Indian leaders to facilitate peace between the Americans and Indians but the meeting was derailed due to British interference. Nonetheless, Douglas was ordered to remain in Detroit to keep an eye on the British.

In a letter dated Feb. 2, 1784, Douglas described the trouble the English made for the Americans with the Indians.

Douglas recounted how a British official, Sir John Johnson, had assembled various western tribes in Sandusky and bribed them with lavish presents to remain loyal to the British. He noted how Johnson appealed to the Indians to remain peaceful – unless the Americans encroached into Michigan.

Johnson told the Indians, "that the King, his and their common father, had made peace with the Americans and had given them the country they possessed on this continent; but that the report of his having given them any part of the Indian lands was false, and fabricated by the Americans for the purpose of provoking the Indians against their father – that they should therefore shut their ears against such reports.... However, as the war between Britain and America was now at an end, and as the Indians had engaged in it from their attachment to the crown and not from any quarrel of their own, he would, as was usual at the end of a war, take the tomahawk out of their hand; though he would not remove it out of sight or far from them, but lay it down carefully at their side that they might have it convenient to use in defense of their rights and property, if they were invaded or molested by the Americans."

And the hatchet would not be buried for years to come.

Feb. 3, 1956
Speeders on guard for first time

For more than 50 years there was no state law that dictated how fast cars could drive on Michigan roads.

As cars gained more horsepower and roads became better, traffic deaths became a larger menace. An estimated 2,000 people died on Michigan roads in 1955. The state decided to conduct a crazy experiment.

Here's how United Press put it, in a wire story that announced the new law to the people of Michigan:

"Michigan's big experiment – the 65-55 mile-an-hour speed limit – will be launched one minute after midnight tonight. Motorists, who have been accustomed to using their own judgment on how fast they can safely wheel along Michigan's highways, will be subject to arrest if they exceed 65 miles-an-hour during the day and 55 miles-an-hour at night."

The state police commissioner announced there would be no sudden crackdown on drivers. Rather, the law would be put into force gradually. He added there would be a leeway of about 5 miles-per-hour, a margin drivers have come to expect to this day.

Police also announced they would put more unmarked cars on the roads and also buy radar devices to measure speed.

The law meant more police needed to be hired, leading to the hiring of 200 road patrol officers. It also meant many more signs were needed on the sides of highways.

"About 2,500 speed signs, placed every six to 10 miles throughout the state by the highway department at a cost of $26,000, will remind motorists of the 65-55 limit," the wire service reported.

Feb. 4, 1902
Lindbergh born in Detroit

Charles A. Lindbergh was born in Detroit at 1120 W. Forest Avenue. His family soon moved to Little Falls, Minnesota and he attended college at the University of Wisconsin, where he proved himself to have exceptional mechanical abilities.

While Lindbergh may have left Michigan at an early age and won fame for his trans-Atlantic flight while a resident of another state, Michigan newspapers treated him like a hometown hero. At least one elementary school and a number of streets are named after him. His mother, Evangeline Land Lindbergh, was born in Detroit in 1876. She graduated from the University of Michigan in 1899. She was the niece of John C. Lodge, a Detroit mayor in the 1920s, and for whom the Lodge Freeway was named. Although Lindbergh's parents never formally divorced, his mother lived in Detroit apart from her husband in Minnesota.

On May 20, 1927, when Lindbergh took off in the Spirit of St. Louis from Roosevelt Field near New York City en route for a 3,600-mile journey to Le Bourget Field near Paris, his historic feat crowded out news of a terrible event that happened two days earlier in Michigan.

The top of newspaper front pages across Michigan screamed over Lindbergh's Atlantic crossing, obscuring news of the deaths of 39 children and teachers in the Bath school disaster, which is described in the entry for May 18.

Feb. 5, 1959
Birth of Michigan's first female govenrnor

Jennifer Granholm may have been born in Vancouver, British Columbia, but she would make her mark in Michigan. Granholm's family moved to California when she was four and she later became a U.S. citizen.

Early on, Granholm attempted to parlay her good looks into a movie career in Hollywood, but that was not to be. Instead she attended the University of California-Berkley where as a Phi Beta Kappa she obtained degrees in political science and French. She went on to earn a law degree, also with honors, from Harvard Law School.

She wound up in Michigan where she clerked for U.S. Judge Damon Keith on the 6th U.S. Circuit Court of Appeals. In 1990, she became an assistant U.S. Attorney for the Eastern District of Michigan and in 1994 she was appointed Wayne County Corporation Counsel. In 1998, Granholm was elected Michigan attorney general, becoming the first woman to hold that position.

In 2002, Granholm became Michigan's first female governor.

She easily won reelection in 2006, despite frustration over the state's economy. Granholm convinced voters that she had the state's interests at heart and that her efforts to reform state politics were stymied by a Republican legislature.

Feb. 5, 1876
End of the Lansing mineral water craze

There was a time when people would come from far-flung places to Lansing seeking for a cure for their ailments. It wasn't Sparrow Hospital or any other medical clinic they sought – it was the mineral water that gushed from a well deep below the ground.

The mineral water was discovered around 1867 when a firm was established to take advantage of a bounty offered by the State of Michigan for salt. The state would pay 75 cents per barrel of brine and the firm Woodhouse and Butler set out to discover brine wells around Lansing.

It was in the old "Upper Town" section of Lansing where the firm made its profitable discovery – but it wasn't brine.

What they did find was mineral water and they found it at a time when it was widely believed that such a liquid could cure scores of ailments from gout to hay fever.

The Mineral Well Hotel and Spa was hastily constructed on the 900 block of River Street and soon attracted people from around the Midwest.

When the well first opened, it spewed mineral water at a rate of approximately 1,600 gallons each hour. Even though the well was prodigious, the folks who arrived with buckets or wagon-loads of barrels seemed determined to run the well dry. So many people sought the well water that the railroad extended its line from the depot on East Michigan Avenue to the hotel.

The mad rush for the water continued into the 1870s and the flow diminished. But just as the water seemed as if it would soon run dry, fire intervened. A blaze destroyed the Mineral Well Hotel and Spa on Feb. 5, 1876, bringing an end to Lansing's mineral water craze.

Feb. 6, 1974
A bad day for truck drivers

S triking truckers made life harrowing for truckers in Michigan who decided to go on with their jobs.

Approximately 100,000 independent truck owners wanted to shut down the nation's highways to protest the rising cost and scarcity of diesel fuel. Because the truckers carried more than half the nation's food, worry spread about food shortages.

Governor William G. Milliken doubled State Police road patrols and ordered the National Guard into the streets as a national truckers' strike threatened to bring violence to Michigan.

Despite the measures, bursts of violence were reported throughout the state as the strike unfolded.

In Washtenaw County, a livestock truck driver was injured slightly by flying glass when someone threw a brick through the trucker's windshield. Two shotgun blasts were fired into the front of a semi traveling on U.S. 12 in Hillsdale County. An egg delivery truck driver reported that someone shot at him at the intersection of I-94 and U.S. 131 near Kalamazoo. A Canadian truck driver was forced off I-75 in Wayne County by a car full of men who fired shots into his windshield. In Holland, a trucker who stopped at an intersection was assaulted and punched in the face.

Feb. 7, 1994
Did Lake Superior completely freeze?

A record cold winter in 1912 in the Upper Peninsula led to a debate among residents whether the largest of the Great Lakes could have completely frozen over.

On one side, Robert Blemhuber of Marquette, contended that the lake was too large to totally freeze, despite that January's average temperature in Marquette had been 1.3 degrees, the coldest in history. There were three consecutive days in the early part of that month when the high temperature never broke zero, another record.

Colonel J. W. Wyckoff disagreed with Blemhuber, arguing that he had proof. Wyckoff said he had boarded a stage in L'Anse that February where he met 20 Englishmen who had been stranded in Canada on the northern shore of Lake Superior. Because the winter came early that year the men, who were in the region to survey the land, did not receive supplies they needed to make it through the winter. In desperation, they hiked from Canada to Isle Royale to the Keweenaw penisula over Lake Superior – proof, Wyckoff believed, that the lake had frozen solid.

Blemhuber countered that the men hiked over a narrow section of Lake Superior and in its middle, to the northeast of the Keweenaw, it would never freeze over. In a back and forth in the newspapers, Blemhuber offered thousand-to-one odds in favor of his theory. Blemhuber believed that the ice absorbed some of the cold from the water leaving the water in the middle of the lake unable to reach a temperature cold enough to allow it to freeze.

In his book, *So Cold A Sky: Upper Michigan Weather Stories*, Karl Bohnak, a meteorologist in Marquette, wrote that satellite images of the lake have sometimes shown it to be completely covered in ice. This may be deceptive, however. For example, it appeared from a satellite image that Lake Superior was completely frozen on Feb. 7, 1994, toward the end of a 50-day cold snap that delivered below zero temperatures throughout Upper and Lower Michigan. While the image shows the lake to be frozen, in its center it apparently was only a very thin layer of ice that covered the water, Bohnak noted, and Blemhuber may not have been entirely wrong after all.

The events of the next couple of days, however, proved that it wasn't frozen solid, because high winds broke up thin ice over the middle of the lake very quickly, exposing open water.

Feb. 8, 1818
Birth of Michigan's Civil War governor

Any politician who spends his life in public office, is repeatedly elected to various positions and winds up a poor man must have the good of the people at heart. Such was the case of Austin Blair, Michigan's Civil War governor.

Blair was born in Caroline, New York on Feb. 8, 1818, where he grew up in a log cabin and helped his father farm the land.

After graduation from Union College in New York and admission to that state's bar association, Blair, like so many men of his generation, moved to the relatively unknown West and found himself in the young state of Michigan.

First he moved to Eaton Rapids where he set up a law practice. Two years later he moved to Jackson, where he became involved in politics, motivated by a disgust of slavery.

After serving a stint in the state House of Representatives, he was elected prosecutor for Jackson County and then to the state

Senate.

He helped form the Republican Party in Jackson and was soon after elected governor of the state, a position he held between 1861 and 1865.

Blair took the governor's job thinking it would be part-time work. The job then paid $1,000 per year. Given the light duties of office, he should have been able to spend most of his time in Jackson with his law practice.

However, the Civil War intervened and being governor suddenly became a full-time job. Blair handled the duties well enough to become known as Michigan's "war-time governor." He was forced to abandon his legal practice and, being an honest man unwilling to profit from his influence, he left office just months before the end of the war an impoverished man.

In the last 30 years of his life, he failed to be elected as a Republican to the U.S. Senate, his life-long goal. In the 1870s, he switched to the Democratic Party.

In 1892, friends took up a collection totaling $4,000 and presented it to Blair at Christmas as "a little aid, not as charity, but as a token of affection."

Blair died in 1894. In 1898, a statue of Blair was erected on state capital grounds at a cost of $7,200.

The statue features an inscription that describes the sacrifice that Blair made to the state: "He gave the best years of his life to Michigan and his fame is inseparably linked with the glorious achievements of her citizen soldiers."

Feb. 8, 1985
Stroh's to stop brewing in Detroit

In the years following Prohibition, there were hundreds of breweries in Detroit. One of them, Stroh Brewing Company, which survived Prohibition by switching production to "near-beer" and ice cream, was the last brewer standing by the mid-80s.

On Feb. 8, 1985, the Detroit institution announced it was leaving Detroit, and the following May it closed its brewery for good.

Competition from larger, national beer companies forced many Detroit brewers out of business and chased Stroh's from the state. However, two decades after Stroh's left, regional brewers like Bell's Brewery Inc. in Kalamazoo, Keweenaw Brewing Company of Houghton, Right Brain Brewery in Traverse City and dozens of others thrive throughout the state.

Feb. 9, 2005
Death of Richard Kearns,
inventor of intermittent wiper blades

Robert Kearns may have invented a product that almost everyone uses, at least when it's raining, but he is better known for the David vs. Goliath patent fight that ensued over his invention with two of the Big Three auto makers.

Kearns was born in Gary, Indiana, but he grew up in River Rouge, in the shadow of the Rouge Ford plant. After serving in the Office of Strategic Services during World War II, Kearns earned an engineering degree from the University of Detroit. He took a teaching job while also tinkering in his basement.

Kearns once said the inspiration for intermittent windshield wipers came to him on his wedding night after he suffered a blow to one of his eyes from a champagne cork. Kearns wondered why a windshield wiper couldn't operate sporadically like his eyelids.

Kearns developed and patented his invention, taking it to several auto makers in the early 1960s. Kearns was unable to strike a deal, probably because he insisted on manufacturing the wipers himself.

When Ford and Chrysler later introduced intermittent wipers similar to Kearns' design, Kearns sued both automakers. The cases dragged on for years and Kearns, who turned down settlement offers, developed a reputation for being eccentric and stubborn.

In the end Kearns prevailed, winning approximately $30 million in damages. His epic struggle against the automakers became the subject of a 2008 film *Flash of Genius* starring Greg Kinnear. He died of cancer on Feb. 9, 2005.

Feb. 10, 1763
Treaty of Paris signed;
Michigan handed from the French to the British

In what would be the first of two documents called "The Treaty of Paris" that would affect who owned Michigan, England and France formally agreed to end the French and Indian War, or, as it was known in Europe, the Seven Years War.

In fact, England had already taken the forts France held in Michigan, at Detroit, Michilimackinac and St. Joseph.

Michigan under French rule never really took off. The French barred non-Catholics from emigrating and they managed to convince only a few hundred French to come to the forts.

They also had a far different notion of what should happen to Michigan and America than the British. The French saw the Michigan wilderness as a bountiful resource that could be exploited for its beaver fur pelts. To clear the land for farms and large-scale settlements would jeopardize this lucrative trade. The British, on the other hand, wanted to clear the land, making it suitable for farms and safe for women and children. That meant controlling or removing Indian populations.

Both sides wanted to control the Great Lakes region in their own way, leading to the Seven Years War, the first between England and France that began in North America.

While the battles of the war were primarily fought in what are now Ohio, Pennsylvania and Canada, residents of Michigan played a critical role in the war. Its outcome would determine whether residents of Detroit and elsewhere in the future state would speak English or French.

Despite having an advantage early on in the conflict, France was outnumbered by English settlers and British forces in the East under the command of William Pitt. He eventually won the war, and Michigan, for England.

Feb. 11 1847
Thomas Alva Edison born

Thomas Alva Edison was born in Milan, Ohio, but within a few years he was in Michigan running a business. When Edison was seven years old, his family moved to Port Huron, then a booming lumber town.

Edison's father, in the grain and lumber business, built a 100-foot observation tower that overlooked Lakes Huron and St. Clair. At age 8, Edison got his entrepreneurial start by collecting 25 cents from anyone who wanted to climb the tower and take in the view.

The business lasted for three years until the tower was taken down. Next, Edison borrowed the family's horse and took to the streets selling onions, lettuce, peas, cabbage, beets and carrots. In the fall, he sold fruit such as apples, pears, plums and grapes.

Meanwhile, Edison became interested in chemistry, setting up a lab that contained hundreds of bottles labeled "poison" at his home.

At around age 10, Edison conducted an experiment on his friend and business partner, Michael Oates. Edison knew that balloons could rise when they contained a gas lighter than air and he set out to test whether this could be applied to humans. He fed his friend some chemicals, which caused severe stomach pain and almost death. Although he was punished, the incident did not deter him from further experimentation.

He later found a job on a train running between Port Huron and Detroit selling snacks and newspapers. He also began publishing his own newspaper, called the *"Grand Trunk Herald,"* on the train.

Drawn back to science, Edison set up a lab on the train – a move that eventually cost him his job. He spilled some phosphorus on the floor of the train that caused a fire. The conductor threw Edison and his belongings off the train at Mt. Clemens, but not before boxing the boy's ears, an assault Edison would later attribute to hearing problems that stayed with him throughout his life. It is more likely that scarlet fever he contracted at a young age caused his auditory problems.

While Edison moved away from Michigan in his adult life, his exploits as a youth indicated ingenuity that would result in such inventions as the phonograph and the light bulb. But he kept close ties to Michigan where his good friend, Henry Ford, lived. The two reveled in conversations about inventions and often went on camping trips with tire tycoon Harvey Firestone. They also shared a love of warm weather, both building winter homes in Fort Myers, Florida across the street from each other.

Feb. 12, 1781
Spanish flag flies over Niles

All of Michigan once was claimed by the British or the French. But only one town also was claimed by Spain, therefore earning its nickname, the Land of Four Flags.

Niles was among the earliest settlements in Michigan because of its strategic location in the fur trade.

A fort was built in Niles by the French in 1691 to control the fur trade in southern Michigan where missionaries and fur traders lived. However, during the French and Indian War, the fort was taken by the British in 1761.

It was during the confusion in the Revolutionary War that a fourth flag entered the picture.

On Feb. 12, 1781, soldiers from Spain, which controlled the territory west of the Mississippi, ran up their flag at the fort for a few hours.

They had entered the Revolutionary War as an ally of the Americans. Taking the British fort was simple since no garrison had been stationed there for 18 years.

Later, the Four Flags hotel in Niles commemorated the distinction.

Feb. 12, 1966
Rabbi Morris Adler shot in front of 900 in synagogue

Rabbi Morris Adler came to Michigan from Buffalo in 1938 when he accepted the position as an assistant rabbi of Congregation Shaarey Zedek in Detroit. He enlisted as an army chaplain in 1943 and he became the first Jewish chaplain to serve in Japan during World War II. He walked the city of Hiroshima after it was devastated by an atomic bomb.

50

When Adler returned to Michigan, he was elevated to chief rabbi in Detroit and later elected as lifetime rabbi for Congregation Shaarey Zedek that had moved to Southfield.

He served on an ethics board for the UAW under Walter Reuther and on an ethics panel for Governor George Romney.

Adler was shot by a deranged student on Feb. 12, 1966 before 900 shocked attendees at his synagogue while delivering a sermon about Abraham Lincoln. The attacker then killed himself. Adler died a month later.

Feb. 13, 1855
Michigan makes a stand against slavery

Before the Civil War and any federal protections for black persons in America, Michigan, along with other Northern states, passed legislation that helped Southern escaped slaves. In 1850, the federal government passed the controversial Fugitive Slave Law. The law made it illegal to help escaped slaves and dictated that slaves, even if they made it to free states in the North, had to be returned to their "owners" in the South.

Many Michiganders opposed slavery and wanted the practice stopped. The Republican Party, founded in Michigan as an anti-slavery party, went to work to on the issue. On Feb. 13, 1855, the Republican-controlled Michigan legislature expressed its anti-slavery position by passing a law that made it illegal to use county jails to detain escaped slaves. The law, called a "personal liberty law," also mandated that county prosecutors use their offices to defend the freedom of recaptured slaves from bounty hunters.

Michigan settlers had stood up to slave owners before.

In January, 1847, when four Kentuckians and a deputy sheriff arrived in town to hunt down an escaped slave, residents of Marshall helped Adam Crosswhite and his family escape to Canada.

As they helped the escaped slaves escape Michigan, the Marshall residents threatened to tar and feather the deputy sheriff and slave hunters.

Feb. 14, 1824
Annarbour founded

By the time John Allen and Elisha Rumsey met each other in Detroit, they had a lot in common.

Both men had come from the East to find their fortune in the wilderness of Michigan.

They were moving West to escape debts they owed in the East. Allen owed money in Virginia and Rumsey bailed out on his family with a loan he took out in New York.

They also each had a wife named Ann.

By the time they became partners in Michigan, they determined that filing land claims would turn their fortunes around. Eventually, they embarked on a successful endeavor that resulted in the creation of a famous Michigan city.

It was winter when the pair headed into the woods west of Detroit by sleigh. They picked a spot of thick woods near a creek that led into a river and they chose a name that reflected the area's numerous burr oaks and the first name of each man's wife – Annarbour.

They staked their claim on Feb. 14, 1824 and registered the plat in Detroit in May. They also arranged for their village to become the county seat of Washtenaw County.

Rumsey died in 1827 before his dreams of wealth were realized.

Allen went on to become a lawyer, postmaster, newspaper editor and village president. Within a decade of founding Ann Arbor, Allen sold land he bought for pennies for hundreds of dollars. Allen later headed to California where he attempted, and failed, to prospect for gold. He finally settled on 20 acres outside of San Francisco where he cultivated a garden. He died on March 11, 1851 "among strangers," according to a newspaper account.

Feb. 15, 1867
Ill-fated county established

Civil War demands for iron caused booming growth in the Upper Peninsula's Marquette iron range. As workers poured in, Ishpeming and Negaunee suddenly became major settlements, creating resentments over the political sway held by their county seat in Marquette.

A state representative from the district attempted to remedy the problem by introducing legislation that would slice out a large portion of western Marquette County and create a new county called Washington. The bill passed on Feb. 15, 1867.

Marquette loyalists immediately started legal proceedings against the law and the Michigan Supreme Court heard the case, People v. Maynard. After a week of deliberation, the Court deemed the bill unconstitutional, meaning that Washington County, which had existed for four months, was dissolved.

Feb. 15, 1935
Birth of an astronaut

From an early age Roger Bruce Chaffee dreamed of flying. He eventually set his goal on flying to the moon.

Born in Grand Rapids on Feb. 15, 1935, Chaffee grew up in Greenville. His father, Don, was a barnstorming pilot who passed on his love of flying and engineering to his son.

Chaffee earned a degree in aeronautical engineering from Purdue University and eventually became a lieutenant commander in the Navy, where he flew RA3Ds, Navy reconnaissance planes.

Over several years Chaffee participated in the grueling application process to become an astronaut. While on a hunting trip in Michigan in 1963, news came to his home in Ohio that he had been selected for one of the scarce spots in the NASA program.

After several more years of hard work he was named pilot of the Apollo I spacecraft.

But during tests of the spacecraft before the mission, on Jan. 27, 1967, as Chaffee sat in the pilot's seat, the Apollo I spacecraft burst into flames and Chaffee and two fellow astronauts were killed. The 31-year-old left behind a wife and two children.

He had earlier described his longing to be in space: "You'll be flying along some nights with a full moon. You're up at 45,000 feet. Up there you can see it like you can't see it from down here. It's just a big, bright, clear moon. You look up there and just say to yourself: I've got to get up there. I've just got to get one of those flights."

Feb. 16, 1897
First all-steel car ferry steams across Lake Michigan

Several companies, including the Ann Arbor Railroad, attempted to run car ferries across Lake Michigan with less than successful results because the ferries were built of wood.

In 1896, the Flint & Pere Marquette Railroad constructed and launched a car ferry built of steel that would set the standard for large open water crossings for years to come.

The *Pere Marquette*, built in Bay City by the Frank W. Wheeler Company, was 338 feet long, 57.7 feet wide and featured two engines. The ferry's design served as a prototype for car ferries around the world for 50 years, whether they sailed on fresh or salt water.

The first Lake Michigan crossing of the boat occurred on Feb. 16, 1897 from Ludington. It arrived the following morning in Manitowoc, Wisconsin.

The first voyage, a V.I.P. affair featuring a brass band, ferried 22 freight cars and the private car of the Flint & Pere Marquette's general manager.

Unlike many car ferries that plied the Great Lakes, the *Pere Marquette* led a mostly uneventful life until it was taken out of service in 1930 and scrapped in Manitowoc five years later. There were only two incidents that blemished the boat's safety record. In 1897, the Pere Marquette struck and sunk a small fishing tugboat at the dock in Ludington. Three years later, in heavy fog, the ship collided and sank a sailing scow some 12 miles off of Manitowoc, killing one person aboard the scow.

Feb. 17, 1864
Black Detroit soldiers mobilize for the Civil War

At the start of the Civil War, black soldiers were prevented from forming fighting units because even Northerners who opposed slavery believed Caucasians could do a better job.

As the war progressed, however, the North was desperate for troops and its leaders became pragmatic.

While laws still prevented states from organizing black regiments, nothing stopped the black soldiers from organizing themselves – and that's just what they did. Volunteers formed a regimental band that toured southern Michigan recruiting soldiers.

The First Michigan Colored Regiment was organized at Fort Ward in Detroit and later became known as the 102nd U.S. Colored Troops. It left Detroit on Feb. 17 with 900 men led by white officers, as were all black regiments who fought during the war.

The black soldiers received less pay than white soldiers and often were not treated well, living in filthy barracks at Fort Ward. The regiment saw more than 1,600 men serve in its ranks over 19 months. According to reports, five were killed in battle, seven died from wounds and 118 died of disease.

The regiment was disbanded in Detroit in October, 1865.

Feb. 18, 1818
Death of Simon Girty, hated man among pioneers

In his memoir, *The Iron Hunter*, Chase M. Osborn, Michigan's 27th governor, described in 1919 the lingering loathing some Michiganders still had for the British official Simon Girty:

"My parents would teach us American history traditionally and they were both well informed. As my father loved or hated so did I come to do. He could not, without rage, think of Simon Girty, who, as an English agent in Canada, had aroused the border Indians, and was charged with paying them fifty cents for the scalp of an American white woman and seventy-five cents to a dollar for the scalp of a man, but only twenty-five cents for a child or a gray-haired scalp. Some of our relatives had met this fate and it has left a bitterness that even I have to struggle against to this day."

But Girty was a more complicated fellow and perhaps not so rabidly interested in the scalps of Americans as was thought.

Whether or not Girty was paid a bounty for the scalps of American settlers, there was a time when Americans took out a bounty for *his* scalp.

Other accounts suggest he pleaded with the Indians for mercy on behalf of settlers and intervened often to save lives.

Girty was born in Pennsylvania but his family was captured by Indians when he was a boy. He was adopted by Seneca Indians and spent seven years away from his family. When he returned, he had come to prefer life as an Indian. More importantly, he had learned Indian languages, setting up his future career as a translator.

In the Revolutionary War, Girty first served on the American side but later became a British loyalist. From then on he was branded a turncoat. After Girty took part in Indian war parties against Americans, an $800 bounty was put on his scalp according to one source.

At the end of the war, Girty settled on a farm in Canada near Fort Malden, or present-day Amherstburg, Ontario, across the Detroit River from Grosse Île.

Girty reportedly took part in the War of 1812, in which the British encouraged Indian attacks on Americans. At the war's end, Girty was in his 60s, in poor health and had failing eyesight. He died on Feb. 18, 1818.

Feb. 19, 1940
Birth of William "Smokey" Robinson

William "Smokey" Robinson was born in Detroit on Feb. 19, 1940. As a youth, Robinson began singing around Detroit and formed a group called the Matadors, later renamed the Miracles.

Robinson's big break came through a chance encounter with Berry Gordy, Jr. that led to a contract with Motown Records.

A 1980 profile in *Time* magazine proves Robinson's foray into music was no sure thing.

"The son of a truck driver and a government worker who died when her only son was ten, William ("Smokey") Robinson was a kid who spent his candy money on music books but figured that the future would be brighter if he followed a more practical bent. He thought about dentistry, considered electrical engineering, 'but between high school and college I met Berry Gordy.'"

The Miracles first hit was "Shop Around" and from there Robinson would go on to score eight gold records in a decade. He made sure no one could think of Motown, the city, without thinking of Motown, the sound.

Robinson left the Miracles in 1972 to become the vice president of Motown where he worked to develop the sound of other artists such as the Temptations, the Four Tops and Marvin Gaye. He continued to write thousands of songs while launching a solo career.

Robinson was inducted into the Rock and Roll Hall of Fame in 1987. Everyone in Michigan said, "I Second That Emotion."

Feb. 19, 1955
Birth of Jeff Daniels

Jeff Daniels, the all-American looking actor, was born in Athens, Georgia, but his name is now synonymous with Michigan. His family moved to Chelsea when he was a boy. He attended Central Michigan University, leaving in his junior year to seek fame and fortune in New York City.

Although he appeared in many Broadway roles, Daniels became a well-known actor after he appeared as Debra Winger's ex-husband in the 1983 Oscar-nominated *Terms of Endearment*. He also appeared in the Woody Allen film *Purple Rose of Cairo* among dozens of other movies. The film left its mark. In 1986, he opened the Purple Rose Theatre in Chelsea, the town where he lives with his wife and their three children.

Daniels made his directorial debut with *Escanaba in da Moonlight* – a play he also wrote – at the theatre. Several other of his plays have been preformed there.

He is also known for his rabid support of the Detroit Tigers.

Feb. 20, 1937
Sit-down strike at cigar maker
Bernard Schwartz Company

For more than a century Detroit had been a cigar and chewing tobacco manufacturing center, a status that was boosted during the Civil War when thousands of troops from Michigan spread Detroit cigars across the country.

Imported tobacco that was rolled into cigars or processed into chewing tobacco was responsible for several fortunes made in the 19th century. The industry lingered in Detroit into the 20th century. During the 1930s when union organization took off in the auto industry, it spread to other work places as well.

In 1937, hundreds of female cigar workers opted to organize a labor action based on a model that had worked for auto workers – they launched a sit-down strike at the Bernard Schwartz Company. The Bernard Schwartz Company was named for its founder, a Jewish immigrant, and it produced R.J. Dunn Cigars. It was one of Detroit's best-known family-run businesses.

The company was about to become better known on Feb. 20, 1937, when some 400 workers stopped working and sat down on the job. The result was a severe response from the Detroit Police Department after the company appealed to the city for help. The women had armed themselves with clubs. Detroit police responded with heavily armed officers ready to clear the factory of its striking workers, using whatever means necessary.

Newspaper photographers chronicled the violent confrontation, which prompted a labor-organized public protest the following month in Cadillac Square.

After the strike, Detroit's cigar manufacturing declined throughout the 20th century when much of the production shifted to Ybor City, Florida, where Cuban immigrants used their expertise to turn it into the country's center of cigar manufacturing.

Feb. 21, 1911
Beginning of brief, ill-fated Cloverland craze

Roger Andrews, who moved to Menominee in 1901 as editor of the *Menominee Herald Leader*, really wanted to see the Upper Peninsula's economy take off.

Andrews called a meeting of business leaders and formed the Upper Peninsula Development Bureau on Feb. 21, 1911, creating the forerunner of the U.P. Travel and Recreation Association.

The organization was formed at a time when residents of the peninsula saw a crisis looming. With the logging days behind them, Yoopers had no idea what could sustain their economy in the future.

The previous November, the Alger-Smith Lumber Company closed in Grand Marais, spelling doom for that village. Telephone lines were yanked from walls and train service that had run for 15 years to the Lake Superior town ceased. The population dropped from 3,000 to 650 in two years and people around the Upper Peninsula wondered if their communities would see the same fate as logging companies, timber mills and mines closed.

Andrews had an idea to turn things around – the Upper Peninsula should be known as "Cloverland."

He soon published a magazine by that name billing itself as "The Only Illustrated Monthly Magazine in the Upper Peninsula." The publisher believed that clover could grow anywhere in the tens of thousands of acres of U.P. land freshly cleared of timber.

Taking good terms on land, sheep herders from across the west bought U.P. land and arrived with thousands of sheep. Meanwhile, the Western Land Securities Company acquired thousands of acres near Seney and planned to drain the swampland and sell off portions to farmers. Some farmers arrived and attempted to plant crops on the drained swamp with no luck.

A company that had attempted to develop the town of New Seney near the site of the once bawdy and bustling lumber town abandoned the project as sheep herders across the peninsula failed to prosper. By 1921, Andrews switched the emphasis of Cloverland to tourism and in 1927 changed the name of the magazine to Hiawathaland, a nod to the famous poem by Henry Wadsworth Longfellow.

Cloverland, it turned out, sounded too agricultural, and Andrews realized the endeavor he had so zealously spent a decade and a half promoting was destined to be a marginal contributor to the U.P.'s economy.

Feb. 22, 1920
Upper Peninsula's whiskey rebellion

A dispute between Iron County and the federal government began when federal agents wanted two brothers charged with possession of 11 barrels of wine discovered in a room above their store.

At an Iron River Town Hall hearing, County Prosecutor Martin S. McDonough sought to have the charges against the brothers dismissed.

He argued that the evidence showed the barrels of wine were for personal use, that the brothers had a surplus of grapes and needed to make them into wine before they spoiled and that there was no evidence the men planned to sell the wine.

The charges were dismissed but that outcome enraged federal officials in Chicago, who believed local Iron County officials were blocking enforcement of Prohibition laws.

Federal officers were sent to confiscate the wine despite what happened in the local court. McDonough and the local police took the confiscated wine from the federal agents and returned it to the brothers. This caused a federal official to announce on Feb. 22, 1920 that Iron County was in revolt and would be made to submit to federal law.

Major A. V. Dalrymple, Supervisor of Prohibition Enforcement for the Central Division in Chicago, asked the federal government for armed men to enforce the law. Dalrymple received the go-ahead from Attorney General Alexander Mitchell Palmer to do whatever he needed.

In a telegram to Washington, D.C., Dalrymple said "My information is that this is not a factional dispute, but an actual revolt against the United States government.... I shall take as many men as are necessary from Chicago and, in cooperation with the Michigan constabulary, I shall put respect and fear of the law into Iron County, cost what it may."

But a day later, the "Whiskey Rebellion of the Upper Peninsula" was no more.

Dalrymple sent in his troops and although McDonough backed down, mine workers throughout the region scurried to hide their stores of alcohol in the hills around Iron River.

Feb. 22, 1922
Great ice storm strikes Cadillac

When the most severe ice storm to strike Cadillac hit in 1922, trees and utility poles collapsed under the weight of the ice. Roads were impassable.

Telephone and electric service was lost for days. The ice-covered town sent photographers into the streets to capture the weather disaster, spawning countless post cards. Streets covered in ice appeared unworldly and looked to be made of crystal. Fallen trees and collapsed utility poles jutted into the city's ice-covered streets.

Feb. 23, 1973
First lottery millionaire announced

The first person to win $1 million in the newly-launched state lottery took his windfall in a very humble manner. Entered into the drawing after winning a $25 weekly prize, the man bought a 29-cent rabbit's foot in a local dime store for good luck.

A United Press International writer put it this way: "Herman Millsaps took the 7:10 Greyhound bus to Lansing Thursday morning with his wife, sack lunch and bottle of coffee. Before the day ended he was a millionaire."

Millsaps, of Taylor, worked as a $176.80-a-week lumber cutter for Chrysler Corporation.

After winning the prize, Millsaps laid out $290.16 for a 14-inch portable color television, saying, "Everyone's seen us on TV except us."

The runner-up was Mary Virginia McCrumb, of Eagle, which is near Lansing. The press dubbed McCrumb the "happiest loser in the state," because while she missed out on the million-dollar first prize, she walked away with $100,000 and planned to take a vacation to Hawaii.

The 50-year-old housewife and nine other lottery finalists were asked to come to a presentation at the Lansing Civic Center for the surprise announcement of who would win the million-dollar prize.

Seven won $5,000 and a prize of $50,000 was also handed out. The winner of the $50,000 prize was the only contestant who failed to turn up at the ceremony. She had been injured in a car accident earlier in the week.

The win was not all roses for Millsaps, however. An ex-wife sued him for a share of the winnings but she did not prevail in the lawsuit.

Feb. 24, 1844
Olivet College founded

Olivet College, located between Battle Creek and Lansing, was founded by Father John J. Shipherd as an institution to provide intellectual, moral and spiritual improvement to students.

Olivet was the first college in the nation to offer education to female and black students.

Its commitment to provide an education to anyone regardless of race, sex, or ability to pay spelled trouble for Olivet in its early years. After its founding, on Feb. 24, 1844, the college was unable to receive a state charter because of the abolitionist beliefs it espoused. Indeed, to offer college education to women and minorities was radical at the time.

In 1859, the school finally received its state charter and in 1863 the school graduated its first class – composed of three female students.

Feb. 25, 1863
Woman arrested for impersonating a male soldier

Some women will go to great lengths to be with the men they love. The *Detroit Advertiser* in its Feb. 25, 1863 edition ran such a story.

"This morning about 11 o'clock, a very pretty woman who gave her name as Mary Burns, was arrested by officer Ven for being attired in soldier's habiliments. It appears that about two weeks ago her lover enlisted in the Seventh Cavalry, and immediately was made a dashing sergeant.

"Mary, with a remarkable love for the Union (of herself and Sergeant) donned soldier's garb and also enlisted in the regiment, with the determination to follow him. She enrolled her name as John Burns. She had been in the regiment indicated for about ten days. She was taken to jail and will be arraigned at the police court.'"

Later that year the *New York Illustrated News* published a story about the exploits of a young woman who enlisted in the military to follow her love called "The Romance of a Poor Young Girl." The story detailed the woman's enlistment with a regiment from Michigan and her successful ploy to hide her identity, act gallantly in the Battle of Pea Ridge and even conceal her true identity from the lieutenant she loved.

That story, supposedly about a woman named Annie Lillybridge, turned out to be a fraud, probably inspired by the story of Mary Burns.

The most famous female soldier who managed to get away disguised as a man also was from Michigan. Sarah Emma Edmonds, a Canadian who moved to Flint to escape an abusive father, enlisted as Frank Thompson with the 2nd Michigan Infantry, seeing battle at Bull Run and elsewhere and serving as a Union spy. She deserted when she came down with malaria and was afraid a doctor would uncover her true identity, although there is evidence that some of the soldiers who served at her side knew she was female anyway.

She became famous with the publication of her memoir, *Nurse and Spy in the Union Army*. She later attended a reunion of her regiment in Flint, where many of her fellow soldiers were shocked to learn, years later, that she had served among them. She died in 1898.

Feb. 25, 1901
Grand Rapids water supply scandal

A plot was hatched early in the 20th century by a few men to profit from a complicated public works scheme in Grand Rapids.

The group planned for the city to authorize bonds for construction of a water pipeline from Lake Michigan to Grand Rapids, about a 30-mile distance. Payoffs in the plot included $100,000 to Lant K. Salsbury, a central figure in the scandal, thousands of dollars to 16 of the city's 24 aldermen and bribes of up to $10,000 to newspaper editors and $500 to a reporter.

On Feb. 25, 1901, Grand Rapids Alderman Christian Gallmeyer called for an investigation into the deal, which he thought suspicious.

Eventually, Salsbury and some of the other conspirators were tried. Salsbury, a lawyer, was convicted, sent to prison and disbarred. He served a federal prison sentence for bank fraud, but before he could serve his state sentence for defrauding city taxpayers, Salsbury told the whole conspiracy story to the prosecutor.

Fourteen aldermen were charged with taking bribes, along with the city clerk, a newspaper reporter, and the mayor. The reporter admitted taking the bribe, although the editors were accused of taking far more money.

After serving his term, Salsbury moved to Memphis, Tennessee and made a fortune brokering cotton. In 1921, the prosecutor who tried Salsbury agreed to help the ex-convict attempt to get back his bar license because he had lived a life for two decades displaying high moral character.

But a Lake Michigan water system for Grand Rapids was doomed. A city commissioner raised the idea at a city council meeting in 1939. The proposal stunned the commissioners. An older commissioner, familiar with the scandal, blasted back that idea wasn't worth the paper it was written on.

Feb. 25, 1861
Albion College: early educational opportunity for women

Albion College was authorized by the state legislature on Feb. 25, 1861 to confer four-year degrees for male and female students.

The school began life as an outpost that offered education to the children of early settlers and Indians. It also was one of the first schools in the Midwest to offer coed education.

A liberal arts school, Albion College now has approximately 2,000 students who choose from 27 academic majors. Its high academic standards make it one of the finest schools in the Midwest.

Feb. 26, 1905
No dance halls, saloons or variety theater
for Ann Arbor youth

Ann Arbor's Mayor Arthur Brown announced on this day that he would instruct the city's police department to crack down on debauched behavior by students.

A newswire story said the mayor planned to enforce a measure passed that year called the "gaming law."

"This means that the lid will be screwed down tighter than ever on Ann Arbor," the reporter wrote.

The law dictated that a student who was a minor and attended any school in the state could not frequent any saloon, bar room, dance house, concert saloon, variety theater, billiard hall or bowling alley in Ann Arbor.

The penalty for violation was a fine of up to $50 and up to 30 days in jail.

"As there are some saloons and billiard halls that draw trade from students who have not yet attained their majority, the new order will have quite an effect," the news report concluded.

Feb. 26, 1800
Birth of Lucius Lyon

In the story of Michigan's growth in the 19th century from a frontier outpost to a thriving young state, the name of Lucius Lyon pops up constantly.

Lyon was born on Feb. 26, 1800 and, like so many of Michigan's early leaders, in an Eastern state, in this case Vermont. As a young man he moved to Bronson, which later became Kalamazoo. He was a land surveyor, an important and well-regarded position in those days. Before land could be owned, it needed to be surveyed and the area mapped.

Lyon, as a representative from the Michigan Territory to Congress, presented a petition requesting statehood for Michigan in

1833. The petition was doomed due to the dispute with Ohio over where the border between the states would be drawn and, particularly, which state would possess Toledo.

Lyon also was the first elected U.S. Senator from Michigan. Due to the border dispute and the delay it caused in allowing Michigan to join the Union, Lyon was forced to sit in the Senate as a non-voting member until Michigan became a state.

South Lyon, Lyon Township (Oakland County), Lyon Township (Roscommon County) and Lyons Township are all named after him. In 1936, Lyon purchased much of the property in a small village in Ionia County and renamed in Lyons, Michigan. However, he never lived there.

He died in 1851 in Detroit.

Feb. 27. 1836
Birth of Russell Alexander Alger;
Civil War hero, lumberman and governor

When Russell Alger was an 11-year-old boy growing up in Ohio, both his parents died, leaving him to care for a younger brother and sister.

Alger found work on a farm in Richmond, Ohio and for the next seven years raised his siblings. At 18, he secured work as a teacher during the winter months.

He became a lawyer by apprenticing at a law firm, which was common in those days, and obtained employment with a firm in Cincinnati. That first job only lasted a few months because Alger suffered from an illness caused by hard work and close confinement.

Alger left the law field and moved to Grand Rapids where he found his fortune in the lumber business.

But his foray into logging was interrupted by the Civil War. He eventually became a brevetted major general in the war after first serving with the 2nd Michigan Calvary, where he earned a hero's reputation. In 1864, at Trevillian Station, Virginia he led a force of 300 men that captured many times that number of enemy soldiers.

General Philip Sheridan mentioned Alger in a report to the War Department:

"The Calvary engagement of the eleventh and twelfth was by far the most brilliant one of the present campaign. The enemy's loss was very heavy. My loss in captured will not exceed one hundred and sixty. They are principally from the 5th Michigan Calvary. This regiment, Colonel Russell A. Alger commanding, gallantly charged down the Gordonville road, capturing 1,500 horses and about 800 prisoners, but were finally surrounded and had to give them up."

Alger went on to a special assignment where he reported directly to President Abraham Lincoln.

After the war, he settled in Detroit where he was known as General Alger. He quickly became one of the largest producers of pine timber in the world, owning extensive pine tracts throughout North America.

Alger also included railroads and copper mining among businesses that made him a wealthy man.

In 1884, he was elected governor, serving from January 1, 1885 to January 1, 1887. He declined re-nomination in 1886. President William McKinley appointed Alger Secretary of War in 1897. In 1902, Alger was appointed by Michigan Governor Aaron T. Bliss to the United States Senate to fill a vacancy left by the death of James McMillan. He was elected to the Senate in 1903, serving until his death in 1907.

A memorial fountain to Alger is in the Grand Circus Park in downtown Detroit. Alger County also is named for him.

Feb. 28, 1977
First high school basketball game televised

Interest in high school basketball had never reached a level that caused a television station to broadcast a game. That changed when a player emerged at Everett High School in Lansing who played the sport at an unimaginable level.

Earvin Johnson, Jr. was born in Lansing and grew up obsessed with basketball. He dribbled a ball around his neighborhood and brought it to bed with him at night. He was so good at the sport that he earned his famous nickname, "Magic", while playing for his high school team.

Johnson scored 27 points in a game against Lansing Eastern High School that was televised on Feb. 28, 1977.

Johnson stayed close to home for college, attending Michigan State University becoming a Spartan. In his sophomore year, in 1979, he led his team to a national title. The following year, he entered the NBA draft and was selected by the Los Angeles Lakers, who had the number one pick. In his rookie season, Johnson led the Lakers to the NBA finals and won the finals' MVP award, the first rookie to do so. Johnson would go on to win four more championships before his Hall of Fame career ended when he announced he was HIV positive in 1992. He would go on to play in the Olympics that year.

He came out of retirement for a short-lived attempt at a comeback in the 1995-96 season, but Johnson shifted his focus to running the businesses he owned, including Magic Johnson Theaters, a nationwide chain of movie theaters located in minority neighborhoods.

Johnson's high profile and work to educate people about HIV helped dispel a misconception that the disease posed a danger only to homosexuals or intravenous drug users

Feb. 29, 1952
Commie witch hunt comes to Michigan

Hearings on communist activity came to Michigan at the height of the "red scare" when the House Committee on Un-American Activities held a hearing in Detroit in early 1952.

An unlikely FBI informant, known to newspaper readers as "Grandmother Bereniece Baldwin," testified about her work as an undercover agent and she outed communists across the state.

Others had been forced to testify before the committee, refused, and were threatened with contempt charges and fired from their jobs.

Baldwin told the committee about communist organizations in East Lansing and Ann Arbor that included teachers at the universities.

She went on to describe communist organizations throughout the state, including a number of Upper Peninsula communities.

A day earlier, future Detroit Mayor Coleman Young had testified. Young didn't shy away from taking on the committee. He accused members of being racist and defended his efforts in working for civil rights.

March

March 1, 1962
Attention Kmart shoppers!

The seeds of Kmart sprung up in Detroit, 1899, when Sebastian Spering Kresge opened a modest convenience store in downtown Detroit.

Kresge sold items for five or ten cents, earning the store the name "five-and-dime." In 1912, the S.S. Kresge Company operated 85 stores.

By the late 1950s, the Kresge Company was run by Harry B. Cunningham, who could tell the landscape was changing and small stores selling a limited number of items for a few coins would not be part of the future.

Cunningham and a team designed a new kind of store – larger and adapted to the suburbs. That led to the opening of the first Kmart on March 1, 1962 in Garden City.

That same year two other stores opened in other states that proved to be the rivals of Kmart over the years – Wal-mart, founded in Rogers, Ark. and Target, which opened in Roseville, Minn.

In 2002, Kmart filed for bankruptcy. It emerged from Chapter 11 in 2003. It then merged with Sears, Roebuck in 2005 to form Sears Holdings, located in Troy. Today Kmart employs more than 130,000 workers.

March 1, 1872
Buck's Opera House opens in Lansing

At the time of the Buck's Opera House opening in 1872, the opulent 1,100-seat venue was considered one of the best in the Midwest and another signal that Lansing had come a long way in a few decades.

One observer commented that "if there is anywhere in Michigan, outside of Detroit, a finer building than the Opera House, we have not seen it," according to Birt Darling, author of *City in the Forest: The Story of Lansing*.

Daniel W. Buck, a one-time Lansing mayor, owned the building on the corner of Washington Avenue and Ionia Street.

At its first performance, Lansing residents saw a production of Macbeth that featured actor Edwin Booth, the younger brother of John Wilkes Booth.

In 1890, Buck sold the theater to James J. Baird, who renamed it the Baird House, and he, in turn, sold the property to Frank Stahl and Fred Williams.

There had been many other owners by the time the building was torn down, in 1939.

March 2, 1972
Hudson hopes to host pandas

The front page of the *Hudson Post-Gazette* blared "Pandas for the People of Hudson." And, for a while, the people of the Lenawee County town of 2,500 hoped that someone half a world away would take them seriously.

The backdrop was a visit by President Nixon to China where he met with Premiere Chou En-Lai, who had given Nixon two pandas as a souvenir of his trip. They were to be awarded to the American zoo that proved they would best be able to provide for their care.

The people of Hudson figured they could get in on the competition, even though they faced some pretty formidable opponents – the National Zoo in Washington D.C., the San Francisco Zoo and the Lincoln Park Zoo in Chicago.

"Why should the big cities get all the good stuff?" City manager Paul Goode said. "When all the little towns are left out in the cold. ... There isn't a zoo in the country that wouldn't sell its soul for those pandas."

Goode and Mayor Ray Curran were not deterred by the fact that Hudson had no zoo. They sent a Western Union telegram to the president and the premiere in China, addressed to "The Great Hall of the People, Peking, The People's Republic of China."

The telegram explained that the people of Hudson wished the honor of "receiving and caring for" the pandas. The push gained national attention, thanks to the public relations flair of the city manager and mayor. The Chamber of Commerce established a "Hudson Panda Fund" to raise money.

The town's high school considered changing mascots. The high school football coach said he was pondering the name change and its psychological impact on players. But the hullabaloo was not to last long.

Within a month, the National Zoo announced it would be home to the pandas and Ling-Ling and Hsing-Hsing were at home by mid-April.

March 2, 1836
Bronson becomes Kalamazoo

In 1826, Governor Stevens T. Mason approved an action by the state legislature changing the name of a town called Bronson to Kalamazoo, a word derived from the language of the Potawatomi.

It may not have been a preference for the sounds of the two words – Bronson or Kalamazoo – that prompted the switch.

The people of Bronson may have wanted to become the people of Kalamazoo because of their animosity toward their namesake.

That man was one of the area's first settlers, Titus Bronson, who bought the land where the county seat of Kalamazoo was founded.

Bronson was viewed as an eccentric by the other settlers.

Prior to settling in Michigan at the age of 41, Bronson traveled around the country for 10 years and was thought of as "an itinerant potato grower," moving from place to place, planting a crop of "Neshannock" potatoes, selling them and moving on. He was known as "Potato Bronson."

Unlike most pioneers, Bronson didn't drink and he denounced those who did. Despite his willingness to sell plots of land in his newly formed village, he hated land speculators. And he was known to mindlessly start whittling things.

Perhaps some of the other prominent landowners around Kalamazoo became fed up or embarrassed by Bronson because they petitioned the legislature to change the name of the city.

The action so offended Bronson that he packed up and moved farther west. He finally settled in Iowa to farm. But in 1842, land speculators swindled him out of his property and he had to rely on his children for support.

Bronson died at the age of 65 on a trip to Connecticut to visit relatives.

March 3, 1875
The nation's second national park founded

Mackinac Island became a national park in recognition of its natural beauty and its pivotal role in early American history.

It was second behind Yellowstone National Park, which Congress organized three years earlier. Twenty years later the federal government turned the park over to the state and it became the first state park in Michigan.

Today it is know for its fudge, Victorian summer homes and ban on motorized vehicles. Tourists must get around by foot, bicycle or horse-drawn carriage.

March 4, 1964
Jimmy Hoffa convicted of jury tampering

James Riddle Hoffa, who became president of the International Brotherhood of Teamsters out of the Detroit local, was 51 years old and head of the nation's largest union when the Kennedy administration set its sights on him.

He was tried in federal court in Chattanooga and found guilty of two counts of jury tampering in a 1962 trial.

It was the fifth time in seven years Hoffa was brought up on

---

charges and he managed to win acquittal, dismissal or a hung jury in each previous case. Attorney General Robert Kennedy became a bitter Hoffa foe.

The charges stemmed from an earlier trial for Hoffa when he was charged in Nashville with accepting illegal payments from an employer. He was accused of taking $1 million from a trucking company to ensure labor peace.

Hoffa and codefendants were accused of offering money and other help to jurors in that trial if they voted to acquit him.

After his 1964 conviction, Hoffa stood outside of the courthouse and told reporters: "If this is justice in the United States, I pity those who don't have the money to pay for an appeal.... This was a railroad job in my opinion."

Hoffa was sent to prison until 1971, when his 15-year sentence was cut short by President Richard Nixon on the condition that he stay out of union activities for 10 years. He disappeared on July 30, 1975 in one of the nation's most famous unsolved mysteries.

March 5, 1902
Birth of Fred Bear

Fred Bear, considered the father of modern bow hunting, is perhaps best known from the Ted Nugent song that takes his name for its title. He was born in Waynesboro, Pennsylvania but was drawn to Detroit for a job in the auto industry, which he found at age 21 with the Packard Motor Company.

It wasn't until his late 20s that Bear first bow hunted, and it took him six years of trying before he harvested his first deer. He developed bow hunting products and became adept at promoting them in national magazines and adventure films he produced. Along the way he became a legendary hunter. Bear lived much of his life in Grayling, where his ashes were spread after his death April 27, 1988.

March 5, 1658
Founder of Detroit born in France

In a French town, St. Nicolas-de-la-Grave, there is a Michigan historical plaque marking, in two languages, the home where Antoine Laumet was born on March 5, 1658. Laumet became known as Antoine Laumet de la Mothe, sieur de Cadillac. Later in life he would move to North America and engage in exploration west from Montreal.

On July 24, 1701, he founded the settlement that became Detroit. Accompanied by one hundred troops of the Compagnie Franche de la Marine and nearly as many Indians, Cadillac claimed Detroit in the name of King Louis XIV, who directed him to establish forts connecting Quebec and New Orleans. Cadillac brought his family to Detroit and remained there until 1710.

In 1717, after serving as Governor of Louisiana, he returned to France. He died in Castelsarrasin in 1730.

In 1972, the Detroit Historical Commission and Society gave the village of St. Nicholas-de-la-Grave $20,000 to purchase and restore his house as a museum.

March 6, 1896
First car driven on Detroit streets

The evening was cold and snowy. It was late before the engine revved up and the car was able to pull onto the street.

At John Lauer's machine shop on St. Antoine St. just south of Jefferson Ave., Charles B. King, a 27-year-old college-educated engineer was getting ready to drive the first automobile on the streets of Detroit.

King's name may be mostly lost to history, but he beat Henry Ford and Ransom E. Olds to the starting line.

King took St. Antoine toward Jefferson to Woodward and made it to Cadillac Square before the engine died.

The short trip got only a little attention in Detroit newspapers.

The following day the *Free Press* mentioned the brief drive on the back page, written by a reporter who apparently was totally unaware of what the automobile would do to Detroit and the world:

"The first horseless carriage seen in this city was out on the streets last night. The apparatus seems to work all right, and it went at the rate of five or six miles an hour at an even rate of speed."

March 7, 1932
"Hunger parade" turns to riot at a Ford plant

Five people were killed and dozens injured on March 7, 1932 when tensions over a sour economy turned on the Ford Motor Company.

The *New York Times* reported that the 3,000 unemployed workers had "communists in their midst" when they marched on the gates of the Ford Motor Company's plant in Dearborn.

However, the protesters were actually regular working class folks who were so frustrated they demonstrated despite bitterly cold temperatures.

The melee began as unemployed residents planned to go to the company's Ford Rouge Plant and, through a committee, ask for work. It started quietly, but before it was over "Dearborn pavements were stained with blood, streets were littered with broken glass and the wreckage of bullet-riddled automobiles and nearly every window in the Ford plant's employment building had been broken," the *Times* said.

A Ford detective was seriously injured as he attempted to drive through the mob and was recognized by some of the demonstrators. The crowd overturned the detective's car, pelted it with stones and someone fired a shot into the automobile.

The police and company officials became more aggressive. They turned fire hoses onto the marchers and fired rounds into the crowd. Five of the demonstrators were killed.

In the aftermath of the riot, authorities mounted a nationwide search for William Z. Foster, national leader of the communist party. The Wayne County prosecutor also announced charges against local communist leaders who were accused of making speeches to the crowd prior to the march.

March 8, 1843
Counties renamed
Keskkauko out, Charlevoix in

Several years after Michigan became a state, the legislature decided that many of the state's counties should be renamed.

Many were named after an Indian word or chief in an act passed in 1840.

Perhaps Michigan would be a more exotic place if the wholesale renaming of so many counties hadn't been approved on March 8, 1843. On the other hand, some counties would have names that would be harder to spell and pronounce.

With the swoop of a pen, Aishcum County became Lake County; Notipekago changed to Mason; Unwatin changed to Osceola; Kautawaubet changed to Wexford; Mikenauk changed to Roscommon; Kanotin changed to Iosco; Negwegon changed to Alcona; Shawono changed to Crawford; Wabassee changed to Kalkaska; Okkuddo changed to Otsego; Cheonoquet changed to Montmorency; Anamickee changed to Alpena; Keskkauko changed to Charlevoix; Tonedogana changed to Emmet; and Kaykakee County became Clare County.

March 9, 1977
The "Burning Bed" burns

Twenty-nine-year-old housewife Francine Hughes had been with an abusive husband for 13 years.

She endured regular beating and attempted to escape from him. But in the 1970s, social workers, police, and the court offered little help for victims of domestic violence.

Hughes finally took the matter into her own hands.

She put her four children into the family's car and poured gasoline on the house where her husband was sleeping. She set the house on fire and burned her husband to death.

Hughes turned herself in. In a trial that took place several months later she was found not guilty of killing her husband based on a temporary insanity defense.

The case attracted national attention and then became the subject of a book called *The Burning Bed*, by Faith McNulty. The case gained more fame when a made-for-TV movie of the same title was aired on NBC starring Farrah Fawcett.

March 9, 1925
The VFW National Home for Children
accepts first residents

Sergeant Edward Pollett was in Detroit to pick up his retirement check at Fort Wayne when he was struck by a streetcar and killed in early March, 1925.

That left his wife and six children, ages 2 to 15, without anyone to support them when Mrs. Pollett learned that his retirement benefits ended with his death. Several days after Pollett's death, his wife and children became the first residents of the Veterans of Foreign Wars National Home for Children, a home created through a national drive to provide support for destitute families of veterans.

The Polletts lived at the home, which was a farm near Eaton Rapids donated by a wealthy cattleman from Jackson.

March 9, 1901
Fire destroys Detroit's first automobile plant

When Ransom E. Olds built a car he called the Oldsmobile in Lansing, he went to Detroit to fund production. There he met Samuel L. Smith who made a fortune in lumber and copper. He agreed to fund construction of a plant in Detroit as long as Olds employed Smith's two sons. Out of this partnership, Olds Motor Works was formed and they sold Oldsmobiles to the wealthy at $2,382 per car.

On March 9, 1901, fire destroyed the Olds plant, including all of the plans and machinery. Olds decided not to rebuild in Detroit and returned to Lansing to build a smaller car.

March 10, 1918
Women warned about Detroit

Social workers publicized a campaign to warn women not to move to Detroit. Women who had flocked to Detroit after the outbreak of World War I to earn big wages had instead found a job shortage. This left many needing to turn to charity or to become prostitutes.

March 11, 1822
Residents of Michigan Territory
fed up with their government

Just a few years before Michigan officially became a state, the territory lacked a legislature and other elected officials. It was essentially run by four men – Lewis Cass, who was the territorial governor, and three judges.

The residents became frustrated with this autocratic system. Often, the four could not agree among themselves about which direction the territory should take.

Cass took office in 1813 and five years later residents voted down a proposal to establish a legislature.

But on March 11, 1822, a meeting at the council house was called and some citizens developed a petition to Congress asking that the power of the Michigan oligarchs be checked. They sought a law "to separate the judicial and legislative power and to vest the latter in a certain number of our citizens."

Congress took no action on the request and later that year another meeting was held amid growing frustration. This time the citizens drew up a "statement of facts" for Congress.

It described Michigan as being run in smoky back rooms, away from the eyes of the public: "The legislative board does not meet to do business at the time fixed by their own statutes for that purpose, and they have no known place of meeting; and when they do meet, no public notice of the time or place is given; and when that can be ascertained, by inquiry, they are found sometimes at private rooms or offices, where none has a right, and few except those immediately interested in the passage of the laws have the assurance to intrude themselves, or can find seats if they should. Laws are frequently passed and others repealed, which take effect from date, and vitally affect the rights of the citizens, and are not promulgated or made known to the community for many months."

Congress decided it could no longer neglect Michigan and it responded with a plan to help allay the faraway settlers' concerns.

In March 1923, President James Monroe signed an act that created a legislature for the territory. Michigan residents were to elect 18 people, and of those the president would select nine to make up a territorial council.

The territory was on its way to becoming a state.

March 12, 1916
The case of the murdered Grand Rapids millionaires

When Arthur Warren Waite and Clara Louise Peck were married in Grand Rapids in the fall of 1915, it was the social event of the season, according to the *Story of Grand Rapids*, a history of the city edited Z.Z. Lydens.

Peck was the daughter of John E. Peck, a millionaire druggist. She and her new husband soon moved to New York City where Waite was to practice medicine. Waite was also a Grand Rapids native. The couple had a promising future and that should have been the end of the story.

But when Peck's mother came to visit the young couple at their home on Riverside Drive in early 1916, the woman became ill and died.

Mrs. Peck's death was attributed to natural causes.

Waite and his bride accompanied the body back to Grand Rapids and it was cremated in Detroit.

In March, John Peck traveled to New York to visit his daughter and son-in-law and he, too, soon died.

Waite determined the cause of death was heart trouble, a reasonable diagnosis as the elder Peck had suffered from heart disease.

But the back-to-back deaths had some members of the Peck family suspicious.

When Peck's body returned to Grand Rapids, Clara's brother made sure it was examined. Traces of arsenic were discovered and Waite was soon suspected of murder.

Detectives in New York confronted Waite about the deaths. There he was caught in a lie and confessed. He admitted he eventually planned to kill his wife because he wanted the family's fortune for himself.

If the Waite-Peck wedding had attracted attention a year earlier, Waite's trial on murder charges in New York absolutely captivated readers in Michigan when it began on March 12, 1916.

A wire reporter described the drama in a story that chronicled Waite's journey to the electric chair, where he was sentenced to die:

"With Dr. Arthur Warren Waite, fashion-plate, bon vivant and globe trotter, a prisoner in Bellevue Hospital looking gruesomely forward to death in the electric chair for his self-confessed share in the poisoning of John E. Peck, his millionaire father-in-law, one of the most amazing poison mysteries in history is being speedily unfolded today. It is a more gripping tale than the chapter on toxicology in Dumas's *Count of Monte Cristo*."

March 13, 1946
Strike ends at GM plant

The strike had lasted 113 days and it enabled the United Auto Workers to flex its muscle. It also provided a national showcase for Walter Reuther, who would be elected president of the union after making a reputation as a tough bargainer.

The strike began the previous November as General Motors and the union sought better positions for themselves in the postwar market, each believing it had been forced to make too many concessions during the war.

GM offered a 10 percent wage increase while the union demanded a 30 percent increase. Reuther wanted the increase along with a pledge from the company that it would not raise prices.

Reuther argued that the workers needed the pay increase to keep their incomes steady as World War II ended and the workers lost opportunities to work overtime.

Reuther demanded proof that the company could not afford a 30 percent increase. He wanted access to the company's books, access that was denied by the company, which argued it was proprietary information.

The standoff led to 175,000 workers walking off the job.

President Harry Truman created a fact-finding board in an effort to end the strike and encourage the sides to negotiate.

The strike ended with compromise. The average hourly pay at General Motors was raised from $1.12 per hour to $1.30 per hour. The raise meant a net pay decrease for the worker, however, because the work week returned to 40 hours from a 48-hour week that was standard during the war.

The raise, plus other improved terms of employment, roughly matched what Truman's board recommended.

At the time it was estimated the strike cost the economy $1 billion in 1946 dollars because of orders GM was unable to fill, lost wages and missed sales commissions for dealers.

March 14, 1920
Fishing for Jack Daniel's

A truck laden with liquor bottles attempted to cross the Detroit River over ice from Windsor and wound up crashing into the water.

When word got out about the liquor bottles in the river, many excited anglers (and non-anglers) decided it was time to go fishing.

When federal agents realized that citizens were fishing bottles of liquor from the riverbed, they issued an order prohibiting the practice.

March 15, 1892
Death of notorious brothel owner Jim Carr

Frontier Michigan produced some deplorable characters. Among the most despicable was Jim Carr.

Carr was a Harrison businessman who ran saloons and whorehouses while attempting to stay ahead of authorities. When he died, it was statewide news.

His obituary in the *Gladwin County Record* offered a look at just how disliked Carr was when he died at the age of 37: "James Carr, known throughout the state, and especially in northern Michigan as of one of the most notorious and wicked of its inhabitants, died in a log camp near Meredith Tuesday morning, unwept, unhonored and unsung by all save his wife, Maggie, who remained faithfully by his side to the last, although every other friend had forsaken him.

"Carr moved to Clare County from Canada about twelve years ago, and for a long time kept a 'stockade ranch' near the village of Harrison, a resort of the vilest character. Herein it was asserted, the worst forces of evil were practiced and the inmates were prisoners, subjected to the grossest cruelty and outrages.

"His reign there continued until the people were aroused by the death of a girl in the place and then Carr was arrested and charged with murder. He was convicted of the crime, but employing able counsel secured a new trial which was never given him for some reason unexplained.

"However, his experience at the time had a salutary effect and he became less conspicuous, moving to a point near Meredith and keeping a place known as the 'State Road Hotel.' Carr was at one time worth considerable money, but the excessive use of liquor and indulgence in other vices caused the loss of it.

"For more than a year back he has been but little better than a pauper, living mostly on the slender earnings of his wife, Maggie, who has stuck to him through thick and thin, and the occasional offerings of some of his friends of better days.

"For a month back, Carr has been failing very fast from the effects of his wild career of dissipation. The county will probably have to assist at his burial."

Carr's wife, Maggie, died in the county poor house a few weeks after her husband's death.

March 15, 1847
Shiawasseetown becomes state capital for a day

A day before Lansing was named the state capital, lawmakers voted to make Shiawasseetown the state capital.

A monument commemorating the novelty of having been the state capital for just a day is all that remains of the move.

The land that had been platted for a capital building became a park in what is now called Shiatown.

March 16, 1847
Swamp becomes state capital

At the time Lansing was named the state capital, there was enough anti-Detroit sentiment in the state that legislators wanted the capital moved from the state's largest city. But that majority reached no agreement on where to locate the capital.

The state constitution of 1835 made Detroit a temporary capital and gave the government until 1847 to name a new place. It was thought in the 1830s that Detroit was too close to the British-controlled Windsor and too vulnerable to attack.

Ingham County's representative, Joseph Kilbourne, saw an opening. Kilbourne's argument for Lansing was its location. It was in the center of the lower peninsula and, therefore, would be equidistant for almost everyone below the Straits of Mackinac. The city had a river that could power mills. And there was a great deal of lumber in nearby woods to build a city.

Kilbourne also had a pledge from an early Lansing settler, James Seymour, that if the state made Lansing the capital, Seymour would give the state the land on which to build it.

There were some reasons the legislators may have wanted to avoid Lansing as a home, however.

There was no road between Detroit and Lansing and much of what later became Lansing was then just a malaria-infested swamp.

In fact, when Kilbourne first proposed his city as the capital, he was met by laughter from other lawmakers.

Kilbourne had enough charisma to keep his peers interested and he kept talking. He talked so well that the legislators focused on the positives and forgot the negatives. They voted to make hard-to-reach swampland the state capital – and their new part-time home – over established communities like Jackson, Marshall or Kalamazoo.

When the bill was first passed, the capital city was called Michigan and was located in Lansing Township.

March 17, 1933
Diego Rivera's murals unveiled at
Detroit Institute for the Arts

Edsel Ford wanted to do something for his hometown. What else would the son of the 20th Century's most successful capitalist do but turn to a renowned Marxist painter?

It was not without controversy that on March 17, 1933 the

Detroit Institute of Arts opened to the public its display of Diego Rivera murals.

According to the *Detroit News*, one of the fiercest critics of the artist was Dr. George H. Derry, president of Marygrove College, who argued that the murals made their way into the city like a dangerous virus:

"Senor Rivera has perpetrated a heartless hoax on his capitalist employer, Edsel Ford. Rivera was engaged to interpret Detroit; he has foisted on Mr. Ford and the museum a Communist manifesto. The key panel that first strikes the eye, when you enter the room, betrays the Communist motif that animates and alone explains the whole ensemble. Will the women of Detroit feel flattered when they realize that they are embodied in the female with the hard, masculine, unsexed face, ecstatically staring for hope and help across the panel to the languorous and grossly sensual Asiatic sister on the right?"

But the angry reaction to the art exhibit was soon countered by support that poured into the museum.

Today the murals remain on display and the museum boasts that they are the finest works of the Mexican muralist movement in the United States.

March 18, 1972
Housing experiment for coeds ends at UM

The 1970s saw a lot of experimenting with new ideas and University of Michigan students sought to stretch boundaries as far as they could.

A group of 29 male and female students embarked on an experiment and moved into a house they called "Xanadu," where they would seek to "break down some of the barriers between the sexes."

This was a time when the notion of male and female students living together in the same house struck people as radical and many persons as immoral.

In this experiment, male and female students didn't just share a house, they shared bedrooms.

The story became national news and the residents received postcards from supporters and detractors, such as one from Columbus, Ohio that read: "What kind of stunt are you and your pals pulling? So – you aren't hippies – just normal people? Baloney!!!"

Another, from a best-selling author of a novel that explored the sex lives of students at a fictional university, offered support: "I am particularly impressed with your joyous method of selecting roommates."

The residents didn't select the roommates themselves, but instead drew lots to determine which member of the opposite sex with which they would share a room.

However, the students quickly tired of the attention from the media. The news coverage wasn't the only trouble faced by the students. Many had problems with their parents.

One girl's parents told her she "needn't bother to come home."

Another female student said she was told she had been disowned and needed to change her last name.

On March 18, 1972, after about three weeks, the students of the Xanadu house disbanded.

March 18, 1837
University of Michigan created

The school was first known as Catholepistemiad, a name coined by Judge Augustus Woodward, an eccentric founding father of Michigan and the namesake of the Detroit avenue. Woodward had written a book that categorized all human knowledge into 13 groups, and he envisioned a school where 13 professors would teach each category to offer a rounded education.

In its early years the school was funded by a 15 percent tax, lotteries and tuition payments. But the institution was not able to live up to Woodward's grandiose expectations and it soon failed.

In addition to the cost, which residents of the territory opposed, its name was regarded as impossible to pronounce and the school became an object of ridicule.

Territorial Governor Lewis Cass is said to have referred to the school as "Cathol-what's-it's-name."

The University of Michigan found new life on March 18, 1837, when the state's first governor, Stevens T. Mason, signed a law authorizing the creation of the school under its new name and at a new location, Ann Arbor.

The university reopened four years later with two professors, one who taught math and another who taught English. It may have started slowly, but the school had an early advantage. Until 1855, Michigan law deemed U of M the only school in the state eligible to grant degrees.

The school, of course, would go on to become one of the top universities in the country. Much credit for that goes to Henry Tappan, who was appointed president of the school in 1852. Despite charges of elitism, Tappan stressed scholarship and science in favor of vocational or agricultural study.

That set the school on course to become one of the premiere research universities in the country.

March 19, 1991
Death of John Voelker
(Hollywood comes to the U.P.)

John Voelker, whose pen name was Robert Traver, was born in 1903 in Ishpeming. He graduated from the University of Michigan law school. After a brief time practicing law in Chicago, he moved back to his hometown where he was elected prosecutor of Marquette County.

His legal career was a huge success, even after he lost a reelection bid for prosecutor. He was appointed to the Michigan Supreme Court by Governor G. Mennen Williams to fill a vacant seat and once won election to the post – but it was his writing career that brought him fame.

He used the pen name Robert Traver – Traver being his mother's maiden name – because when he became a published writer he was also the county prosecutor and he didn't want people to think he was "spinning yarn on company time," according to the Michigan Bar Association.

His first books, *Troubleshooter* and *Small Town D.A.*, drew upon his experience as a prosecutor, as did his most famous work, *Anatomy of a Murder*.

He served as prosecutor for 14 years until, after six wins at the polls, the residents of Marquette County voted him out of office. He figured that a prosecutor in a small town could only last so long because he convicted enough people to turn a majority against him.

But he credited the loss for giving him the opportunity to write his greatest work.

"Being voted out of office probably turned out to be the best thing that could have happened to me," he once said. "Because if I hadn't been, I would have had to prosecute a certain case instead of defending it."

That case was the basis for *Anatomy of a Murder*, which went on to become a best-seller and the basis for a classic Hollywood movie filmed in Marquette County. (See entry for July 1.)

Voelker also wrote *Laughing Whitefish*, a historical novel exploring a 19th Century case of an Ojibwa woman's efforts to collect a debt owed to her father, and *People Versus Kirk*, which dealt with the use of hypnosis in the courtroom.

In addition, he also wrote several books on fly fishing, a sport he remained passionate about throughout his life.

March 20, 1900
Calumet Theater opens
(Lillian Russell, Sarah Bernhardt, John Phillip Sousa
come to town)

At the turn of the century, as the Keweenaw Peninsula basked in the height of the copper mining boom, the village of Calumet found itself in an enviable position – the village coffers overflowed with taxes and it needed something to do with the money.

Community leaders settled on an opera house to attract high-brow culture to their far-flung home where about 35,000 people lived.

The theatre opened on March 20, 1900. Its first production was "The Highwaymen," a touring Broadway show by Reginald DeK-oven.

In the following years, the theater became a stop for famous actors and productions as they toured the country. The theater staged performances by Madame Helena Modjeska, Lillian Russell, John Phillip Sousa, Sarah Bernhardt, Douglas Fairbanks, Sr., Lon Chaney, Sr., Jason Robards, Sr., James O'Neill, William S. Hart, Frank Morgan, Wallace and Noah Beery, and Madame Schumann-Heink.

Just as the copper created a boom, however, it also brought a bust. By the late 1920s fewer tours put Calumet on their schedule. Its operators adapted and showed movies.

Starting in 1958, the theater played summer stock productions for 10 years but the theater declined as it entered old age. In 1975 there was a renovation to mark the village's centennial.

In 1983, the Calumet Theatre Company took over the theater and now oversees 60 to 80 year-round events.

March 20, 1970
State civil rights commissioner assassinated

He was known as a tough fighter for minority rights who wasn't afraid to make enemies to further his goals.

When Burton I. Gordon was found dead, shot three times in the chest at close range in a secluded parking garage three blocks from a Detroit Police station, authorities said they could not determine a motive for his murder.

While police said they could find no evidence that the head of the Michigan Civil Rights Commission's death was connected to the work he devoted his life to, they also said they could find no evidence that his murder was part of a robbery. Whoever shot Gordon left a wallet and a brief case untouched.

Gordon, who was white, headed the civil rights commission since it was created six years earlier.

Under Gordon, the commission investigated claims of employment discrimination across the state. The commission also sent teams to investigate discrimination in housing or at hotels.

Because of his willingness to criticize local government and police, Gordon was not popular in a lot of circles.

His murder was never solved, but many believed he was assassinated for his tough stands on civil rights.

March 21, 1837
Michigan dreams big

Michigan had just become an official part of the United States and it was hard not to plan big things for the fledgling state.

Governor Stevens T. Mason had proposed some big ideas, such as a canal to create a navigable waterway between Lake St. Clair and Lake Michigan. This was in addition to three railroads that were to stretch around the state to be constructed with public money.

While a canal across lower Michigan may have been a pipe dream, Mason proposed one idea that would not go away and would become reality long after his death – the Soo Canal.

In January 1837, soon after he took office, Mason spoke at length about the need for a canal around the St. Mary's Falls and said if the state could not obtain federal funding for the enormous project, it should find a way to pay for it itself.

The legislators were sold on the Soo project. On March 21, 1837 they passed a measure enabling the state to take out a loan of $5 million for improvements in Michigan.

It turned out, however, it was a bad time to go into debt.

The Michigan economy spiraled downward amid the Panic of 1837 when many banks closed. The company founded to make some of the improvements failed and Michigan was faced with millions of dollars of debt and nothing to show for it.

This led to the downfall of Mason, as described in the Jan. 4 entry which memorializes his death.

March 22, 1884
Prominent U.S. Senator born into poverty

Arthur H. Vandenberg, born in Grand Rapids on March 22, 1884, grew up in an impoverished family and was forced to work a variety of jobs as a youth.

But he had intelligence and a good work ethic, and by age 22 he found himself working as the editor of the *Grand Rapids Herald*.

He made a name for himself in that job, acquiring a good reputation among powerful people. In 1928, Vandenberg was appointed to the United States Senate by Governor Fred Green. He held that position until his death in 1951.

Vandenberg served as a senator through the Great Depression and helped foster the Federal Deposit Insurance Corporation, which restored people's belief in the safety of banks.

He favored isolationism, but after World War II he supported the creation of the United Nations in the hope that cooperation among nations could prevent worldwide war from breaking out again.

March 22, 1966
GM apologizes to Nader

James M. Roche, president of General Motors, apologized before a Congressional committee for the company's hiring of private detectives to investigate the personal life of Ralph Nader, a Washington lawyer then best known for being a consumer advocate.

GM apparently wanted to get some lurid dirt on Nader, who had just published a book, *Unsafe at Any Speed,* critical of the automotive industry.

The GM investigation of Nader involved interviews with up to 60 of his acquaintances and family members. Those questioned were asked about Nader's sex habits and his opinions about Jews. The representatives who took GM to task for the investigation said they learned that GM had come up with nothing unsavory on the activist.

The GM investigation came to light while Congress investigated auto safety and brought in Nader to testify about the industry. That meant GM could have been found criminally at fault if it was determined its action against Nader was meant to intimidate a witness before Congress.

Nader complained to Congress that twice he had been approached by young women while he was shopping and the women asked Nader to come back to their apartments.

GM denied using women to lure Nader into a compromising position as part of their investigation.

March 23, 1984
Michigan Homemaker of the Year
convicted of murdering husband

Dorothy Andrews, a 43-year-old Owosso woman who was crippled by multiple sclerosis, had been married to her husband Terry only 11 months before she decided she had had enough.

In a trial, the woman testified that Terry abused her constantly, causing her to snap. She got a .22-caliber rifle, propped it on the handle of her motorized wheelchair, and fired a shot at her husband as he lay sleeping in bed.

Terry, a 28-year-old on parole for armed robbery, died four days later of wounds to his head and neck.

Just two years earlier she won the Michigan Homemaker of the Year award at the Michigan State Fair.

Despite the evidence against her, the woman fought the murder charge and a 1982 jury was unable to reach a verdict after a five-week trial and 30 hours of deliberation.

Two years later, after prosecutors readied to try the homemaker again on murder charges, Andrews agreed on March 23, 1984 to plead guilty to manslaughter and accept a sentence of up to 15 years in prison.

In her plea, the Associated Press reported that Dorothy told the judge: "I intentionally killed Terry. ... I shot him while he was in bed. He was asleep."

March 24, 1956
Steve Ballmer born

Steve Ballmer was born in Detroit where his father, a Swiss immigrant, worked as a manager at the Ford Motor Company. Ballmer grew up in Farmington Hills and attended Detroit Country Day School before he earned a bachelor's degree in mathematics and economics at Harvard.

It was at Harvard where Ballmer met Bill Gates, who lived down the hall from him. Gates, who left school to found Microsoft, hired Ballmer in 1980. He was named chief executive officer of Microsoft 20 years later, on his way becoming a billionaire.

March 24, 1680
The mystery of the missing Griffon

Frenchman Rene-Robert Cavelier, siuer de La Salle was among the first Europeans who made it into the Michigan region and was the first to sail a large vessel on the Upper Great Lakes.

La Salle was a well-educated man who arrived in Canada from France in 1666 at the age of 23. He arrived at Montreal to farm but his thirst for exploration kept him moving west.

La Salle wanted to explore the Mississippi and erect a chain of forts throughout the heart of North America to claim that land for the French, keeping the English out. La Salle obtained permission from King Louis XIV to embark on his adventure, but he would get no funds from the French government. He would need to pay for the project himself by engaging in fur trading as he went along.

In order to have a ship large enough to carry the furs, La Salle had a wooden ship constructed above the falls at Niagara to sail on the Upper Great Lakes. On its prow, the ship had a carved figurehead of a monster with an eagle's head and a lion's body. The ship was named after this figure, a griffon.

The Griffon made its way to where Detroit would one day be settled and into Lake Huron and Lake Michigan.

La Salle and his expedition traveled to Green Bay where they collected a load of pelts. He instructed his captain to take the furs back to Niagara on the Griffon and return to meet him at the mouth of the St. Joseph River on Lake Michigan.

La Salle took a party of men in four canoes, making their way to the mouth of that river. At St. Joseph, he built Fort Miami and awaited the return of his ship so he could continue with his expedition. The ship never returned, however. La Salle left for the Illinois River, where he built another fort. He returned to Fort Miami in hopes of finding his ship.

Finally, after sending men to look for signs of the ship and coming up empty handed, La Salle decided the ship was lost. He set out on foot across lower Michigan, returning to Lake Erie and finally Montreal.

Over the centuries, claims have been made that evidence was discovered shedding light on the Griffon's fate. However, it remains one of the Great Lakes greatest and longest-running unsolved mysteries.

March 25, 1942
Aretha Franklin born

The Queen of Soul was born in Memphis, Tennessee on March 25, 1942. Her father, the Reverend C.L. Franklin, became pastor of the New Bethel Baptist Church in Detroit, a 4,500-member congregation, where she and her sister were brought up singing in the gospel church choir. Franklin moved to Detroit with her family at around age six.

She made her first recordings at age 14, but when Berry Gordy Jr. attempted to sign her to his Motown label, her father refused. Franklin later reconsidered switching from gospel to pop, however, and wound up signing with Columbia Records. After a move to New York City, her first several singles, "Today I Sing the Blues," "Won't Be Long," and "Operation Heartbreak" did well on the R&B chart.

Franklin had little mainstream success, however, until she switched producers and record companies, signing with Atlantic in 1966. It was there that she recorded "Respect," "Think," "Chain of Fools," "Since You've Been Gone" and "Baby I Love You." Franklin's career spans decades and she became known as the

"Queen of Soul." She moved back to the Detroit area in 1982 and became the first women inducted into the Rock and Roll Hall of Fame in 1987.

March 25, 1890
Suomi Synod founded, paves way
for U.P.'s Finnish University

In the late 19th Century, Finnish immigrants flocked to the Upper Peninsula. The climate was familiar and the newcomers could take part in a burgeoning mining and lumber boom. Roughly 1,200 persons formed nine Lutheran congregations.

On March 25, 1890, they united the congregations, an accomplishment memorialized in a Michigan historical marker located in Hancock. Members of the church established the Finnish Evangelical Lutheran Church of America, or the Suomi Synod. But they soon feared their pastors would get old and their young people would forget their culture.

To prevent this, Rev. Juho K. Nikander, founded Suomi College in 1896 to ensure seminary training and preserve Finnish culture in America.

Today the college is named Finlandia University and has about 600 students. It is located in Hancock.

March 25, 1936
Longest Stanley Cup game in NHL history ends...finally

Three periods were played between the Detroit Red Wings and the Montreal Maroons in a Stanley Cup semifinal game and not a goal was scored, sending the teams to overtime. What the players probably didn't realize as they took the short break between the third period and the first overtime period was that their evening had just begun.

The game would last six more periods. In all, hockey was played for 176 minutes and 30 seconds in this game one match up.

Norman Smith, the goalie for Detroit who Montreal players thought would be easy to beat at the outset of the game, saved 92 shots, enough to earn him a place in the *Guiness Book of World Records*.

Finally, well into the sixth overtime period, rookie Moderre "Mud" Bruneteau, a Red Wing who had scored just two goals during the regular season, shot a puck into Montreal's net. The game lasted until nearly 2:30 a.m.

The Red Wings went on to win the series and then beat the Toronto Maple Leafs 3-1 in the Stanley Cup final.

March 26, 1922
Birth of William G. Milliken,
Michigan's longest serving governor

William Milliken was born into a prominent family and raised in Traverse City. His father was once mayor of the city and served as a state senator. The Millikens ran a successful department store on Front Street.

Milliken left his small home town when he attended Yale University, studies that were interrupted by World War II. Milliken flew more than 50 combat missions as a waist-gunner in a B-24 bomber. He survived two crashes, suffered shrapnel wounds and was once forced to bail out of his plane over Italy.

Once out of school and back home, Milliken plunged into the family's department store business before following his father into politics. After Milliken took over the business he expanded it, opening department stores in Manistee and Cadillac.

At age 37, Milliken was elected state senator. In the senate, Milliken earned a reputation as a moderate Republican who could bring people together. Milliken believed in civil rights and environmental conservation, working across the aisle.

In 1964, Milliken successfully ran for lieutenant governor along side Governor George Romney. In 1969, when Romney stepped down to take a place in the cabinet of the Nixon administration, Milliken became governor.

Milliken's good nature and charm would make him an enormously successful governor. He would go on to be elected in 1970, 1974, and 1978. He served from 1969 to 1983, making him the person to hold the position longer than anyone else in the state's history.

His tenure was marked by progressive politics and a commitment to environmental causes. He loved northern Michigan and he was committed to protecting its natural beauty. He also fought for programs to help the state's cities, including Detroit, which made the man from a small city in northern lower Michigan an unlikely ally of Detroit Mayor Coleman Young.

March, 26, 1944
Diana Ross born

Born in Detroit, Diana Ross attended Cass Technical High School and while still a teenager began singing with a group of friends, Mary Wilson, Florence Ballard, and Barbara Martin. Later Martin dropped out and the group went on to international success as The Supremes.

They recorded 12 number one hits, including "Stop! In the Name of Love," "Where Did Our Love Go?" and "Someday We'll Be Together."

Ross left the Supremes in 1969 for a solo career. She had numerous chart-topping singles as a solo artist, including "Ain't No Mountain High Enough" and "I'm Coming Out." She also embarked on an acting career that included an Academy Award-nominated performance in *Lady Sings the Blues*, a biopic about Billie Holiday.

March 27, 1670
Stone idol perched on the banks of Detroit River destroyed by priests

Of the lesser known early explorers to make their mark on Detroit, Francois Dollier de Casson and Abbe Brehant de Galinee blundered into the region from their posts in Montreal before the settlement of Detroit had been established and immediately did what they could to antagonize the Indians.

Upon arrival into the region along the Detroit River, Galinee was troubled by a rock formation he found along the riverbank.

He did not like the pagan stone idol and believed its blasphemy was responsible for a storm his party encountered in Lake Erie during which the expedition lost three canoes.

He wrote: "At the end of six leagues we discovered a place that is remarkable and held in great veneration by all the Indians of these countries, because of a stone idol that nature had formed there. To it they say they owe their good luck in sailing on Lake Erie, when they cross it without accident, and they propitiate it by sacrifices, presents of skins, provisions, etc., when they wish to embark on it. The place was full of camps of those who had come to pay homage to this stone, which had no other resemblance to the figure of a man than what the imagination was pleased to give it.

"However, it was all painted and a sort of face had been formed for it with vermilion. I leave you to imagine whether we avenged upon this idol, which the Iroquois had strongly recommended us to honor, the loss of our chapel. We attributed to it even the dearth of provisions from which we had hitherto suffered. In short, there was nobody whose hatred it had not incurred. I consecrated one of my axes to break this god of stone, and then, having yoked our canoes together, we carried the largest pieces to the middle of the river and threw all the rest also into the water, in order that it might never be heard of again. God rewarded us immediately for this good action, for we killed a roebuck (a male deer) and a bear that very day."

It seems this priest wanted it both ways – he looked down on the Indians for thinking the rock formation brought them luck, yet he held superstitious feelings about the idol himself.

The rock is described as having been located just south of the present-day Ambassador Bridge.

Its destruction gave rise to an Indian legend. After the two priests had moved on, a company of Indians came to the site of the idol with gifts and found only fragments of stone remaining. The Indians were crushed. But a medicine man instructed each of them to take a small fragment in his canoe and let it guide them. The fragments led each man to Belle Isle, where the spirit of the idol had taken residence. The spirit instructed the Indians to discard each fragment on the island. They complied and each fragment supposedly turned into a rattlesnake that would protect the island from the encroachment of the white man.

March 27, 1960
Last commercial steam locomotive

The Grand Trunk Western Union Depot in Durand was once a grand depot, the largest in rural Michigan and one of the biggest in a small town anywhere in the country.

It featured a large waiting room, a dining room and a lunch counter.

On March 27, 1960, the last regularly scheduled passenger train powered by a steam locomotive pulled away from the station.

March 28, 1985
Long-time dispute over Indian fishing boundaries settled

By the middle of the 1900s, the majority of Michigan's Indian population had moved into mainstream culture. Many lived and worked in urban areas.

In northern Michigan, however, some Indians clung to a more traditional life.

In order to do that, they needed to assert rights granted them in age-old treaties.

In the 20th century, Indian tribes increasingly began to assert rights granted by those treaties. This brought the Indians increasingly into conflict with non-Indians when tribes demanded fishing rights.

The dispute came to a head when, in 1980, a federal court sided with Native Americans and agreed that Indian tribes that operated commercial fishing businesses were exempted under an 1836 treaty from fishing restrictions imposed by the state.

This led to confrontations, sometimes violent, between white sportsmen and Indians in northern Michigan. With no clear end to the conflict in sight, Indian fishermen, non-Indians, tribal leaders and state officials sat down to work out a deal.

The deal, the Indian Fishing Agreement, was reached on March 28, 1985. The tribes agreed to limit commercial fishing operations, which tended to go after whitefish, to the northern parts of lakes

Michigan and Huron and the eastern end of Lake Superior, leaving the rest of the lakes free for sports fishermen, who preferred to fish for salmon.

March 28, 1859
Adrian College chartered

Like so many colleges in Michigan, Adrian College was founded by a religious group that wanted to bring education into the isolated inner reaches of the state.

Adrian College traces its roots back to the small town of Leoni, located just east of Jackson, where the Wesleyan Methodist Theological Institute was founded in 1845. Legend has it the administrators of the school soon looked for a new locale because of the debauchery of Leoni, which was then nicknamed "Whiskey Town."

It so happened that the town of Adrian, about 40 miles to the southeast, was looking to establish its own college. An agreement was struck and the books of the college library were taken by oxcart to their new home. Adrian College received its charter from the state legislature on March 28, 1859. It's first president was Rev. Asa Mahan, an anti-slavery leader who negotiated the relocation of the college to Adrian.

Over the years the college, which kept its ties to the United Methodist Church, has grown to 100 acres that are home to 21 academic buildings and 10 residence halls.

Today the liberal arts college has a population of approximately 1,000 students.

March 29, 1850
Isolated U.P. opened by road

On March 29, 1850, the legislature approved the construction of a plank road between Rockland and Ontonagon by the Ontonagon Plank Road Company. Previously, contact with the outside world for the people of Ontonagon was by way of Lake Superior that, for six months out of the year, became an impassable ice shelf.

This was a tenuous and perilous connection with the rest of civilization.

Over 50 years ago, local historian, James K. Jamison, attempted to describe the horrible feeling a person would have when the western U.P. was cut off for another winter from the rest of the world: "If you want to try to relive for a moment the life of our people during those foundation years, go down to the harbor on a November day when a gale is blowing and plant your feet solidly to withstand the buffeting of the wind. Lake Superior will be in a perfect frenzy of excited waters as though it were taking a last fling before the quiet imposed on it by the winter's ice. Tell yourself then, 'This is winter; I am now cut off from the world for six months. No news will come to me. My kin may die and be in their graves and I shall not know it. Behind me there is a settlement. There are no roads, the world is beyond and I am here. Ah, Spring!' With that sigh snatched from your lips by the first storm of winter, you may turn back to make whatever adjustments to the inevitable is possible."

Given their remoteness, the residents of Ontonagon lobbied state and federal officials for a road that would connect Green Bay and Fort Wilkins, at the northern tip of the Keweenaw Peninsula, via Ontonagon.

First, they won winter delivery of mail via dog sleds from Green Bay.

But the area's inhabitants were so desperate they exaggerated or invented "Indian scares" to hasten the construction. One of the first roads leading out of Ontonagon was constructed by the Ontonagon Plank Road Company. However, it took nine years from its establishment in 1850 for the road to Rockland to get planked. It operated as a toll road. By 1877 a daily stage coach operated between Ontonagon and L'Anse, which was connected to the outside world by a railroad. Residents of Ontonagon finally received daily mail and some sense of security.

March 30, 1979
Kellogg defends targeting sugary cereal at children

B reakfast cereal was born by accident in Battle Creek in 1896 when brothers W.K. Kellogg and Dr. John Harvey Kellogg attempted to process wheat into flour and were interrupted by other matters at the Battle Creek Sanitarium, a hospital and spa for wealthy clients.

When they returned, they found the wheat had gone stale. They processed it anyway and discovered thin flakes of wheat. Once baked, the flakes made a novel and nutritious meal.

That was especially interesting to Dr. Kellogg, who spent a career in search of healthy food that could be served off the shelf.

Suspecting they might be on to something, they experimented with corn and,,, voila! – cornflakes.

Corn flakes sold commercially beginning in 1906, after W.K. Kellogg organized the Battle Creek Toasted Corn Flake Company, later to be known as Kellogg Company. The Kelloggs spent several years watching others, like Charles W. Post, make fortunes from their ideas.

Corn Flakes took off, packaged in a gray box with the slogan "The Genuine Bears This Signature – W.K. Kellogg" to distinguish it from competitors who copied the Kelloggs' idea.

Over decades the company grew and offered a wide range of cereals. They introduced Pop Tarts in the 1960s.

By the 1970s, questions were raised about the sugar levels in some cereals offered by Kellogg and other cereal companies and the use of colorful advertisements featuring cartoon spokesmen that aired during children shows.

A month-long hearing before the Federal Trade Commission over whether the advertisements should be banned concluded on March 30, 1979 with testimony from a Kellogg Company executive about the nutritional value of the cereal. The executive noted that the sugary cereal contained less sugar than some other products regularly consumed by children, such as fruit-flavored yogurt or apple pie.

The ban on the advertisements never materialized, but nearly three decades later the company took voluntary measures to limit its marketing of certain types of cereal directly to children.

In 2007, the company announced it would no longer market certain products to children under 12, such as Froot Loops, Cocoa Krispies and Apple Jacks.

March 31, 1918
Death of Major Edward Edgar Hartwick

In life, Edward Hartwick was a soldier and a businessman. In death, he's remembered for Hartwick Pines State Park.

He was born in St. Louis, Michigan in 1871 and his family moved to Grayling when Hartwick was a boy. Hartwick went on to graduate with honors from West Point and served in the Spanish-American War.

After the war, Hartwick returned to Grayling, married and became involved in the lumber and banking business, becoming quite wealthy. He then moved to Detroit before serving in the military after the outbreak of World War I. He was made a major in the 20th Engineers and headed to Europe. There, on March 31, 1918, he died of meningitis at the age of 46 near Bordeaux, France.

His wife, Karen, used some of her family's wealth to buy 8,000 acres of land near Grayling that included 85 acres of virgin forest, a rare commodity that became almost extinct in 20th century Michigan.

It was the last virgin pine left in the Lower Peninsula and Karen Hartwick donated it to the state in her husband's name, leading to the Hartwick Pines State Park.

March 31, 1928
Gordie Howe born

B orn in Floral, Saskatchewan, Gordie Howe was signed by the Detroit Red Wings at age 16. After several seasons with development teams, Howe would spend 25 years with the Wings, many of them as part of the "Production Line," with Ted Lindsay and Sid Abel, considered one of hockey's greatest-ever combinations. He retired from the Red Wings in 1971 but he couldn't leave hockey behind. He signed with the Houston Aeros of the World Hockey Association in 1973 where he had a successful season despite his age.

In 1979, he returned to the National Hockey League and played for the Hartford Whalers for one season. He made a final professional hockey appearance in 1997 when he played a game for the Detroit Vipers of the International Hockey League and became the only player to have played professional hockey in six different decades. After retiring, Howe moved to Traverse City and later to metro Detroit.

April

April 1, 1889
Sawmill on the run from creditors

In 19th century Michigan, a sawmill was often the reason a town existed. On this date the village of De Tour in the Upper Peninsula saw the beginning of the end for its facility.

The first steamboat of the season showed up at the dock, towing two barges and skippered by a nephew of the Moiles brothers, the men who ran the sawmill in De Tour.

When the tug, the *Tom Dowling*, failed to blow its whistle to announce its arrival, some of the villagers became suspicious.

They became more wary when 15 burly men emerged, saying they were there to retool the mill's machinery.

The next morning the townsfolk awoke to find the men dismantling the mill and loading it onto the barges.

The Moiles brothers' mill produced 150,000 board feet of lumber per day and employed approximately 100 men in the spring.

The sawmill may have been known as the Moiles Brother's Mill, but the brothers had mortgaged it through a firm in Chicago. When the burden of the mortgage became too much, the brothers endeavored to take the mill to Canada, out of reach of their creditors. No one was fooled when the brothers insisted they were merely taking the mill to Saginaw for repair.

When someone in De Tour attempted to call the sheriff in Sault Ste. Marie, they found the village's telephone line to the outside world had been cut.

A boy, Bill Jones, was sent on horseback to Pickford, 40 miles away, to notify the authorities of what was taking place.

Days later, the sheriff, on a steamer, caught up with the *Tom Dowling* as it churned its way through the ice toward Canada. One of the Moiles brothers appeared on deck with a rifle and warned the sheriff that he had left U.S. waters and anyone who tried to board his tug would be shot. The sheriff, unsure if he was in Michigan or not, backed off. The sawmill wound up in Canada, on John Island, just north of Manitoulin Island. But the Chicago mortgage holders got even – they went to Canada and secured logging rights to the land around the mill, putting an end to the Moiles brothers' business.

April 1, 1875
Five bridges collapse in Lansing

As a hard winter receded, it left behind a huge ice floe on the Grand River that battered the newly constructed Mineral Wells Bridge on April 1, 1875. The folks in Lansing believed for a time that the iron span could withstand such a beating.

Hours passed as ice and debris pounded the bridge. Finally the center span caved, collapsing into the water with a loud crash and sending a geyser into the air.

Horrified spectators realized it could be just the beginning.

They rushed to keep up with the Mineral Wells Bridge as it turned into a barge floating down the river to the north. Hundreds watched as the detached bridge came upon the Michigan Avenue Bridge, ready to crash it into the water. The Mineral Wells Bridge ground and scraped the Michigan Avenue Bridge, but ultimately passed under without bringing it down.

Residents cheered as they realized the bridge had been spared because it had been constructed without a center pier.

There was little time for celebration, however. The next bridge, at Shiawasse Street, was hit and crashed into the river.

What happened next was like a snowball gaining mass as it rolls down a hill: The Saginaw Street iron span was hit and fell into the river, followed by the Franklin Street span, which took 15 minutes of pounding before it relented. Next came the Seymour Street Bridge, which buckled under the pressure of the four bridges that crashed upon it. The following August, Lansing residents approved a $14,000 bond issue to pay for new bridges.

April 2, 1881
Hudson's opens for business

Joseph Lowthian Hudson was 35 years old when he opened his first store in 1881 in a leased space at the Detroit Opera House, selling men and boy's clothing. The popularity of the store grew. But rather than focusing on expanding his store, Hudson decided to branch out into automobiles, providing the cash for his eight partners – most notably Roy D. Chapin – to start up the Hudson Motor Car Company to compete with Ford and Chevrolet.

That venture started in February 1909 and began production on low-cost autos. The cars were well received and at the height of the company's popularity, in 1929, it produced more than 300,000 cars. In 1954 the company merged with Nash-Kelvinator to become American Motors Corporation.

Hudson didn't live to see the success of his store or his car company. He died in 1912 while vacationing in England. A lifelong bachelor, the store was turned over to his four nephews who charted a new course.

In 1923, Hudson's relocated to its own building on Woodward Avenue. By 1920, J.L. Hudson's was the third largest department store in the country. Its sales were behind only Marshall Field and Macy's.

Hudson's became more than a place to shop. It was also a reflection of Detroit. The store sponsored the city's annual Thanksgiving Day Parade. It was one of the first stores to employ minorities. In 1960 Diana Ross, then a Cass Tech student before she gained the world stage as the leader of Motown's Supremes, hired in as a bus girl in the cafeteria.

Hudson's also was the first major retailer to establish itself in a new retailing concept – the mall. When Northland Mall opened in 1954, it was among the first cluster of shops in the country. Hudson's was a cornerstone of that mall's success.

Other malls opened throughout the metropolitan Detroit area in the next two decades, signaling the reduction of suburban shoppers to the downtown Detroit facility. The Detroit store closed in 1983 and the building was demolished in 1998. In 2000, the Hudson's chain was purchased by Marshall Field and the name "Hudson's" disappeared.

April 3, 1871
One woman gets the vote – and continues to vote

Long before women gained the right to vote in 1920, a tenacious Detroit resident managed to register and vote.

Nannette B. Gardner went to her ward to register, arguing that she was a "person" in the context of the 14th Amendment and thereby had the right to vote. She was a widow and a taxpayer and, therefore, had no representation, she argued. Inspector Peter Hill thought Gardner had a reasonable argument and he put her name on the voting list.

Voting records show that Gardner continued to vote in elections as long as she remained in Detroit.

April 3, 1933
Crime, corruption and carnage makes
Michigan first state to repeal Prohibition

Michigan hopped on the temperance wagon early and forbade its residents to drink alcohol beginning in May of 1918, long before the 18th Amendment prohibited drinking across the nation in 1920.

But Michigan was geographically situated to become the epicenter of the underworld's effort to exploit Prohibition and sell bootlegged liquor. It was only a matter of bringing in loads of booze across the Detroit River from Windsor, where liquor remained legal. Whether through open waters or across the frozen ice in winter, rum-running was common.

Also, any thirsty resident could find what they needed to make their own beer at ordinary "dime stores."

This meant efforts to enforce Prohibition were particularly troublesome in Michigan.

At times, the federal government spent as much as 27 percent of its entire annual enforcement budget in a futile effort to stem the tide of alcohol flowing into Michigan. By 1927, smuggling, manufacturing, and liquor distribution was second only to the auto industry in Detroit in terms of revenue – $215 million.

The Purple Gang was notorious for its run of the town and ruthlessness. The Tommy gun ruled. Policemen, politicians and judges were allegedly on its payroll. The Purple Gang, a group of local killers and thugs, was so influential that it told Al Capone to stay out of eastern Michigan.

The rampant crime, flouting of the law and pressures of the Great Depression persuaded many residents that booze should be legal again. On April 3, 1933, by a vote of 99-1 Michigan lawmakers legalized the flow of alcohol in the state, making Michigan the first state to approve the 21st Amendment that repealed prohibition.

The amendment took effect in December of that year but Michigan returned to its non-Prohibition ways months earlier when in May the state government legalized the sale of 3.2 percent beer and wine.

April 4, 1957
Savage Straits of Mackinac storm

In the background, the towering Mackinac Bridge loomed; construction almost completed, but its opening date still months away. Dozens of passengers crossing the straits the old fashioned way, on the Vacationland Ferry, found themselves in a horrific spring blizzard.

The Vacationland boasted the second most powerful engine on the Great Lakes, but the engine wasn't strong enough to outrun the storm. High winds and crushing waves tossed the ferry and its 91 passengers onto an ice floe 25 feet thick. The vessel was stranded overnight hundreds of yards off shore. The Coast Guard rescued the crew and passengers the following day.

It was a brutal spring in northern Michigan. More than a week later, an ice field as large as 60 square miles stranded 35 freighters in Whitefish Bay.

April 4, 1882
The Battle of Manton

Of all the disputes over which town should become its county's seat, Manton, in Wexford County, has perhaps the best tale.

It started with a compromise between Cadillac and the town of Sherman that made Manton the county seat in 1881.

Cadillac residents, however, were never satisfied with the result.

The following year the matter was brought to the polls, and in early April Cadillac won the right to the county seat.

A party of 60 men from Cadillac, including the county sheriff, arrived in Manton April 4 on a special train to take the county records, the *Manton Tribune* reported. They were prepared to use force, if necessary.

Before the people of Manton realized what was going on, nearly all the records had been transferred from the county building to the train.

A short hand-to-hand fight broke out and, even though one of the Cadillac men was armed with a revolver, the few Manton men chased the Cadillac men back to their town.

Later that day some citizens of Cadillac returned, this time ready for a fight.

The paper wrote: "At noon they were back at Manton with 500 drunken men and boys. One barrel of whiskey was consumed by the brutes during the twelve-mile ride and when they marched through our streets a more disgusting and beastly sight was never witnessed in the State. Boys not a dozen years old drunk as sots, each armed with a club ready to assault the first man that got in their way, while the sheriff and Cadillac's mayor, with others prominent in that burg, brought up the rear."

At the courthouse, the mob was met by Manton resistance, leading to a fight. The Manton men who had fought off the earlier Cadillac delegation were singled out and beaten with clubs and crowbars.

Whether underhandedly or legitimately, through an election, Cadillac won the fight and the Wexford County courthouse remains there today.

April 5, 1778
Daniel Boone arrives as prisoner in Detroit

During the Revolutionary War, when the Indians were aligned with the British, the famous pioneer and frontiersman Daniel Boone and his settlers were particular enemies of the Indians because of their Westward movement.

In early 1778, while on an expedition to collect salt for his settlement, Boone was captured by a band of Shawnee Indians.

Boone's captors brought him to Detroit, where he arrived as a prisoner on April 5, 1778. There, British commander Lieutenant Colonel Henry Hamilton wanted Boone as a prisoner for himself because of Boone's celebrity

Hamilton offered the Indians 100 pounds for their prisoner, but they refused.

The Indians took Boone to Ohio, where he escaped.

April 6, 1808
American Fur Company founded

One of the most important companies in the early development of the United States had its headquarters on Mackinac
Island in the early 19th century.

Founded in New York on April 6, 1908, John Jacob Astor ran
the American Fur Company from a building on Mackinac Island,
strategically located for controlling the comings and goings of fur
traders.

Astor obtained a monopoly in the fur trade for his company
after the War of 1812, when control of Northern Michigan shifted
into American hands from the British.

For many years the company was run on the island by Astor's
trusted aide, Ramsey Crooks. Crooks brought great efficiency to
the industry and went after competitors with a ruthlessness that
any business tycoon of the late 19th century would have admired.

April 6, 1892
Never say die

Private George Sidman, a 17-year-old drummer boy from
Owosso, received the Congressional Medal of Honor on
April 6, 1882 for heroism displayed on a Civil War battlefield in
June, 1862. He was the youngest man in the state to receive that
commendation.

The citation declared that Sidman "rallied his comrades to
charge a vastly superior force until wounded in the hip."

Sidman was small and young when he enlisted with the 16th
Michigan Infantry at age 16 as a drummer boy, even though he
couldn't play the instrument properly. His regiment kept him
around despite his musical inability in hopes that eventually he
would become a soldier.

He earned a soldier's reputation at Gaines Mill, Virginia a year
after he enlisted. Sidman fought off the enemy and added encour-
agement to the battle until a mini ball struck his hip. He continued to fight until he fainted.

According to one witness, Sidman dragged "himself to an open
ditch in the rear, he clubbed his musket over a stump to destroy
its usefulness to the enemy, and throwing his accoutrements in
the ditch, he crawled on his hands and knees off the field of battle
and through the Chickahominy Swamp."

Sidman was captured and then exchanged. He twice escaped
from hospitals and managed to rejoin his unit. He was given the
honor of carrying the 3rd Brigade's new flag in the charge on
Marye's Heights at Fredericksburg where Sidman was wounded
again.

He was promoted to corporal and wounded again at the Battle

of Middleburg, where he was shot in the foot on June 21, 1863. He was hospitalized for several months and over his objections was transferred to the Invalid Corps until his discharge in 1865.

April 7, 1947
Death of Henry Ford
Born without electricity, died without electricity

Henry Ford represented the industrial revolution that brought a modern age to the world, but the night he died he lay at Fair Lane, his Dearborn home, in a room lit by two candles and an oil lamp, without the comfort of electricity or telephone.

A torrential storm raised the River Rouge above its banks and brought a power outage after the home's hydroelectric plant failed due to flooding.

Ford died with his wife, Clara Bryant Ford, and maid, Rosa Buhler, at his side.

At age 83, Ford's health had been in serious decline for three years. However, the day he died, he insisted on inspecting the damage caused by the flood.

Ford was born July 30, 1863 at his parent's farmhouse, lit by oil lamps, in Dearborn.

April 7, 1939
Francis Ford Coppola born

Francis Ford Coppola was born in Detroit to mother Italia and father Carmine, who was a composer, musician and the first flautist for the Detroit Symphony Orchestra. His father's flute-playing ability took the family to New York City two years after Coppola's birth, where the family settled in Woodside, Queens.

Coppola would go on to become a legendary filmmaker, directing movies such as *The Godfather*, *The Godfather Part II* and *Apocalypse Now*. He also directed *Tucker: The Man and His Dream*, based on the life of the Michigan automaker.

April 8, 1871
First roller coaster in Michigan

Grand Ledge incorporated on this day and immediately created a plan to make it a resort destination.

The resort business began when John Burtch launched a steamer in the Grand River called *Dolly Varden*, named after a Charles Dickens character, for the purpose of taking passengers to the city's Grand Island. There were trees, the running water of the

Grand River, and the sandstone ledges along the riverbanks. That natural beauty was enough to convince Burtch he had the makings of a resort and he founded the Seven Islands Resort.

Burtch built a hotel on the island and in 1877 sold the resort to S.M. Hewings, who launched a steamer called *Gertie*, named after his daughter. Hewings upgraded the resort by building a luxury hotel on the site.

The Island House Hotel was 144 feet long and 25 feet wide. It featured a veranda and a ballroom on its second story.

Hewings also built a dam made of stones and logs to allow for deeper water for boating.

According to the Grand Ledge Historical Society, one 1880 account noted the opulence of the resort: "Mr. Hewings, being a man of taste and means, is doing a great deal to add to the attractions of the vicinity, a spacious hall, beautiful little steamer, row-boats, bathhouses, bathing-suits, hammocks, archery, croquet-grounds, swings, rustic-seats, fountains, animal-parks, refreshment-stands, and everything for the pleasure and comfort of visitors, are provided. Beautiful camping-grounds with plenty of pure spring water. No liquors sold on the grounds. There is a fine mineral spring on one of the islands, said to possess curative properties of a high order...."

In 1886, J. Scott Mudge bought the resort and built a roller coaster, which became a hit. It is believed to be the first roller coaster in Michigan.

By the time Mudge was finished, Grand Ledge was the second most popular resort town in Michigan, behind Petoskey.

Until 1910, trains brought folks from around Michigan to enjoy the ledges, the swimming, the fishing, a roller coaster, a vaudeville theater and steamboat rides.

In the 20th century, the development of the automobile proved an end to Grand Ledge's popularity as a resort destination.

April 9, 1871
Alpena: Phoenix of the North

Near midnight on April 9, 1871, the most disastrous fire Alpena had seen destroyed the business district of the city north of the Thunder Bay River. More than 100 residents were left homeless and Alpena was left without a place for public entertainment or gatherings.

This fire, and a fire on Dec. 12 of the previous year that destroyed the courthouse and nearly all of the county records collected since 1863, probably motivated the citizens of Alpena to organize a fire department.

A local newspaper reported on the devastating impact the fire had on the psyche of the young city: "Our city has received a severe loss, and one that it will take years to recover from. The public also sustained a great loss, in the destruction of our two principal hotels, the Huron House and Star; and in the burning of the Evergreen Hall, we are deprived of any place for public entertainments or public gatherings, since the courthouse was destroyed last winter, the Evergreen Hall was the only building of the kind left in the place."

The newspaper writer urged a group of newly elected officials to organize a fire company, "so that in the future, we may not be entirely at the mercy of the devouring flames."

The fire company was organized, but it didn't put to an end a history of devastating fires that visited the town. The pumper purchased by the city was no match for a fire in July of 1872, which burned some 15 acres and took with it almost 70 buildings.

According to an account from the *Alpena Pioneer*: "Every minute seemed an hour. In seven and one-half minutes after leaving the engine house the steam was up, but the fierce flames had already wrapped their devouring arms around the Sherman House, and were darting a hundred fiery tongues into the air. The engine commenced to play, but it was evident that one little engine was fighting against fearful odds. The buildings were all built of pine wood, and burnt like tinder. Despite the volume of fire, and the frantic effort of citizens to douse the flames as they spread around by rapidly changing high winds, only three lives were lost."

But the city endured yet another fire in 1888 that burned 200 buildings and left 1,500 homeless. That fire took one life.

Alpena began life as a lumber town in the tinderbox of northeast Michigan and grew to include other industries, such as pulp production for the manufacturing of paper.

April 10, 1922
Horse-drawn firefighters answer final alarm

More than 50,000 people poured along Woodward Avenue to watch the end of an era.

In the previous decade people watched as cars and trucks overtook horse-drawn modes of transportation thanks to the auto industry that developed in Detroit. On April 10, 1922, the crowd watched horses draw fire engines through Detroit for the last time.

The star of the parade was Ned, a horse that had worked to haul equipment to fires for 14 years. All of the horses were taken to Belle Isle to spend their retirement in comfort.

Parade goers also got a glimpse of the future – rounding out the back of the procession was a shiny, fire-red motorized fire engine that drove down Woodward Avenue with its siren blaring.

April 10, 1915
Harry Morgan born

Born Harry Bartsburg in Detroit, Harry Morgan graduated from high school in Muskegon and earned distinction on his school's debate team. He began his film career in 1942 with a role in *The Shores of Tripoli*, and he would go on to appear in a dozen other movies.

It was on the small screen that Morgan would really break through, however, as officer Bill Gannon on *Dragnet* and Colonel Sherman T. Potter on *M*A*S*H*.

April 11, 1949
Death of Michigan's sole U.P. governor

Chase Osborn began his professional career as a reporter at the *Chicago Tribune*.

He was born on Jan. 22, 1860 in a log cabin in Indiana. Initially, the family lived quite comfortably, but at age eight his father lost all their money and the family lived in poverty. In his autobiography, *The Iron Hunter*, Osborn said he had no idea what happened, only that suddenly all the family's possessions were taken away.

"It was one of those occurrences that are continually happening and directly or indirectly, mostly the latter, exert a great influence both upon individuals and society, serving to cure pride and remind man in a decisive manner of his self-insufficiency," he wrote.

As a boy he fought a lot and did not do well in school.

"I was the most depraved youth in Indiana according to their ideas," Osborn said. "Parents forbade their daughters to speak to me and ordered their sons to shun me.

He attended the first class of Purdue University but he left for Chicago before graduating and, after working as a laborer, eventually found a reporting job at the *Chicago Tribune*.

Later, Osborn convinced an investor to help him start a newspaper in Florence, Wisconsin, where he took on corrupt local officials and prospected for iron.

He later moved to Sault Ste. Marie, where he ran the *Sault News* and became involved in politics, first as a postmaster and then as State Fish and Game Warden. Governor Hazen Pingree named him Commissioner of Railroads. Osborn was known for fighting political corruption and refusing bribes such as one he was offered when he sought lower fares on the railroads.

He was elected governor of Michigan in 1910 as a Republican and served a two-year term. He was the only governor to come from the Upper Peninsula.

Osborn ran for governor again but lost. He also lost bids to become a U.S. senator and a candidate for vice president.

After his term as governor, Osborn traveled the world. He was particularly interested in visiting foreign iron mining operations. Osborn loved iron so much he devoted 10 chapters in his autobiography to it. One chapter is titled "The Poetry, Charm, Romance, and Usefulness of Iron Ore."

He was a vocal proponent of the Mackinac Bridge. However, he died on April 11, 1949, missing the construction and completion of the bridge by almost 10 years.

April 11, 1884
First brown trout in the United States

The first effort in the United States to introduce brown trout took place on April 11, 1884, in Lake County.
The Northville station of the Federal Fish Hatchery planted trout eggs into the Pere Marquette River system near Baldwin.

The 4,900 fry were obtained from Baron Friedrich Von Behr of Berlin, Germany by Fred Mather, superintendent of the Cold Springs Harbor Federal Fish Hatchery at Long Island, New York.

The brown trout, known as Bachforelle, took hold and spawned a sport fishing industry throughout Michigan.

April 12, 1955
Old Mariners' Church saved

For a city where so many old buildings have been demolished, it's notable when Detroit goes out of its way to save an old structure.

Such was the case with Mariners' Church, the oldest stone church still standing in Detroit. It was erected in 1842 when Detroit was still a busy seaport.

The church holds a special service each March called "the Blessing of the Fleet" in anticipation of the coming shipping season. In November, the church holds the "Great Lakes Memorial Service," when its congregation remembers those who have been lost to the lakes. In November 1975, a day after the loss of the Edmund Fitzgerald, church members sat silently as the church bell rang 29 times for each man lost in the wreck, giving Gordon Lightfoot a lyric for his song.

The Mariners' Church was in the way when planners were looking for a location for a new convention center to be called Cobo Hall in the 1950s. But preservationists won and the church was moved stone by stone from the foot of Woodward Avenue, in what used to he heart of the dock and warehouse district to its new location beginning on December 13, 1954. It was completed on April 12, 1955. It now stands at East Jefferson Avenue at Randolph

April 12, 1997
World's largest black history museum opens

The idea for the museum began when Dr. Charles Wright, an obstetrician and gynecologist, visited a World War II memorial to soldiers in Denmark. That visit sparked the notion that African-Americans needed to preserve the history of black people in America.

Wright worked with 30 others in 1965 and established the International Afro-American Museum that opened on West Grand Boulevard and featured dozens of exhibits. The museum held items such as masks from Nigeria and Ghana and the inventions of Elijah McCoy, items that toured the country the following year as a traveling museum in a converted mobile home.

But the scope of what was to be preserved soon outgrew the space of the small building. Throughout the 1970s and 1980s, funds were raised to build a larger museum.

A 28,000 square-foot museum opened in the 1980s, but soon even that was too small.

Voters in the city approved funds for an even larger building at East Warren Avenue and Brush Street in the city's Cultural Center, which also includes the Detroit Art Institute and the Detroit Science Center. On April 11, 1997, doors opened to a 120,000-square foot facility called the Charles H. Wright Museum of African American History.

The museum houses more than 30,000 artifacts and archival materials and is home to the Blanche Coggin Underground Railroad Collection, Harriet Tubman Museum Collection, Coleman A. Young Collection and the Sheffield Collection, a repository of documents of the labor movement in Detroit.

April 13, 1978
Michigan refuses to return Alabama prisoner

Lizzy Williams was a harmless looking 60-year-old Detroit resident when it was discovered she was actually an escaped convict from Alabama.

Williams was sentenced to a 218-year term on a prison farm in 1942 for lying to police to protect her boyfriend from robbery charges. She walked off the farm in 1951, settled in Detroit, and lived the life of a respectable citizen for 27 years, making a living as a cleaning lady.

She lived this life until she was discovered by Alabama authorities who said they wanted her returned to Alabama to serve the remainder of her sentence.

Governor William G. Milliken moved quickly to hold an extradition hearing and within a day he denied the request of Alabama Governor George Wallace. Milliken said he determined that since the woman had lived a law-abiding life in the decades since she had come to Michigan, the interest of justice would not be served by sending her back to prison.

The following day Wallace's office backed off and said they did not want the woman returned to prison anyway. A Wallace aide said the governor had "no personal interest in the case whatsoever."

April 13, 1890
Frank Murphy, governor, U.S. Supreme Court justice, born

Frank Murphy was born at Harbor Beach, in Michigan's thumb. He followed his father into law, attending school at the University of Michigan.

He served in the U.S. Army during WW I, achieving the rank of captain with the Occupation Forces in Germany.

His political life began in Detroit when he was elected mayor in 1930. In 1933, he organized the first convention of the United States Conference of Mayors. In the mid-1930s, Murphy was appointed by President Franklin D. Roosevelt as High Commissioner of the Philippines before he returned to Michigan to run for governor.

Murphy was governor of the state in 1937 when the General Motors sit-down strike took place in Flint. Although he ordered National Guard troops to the site, he refused to send them into the plant to remove workers because he wanted a peaceful end to the strike. He helped mediate the strike and win a victory for the United Auto Workers.

Two years later Roosevelt appointed Murphy Attorney General of the United States and in 1940 he was named a U.S. Supreme Court justice. Among his most famous dissents regarded a decision upholding the forced relocation of Japanese-Americans during World War II. He said the court was sinking into "the ugly abyss of racism."

Murphy died July 19, 1949 in Detroit at 59 of a heart attack. More than 10,000 persons attended his funeral.

April 14, 1972
Discovery of long lost car ferry

The car ferry *Milwaukee* was built in 1903. The boat was 338 feet long and first named the *Manistique Marquette and Northern No. 1.*

In 1908, the car ferry was damaged in heavy ice near Manistique. After it was salvaged from the bottom of Lake Michigan, she was renamed the *Milwaukee.*

The *Milwaukee* sailed the Great Lakes until a storm in October of 1929 brought her permanently to the bottom of Lake Michigan.

The captain, Robert "Heavy Weather" McKay, fought through high wind and pounding waves to make the voyage from Grand Haven to its port in Milwaukee, Wisconsin where the boat was loaded with cargo bound for Michigan. There, railroad cars full of automobiles, canned peas, lumber, cheese and bathtubs were loaded onto the *Milwaukee*.

Even with the cargo loaded, the crew did not believe the boat would leave port because the weather had turned so bad. But somewhere past 3 p.m., "Heavy Weather" McKay piloted the boat out of the harbor in Milwaukee to the disbelief of those who remained on shore.

The crew of a ship anchored three miles offshore was the last to see the *Milwaukee*. Debris and a lifeboat were later found near Holland. The bodies of four crewmen were soon recovered. In all, 52 lives were lost.

A U. S. Coast Guard officer found a message left by a purser, A.R. Sadon, in a waterproof container containing his last thoughts: "The ship is taking water fast. We have turned around and headed for Milwaukee. Pumps are working but sea gate is bent in and can't keep water out…. Seas are tremendous. Things look bad. Crew roll is about the same as on last payday."

Where the *Milwaukee* went down remained a mystery, as did whether the captain set sail on his own accord or was ordered by his company to make the return trip across the lake.

Then on April 14, 1972, a crew using sonar equipment were investigating an area where local fishermen complained of snagged lines. The crew discovered a bulk on the lake floor and lowered video equipment into the water.

Divers discovered that the railroad cars inside the ferry probably came loose during the storm and crashed through the ship's storm gate, dooming the vessel.

April 14, 1898
Ypsilanti: Pay your water bill or go to jail

The landmark water tower in Ypsilanti was built in 1890 for a little more than $21,000. In its first year, it supplied water to the town's 471 residents.

City officials must have worried about people receiving more than their share of water because on April 14, 1898, they passed a complicated annual rate schedule for water usage.

People paid $5 per faucet in their house and a private bathtub cost an added $2. Saloon owners were forced to pay $7 for one faucet and, oddly, $1 for each billiard table. A person owed $1 for each cow they owned. Failure to pay the rates subjected a resident to a $50 fine and 90 days in jail.

In 1975, the 147-foot tower was designated an American Water

Landmark by the American Water Works Association.

April 15, 1942
Liquor permit issued to Paradise Club at Idlewild; Black resort brought in Jackie Wilson, Della Reese, the Four Tops

The resort of Idlewild in Lake County was known as the luxury resort that discrimination built, since it was one of the few places in the country where blacks were able to freely purchase land and vacation during the segregation era.

The Michigan Liquor Control Commission issued a permit on this day to John Simmons for his 2,500-square foot clubhouse, the Paradise Club. The permit meant vacationers could drink and dance while enjoying such performers as Della Reese, Al Hibbler, Bill Doggertt, Jackie Wilson, T-Bone Walker, Sarah Vaughn, Aretha Franklin, Bill Cosby, George Kirby, Roy Hamilton, Brooks Benton and Choker Campbell. The Four Tops got their start at Idlewild, singing at the Paradise and three other clubs. They later toured the country with Arthur "Big Daddy" Braggs' Idlewild Revue.

Idlewild had been a resort for well-off black families for decades, since a real estate developer bought 2,700 acres of land in Yates Township and advertised small lots in black newspapers around the Midwest. It contained many businesses and had its own post office.

It really caught on and became a place of status after Dr. Daniel Hale Williams bought land at Idlewild. Williams performed the world's first successful open heart surgery in 1893 at a hospital he founded in Chicago to serve the black community. Williams retired to Idlewild and died there in 1931. Madame C. J. Walker, the first self-made U.S. woman millionaire, also owned property at the resort.

In the 1940s and 1950s, Idlewild developed a reputation as a national center for blacks that attracted entertainers from across the country.

The Civil Rights Act of 1964 barred discrimination against blacks in public places and led to the demise of the resort as a national attraction.

April 16, 1912
Michigan-born woman is first female to fly over the English Channel

Famous aviator Harriet Quimby was born in May, 1875 in either Arcadia or Coldwater – they both claim her as their own. Quimby disowned Michigan, saying later in life that she was born in California.

However, there is solid evidence that, as a girl, Quimby lived in a farmhouse in Arcadia Township near Bear Lake, which is near Lake Michigan in Manistee County. If fact, her mother left behind evidence of the family through advertisements in the *Manistee Daily News* for patent medicine, "Quimby's Liver Invigorator."

At the turn of the century, the family moved to San Francisco after the Michigan farm failed. In California, she pursued a career in journalism, working for the *San Francisco Call*. She also wrote five screenplays for silent movies. But always ready for a new adventure, she moved to New York where, from 1903-1912, she worked at *Leslie's Illustrated Weekly* as a photojournalist, theater critic and reporter, focusing mainly on household stories. She was also the darling of movers and shakers in the Big Apple, frequently in the public eye.

During this time, Quimby developed an interest in flight, becoming the first woman in the United States to obtain a pilot's license and only the second in the world in 1911. She highlighted her beauty, style and charm by wearing tight-fitting purple silk jump suits. She earned lucrative fees at air meets, where people turned out to see this celebrity of the skies. Quimby also showed her flair by flying over a crowd of some 15,000 spectators on Staten Island during a moonlit night becoming the first woman to make a nighttime flight in September 1911.

On April 16, 1912, Quimby became the first woman to fly solo over the English Channel, taking a route from Dover, England to Calais, France, and completing the flight in just less than an hour. Her feat would have received more coverage had the Titanic not sunk a few days earlier and dominated the pages of newspapers in North America and Europe.

Her passion for aviation eventually cost her her life at the age of 37. On July 1, 1912, at the Third Annual Boston Aviation Meet in Massachusetts, one of the event's organizers insisted on joining her in a flight. Thousands of spectators watched in horror as the plane shifted unsteadily in the air, finally pitching forward. Quimby lost control, falling with her passenger from the sky into the shallow waters of Dorchester Bay. It has been suggested that Quimby lost control of the delicately balanced plane when the passenger, a very large man, leaned forward to ask her a question.

April 17, 1890
Benzie "millionaire" kills sheriff and doctor

In a now-nonexistent town called Aral at Otter Creek, which today is part of Sleeping Bear Dunes National Lakeshore, C. T. Wright, a lumberman, shot and killed local Deputy Neil Marshall and Dr. Frank Thurber.

Wright leased a mill in the small town in the late 19th century. At the time, the town consisted of a few houses, a general store, a post office, a few boarding houses and a nearby Indian camp.

Wright, who came to northern Michigan from Racine, Wisconsin, employed approximately 200 men who cut trees, rolled logs into the stream for floating to the mill and sawed logs.

Wright drank heavily, often resulting in disputes with his neighbors. Benzie County's prosecutor described Wright's troubles as the source of half the county's legal business. In nine cases out of 10, he was the defendant.

Wright's disputes extended to battles with the county government; he maintained it was overtaxing him on his property. Benzie County officials believed Wright was a millionaire lumberman and taxed him at a "millionaire's rate." Wright, in fact, had amassed no fortune.

Sheriff A.B. Case was dispatched to collect the taxes in the form of 250,000 board feet of uncut lumber worth $900. Case deputized Marshall and sent him to guard the lumber until it could be collected. But when Marshall arrived in August 1889, he found a drunk Wright toting a rifle.

Wright's men stood atop a pile of logs, ready to roll them into the stream to be taken to the mill. When Marshall ordered them to stop, Wright said he would shoot Marshall if he didn't move. Marshall left, but returned shortly with Dr. Thurber, a well-liked doctor and schoolteacher.

They were met by a riled-up Wright, who had spent the day drinking. Marshall and Thurber were shot and killed in front of two witnesses. Wright immediately took off.

A manhunt ensued and a lynch mob formed. After Wright was found on a Lake Michigan beach and arrested, he was taken from the Frankfort jail to the Manistee one for his own safety. A rumor that he was taken to Traverse City brought a Benzie County lynch mob there.

His trial began on April 17, 1890, including 10 days of jury selection to find an impartial panel.

Wright was found guilty and sentenced to life at hard labor. His sentence was later commuted to 17 years by Governor Hazen Pingree and, over the objections of the slain men's widows, Wright was released from prison in May, 1902.

April 18, 1837
Grand Rapids' first newspaper published

A wrecked steamer, sailboat and dog sleds were involved in getting one of the state's first newspapers to print.

One of the earliest challenges that faced the *Grand River Times* was getting a press purchased from the *Niagara Falls Journal* of New York to Grand Rapids.

In Niagara Falls, the materials were put aboard the steamer *Don Quixote* and carried through Lake Erie and into Lake Huron. But the steamer wrecked near Alpena.

The equipment was recovered and put aboard a sailboat for Grand Haven. There, the press and equipment were transferred from sailboat to dog sleds with six-dog teams trudging the rest of the way to Grand Rapids. The press had to be recovered one more time from icy water when a sled crashed through ice on the Grand River.

On April 18, 1837 the weekly's first edition hit the streets.

Louis Campau, one of the founders of Grand Rapids, bought 500 copies of the first edition for $2 per paper. The Kent Company, which initially invested $4,000 in the newspaper, did the same. Other prominent citizens paid for copies by the dozen.

Despite such civic interest, the *Grand River Times* suffered because national news took days to reach the newspaper's office from Detroit. And local news, by the time it reached the front page, was already well known around town.

George W. Pattison, who bought the paper for $4,100 from the Kent Company when the equipment was on the sailboat to Grand Haven, sold the paper within 18 months. The paper folded and the plant became a printing shop.

April 19, 1973
There's oil in them thar' craters

Readers of the *Traverse City Record-Eagle* were greeted with an unsettling headline on April 19, 1973: "Craters open up in Grand Traverse County."

Fifty families were evacuated from their homes around Williamsburg after boiling craters of gas and water erupted through the surface of the earth in a two square-mile area. One of the craters erupted on the shoulder of M-72 and it amassed into a 40-foot circle of bubbling dark water.

In Lansing, United Press International could not get an explanation from officials at the Department of Natural Resources.

"At this point we don't know how to assess it," an official said.

In addition to having to leave their homes, residents worried about the safety of drinking water and the natural gas stench that made the air seem flammable. The geological event also killed fish in Williamsburg Creek. Traffic was detoured and no smoking signs erected around the affected area.

Attention soon turned to an oil well site operated by a subsidiary of Standard Oil Company four miles south of Williamsburg. But the following day, Standard Oil officials assured residents that the bursts from the ground were not a big problem.

It was finally determined that natural gas traveled four miles underground from the oil drilling site to Williamsburg, where it broke through areas where the groundwater pressure above the gas could no longer contain it inside the earth.

April 19, 1836
"Biddle City," home of state capital, founded

B rothers William and Jerry Ford left New York for Michigan looking for fortune in the 1800s. They settled first in what was called Jacksonburgh, now the city of Jackson, where they purchased a plat, cleared the land, and constructed a mill and water power facility.

They were confident that, having licked nature once, they could do it again by starting their own city. The two men looked 40 miles to the north, near the convergence of the Grand and Red Cedar Rivers, for their venture.

On April 19, 1836, the brothers executed the plat for "Biddle City" at the state land office and drew up plans for proposed streets and town squares at the site of what is now Lansing.

But travel to the fledgling town in the 1830s was difficult. That led speculators, not pioneers, to purchase the lots, preventing the establishment of "Biddle City."

April 20, 1909
First mile of concrete in USA

I t was fitting that automotive-driven Wayne County should be the first in the nation to lay down a mile of concrete for a highway.

Work on the road began on April 20, 1909, with the surface of Woodward Avenue to be paved between Six and Seven Mile Roads.

The highway, constructed under the administration of the state's first highway commissioner, Horatio "Good Roads" Earle, was 18 feet wide and cost $13,357.

At the turn of the century, Earle was a young entrepreneur and bicycle enthusiast who was president of the League of American Wheelmen, a group founded in 1880 to fight for better roads. This group convinced lawmakers to create a state highway commission in 1892.

In 1901, Earle advocated a system of roads to connect all major cities and in 1905 he helped convince Michigan voters to approve an amendment to the state constitution allowing state expenditure for roads. The amendment also created the state highway department, with Earle as its first commissioner. There he declared war on mud, a great impediment to travel before paved roads. The concrete experiment was closely watched across the country by others who were interested in building better roads.

The pavement also became a tourist attraction. The original concrete was replaced in 1922.

April 21, 1947
Birth of James Newell Osterberg, Jr. – Iggy Pop

James Newell Osterberg, Jr., also know as punk rocker Iggy Pop, was born in Muskegon and raised in a trailer park in the Ann Arbor area.

At the trailer park, the Osterbergs was probably the only family led by a college-educated father. Iggy's supported his creative energies and when they discovered the only place in the trailer that would fit a drum kit was the parents' bedroom, they moved out to let Pop explore his talents.

His stage name came from a band he started at high school in Ann Arbor called the *Iguanas*; the name Pop he borrowed from a friend.

Although never a great commercial success, he would put an enormous imprint on music. He's credited with inspiring the birth of punk and of grunge. Songs he wrote decades ago remain fresh today as commercial jingles, such as "Lust for Life" in ads for Royal Caribbean Cruises.

Pop, accompanied by his band, The Stooges, unveiled stage antics that would make him famous, such as smearing his body with peanut butter or raw meat, or cutting himself with broken glass. He's also thought to be the first performer to throw himself into the audience.

The band was signed to Elektra and made two albums that would be loved by fans of punk rock but were commercial failures.

Drug abuse caused fits and starts in Pop's career. As Pop recovered from heroin addiction, a chance encounter with David Bowie in New York City changed his career. Bowie visited Pop after he had committed himself to a mental hospital in Los Angeles.

In the mid-1970s Bowie and Pop lived in Berlin for three years and collaborated on Pop's albums, *The Idiot* and *Lust for Life*. In the late 1970s, Pop toured the country with Bowie on keyboard. They later co-wrote "China Girl," a song released by Bowie that was Pop's first commercial success.

Pop released solo projects through the 1990s. In 2003, The Stooges reunited.

By the 21st Century, Pop had become an icon. When the satirical newspaper *The Onion* ran the headline "Song About Heroin Used To Advertise Bank," it was satire that was very close to reality.

As for the use of his songs in commercials, Pop told *Rolling Stone* magazine he's just glad to reach a larger audience.

April 22, 1833
State's oldest college founded

On April 22, 1833, the Michigan and Huron Institute was granted its charter, although classes didn't begin until two years later. It eventually became Kalamazoo College in 1855.

The school was founded by Baptists and residents of the village of Bronson, soon to become Kalamazoo. The founders promised funds for construction of the school.

Kalamazoo College is the oldest institution to continuously offer college-level instruction in the state.

The University of Michigan was chartered in Detroit in 1817 but didn't open in Ann Arbor until 1837.

April 22, 1833
First railroad in the West

The Erie and Kalamazoo, chartered on April 22, 1833, was the first railroad to operate west of the Alleghenies. The railroad would connect Port Lawrence, now Toledo, with the Kalamazoo River via Adrian.

It took three years to lay the rail. The first train trip between Toledo and Adrian was in a car drawn by a horse in November, 1836.

In 1837, the railroad became the first to operate a steam locomotive in Michigan.

The locomotive was built in Philadelphia and was called the Adrian No. 1. The engine ran on wood and was cooled by water. If the train ran out of either, the passengers were expected to head into the forest to collect wood and fetch water. It took one day to travel between Toledo and Adrian.

The line was later known as the Michigan Southern Railroad, part of a system that linked the East Coast and Chicago.

April 23, 1954
Filmmaker born in Flint

During the George W. Bush administration, Michael Moore became almost as polarizing to Americans as Bush himself. During Bush's re-election campaign, Moore attended the Republican National Convention and taunted the crowds, answering their cheers of "four more years" with "two more months."

Love him or hate him, there is no question Moore loves Michigan and has remained committed to his home state.

He founded the Traverse City Film Festival in 2005, an event that annually brings thousands of visitors and millions of dollars to northern Michigan. He led a successful effort to restore the State Theater in 2007 in Traverse City, bringing new life to the downtown.

Moore was born in Flint in 1954 to a mother who was a secretary, and a father who worked on the line at a General Motors factory.

Moore got his start in politics early when he won a local school board seat at age 18, making him one of the youngest public officials in the country.

Moore left for the University of Michigan in 1976 but spent less than a year there before dropping out to focus on activism. He took a job with General Motors and quit after one day in the factory.

Next, Moore became editor of an alternative newspaper called the *Flint Voice*, which later became the *Michigan Voice*.

Moore parlayed that experience into a job as the editor of *Mother Jones*, a liberal magazine where Moore was fired in a dispute with his publishers after he refused to run a piece he believed gave credit to the Reagan administration's policies in Latin America.

Moore sued after he was fired and won a settlement of $58,000. He used the money to fund the filming of the documentary *Roger & Me*, a movie about the devastation brought to his hometown when General Motors closed its Flint plant. The film featured Moore's futile attempts to interview G.M. Chairman Roger Smith.

Moore produced television shows with a consumer activist bent and in 2002 directed *Bowling for Columbine*, a film that won the jury award at the Cannes Film Festival and the Academy Award for best documentary film

His next movie, which attacked the Bush administration, *Fahrenheit 9/11*, became the highest grossing documentary film of all time.

Moore premiered his film *Sicko* in 2007 at a small movie theater in Bellaire, near his home on Torch Lake where Moore lives with his wife, producer Kathleen Glynn.

April 24, 2007
Inventor of airport rental cars dies

Warren Edward Avis, a Bay City native, returned from World War II a decorated U.S. Army Air Corps pilot with a new business idea.

As a pilot, he experienced the frustration of arriving at European airports unable to find ground transportation. He eventually put motorcycles on the bombers so he could travel to see local towns.

With $85,000, two employees and fewer that 200 cars he started a car rental company in 1946 at Willow Run Airport in Ypsilanti and another at Miami International Airport. The company used new cars and attractive women at rental car counters to attract customers. Avis Rent-A-Car was up and running.

Avis became the world's largest car rental company until the title was taken by Hertz after years of competition.

Avis hobnobbed with the social elite of his day, making friends with actor Cary Grant, hotelier Conrad Hilton Jr., and entertainer Sammy Davis, Jr.

"You knew when he walked in the room he was somebody; he had that presence," Patrick Kalmbach, president of Avis Enterprises, told the *International Herald Tribune* upon Avis' death. "He was shrewd but he truly believed in the team approach and listening to people at all levels."

He sold Avis in 1954 for $8 million and went on to form a company that invested in high tech enterprises.

He died at his farm near Ann Arbor at the of age 92.

April 24, 1941
Detroit: The arsenal of democracy

During World War II, when production in Detroit shifted from automobiles to the machinery of war, famous Detroit architect Albert Kahn was hired by the Chrysler Corporation to design a self-contained tank plant.

A crowd cheered on April 24, 1941 as the first tank rolled off the line at the Detroit Arsenal Tank Plant. Shifts worked around the clock at a blistering pace.

The plant made more than 22,000 tanks during the war, more than a quarter of the country's production. It continued to produce tanks through 1997.

April 25, 1696
King Louis XIV abandons Michigan

The French who filtered into Michigan in the early days were in two camps.

There were the Jesuits, who believed settlers and fur traders should not be allowed into the region because they corrupted the Indians when they traded rum for beaver pelts.

Those in the fur trading business believed no such thing. They also worried that if France didn't settle the region, the English would.

In acquiescence to the Jesuits, King Louis XIV issued a decree on April 25, 1696 requiring all of the western posts of New France to be deserted. The missionaries could stay but all other Frenchmen were to return East.

This decree disturbed Antoine Laumet de la Mothe, sieur de Cadillac, commander of the fort at Mackinac while the French and the English were at war.

Cadillac and the Jesuits were often at odds. The evacuation of the French created a vacuum the English traders were more than happy to fill.

The Indians became dependent on such wares as gunpowder and rum from the white men. Why would they travel to Montreal for trading when the English were willing to come to them?

Cadillac saw that France would lose the region if the decree was not reconsidered, so he traveled to France to plead his case. Cadillac argued that to protect the interests of France he should be allowed to establish a fort and settlement at the bend in the river between Lake Erie and Lakes St. Clair and Huron.

Cadillac won his case and went on to found Detroit at the bend.

April 26, 1835
Michigan and Ohio go to war

Long before the University of Michigan and the Ohio State University developed a bitter rivalry, Michigan and Ohio went to war over Toledo (see also Dec. 14).

The dispute had its origins over where the boundary line between the state of Ohio and the territory of Michigan lay, and which would claim the mouth of the Maumee River. The mouth of that river was considered enormously valuable because of the shipping trade going through the Erie Canal.

The Northwest Ordinance put the strip of land in question inside the Michigan Territory.

Officials in Ohio balked at that action. So in 1817, in accordance with an act of Congress, they sent out their own surveyor who determined the land belonged in Ohio.

Nonetheless, Michigan continued to exercise jurisdiction over the territory, passing a law that made it a criminal offense for anyone other than a Michigan official "to exercise any official authority in the disputed territory." The penalty was five years in prison and a $1,000 fine.

This set up the showdown of 1835.

Ohio scheduled elections in Toledo to select town officers. Territorial Governor Stevens T. Mason of Michigan sent a militia from Monroe to Toledo to arrest those who participated in the election. Two arrests were made but the Ohioans posted bail and returned to their state.

Weeks passed until a Michigan militia patrolling the area encountered a group of Ohio officials busy marking the state line as they saw fit.

Shots were exchanged on April 26, 1835, although some sources say it was a day earlier. No one was injured but the Ohio officials were arrested. This caused Ohio Governor Robert Lucas to order his own militia into the region but the two militias avoided meeting each other on the battlefield.

In July, Michigan officials returned to Toledo and Sheriff Joseph Wood of Monroe County arrested several Ohioans. The arrest of Major Benjamin Franklin Stickney led to the only blood spilled during the war. Stickney had two sons, named One and Two. Two Stickney attempted to rescue his father, stabbing Wood in the thigh with a knife.

During this period, Michigan petitioned to become a state. Ohio insisted that as a condition of statehood the new state should surrender the Toledo strip.

President Andrew Jackson depended on Ohio's support in the 1836 election and sided with Ohio.

Michigan gave up its claim to the Toledo strip in exchange for entrance into the Union and the western two-thirds of the Upper Peninsula, land which would decades later offer fortunes in copper and iron.

April 27, 1763
Pontiac's council

Once the English took over the Great Lakes region from the French, Indians became frustrated with the new caretakers. The French and the Indians had come to an understanding – the Indians respected the French military power and the French were generous with the Indians, regularly giving them gifts and paying good prices for furs.

The English, on the other hand, did not want their relationship with the Indians to be too expensive. They rarely made offerings of gifts, paid as little as possible for furs and charged exorbitant prices for their goods.

After three years of English rule, an Ottawa chief, Pontiac, decided he'd had enough. He resolved to remove the British from the region, enlisting other tribes for help.

On April 27, 1763, he held a council of Ottawas, Potawatamis and Hurons at Ecorse, about 10 miles southwest of the fort in Detroit. Pontiac said the Great Spirit urged him and his followers "to unite for the extermination or expulsion of the white invaders and the recovery of their hunting ground."

Pontiac secured the assistance of the tribes and received promises of aid from some French inhabitants of the area. At the meeting, the tribes planned an attack on the British holdings. Tribes were assigned posts to attack. They were expected to remove the garrison and take over the posts.

Pontiac himself would lead the attack on the fort, which is described in the entry of May 7.

April 28, 1941
Gambling and vice in Wayne County

A story of corruption in Detroit was almost drowned out by news of World War II. Nonetheless, Michigan residents ate up the news.

Among 26 defendants caught in an illicit gambling operation were former Wayne County Prosecutor Duncan C. McCrea and former Sheriff Thomas C. Wilcox.

Twenty-five of the suspects, including McCrea and Wilcox, were convicted on April 28, 1941, of "conspiracy to permit gambling and vice to flourish in Wayne County."

The trial took three months and was thought at the time to have been the state's longest-ever circuit court trial.

The officials were accused of running a large gambling operation and using their authority to eliminate competition.

McCrea was said to have netted more than $100,000 from the operation and Wilcox over $70,000, according to a United Press report.

Other defendants included the former president of Grosse Pointe Park, a division chief at the Wayne County Sheriff's Department and the former Inkster chief of police.

These officials were convicted along with 14 others. Four defendants were accused of operating "disorderly houses."

McCrea and Wilcox received maximum sentences of four-and-a-half to five years in prison and a $2,000 fine when they went before a judge a month later.

April 29, 1895
Traverse City murder mystery

Julia Curtis was not considered especially good looking but she was well liked among her community on the Old Mission Peninsula in Grand Traverse County.

When the 22-year-old daughter of a fruit farmer set off to spend a spring afternoon to look for trailing arbutus and failed to return, people in the town formed a search party. They plodded the peninsula throughout the night.

The following day with no sign of Julia, 40 more men joined the party.

Within a few hours the young woman was found with her feet crossed and her hands lying naturally across her breast. Beside her was a basket filled with flowers and a half-full bottle of laudanum, an opiate.

At first there appeared to be no sign of foul play. Perhaps the young woman had taken her own life.

Closer inspection by a coroner, however, determined, that Julia had been strangled and that she was two months pregnant. The theory that she had killed herself with laudanum in distress over the pregnancy was put to rest and a search for her killer began.

That search quickly centered on Woodruff Parmalee, a fruit farmer in his mid-30s who was twice divorced and had demonstrated his capacity for violence with an earlier wife.

It came to light that Parmalee had been seeing Julia for about a year.

Parmalee was arrested and brought quickly to trial on the testimony of another resident who claimed he saw Parmalee head off in the direction of the location of Julia's death the day she disappeared.

The trial brought crowds to the Grand Traverse County courthouse as dozens of witnesses were ushered in and out of the courtroom. During deliberations, when it was leaked that the jury was hung 11-1 in favor of conviction, the sentiment of the crowd turned to street justice and several shouted that Parmalee should be lynched on the spot.

This talk may have echoed into the jury room because soon after the lone holdout changed his position Parmalee was convicted of first-degree murder.

Parmalee maintained his innocence to the end and, at his sentencing hearing, Parmalee said: "Your Honor, I don't know as anything I might say would make any difference, but there has been a terrible mistake made. I have been robbed of my home, robbed of my family; I have been robbed of everything except a clear conscience. I have never committed murder."

Parmalee served 20 years in prison and was paroled by Governor Woodbridge N. Ferris in 1915.

Parmalee returned to Traverse City where he lived until the age of 89, when he died of pneumonia at the Traverse City State Hospital.

April 29, 2004
Final Oldsmobile produced

Oldsmobile had been making cars for 106 years. In the later years, however, the people who bought the cars – like the name – got older and older.

In the end, the brand couldn't shake its reputation as a car for blue-haired women.

The last Oldsmobile produced was a metallic cherry red Alero that rolled off the line at the Lansing Car Assembly Plant at 10 a.m. on April 29, 2004.

General Motors said it discontinued the line because it became unprofitable.

April 30, 1878
"The man with the branded hand" dies in Muskegon

Captain Jonathan Walker was made famous by the John G. Whittier poem, "The Branded Hand."

An abolitionist who was caught helping slaves to freedom, Walker was convicted in 1844 in a Florida court as a slave stealer. He had the letters "S.S." branded on his right palm.

Born in Cape Cod in 1799, as a teenager Walker worked at sea and traveled the world, narrowly escaping death at the hand of pirates and yellow fever.

He lived with his family in Florida for six years until 1844, when some slaves who knew of his abolitionist leanings asked for help. He and seven slaves set off in an open boat for a British-owned island near the Florida coast but Walker became overcome by heat. The slaves were unable to navigate to their freedom.

After a $1,000 reward was offered for the capture of Walker, a U.S. revenue cutter came upon the drifting boat.

Influential friends in the north finally secured his release after months in a Pensacola jail but not before he was branded and endured other tortures.

After his release, Walker wrote a book about his experience and traveled the North giving abolitionist lectures. When the Emancipation Proclamation was signed, Walker withdrew from public life and bought a small fruit farm near Muskegon, according to the *Muskegon Chronicle*.

In his later years Walker and his wife became destitute. At that point, Henry H. Holt, a Muskegon lawyer and one-time lieutenant governor of the state, wrote an article about Walker that was published in newspapers across the country.

Money poured in, including a generous donation from the poet Whittier.

Upon his death, a U.S. Navy chaplain offered to pay for a monument to Walker at the Evergreen Cemetery in Muskegon.

When the monument was unveiled, more than 6,000 people showed up on a steamer from Chicago and a train from Allegan.

May

May 1, 1981
General Motors takes over Poletown

General Motors' slogan at this time was "Mark of Excellence" but Poletown's Immaculate Conception Church had a different view, reflected in a sign that read: "GM: Mark of Destruction."

The automaker worked out a deal with the cities of Detroit and Hamtramck to purchase 456 acres of land to build a $500 million Cadillac plant.

Much of the deal involved the shuttered Dodge Main plant, which had left thousands out of work when it closed 15 months earlier.

However, the land was not vacant. On 250 of the condemned acres, approximately 3,500 residents lived, ran small businesses and attended school.

Detroit faced an 18 percent unemployment rate and the 6,000 new jobs to be created when the plant opened in 1983 were needed desperately.

Most of the residents readily agreed to sell – the city paid market price for their property. In addition, Detroit paid $15,000 to homeowners and $4,000 to renters to cover moving expenses.

Some wouldn't budge, however. They recruited consumer advocate and long-time GM foe Ralph Nader to run interference on the project.

Nonetheless, GM and the city prevailed in a landmark court case that said the use of "imminent domain" could include economic stimulus. (Until then, imminent domain only applied to razing structures for government purposes, such as street widening or building parks.) On May 1, 1981, the automaker received title to the first 75-acre parcel. Three days later, crews fired up bulldozers and began to raze Poletown.

May 1, 1903
Israelite House of David opens

Benjamin Purnell was a charismatic, roving preacher who settled in Benton Harbor in 1903.

Purnell, along with his wife Mary, opened the Israelite House of David, a religious colony whose members believed they were descendants of the 12 Lost Tribes of Israel.

The members, numbering in the 700s by the mid-1920s, lived communally.

Purnell and his followers believed the second coming of Christ was imminent and they gathered in Benton Harbor to prepare.

In the meantime, the followers managed a farm and a popular amusement park with a miniature train, zoo, ice cream parlor, hotel, vegetarian restaurant, souvenir stands and tourist cabins.

Michigan Every Day

They became famous nationwide for their baseball team that traveled the country, with players sporting long hair and beards that reached down to their chests. They played amateur and semi-pro teams in exhibition games. In 1933, the House of David beat the St. Louis Cardinals 8-6.

Purnell was accused of "public immorality" in 1923. Thirteen women swore in court to having sex with the leader, which was forbidden by the commune. The case led to a conviction and Purnell's banishment from the colony. He died in 1927 and the colony split into two factions, The House of David and Mary's City of David.

Since then the groups have declined in members.

May 2, 1939
Don't put me in coach; I don't want to play today

The New York Yankees arrived by train in Detroit to check into the ritzy Book Cadillac Hotel.

At the time, Yankee Lou Gehrig held what was thought to be an unbreakable streak – he had started in 2,130 consecutive games for his team.

When interviewed by a *Detroit News* reporter about his performance, he admitted that he wasn't playing well at all.

Gehrig found his manager, Joe McCarthy.

"'Joe, I'd like to talk to you,' said the burly first baseman," the *New York Herald-Tribune* reported the following day.

"'Sure thing, Lou, c'mon around the corner here and sit down.' Joe knew what was coming. He had been waiting for it ever since the 1939 season opened.

"'Joe,' Gehrig began, 'I'm not helping this team any. I know I look terrible out there. This string of mine doesn't mean a thing to me. It isn't fair to the boys for me to stay in there. Joe, I want you to take me out of the line-up today.'"

And so ended the streak of the player who was known as the "Iron Horse."

When the Yankees took the field to play the Detroit Tigers at Briggs Stadium, Gehrig was not in the lineup. However, it didn't hurt the Yankees performance. They trounced the Tigers 22-2.

In an odd coincidence, the player whom Gehrig replaced to begin his streak in 1925 was in the stands and discovered by reporters that day. Wally Pipp, by then a Grand Rapids businessman, congratulated his former teammate and joked that he was sorry he wasn't in shape to get into the game to take Gehrig's place.

May 2, 1933
Michigan's Civilian Conservation Corps

The Great Depression left a lot of young men no money, no job and a lot of time on their hands.

President Roosevelt created the Civilian Conservation Corps to create employment and to restore the county's natural beauty by planting trees in areas ravaged by loggers.

The first such camp in Michigan opened on May 2, 1933 in the Hiawatha National Forest near Sault Ste. Marie.

Eventually, there were 41 such camps throughout Michigan.

Camp Raco in the Upper Peninsula between Brimley and New-berry became home to 200 men from Detroit between the ages of 19 and 23.

Upon arrival, the men received a blue denim work suit, shoes, socks, underwear and a toiletry kit. They were paid $30 per month and they were required to send at least $22 home to help their families.

In addition to planting trees, the workers built roads, ran telephone wire, cleared fire breaks, planted fish, built camp sites and fought forest fires.

A few miles away, Camp Germfask turned 95,000 acres of swamp into habitat for migratory birds in what is now the Seney National Wildlife Refuge.

Camp Raco closed in 1942 but later reopened as a prisoner-of-war camp for captured German soldiers.

May 3, 1942
Lights out in Detroit

During World War II there was real concern that Detroit would become an enemy target because it was the industrial heart of the American war machine.

To prepare for a potential onslaught of bombs, civilian defense authorities scheduled a blackout over a 1,500 square mile area.

Residents and businesses were instructed to go dark at 10 p.m. on May 3, 1942, a Sunday. They could turn their lights back on 15 minutes later.

During the blackout, the air raid wardens patrolled the streets in gas masks and steel helmets. Anyone who didn't have permission to be on the street was forced back inside.

United Press reported that most residents complied.

"Observers from patrolling airplanes reported the business section conformed strictly with blackout requirements but that lights could be seen in homes in the residential districts," the wire service reported.

Windsor and neighboring Ontario communities also participated in the blackout.

The exercise was just one example of measures employed in Detroit during the war to protect the strategically important city.

The day after Pearl Harbor was bombed in 1941, U.S. Army guards from Selfridge Field were assigned to the Detroit-Windsor Tunnel and the Ambassador Bridge.

Anti-aircraft batteries were installed in parks around the city and air raid sirens were attached to buildings.

More than 100,000 persons were trained as air raid wardens, medical responders, police officers and firefighters.

May 4, 1935
Nation's first freeway state welcome center

Michigan not only loves cars but it also loves people who drive those cars, especially when they're coming here to visit. Appropriately, Michigan opened the nation's first gateway welcome center to greet travelers, offer directions and give them a chance to stretch their legs.

On May 4, 1935, the nation's first state welcome center opened on US-12 at New Buffalo to welcome travelers to Michigan.

The Michigan State Highway Department, later the Department of Transportation, built the novel center. The welcome center was moved to a more modern building nearby in 1972 with the opening of I-94.

Other states have since adopted the idea. By 1985, there were 251 travel information centers across the country, according to a historical marker at the New Buffalo site.

May 5, 1831
Michigan's oldest existing newspaper debuts

There were approximately 2,500 people living in the fledgling town of Detroit when Sheldon McKnight published the first edition of the *Detroit Free Press*.

At that time it was called the *Detroit Free Press and Michigan Intelligencer*, a weekly made up of four pages.

That first edition announced the politics of the newspaper: Democratic.

"The Democratic citizens of this territory, having found the two newspapers already established here completely under the control of the city aristocracy, have been compelled to set up an independent press," McKnight wrote in the paper's first editorial.

The paper was first published in a small wooden building near where the tunnel entrance to Canada is located today.

The name of the paper changed in 1835 to the *Detroit Daily Free Press* when it became the state's first daily.

In 1836, McKnight sold the paper, nine days after he was acquitted of a manslaughter charge stemming from a brawl in the Bull & Beard's Saloon.

The paper was an ardent supporter of statehood. Unfortunately, a fire destroyed its offices in January 1837 and the paper was unable to publish for six weeks, which meant it could not report that Michigan had become a state.

The newspaper credits an early publisher with bringing many innovations to the pages of the *Free Press*.

Wilbur F. Storey, who took over in 1853, expanded the telegraph service so the newspaper could offer news from around the country faster than before. He also created a "city desk" to cover Detroit. And he instructed a reporter to walk the length of the port each day to collect shipping news, creating the first beat reporter.

The paper distinguished itself during the Civil War, sending reporters to the battlefield and becoming a vital link between the war and the citizens of Michigan.

In 1881, publisher William E. Quinby launched a London edition of the *Free Press*, making it the first American newspaper to publish in Europe.

May 6, 1945
Birth of Bob Seger

B ob Seger's gritty sound is synonymous with Detroit. The rocker grew up listening to James Brown and Elvis Presley. At 16, he started a band called the Decibels, and wrote his first song.

Beginning in the mid-1960s, Seger spent about 10 years playing small bars and clubs in the Detroit area before he struck it big with his Silver Bullet Band. Anyone growing up in metro Detroit has memories of Seger playing at local ice arenas, school dances and at VFW halls.

Appropriately, he gained national attention for his album "Live Bullet," which was taped during two concerts at Detroit's Cobo Hall on Sept. 4 and 5, 1975.

Seger's songs such as "Night Moves," "Like a Rock," and "Old Time Rock and Roll" celebrated blue collar life and became staples of classic rock stations. He has sold about 50 million albums worldwide and won Grammies in 1980 and 1993.

Governor Jennifer Granholm proclaimed March 15, 2004 as Bob Seger Day in Michigan. "Seger is the unmistaken voice of Michigan rock and roll and a treasure to our state," she said.

He was the 18th Michigander to be inducted into the Rock and Roll Hall of Fame in Cleveland.

May 7, 1763
Pontiac's siege of Fort Detroit begins

Chief Pontiac convinced other tribes around Michigan to join in an uprising against the British, who took control of Detroit from the more friendly French.

Pontiac resolved to kill or drive the British from the region so the Indians could reclaim their hunting grounds.

Pontiac and bands of Indian warriors planned to take forts throughout the Great Lakes by surprise. Their first adventure would be to capture Fort Detroit through a detailed attack. They would enter seemingly in peace, with knives, tomahawks, and muskets, shortened with files, concealed under blankets. Then they would kill the guards or take them prisoner and drive the British away.

Pontiac and some 40 of his men visited the fort a few days before the attack. The garrison became suspicious and would not let the full contingent into the fort. Negotiations ensued, with Pontiac assuring they had come to perform a peace-pipe dance for the commandant.

Some were allowed in and performed the dance. Meanwhile, others casually made their way around the fort, inspecting the defenses and sizing up their task.

Major Henry Gladwin, fort commander, found out about the conspiracy.

He was prepared when Pontiac and 60 warriors arrived at the gate of the fort and asked for a council with the commandant. They were let in and brought to a house where Gladwin met with them as the soldiers of the fort assembled. Other Indian warriors were supposed to casually filter through the gate after Pontiac to lend added power to the uprising.

Just as Pontiac prepared to let out a war cry, he stepped out of the house, expecting to see his warriors ready for a surprise attack. Instead, he found the entire garrison ready for a fight.

Pontiac realized his plot had been discovered and he called off the attack. For that day, at least.

May 8, 1933
Grand Rapids police chief fights for his job

Grand Rapids Police Chief Albert "Ab" Carroll, a stern and autocratic man, was first hired in 1914 to modernize the detective bureau by instituting policies barring abusive interrogation techniques.

By 1933, a newly hired city manager thought Carroll, at age 67, was too old for his job and should be released.

Ernest T. Conlon suggested this to state Senator Earl W. Munshaw, who happened to be Carroll's nephew. When Caroll heard the news, he went to the press and launched a preemptive campaign for his job, saying Conlon was out to get him.

Conlon backed off and told the press he had merely expressed his thoughts privately and he seemed prepared to let the matter go.

The affair was far from over, however.

The following weekend, Conlon and five of the seven city council members scheduled a trip to Chicago. The editor of the *Grand Rapids Press*, Lee M. Woodruff, was suspicious. He believed the Chicago trip might involve more pleasure than business and asked Carroll to have the Chicago police discretely check on the men while they were in town.

Police in Chicago went a step further and confronted the men in their hotel room, leading to an ugly scene. Conlon decided it really was time to force Carroll out. At the next council meeting, on May 8, with the five politicians who had been embarrassed in Chicago present, the council voted 5-2 to suspend Carroll for insubordination.

That vote was overturned by the State Supreme Court, which held that the charges against Carroll were frivolous.

Conlon's next move was to fire Carroll again, on the grounds that he was too old and unable to cooperate with his superiors. The city commission rejected that attempt and, instead, it created a new position for Carroll that carried the same salary but stripped him of any power.

Carroll rejected that offer. By the following April, new members on the city commission voted to restore Carroll to the position of police chief and Conlon resigned. Carroll retired 18 months later.

May 8, 1813
British naval commander dies at home in Detroit

Alexander Grant was born in Scotland in 1734 and came to America during the French and Indian War. Although uneducated, he found himself in the Royal Navy and rose in the ranks, eventually becoming commander of one of the navy's vessels.

Grant arrived in Detroit and was put in command of the dockyard in 1771.

He settled in Grosse Pointe, cleared land for a farm and built what became known as Grant's Castle.

Grant was "an old Scotchman," one observer wrote. "A large stout man, not very polished, but very good-tempered, (who) had a great many daughters, all very good-looking, all very lively, all very fond of dancing, and all very willing to get married as soon as possible." In fact, Grant had 11 daughters and one son.

Perhaps it was because he was such a likeable character that he was allowed to remain on his farm when the British handed over the Michigan Territory to the Americans in 1796. He was still on active duty, holding powerful political posts in Canada for the British while living in Detroit.

Not only was Grant probably one of the first commuters to live in Detroit and work across the river in Ontario, but he was possibly one of a handful of military commanders to live openly in the country of his enemy.

As the War of 1812 approached, Grant's leadership and his age – nearly 80 – came into question and Grant retired in March of 1812.

Grant died on May 8, 1813, at his farm in Grosse Pointe.

May 9, 1990
Freak Upper Peninsula snowstorm

Spring brought unusually warm temperatures to the Upper Peninsula in 1990.

The National Weather Service recorded an official high temperature that broke the record for May 8: 76 degrees Fahrenheit.

In the previous 16 days, the Upper Peninsula saw six record highs. But just as residents were thinking of beach towels and bathing suits, one of Michigan's famous weather swings swept in from the North. A thunderstorm brought with it a belt of cold air to upper Michigan.

The morning of May 9 dawned with temperatures in the 30s and 40s and the day didn't get much warmer. Some rain and ice fell as the day wore on. Later in the day, snow began to fall and it fell throughout the night and into the morning. The following day, rain turned to snow in Marquette, where eight inches accumulated. In Negaunee Township, 22 inches were reported.

In Menominee the snow was so heavy and the winds so strong that power lines were cut.

The fickleness of a Michigan spring was apparent a day later when there was sunshine and temperatures in the 50s. Soon evidence of the aberrant winter storm melted into streams and puddles on lawns.

May 9, 1970
Walter Reuther dies in northern Michigan plane crash

Union leader Walter Reuther, his wife May, and four others chartered a Lear jet from Detroit to the United Auto Workers retreat on Black Lake, near Onaway.

When the plane reached the northern portion of the lower peninsula, the pilot found fog and rain. The aircraft was cleared for landing, but when it broke through the cloud ceiling 400 feet from the ground, the plane was well short of the runway and clipped treetops. The jet crashed in flames as it attempted to land near Pellston at 9:30 p.m. on May 9, 1970, killing everyone aboard.

In addition to being a union leader, Reuther was involved in social change movements. With Martin Luther King, Jr., he helped lead the 1963 civil rights march in Washington D.C. He spoke out against the Vietnam War, proposed a national health care system and brought environmental concerns into the negotiations between the union and auto companies.

Reuther's bargaining prowess resulted in pensions, cost-of-living raises, and benefits for laid-off workers.

President Richard M. Nixon issued a statement on Reuther's death, saying it was "a deep loss not only for organized labor but also for the cause of collective bargaining and the entire American process. He was a man who was devoted to his cause, spoke for it with eloquence and worked for it tirelessly. While he was outspoken and controversial, even those who disagreed with him had great respect for his ability, integrity and persistence."

Reuther had survived earlier assassination attempts and a similar plane crash months earlier, leading some to speculate that Reuther's death was no accident.

May 10, 1865
Michigan soldiers capture Jefferson Davis

It was the close of the Civil War and the 4th Michigan Calvary found itself in the deep South.

The regiment, under the command of Colonel Benjamin D. Prichard of Allegan, occupied Macon, Georgia. There, he learned that Jefferson Davis, president of the Confederacy, was in southern Georgia, planning to flee the country.

Prichard led his men to Irwinsville, Georgia in the early morning of May 10, 1865 in search of Davis. He learned that the president had set up camp less than two miles away.

The Michigan 4th surrounded the camp and captured Davis, who in haste to escape had grabbed his wife's coat, leading to a legend that Davis disguised himself as a woman in order to evade capture.

A regiment from Wisconsin was also in the area looking for Davis, who had a $100,000 bounty on his head.

The soldiers from Wisconsin and Michigan mistook one another for a renegade band of Confederate troops and a skirmish ensued, leading to the death of two Michigan soldiers.

After the mistake was discovered, Prichard and his staff delivered Davis to Fort Monroe, Virginia, where he received a receipt for the prisoner.

But the bounty took some time to collect. After three years of delays, it was determined soldiers from Michigan would have to share the money with officers and soldiers from other units who also had been searching for Davis.

May 11, 1861
The 1st Michigan Infantry gets its colors

At the start of the Civil War, the United States only had a small standing army. President Lincoln called on the states to organize and provide infantrymen.

Lincoln expected 75,000 men to sign up for three months of service. Michigan filled the quota after it sent 10 of the state's 28 militias into federal service.

All of the companies assembled in Detroit by April, 1861, commanded by Orlando B. Willcox, a 38-year-old Detroit attorney and West Point graduate.

While in Detroit, the men of the 1st Michigan Infantry practiced marksmanship, worked on formations and received new federal uniforms.

They received a ceremonial send-off on May 11, 1861.

The soldiers traveled by steamship and rail to Washington where Lincoln was in desperate need of reinforcements.

When the regiment arrived on May 16, Lincoln reportedly exclaimed, "Thank God for Michigan."

Soon enlistments of three years rather than three months were required, and Michigan would go on to send 45 regiments into the battle. Approximately 90,000 Michigan soldiers served in the Civil War, with about 75,000 surviving.

May 11, 1835
Michigan takes control of its salt

In pioneer life, salt was a vital component of everyday life. It wasn't merely used to add flavor to food. Early settlers needed it to preserve fish, cure meats and tan hides.

On May 11, 1835, delegates at the State Constitutional Convention recognized Michigan had an abundant supply of this important resource and they dictated that the state would control its salt springs and the salt under its land.

Two years later, when the state legislature met for the first time, a geological survey was authorized, with Douglass Houghton named state geologist.

Houghton would go on to catalogue Michigan's underground riches, including salt, copper, iron, coal and gypsum.

May 12, 1924
Founder of the nation's oldest
university botanical garden dies

William James Beal, a celebrated botanist, was born in Adrian in 1833. He attended the University of Michigan, Harvard and the University of Chicago, where he later served as a professor of botany.

In 1871, Beal was lured to Michigan Agricultural College, which later would become Michigan State University. There he was a professor of botany and a museum curator.

Beal pioneered the development of hybrid corn. He also helped found East Lansing, which was supposed to be called Collegeville. But he is perhaps best remembered as founder of the W. J. Beal Botanical Garden, the oldest continuously operated such garden in the country.

The project began in 1872 as a nursery. An arboretum followed two years later.

The Beal Botanical Garden covers five acres of the MSU campus where thousands of plant species are displayed to the public year around.

Beal retired to Amherst, Massachusetts, where he died on May 12, 1924.

May 13, 1857
America's first land grant college opens

Although Michigan State University claims 1855 as its founding date, it officially opened on this date – two years after the Michigan Legislature passed legislation creating the Michigan Agricultural College.

The first land grant college in America offered instruction in scientific and practical agriculture

At its inception, it almost became part of the University of Michigan. As state legislators debated details of establishing an institution for the study of agriculture, University of Michigan President Henry P. Tappan lobbied for his school to receive the 22 sections of land to be set aside for the farm college.

Tappan was unable to muster enough support and the school opened near Lansing in the location that would become East Lansing 50 years later.

MSU has grown into a world-class university that boasts 46,000 students and more than 4,800 faculty members in 200 academic areas. The 5,200-acre campus houses 576 buildings, including the world's largest non-military cafeteria.

May 13, 1980
Tornado rages through Kalamazoo

On the afternoon of May 13, 1980, a storm struck Kalamazoo and brought with it a tornado that zeroed in on the city's downtown.

It first touched down at 4 p.m. about eight miles from the city. For nearly a half hour, the tornado whirled east, into the heart of Kalamazoo, and left a swath of destruction 12 miles long. Homes in the Westwood neighborhood were destroyed. Monuments in Mountain Home Cemetery were overturned. The twister knocked down 26 century-old oak trees in Bronson Park, including one that had shaded Abraham Lincoln when he made his only speech in Michigan.

The storm's toll was enormous: five dead, 79 injured and an estimated $50 million in damage.

May 14, 1936
Ford Rotunda opens to the public

The Ford Rotunda, shaped like a giant gear, attracted visitors from around the world. In the 1950s, it was the fifth most popular tourist destination in the United States, ahead of such places as the Statue of Liberty and the Washington Monument.

The circular building was originally an exhibition by the Ford Motor Company at the 1933 World's Fair in Chicago. At the fair's end, the building was packed up brick-by-brick and shipped to Dearborn where it was reconstructed as a permanent structure. It opened to the public on May 14, 1936.

It was located on Schaefer Road across from the Ford administration building.

The Ford Rotunda featured exhibits that highlighted Ford products. The grounds contained reproductions of historic roads from around the world. The structure was best known, however, for its elaborate Christmas displays.

Workers were preparing for the 1962 Christmas display, applying tar to the dome as a buffer from cold weather, when a heater set the tar on fire and the building burst into flames.

Columns of flames shot 50 feet into the air and black smoke could be seen for four miles, according to the *Detroit News*. The Ford Rotunda lay in smoldering ruins in less than an hour.

May 15, 1911
Grand Rapids riot

By the early 20th century, Grand Rapids had become the furniture manufacturing capital of the world.

But with prosperity came labor troubles.

In early 1911, some 4,000 furniture workers walked off their jobs at 35 plants. Better pay and working conditions were the aims in this workers' strike that lasted 19 weeks. Backers of the furniture shops sent in armed guards to deal with the situation but before violence could break out, Grand Rapids Police Chief Harvey O. Carr sent in officers to keep the peace.

The officers disarmed the guards.

Carr may have had a soft spot in his heart for the cause of labor – he was appointed police chief in 1893 based on his political connections, stemming from his experience as a member of the board of public works and former president of the powerful printers' union. But some interests were not content to let the strike carry on peacefully.

Men with weapons, probably professional strike breakers, continued to intimidate the workers and the threat of widespread violence simmered.

On May 15, 1911, a riot broke out that was finally quelled by fire hoses.

Carr called in "special police" to patrol the factory areas. The strike continued, but Carr's move ended the violence.

May 16, 1891
Fire destroys Muskegon

The owner of a stable that housed 59 horses had just purchased 140 bushels of oats and hay.

On a warm, dry spring day, that was good fuel for a fire.

When the stable burst into flames, an alarm went out and every fire department in the region rushed to the scene.

By the time men with buckets of water arrived, the fire at the livery raged out of control and had begun to spread up Pine Street, consuming houses and businesses as it went along.

Panic-stricken residents shoved whatever belongings they could into carts and fled. Many left their valuables on the courthouse lawn, believing that place would be safe from the fire.

But flames hopped through town over rooftops and eventually reached the courthouse, burning its roof, too high for firemen to douse with water.

Only courthouse documents stored in a vault were saved. Prisoners locked in the basement jail were released. Two helped fight the fire while the remaining 10 were taken to another lockup.

When the fire was done six hours later, 17 city blocks and 250 buildings were destroyed.

The vaults and partial walls of the courthouse were all that remained.

That night many residents slept in a farmer's field outside town. Muskegon already was suffering the loss of the timber industry. Now there were hundreds of homeless and destitute.

This was the second fire to lay siege to the city.

On August 1, 1874, a fire destroyed 12 city blocks. Two hundred businesses and about 100 homes were in ashes.

This fire was believed to have been arson, with two men seen running from a shoe store where the fire started in a barrel of shavings.

Despite the lesson of the great Chicago fire three years earlier, and the fact that Muskegon was a town consisting of sawmills and sawdust, there was no city waterworks system.

May 17, 1673
Joliet and Marquette head out to explore

In the early 17th century, French priests traveled to Michigan for the first time from the French settlements of Quebec and Montreal intent on saving the souls of Indians.

Accounts of these first interactions between the Europeans and the native people of North America indicate that the relations between the Jesuits and the Indians were peaceful.

The Jesuits blazed a trail for the fur traders and the white settlers who would follow, leading to all sorts of trouble for the Indians. But in the beginning, the Indians learned from the Jesuits and the Jesuits learned from the Indians.

One important thing the Europeans learned in 1665 was the existence of a great river, eventually named the Mississippi, to the west that no European had ever seen. It would prove to be of great strategic and economic importance.

Several years passed before France and the Indian tribes of the region signed a peace treaty, allowing Father Jacques Marquette and Louis Joliet, a fur trader skilled in navigation and mapmaking, to find the great river.

They left St. Ignace in two large canoes on May 17, 1673. Along with five voyageurs, the party headed out of the Straits of Mackinac and into Lake Michigan. They crossed the lake and paddled into Green Bay, up the Fox River, and by portage over to the Wisconsin River, where they traveled until they found the Mississippi about a month after setting out. They hoped the river would lead west, to the Pacific, but it soon became clear this river would empty into the Gulf of Mexico.

By the time the party had traveled to the mouth of the Arkansas River, they encountered unfamiliar Indians and evidence they were venturing into a region controlled by Spain. The party then turned around, leaving the exploration of the lower end of the river for another time, unaware that that part of the river had already been discovered by Spanish explorer Hernando DeSoto.

The party returned via the Illinois River to the Chicago River and found themselves on the southern end of Lake Michigan.

Marquette traveled to Green Bay and returned to spend the following winter in what is now Chicago, where his health deteriorated. The following spring, he resolved to return to his beloved St. Ignace before he died, but he was unable to reach his destination in time, as described in the May 18 entry.

May 18, 1675
Father (Pere) Jacques Marquette dies in Ludington or Frankfort...or somewhere along Lake Michigan

Father Marquette had accomplished much in his 37 years. He founded St. Ignace, the first European settlement in Michigan. He devoted himself to helping the natives of the region in the way he believed best. And he discovered the northern part of the Mississippi River.

Marquette, on his return journey to Mackinac, reached Chicago in December, 1674, where he began suffering symptoms of tuberculosis. He remained in a hut built on the south branch of the Chicago River until the end of March, when he set out for the Straits of Mackinac.

He and two voyageurs made their way along the eastern shore of Lake Michigan and Marquette's health deteriorated further.

He became terribly ill on May 18, 1675 and his party pulled ashore near the mouth of a river. Within a few hours Marquette was dead and his body was buried. When he died was documented; where he died and is buried remains a mystery.

Ludington and Frankfort both claim to be the locale, although most writers of Michigan history place the site at Ludington.

Nonetheless, both cities have official state historical markers staking their claim.

May 18, 1927
Forty-five killed in Bath School disaster

Newspapers called it a "diabolical deed" committed by a deranged member of the school board.

"A maniac today blew up the village school of Bath and killed perhaps as many as 30 children while they sat in school rooms busy with their studies," a reporter for United Press wrote.

It turned out that 39 children and teachers were killed on May 18, 1927.

The culprit was Andrew Kehoe, treasurer of the school board, who was enraged over school taxes.

Kehoe burned his own home, murdered his wife and then set off bushels of dynamite he secretly placed under the foundations of the school.

In the aftermath of the explosion, residents rushed to the school to rescue the injured.

Martin Milliman, a 72-year-old who was among the first on the scene, told a harrowing story of attempting to save as many lives as he could in the rubble if the school:

"But I couldn't take it for long," he said. "I had taken four bodies out of the ruins when Kehoe, believed by everyone to have planned the entire disaster, drew up to the curb in front of the wrecked school and called out to Emory E. Huyck, superintendent, who was supervising the rescue.

"Both of the men stood talking on the curb for a few minutes when suddenly Kehoe's automobile was blown to bits. He and Huyck were killed outright."

A passerby and Bath Postmaster Glenn Smith also were killed in the explosion, bringing the death toll of Kehoe's murder spree to 45. Smith was killed in front of his wife.

Milliman said it was too much for him to witness all of these murders.

"When I saw Mrs. Smith rush over to her husband and gather his broken form into her arms, somehow I lost all the strength I had. I was trying to saw a heavy plank that held a little girl of five in the wreckage, but I couldn't work the saw, and a man working beside me said, 'You had better get home,' and I did."

Others witnessed the arrival of mothers and fathers who came to the school to learn their children had been killed.

Kehoe had been a farmer, struggling to pay the tax bill brought on by the construction of a new school. His home had recently been put into foreclosure.

May 18, 1846
Michigan first in nation to ban death penalty

In its first 50 years as a territory and as a state, the penalty for first-degree murder in Michigan was death by hanging. Despite that law, the death penalty was employed only twice.

A turning point in capital punishment came in 1830 when Stephen Simmons was hanged for killing his wife in a drunken rage. At first citizens clamored for Simmons' death but when he appeared at the gallows as a sympathetic fellow, the public mood changed. Some people were horrified at his execution, which is described in the Sept. 24 entry.

Between Simmons' execution and the state abolition of the death penalty, the state moved gradually toward a more civilized approach to criminal punishment. Six months after the hanging, the territorial government abolished whipping as a legal punishment.

The public whipping post in Detroit's marketplace was abandoned and 10 lashes were no longer meted out as punishment for disorderly behavior. The whipping post was used rarely, but up until 1830, it could be used for anybody found to be "vagrant, lewd, idle or disorderly persons, stubborn servants, common drunkards, common night-walkers, pilferers, or any persons wanton and lascivious in speech, conduct or behavior, common railers or brawlers, such as neglect their calling and employments, misspend what they earn, and do not provide for themselves or their families."

When Michigan drew up its constitution in 1835, capital punishment was nearly banished. A provision to abolish it failed in a vote of 38-35.

In 1838, the state followed New York, New Jersey and Pennsylvania and barred public executions.

But the impetus to ban all executions came from across the Detroit River in Windsor. There the death penalty was used often, including for crimes other than murder. Resentment stirred in Detroit, especially during the Patriot War when its own citizens were sent to the gallows in Canada.

In 1846, the state government passed a bill to abolish capital punishment except in cases of treason. In a compromise, the legislature deemed that in lieu of death, those convicted of first-degree murder would be sentenced to life in prison in solitary confinement at hard labor, even though at the time the state lacked a prison system that could enforce such a punishment.

Governor Alpheus Felch signed the bill on May 18, 1846, making Michigan the first government in the English speaking world to bar capital punishment

Over the years efforts to reinstate the death penalty were sometimes only narrowly defeated. In 1964, the abolition was made part of the state constitution, meaning that it would take a vote of Michigan citizens to reinstate capital punishment.

May 19, 1677
Marquette exhumed

In addition to disagreement over where Pere Marquette died, there is also no consensus over what happened to his body.

Some claim that Marquette's body was exhumed on May 19, 1677 by a group of Indians who loved the priest.

The Christian Indians passed by Marquette's supposed resting place in Frankfort two years after he died. They determined that a more fitting place for Marquette would be at his own mission in St. Ignace so they exhumed his body and prepared it for a return to the mission at the straits of Mackinac.

Father Claude Dablon, Marquette's superior at Quebec, provided an account of Marquette's exhumation in *The Jesuit Relations*, saying "the Indians opened the grave, and uncovered the Body; and, although the Flesh and Internal organs were all Dried up, they found it entire, so that not even the skin was in any way in-

145

jured. This did not prevent them from proceeding to dissect it, as is their custom. They cleansed the bones and exposed them to the sun to dry; then, carefully laying them out in a box of birchbark, they set out to bring them to our mission of St. Ignace."

May 19, 1903
Buick Motor Company incorporated
Foundation of General Motors

David Dunbar Buick incorporated Buick Motor Company in Detroit on May 19, 1903 but by the end of the year, the operation moved to Flint.

The following July, the company's first car was driven from Flint to Detroit and back. *Motor Age* magazine called the car "a little machine that attracted an immense amount of attention… owing to its high power and low price.

William C. Durant took over management of Buick and moved the company to Jackson in 1905. In three years, Buick produced more cars than any other company in the nation – 8,820.

That success was the foundation of General Motors, which Durant established that year.

Durant added two smaller Detroit car companies – Pontiac and Cadillac – to the GM stable before he resigned from the company in 1920. He started his own Durant Motors but that company never took off.

Today, Buick, along with Cadillac, remain the luxury brands in the GM collection.

May 20, 1970
Student takeover of MSU building ends

As political strife over the Vietnam War heated up around the country, students at Michigan State University joined the action.

Student protesters organized a class strike that took over university buildings.

At the beginning of the strike, in early May, Governor William Milliken held a news conference and met with the students to send them a message – it was OK for them to strike and make their feelings about the war known but it was not OK for them to prevent students from attending class.

"Students have the right to stay out of classes if they wish to," Milliken said. "I'm very pleased that President (Clifford) Wharton takes a very strong position on this . . . no student should be denied the opportunity to attend class by intimidation or otherwise."

Approximately 15 percent of the school's 40,000 students were skipping class. The impetus for the protest was not just Vietnam but also the recent incident at Kent State University where four students were killed by members of the Ohio National Guard.

Milliken did not want the same kind of violence at a Michigan school and he resisted sending in the state police or the National Guard to break up the strike.

"The lessons of Kent State have not been lost on me," Milliken said.

Between May 7 and May 20 students took over university buildings, among them the home of the Reserve Officers' Training Corps.

Wharton finally ended the protest when he called in the police, who arrested 127 students. By May 20, 1970, the strike was over.

Michigan played a large role in student activism. Tom Hayden, a University of Michigan student, was one of the founders of the Students for a Democratic Society. He launched the group's Port Huron Statement, so named because it was adopted in that Michigan city at its convention June 11-15, 1962.

The statement outlined a student's obligation to reform society into one driven by the American people. The lengthy treatise included endorsing peace, ending bigotry and ensuring a participatory democracy.

May 20, 1918
Black hospital opens

After World War I, black Detroiters realized the health care they received was substandard compared to that afforded to whites.

In addition, black doctors were not allowed on the staffs of Detroit hospitals and needed the permission of a white doctor before a black patient could be admitted.

On May 20, 1918, 30 black doctors, members of the Allied Medical Society, incorporated Dunbar Hospital, the city's first nonprofit hospital for the 30,000 black residents of Detroit.

The hospital also offered a nurses' training program.

The hospital was located in a neighborhood on Frederick Street, near the city's cultural center. Later in that decade, the hospital moved into a larger facility and was renamed Parkside Hospital.

May 21, 1892
First car in nation sold for export

Ransom E. Olds got his start tinkering at the Olds and Son's Engine Works, an engine manufacturing and repair shop owned by his father in Lansing.

There he helped develop an experimental steam-powered vehicle by 1887.

In 1892, an updated version proved novel enough to be featured in the magazine *Scientific American*, in its May 21, 1892 issue.

A company in London saw the article and bought the car, making it the first American-made car to be sold for export. It may also have been the first instance in the world when a car was sold.

The article gushed about the two-passenger vehicle: "The boiler and engines at the rear end are enclosed by curtains which shut out all view of the machinery, so there is nothing about it to scare horses and they do not seem to mind it any more than an ordinary carriage. Its usual speed on good roads is fifteen miles per hour, and it will ascend any ordinary grade. The vehicle as a whole includes many new merits."

Olds went on to form the Olds Motor Works, which sold 4,000 Oldsmobiles by 1903.

The company claimed in an advertisement that its first production model could travel at speeds up to 25 miles per hour and get 40 miles per gallon of gasoline.

May 21, 1891
Last county established

The 83rd and final Michigan county was organized in the Upper Peninsula after John Lane Buell discovered one of the richest deposits of iron ore known in the world.

The Menominee Iron Range led to the founding of Dickinson County, which was established by an act of the state legislature that was passed on May 21, 1891. The county consists of land that had formerly been part of Marquette, Menominee and Iron counties.

The county was named after Donald Dickinson, a Detroit attorney who served as postmaster general in the administration of President Grover Cleveland.

May 22, 1900
Mass-market player piano invented

Pianos were an important part of well-to-do homes in the 19th century and into the early 20th century. But the instrument was difficult to play, requiring years of practice and people struggled with a way to make a piano play itself.

The first inventors tinkered with contraptions that could be rolled up to ordinary pianos and made to tap the keys with hammers. There were some inventors in Europe, particularly in Italy, who had some luck, but their inventions were too expensive to appeal to a large market.

"A lot of people were bent on producing a piano that could

play by itself, and a number of machines were built to do just that," Joseph Fox wrote in *American Heritage* magazine. "But it took a special combination of skill, timing, perspicacity, and a certain Barnum-like quality to bring the self-playing piano into its own."

Enter Detroit resident Edwin S. Votey, who invented a version of the pneumatic piano player. He patented it on May 22, 1900, and convinced the Aeolian Company to build and sell it.

The instrument was called the Pianola and it became a huge success.

The success created such a craze that soon there were dozens of companies building and selling player pianos.

Votey's device would be rolled up to an ordinary piano and would bang out a tune based on a roll of paper that was encoded with perforations.

Later Aeolian and countless other companies incorporated the technology into the piano so that a player piano would appear to be playing itself, or perhaps appear to be played by a ghost.

When the phonograph came along, its early recordings of piano music were considered inferior to the player pianos, which had become complex and sophisticated enough that by the 1920s they could mimic a particular piano player's style.

By the late 1920s, better recordings and radio killed the player piano business.

May 23, 1893
Last lynching in Michigan

Stories vary over what 27-year-old William Sullivan was doing at a farm owned by Layton Leech in Durand around New Year's Day 1893. In some versions, Sullivan was a laborer on the farm. In others, he appeared at the farm to beg for food.

Not in dispute are the awful crimes Sullivan committed – he killed Leech with an axe before raping and shooting the man's wife, though she survived to identify her attacker.

Sullivan fled the scene, setting off a massive manhunt.

Posters circulated around the state offering a $1,000 reward for his capture.

The campaign paid off on May 21 when Sullivan was spotted drunk and slumped over in a Detroit saloon. He was arrested and at first insisted the police had the wrong man but later confessed to the crimes.

The easy parts for the police, as it turned out, were the arrest and confession. What wouldn't be so simple was getting Sullivan back to Shiawassee County for a trial.

Word of his arrest reached Durand and soon 200 men appeared in Detroit with a lust for revenge.

They surrounded police headquarters and demanded that Sullivan be turned over to them.

The Detroit police were able to stall the crowd, sneak Sullivan out of the station and get him on a train bound for Corunna, not far from the scene of the murder.

In Corunna an even larger crowd gathered. The officers who transported the prisoner anticipated this, slowing the train before it reached town. They jumped out with Sullivan.

When the mob realized they had been tricked, Sullivan was already in jail.

On the morning of May 23, Sullivan pleaded guilty and was sent back to jail, which later that day was surrounded by a mob of more than 2,000 angry people.

The rabid crowd sent a delegation of 20, who wore masks, to meet with Sheriff Ed Jacobs, to demand that Sullivan be handed over.

The sheriff pulled his weapon, ordering his deputies to stand their ground but the officers were overtaken. Soon the crowd had their hands on Sullivan, who was strung up and hanged from a tree near the jail. His corpse then was dragged through town behind a buggy, the rope still tied around his neck. The rope eventually was collected by an enterprising hardware store owner, who cut it up and sold pieces as souvenirs.

Sheriff Jacobs had to face charges that he only put up token resistance to the mob and had in fact enabled the lynching, which turned out to be the last in the state's history.

One observer claimed that Sullivan was dead before he was lynched, having been bribed with a bottle of whiskey in exchange for an interview with a reporter. He broke the bottle and slashed his own neck before the mob pulled him from the jail.

Nonetheless, the mob justice brought condemnation from newspapers from around the country, including the *New York Times*.

None in the mob ever was charged with any crime. The sheriff was investigated by the state and avoided charges. The following year the sheriff was reelected by a two-to-one margin.

May 24, 1820
Michiganders explore the state

Governor Lewis Cass and Henry Rowe Schoolcraft, along with a party of French Canadian voyageurs, Chippewa and Ottawa Indians, about a dozen soldiers and a group of scientists set out from Detroit on May 24, 1820 to explore Lake Superior and the vast lands that would become the state of Michigan.

The party of 40 men traveled in three large canoes about 30 feet long and as much as six feet wide.

The vessels were equipped with sails. In inclement weather they were taken ashore, unloaded and tipped on their sides. The party did not make it far before they found trouble at Lake St. Clair, where they ran into a violent storm, requiring them to camp for two days.

The trip to Mackinac took 14 days. They expected trouble at the Sault so in Mackinac the party took on an additional 22 soldiers. They ascended the rapids of the Saint Marys River and arrived at the Sault on June 14 in time to make camp in an open field before nightfall.

Two days after his arrival, Cass had a council with the Chippewas and announced the intention of the United States to erect a fort there.

The Americans believed they were entitled to the same land the French used to construct their fort but the Indians did not see things that way. The head chief, Shin-a-ba-was-sin, while opposed, did not want a confrontation. But another, Sassaba, reacted violently. Sassaba, wearing a scarlet British soldier's uniform, thrust his war lance into the ground, delivered an angry speech, and then kicked over the gifts given to the Indians before storming out.

Sassaba made off to the Indian village a few hundred yards away and raised a British flag. When Cass saw the flag he pulled it down and stomped upon it. A standoff ensued, with the American soldiers awaiting a battle. However, another council was hastily formed and the Indians agreed to turn over a large tract of land for an American fort.

Later, Colonel Hugh Brady built what would come to be known as Fort Brady in Sault Ste. Marie.

There is another version of this story that saw Cass behave less diplomatically.

According to the Bay Mills history department, Cass told the Indians that if they resisted "he would put his boot to their necks and kill every last man, woman, child and dog among them."

May 24, 1917
First American killed on German soil in World War I

Joseph W. Guyton worked as a farmer, a plumber and a well driller in Evart. He earned distinction far from that town however.

Guyton was drafted into the Army when America entered into World War I. At the time, he was 28-years-old with a wife and a child.

On May 24, 1917, Guyton, serving with the 126th Infantry Regiment of the 32nd Red Arrow Division, was hit by machine gun fire shortly after he reached the front lines in the Alsace region of Germany.

Guyton became the first American to die on German soil during the war.

Guyton received the *Croix de Guerre* from France. He was buried in a German cemetery. But later his remains were returned to the United States where at a memorial ceremony in New Jersey President Warren Harding laid a wreath on Guyton's casket as a symbolic way of honoring all of the war dead.

Newspapers reported that 10,000 people attended his funeral when his body was returned to Evart, where he was laid to rest at the Forest Hill Cemetery.

May 25, 1977
Darth Vader finds his voice in Michigan

James Earl Jones was born in Mississippi, but he moved to Jackson, Michigan at age five, where the trauma of being adopted by his maternal grandparents caused Jones to stutter and kept him nearly silent for years. Jones' family later moved to Dublin, in Manistee County, where Jones attended a one-room schoolhouse and worked on his family's farm.

Jones had a tough time speaking until he attended high school in Brethren, also in Manistee County, where an English teacher, Donald Crouch, goaded Jones into public speaking.

Crouch, who had been an English professor before he retired to northern Michigan and turned to the local high school out of boredom, once discovered a poem, "Ode to Grapefruit," that Jones had secretly written.

Crouch told Jones he thought the poem was too good for him to have written it, and asked the student to stand up and read it from memory to prove he was the author.

Jones so much wanted to vindicate himself he forgot his stuttering problem and recited the poem. From then on, he was able to speak in public.

In high school, he first appeared on stage as the rear end of a horse in a "horse opera." Jones didn't have a speaking part. But better things lay ahead.

Jones attended the University of Michigan, where he studied pre-med, and he served in the Army during the Korean War, although he was never deployed overseas. After that, Jones turned to acting over the objections of his grandparents, who wanted him to pursue a more conventional line of work.

For a while, Jones returned to Manistee, where he worked at the Ramsdell Theater, but he had bigger plans.

He won small roles in television and film before he landed a more substantial part in the film *Dr. Strangelove.*

Later Jones starred as a prizefighter in "The Great White Hope," a performance for which he won a Tony and reprised in the film version of the play.

In a career that spans decades, Jones became the famous, baritone voice of CNN, he stared in *Field of Dreams, Coming to America,* and dozens of other movies. He continues to act well into his 70s.

Perhaps his most famous role, one for which, at first, he was not credited, was the voice of one of the most iconic movie characters of all time – Darth Vader.

Star Wars, the first film featuring Darth Vader, was released on May 25, 1977.

May 25, 1845
Birth of Mother Mary Mayo

It's a stretch today to associate home economics with the feminist movement. The notion that a young woman would attend college to study how to be a good wife is today antiquated but in the 19th century Mary Mayo fought for women's education at the Michigan Agricultural College.

Born on May 25, 1845, Mary Anne Bryant grew up on a farm near Battle Creek, when life in Michigan was hard work.

Her family believed everyone should have an education, so Mary attended a private school where two of her aunts taught and she became a teacher after high school.

When she met Perry Mayo, a Civil War veteran, Mary left teaching to become a wife.

It may have been a sly insult that motivated Mayo to do something more with her life.

"A chance encounter with a former classmate in a Battle Creek store helped to provide direction for Mary Mayo's future life," Marilyn Culpepper wrote in a chapter about Mayo in *Historic Women of Michigan: A Sesquicentennial Celebration*. "In recalling the incident, she explained how the acquaintance had patronizingly remarked that 'as I had married a farmer, about all I had to do, or did do, was to work hard and make lots of good butter. While riding home with Mr. Mayo, I kept thinking it over. I knew that I did work hard and that I made good butter, but it made me indignant to think that this was the measure of my life and that of every farmer's wife. We both decided we would do something.'"

She became active in the Grange, or the Order of the Patrons of Husbandry, an organization devoted to improving rural life. For women who lived on farms, Grange membership may have been the only social outlet they had.

Mayo rose quickly in the organization because she was a gifted speaker.

She used her position to advocate the creation of a program for women at the state college near Lansing. She also promoted the construction of a women's dormitory.

She traveled the state and prodded her audiences to join her cause. She was critical of the curriculum offered at the school, believing it provided little for women who lived on farms and even less for women who lived in cities.

Women were allowed into the school as early as 1870 but they were required to find their own housing off campus and there were no courses tailored to them.

At the time the school, which would become Michigan State University, offered courses in plowing, maintenance of farm equipment, crop fertilization and dairy hygiene. Mayo convinced the school to begin offering courses that would help women run a farmhouse.

Mayo saw her work pay off in 1896, when a women's course, home economics – or domestic science – was instituted at the college, and in 1900 when a woman's building was opened. When the women's dorm opened it housed 120 female students.

May 26, 1937
Battle of the overpass

The United Auto Workers union managed to organize workers at General Motors and Chrysler, but Henry Ford's company proved more stubborn. Blood would spill before the Ford Motor Company would go union.

On May 26, 1937, the UAW planned a leaflet campaign at the Miller Road overpass near the Ford Rouge plant.

Early that afternoon, union organizers, led by Walter Reuther and Richard Frankensteen, planned to hand out flyers that proclaimed "Unionism" over "Fordism." As Reuther and Frankensteen posed for a *Detroit News* photographer, members of the Ford "service department," headed by notorious Ford boss Harry Bennett, stormed in.

Around 150 company men, hoodlums, retired police, boxers and wrestlers recruited by Bennett descended upon the union organizers.

"One called out that we were on private property and to get the hell out of there," Reuther later testified at a National Labor Relations Board hearing. "I had hardly taken three steps when I was slugged on the back of the head. I tried to shield my face by crossing my arms. They pounded me over the head and body."

Reuther went on to describe a prolonged and intense beating.

Meanwhile, as the union organizers were pummeled, Dearborn police stood by and made no effort to end the violence.

The bloody turmoil was captured by newspaper reporters and photographers. The story shocked the nation.

Nonetheless, the company's ardent resistance to the union lasted a few more years. Fear of losing their jobs and whatever consequences Ford's goons might have in store for them kept the factory workers out of the union.

It was not until April 1941 that the UAW struck a Ford plant and won representation of the workers.

May 26, 1927
Fifteen millionth Model T produced

Exactly ten years before the Battle of the Overpass, Ford Motor Company celebrated a banner day.

Henry Ford, with his son Edsel at the wheel, drove the 15 millionth Model T out of the factory.

It was basically the same car that had emerged 19 years earlier. But times had changed and production of the Model T was coming to a close. After car production was halted for months to retool for a different model, the Model A was introduced in early 1928.

May 26, 1943
Edsel Ford dies

Henry Ford's only child, Edsel was 49 years old when he died of cancer in Detroit. He took over the company but struggled for control with Harry Bennett, one of his father's right-hand men, and some biographers say Henry Ford drove his son to an early grave.

Edsel gave Ford its luxury division, purchasing the Lincoln Motor Car company. He also was instrumental in the design and naming of the company's Mercury division. He was the father of four children: Henry Ford II, who led the company for years; Benson; Josephine; and, William Clay, who now is most noted as the long-time owner of the Detroit Lions football team.

May 27, 1913
Former president testifies in Marquette
about his drinking habits

When a newspaper editor in the Upper Peninsula accused Theodore Roosevelt of excessive drinking, the former president could not let it go. Four years after he left the presidency, Roosevelt was characterized as a heavy drinker and he was going to fight that image.

He sued the editor for libel and travelled to northern Michigan to testify before a jury made up of miners, teamsters, farmers, a lumberman, a blacksmith and a locomotive fireman.

The editor had written that Roosevelt "gets drunk, and not infrequently curses and uses foul language."

"Col. Roosevelt, who was the first witness in the trial of his libel suit against George A. Newett of Ishpeming, came as near as he could to giving a complete record of all the drinks he has taken in his life," reported the *New York Times*, which featured hundreds of inches of coverage of the trial.

Roosevelt outlined exactly what and when he drank – wine or champagne with dinner – and maintained that he never had cocktails or high balls, drank mint juleps on a couple of rare occasions, and never drank whiskey unless it was prescribed by a doctor.

People were fascinated by the trial because the former president described in detail his daily habits, including how he spent his days in the White House.

Roosevelt may have prompted people to believe he was drunk due to peculiar mannerisms, such as bearing his teeth or using a falsetto to emphasize a point. It was not uncommon for people at the time to believe Roosevelt drank a lot.

Roosevelt took the trial seriously, believing his reputation was at stake.

"I have never been drunk or in the slightest degree under the influence of liquor," he told the jury when he took the stand on May 27, 1913.

The trial brought a parade of luminaries to Marquette.

"Yesterday you couldn't throw a brick in the courtroom without hitting an ex-Cabinet officer, an ex-Governor, or somebody like that," the reporter noted about jury selection day. The long list of Washington elites all testified that Roosevelt did not drink.

When it came time for Newett, the editor to testify in his defense, he took the stand and said he had searched the country for a witness who would testify that Roosevelt drank in excess and that he could find no one. He said he believed he was wrong when he wrote that Roosevelt drinks.

Roosevelt addressed the court and said he had nothing against Newett. He asked for only nominal damages.

Newett was ordered to pay Roosevelt six cents.

May 27, 1915
Henry B. Joy embarks on cross-country automobile trip

Henry Joy, president of Packard Motor Company, was an early advocate of paved roads that would cross the country.

He became president of the Lincoln Highway Association that sought to promote the idea. On May 27, 1915, Joy and two associates left Detroit for San Francisco over the various roads that then made up the Lincoln Highway.

It turned out to be tough journey. His car became stuck in mud in Tama, Iowa. On June 7, he veered off the road in Nebraska and it took him and his associates, several farmers and a team of horses to pull the car out.

He eventually made it to California and his trip served its purpose of bringing attention to the terrible conditions on many of the nation's roads.

May 28, 1837
Onslaught of immigrants come to Detroit

Detroit Mayor Charles C. Trowbridge wrote to former territorial governor Lewis Cass, who was in Paris, about the throngs of émigrés coming to his city.

"The opening of navigation has brought us immediate crowds of old fashioned immigrants with their wives and babies and wagons and spinning wheels, and a hundred dollars to buy an eighty acre lot for each of the boys," Trowbridge wrote. "I have never seen more crowded boats."

Trowbridge recorded the arrivals into the Detroit port for May 28, 1837: eight steamboats, one ship, three large brigs and nineteen schooners. A day before, seven steamboats had arrived.

One day that month, Trowbridge counted 2,400 settlers entering Detroit.

The Erie Canal was completed in 1825 and opened the upper Great Lakes to navigation. It connected Lake Erie with the Hudson River north of New York.

Immigration escalated as steamboat traffic flourished and Michigan gained a reputation as a place where persons could come with little money but, with a willingness to work, create a comfortable life for themselves.

When the Erie Canal opened, the *Detroit Gazette* bragged: "We can now go from Detroit to New York in five and a half days."

Prior to that, the trip took two months or more.

May 29, 1848
Michigan's first presidential candidate falls short

Lewis Cass, once the territorial governor of Michigan, was elected to the United States Senate from Michigan in February 1846.

Cass had become the most prominent Michigan resident on the national stage but as a senator he strayed from the will of the people he represented.

When Cass entered the senate, the nation was preoccupied with westward expansion – obtaining Texas and California from Mexico and claiming as much land as possible in the Northwest, where the British were also looking to expand.

A resolution to appropriate $2 million to acquire Texas on condition the new territories be anti-slavery was proposed. Cass was pragmatic. He wanted his country to acquire the land and feared that injecting the slavery issue into the transaction could derail the whole thing.

He supported leaving the slave matter to the new governments after they were formed.

This was in direct opposition to the mood of the people of

Michigan, who had passed a measure condemning the spread of slavery.

The difference of opinion between Cass and his constituents may be understood as a generation gap. By the time Cass reached the senate, Michigan was filled with citizens who had not been around decades earlier when Cass was a territorial governor preoccupied with forging Michigan into a state.

His locally unpopular views did get him noticed by national leaders and positioned him to get the Democratic party's nomination for president on May 29, 1849.

Cass lost to Zachary Taylor, the Whig candidate, in an election that was complicated by a third party, the Free Soil Party, which ran Martin Van Buren for president and captured a significant amount of the Northern vote.

May 30, 1763
The terrible fate of the Cuyler party

The residents of Detroit were three weeks into a siege launched on Fort Detroit by Indians led by Chief Pontiac.

The morning of May 30, 1763, Detroiters were tired, hungry and anxiously awaiting a supply of provisions to help them get through more weeks of fighting.

A sentinel on the fort flag bastion saw several barges slowly moving up the Detroit River toward the fort. This was an expedition that had left Niagara on May 13 with nearly 100 men, 10 flat-bottomed boats and 139 barrels of provisions, headed by Lieutenant Abraham Cuyler of the Queen's Company of Rangers.

The sentinel gave the alarm alerting the residents that supplies had arrived. As the convoy drew closer, however, the sound of war cries coming from the barges changed the mood in the fort from joy to gloom.

The sight and sound of the Indians who had taken over the boats and paraded them past the fort must have been a serious blow to the morale in Detroit.

The Indian warriors won this strategic victory after they learned of the convoy and awaited its appearance at Pelee Point on the shore of Lake Erie, not far from the mouth of the Detroit River.

The convoy happened to use that spot to drop anchor for the night. The Indians waited patiently until the first light of dawn.

Fifty-nine officers and troops and one child and one woman were killed in the attack.

Cuyler and a party escaped with five barrels of provisions and two boats but everything else was captured, along with several prisoners.

When the string of barges arrived opposite the fort in the hands of the Indians, four Englishmen on one of the barges made a break for freedom.

Two shots were fired at pursuing Indians, which halted their chase, but one of the Indians was able to pull one of the Englishmen with him into the river where both drowned.

The remaining three were able to reach the fort with their lives and a small portion of the provisions.

The remaining English prisoners were taken to Pontiac's camp where, except for a small number of them, they were killed.

May 30, 1944
Michigan prisoner of war camps

There were 25 prisoner of war camps created in Michigan during World War II.

One of them was Camp Owosso, set up on an unused dirt race track at the corner of M-21 and Carland Road.

The camp consisted of tents surrounded by a barbed-wire fence. At night, the camp was illuminated by floodlights. The tents, guarded by a garrison of 30 military police, had cement floors, showers and toilets.

On May 30, 1944, the U.S. government brought 200 German prisoners to Camp Owosso. They were soldiers who fought in Field Marshall Erwin Rommel's Afrika Korps. Most of them were men in their 20s.

The public was not allowed to visit. A sign on M-21 alerted motorists that stopping or parking was prohibited.

The prisoners had the option of staying at the camps or working at area farms during the day for pay.

Most of the prisoners opted to take the work. They earned extra food and about 80 cents per day.

According to the Shiawassee County Historical Society, the Germans apparently enjoyed being prisoners away from the danger of the battlefield. As they were transported from camp to field in the back of trucks, they would sing and wave happily to anyone.

During the winter, they were taken to Camp Custer where they stayed indoors.

The camp received national attention when two prisoners walked away from a canning factory and met two women who were waiting in a car.

A massive manhunt ensued and the following day all four were arrested near Colby Lake.

May 31, 1855
Soo Canal completed

Almost as soon as explorers made their way up the rapids of the St. Mary's River between Lake Huron and Lake Superior, men dreamed of dredging a canal to enable navigation of the passage.

When the first two Soo locks were turned over to a state superintendent on May 31, 1855, after just two years of construction, it was considered one of the greatest engineering feats of the era.

The project cost just under $1 million, which is comparable to $34 million today.

The one-mile canal enabled ships to travel between Lakes Huron and Superior despite the 22-foot difference in elevation.

The first ship to pass through, the *Illinois,* made the trip the following month.

The canal was first officially sanctioned by the State of Michigan under its first governor, Stevens T. Mason.

Mason pushed the canal as part of a package of improvements he wanted to see completed in the state.

During an early effort to build the canal, a contractor and the War Department skirmished over the project. The commander at Fort Brady in Sault Ste. Marie did not like the plans, which he thought would stall construction of a millrace at the fort.

An order that the canal could not jeopardize the mill forced a showdown between the contractor and the commander. The contractor immediately began work in defiance of the order and soldiers were called to run workmen off the grounds.

The contractor may not have been motivated by an eagerness to see the canal completed, however.

It's more likely he started work in defiance of the order because he had received an advance of $5,000, and as long as he started work, he would not have to refund the deposit.

It took 12 years before Congress granted Michigan a right-of-way through Fort Brady and construction of the canal could begin in earnest.

June

June 1, 1922
Women in knickers descend on Traverse City

The mayor of Traverse City noticed that a growing number of women were wearing pants and he feared the effect on male citizens of his town would not be good.

On June 1, 1922, Mayor Lafayette Swanton, a medical doctor, issued an order to Police Chief John Blacken to arrest any woman found on downtown streets wearing knickers or behaving in an unladylike fashion.

"Young men and boys have been severely criticized for accosting women on the streets, and I believe that much of this is because of the actions of the women," Swanton said in a public statement.

The mayor was also opposed to one-piece bathing suits for women as well as those who wore "somewhat fashionable trimmings."

He left it to the police chief to determine what constituted unladylike displays or fashionable trimmings.

The proclamation prompted rebellion.

The following day women from the upper class to store clerks to high school students announced plans to march down Front Street dressed in knickers.

Wire services picked up the story and it spread across the country. Swanton became hard to contact, but he didn't back down.

Next, the chamber of commerce and downtown merchants expressed outrage at the proclamation. Finally the mayor gave in.

But he refused to make an apology to the local newspaper, which had chastised him for ignoring more important issues and concentrating on women's fashion. Instead he delivered a statement to a newspaper in Grand Rapids.

June 1, 2007
Dr. Jack Kevorkian paroled

Jack Kevorkian spawned countless jokes, taunted police and prosecutors, and ended nearly a hundred lives.

The assisted suicide advocate began his campaign, which he characterized as a treatment to end suffering, in the late 1980s. Although the state of Michigan revoked his medical license in 1991, he continued to end patient's lives, using an invention that enabled patients to cause their own death.

Kevorkian was tried on homicide charges several times in Oakland County but managed to win acquittal each time. That changed in 1998, after he provided a video of an assisted suicide he performed to *60 Minutes*. In the show, he taunted prosecutors to come after him.

This suicide was different from the others in one aspect – because the patient had advanced ALS disease, the man could not operate the machine himself. In this case Kevorkian "pulled the trigger" and ended the man's life.

Kevorkian represented himself at trial and was unable to win acquittal. He was convicted of second-degree murder and sentenced to 10 to 25 years in prison.

Kevorkian was finally paroled on June 1, 2007, at the age of 79. He pledged he would no longer perform assisted suicides but instead devote himself to their legalization.

June 2, 1763
Massacre at Mackinac

There was plenty of evidence to indicate relations between the European settlers and the Indians were strained and could boil into violence in Detroit.

Violence had already broken out in Detroit, where Chief Pontiac and his Indian warriors held the fort under siege for nearly a month.

Nonetheless, when word of an Indian uprising reached Mackinac, its post commander, believing he had friendly relations with the Indians, refused to believe his fort was in danger.

So when the Indians attacked the fort, they employed a brilliant strategy and the English were taken by complete surprise.

The strategy of the attack is credited to a Chippewa chief named Minavavana.

Minavavana cultivated the friendship of Captain George Etherington, commander of Fort Mackinac. He convinced Etherington that the Indians were his friends and Minavavana proposed a celebration on June 2, 1763, the birthday of King George III.

The festivities included a game of lacrosse staged outside the fort between a group of Chippewa and visiting Sac Indians from Wisconsin.

On the sidelines, Indian women sat and watched, covered in blankets despite the heat of the day.

The game went on for some time and the British soldiers relaxed. Eventually the ball was hit into the fort, seemingly by mistake. As the Indians rushed in to retrieve it, the women handed them weapons they had concealed under the blankets.

French traders were allowed to escape, but the Indians killed 20 British soldiers and one English trader.

Alexander Henry, an English trader, had been warned about the attack in a cryptic manner by an Indian friend. Henry, who wrote an account of that day, sought shelter with a French family and wound up in a room that overlooked the fort, offering a good view of the drama as it unfolded.

Henry, able to escape detection at first, was finally given up to the Indians by his French keepers.

164

The Indians kept Henry and other English prisoners for a time. However, Henry escaped death when an Indian friend intervened and claimed him.

June 3, 1856
Federal law paves way to clear Michigan of trees

The fate of Michigan's virgin forests was sealed once European settlers landed in the New World.

After the United States gained independence, it needed wood to construct buildings, roads, and to fire steam engines. (The country's first improved roads consisted of wood: plank roads when they consisted of planks and corduroy roads when they were made of uncut logs.)

It was inevitable that Michigan's rich forests would be swept away in a frenzy of logging operations.

To make it happen, and to encourage the construction of railroads, Congress passed the "land-grant law" on June 3, 1856.

Under the law, a company that built a railroad would be awarded land around the railroad from the federal government. This meant that a railroad line built from southern Michigan to the north didn't necessarily need passengers and freight to make money as long as the line travelled through well-forested areas.

The law spurred development of the state, but the leveling of the state's forests that ensued was still evident in the middle 20th century.

June 4, 1910
Custer monument dedicated in Monroe

General George Armstrong Custer was born in Ohio but was raised in Monroe and that city has long adopted the Civil War hero and famous general as their own.

Custer led Michigan men into battle during the Civil War and made "Come on you Wolverines!" his battle cry, including when he and his men fought at Gettysburg.

Custer became notorious in the Battle of Little Big Horn when he and 266 others were surrounded by plains Indians and killed.

An equestrian statue commissioned of Custer was dedicated in Monroe on June 4, 1910 by President William Howard Taft and Michigan Governor Fred M. Warner.

June 5, 1920
"Sweet Singer of Michigan" dies

Julia A. Moore, born in Plainfield Township just north of Grand Rapids, the granddaughter of a pioneer, came to be known as the "Sweet Singer of Michigan."

She would go on to become a nationally-known poet. Unfortunately for Moore, she earned her literary fame because she was a really, *really* bad poet.

Here is a sample of her work, a poem about the Great Chicago Fire:

> *The great Chicago Fire, friends,*
> *   Will never be forgot;*
> *In the history of Chicago*
> *   It will remain a darken spot.*
> *It was a dreadful horrid sight*
> *   To see that City in flames;*
> *But no human aid could save it,*
> *   For all skill was tried in vain.*

To be fair to Moore, she never had any training as a poet. Her formal education ended at the age of 10, when her mother became ill and, as the oldest sibling, Moore was forced to assume a maternal role in her home.

She continued to educate herself through reading and developed a love of writing, especially in rhymed verse.

She was inspired to write poems about children and acquaintances who had died and newspaper accounts of disasters. A book of her poems, "The Sentimental Song Book," was published in 1876.

Her first book gained national fame after a publisher in Cleveland obtained a copy, fell for the awkward rhymes and republished it as *The Sweet Singer of Michigan Salutes the Public.* The publisher sent copies to newspapers around the country with a press release filled with sarcastic praise for Moore's work.

The collection became a bestseller but Moore's career soon ended at the insistence of her husband, who was horrified at the jeering his wife received during a performance at an opera house in Grand Rapids.

Moore moved to Manton in 1882, in part to escape her notoriety.

There, the locals respected her privacy and refused to cooperate with any reporter who wanted to rekindle the Moore story.

She died on June 5, 1920.

In 1997, Governor John Engler dedicated a week in December as Julia A. Moore Week.

June 6, 1822
The hole in St. Martin's stomach

A musket filled with powder and duck shot accidentally discharged, sending its load into the stomach of Alexis St. Martin, a French Canadian fur trader who worked for the American Fur Company.

The shooting happened in the company's store on the corner of Astor and Fort streets on Mackinac Island.

Dr. William Beaumont, an Army surgeon stationed at Fort Mackinac, was called in to treat St. Martin. When the patient recovered but his wound failed to completely close, Beaumont convinced his patient to let him study the digestive system through the flap in his abdomen.

The doctor became the first person to study human digestion as it occurred in the stomach. Beaumont tied a variety of pieces of food to a silk string and dangled it inside the stomach hole. The doctor pulled the string out one, two and three hours later to observe the rate of digestion for the different foods. As the years passed, he tried other gastric experiments with his patient.

Beaumont went on to become famous for his research in the field of gastric medicine. St. Martin remained healthy, married and fathered 17 children. He lived to the age of 76.

Beaumont is the namesake of a large hospital in Oakland County.

June 7, 1897
Nineteenth Century diving contraption
reaches the shipwreck *Pewabic*

The *Pewabic*, which went down in 1865 with a loss of 125 lives, was for years one of the most sought after shipwrecks in the Great Lakes. The *Pewabic* sunk while she attempted to pull alongside another ship to exchange messages. The wooden ships crashed, sending the *Pewabic* to the bottom of Lake Huron.

At least five divers died attempting to get to the boat, which was carrying tons of Upper Peninsula copper and iron when it went down.

In the 1890s, a well-financed operation arrived in Alpena determined to succeed where others had failed.

They brought with them an invention they called a "diving bell," an enclosed vessel able to take people deep into the lake.

The American Wrecking and Salvage Company of Milwaukee led by Worden G. Smith, one of the contraption's inventors, arrived in July of 1896 with the intention of raising the *Pewabic*.

On June 7, 1897, the company located the *Pewabic* and began salvage operations. But the work was postponed in September when autumn and winter weather moved in.

The enterprise however, would end in tragedy, as if the *Pewabic* were cursed. When the diving bell returned the following summer, two men, George S. Campbell, who co-invented the bell with Smith, and his associate Peder Olson, were killed inside the bell when a window broke.

Later that same year, Oliver Pelky died while attempting to examine the wreck wearing an armored diving suit of his own creation.

In May 1917, another man came along with an armored diving suit and this time located the wreck and successfully salvaged much of the copper and iron ore. Unfortunately for B.F. Leavitt, founder and inventor of the B.F. Leavitt Diving Armor Company, he was short on cash and was forced to cease salvage operations in August. The iron and copper he salvaged was worth less than the cost of the expedition.

The most successful salvage operation was conducted in 1974 by Busch Oceanographic, according to the Thunder Bay National Marine Sanctuary. Some of the artifacts from the ship are on display at the Jesse Besser Museum in Alpena.

June 8, 1854
Early communication on the lake: by bottle

When Alonzo J. Slyfield, the lighthouse keeper on South Manitou Island, saw a ship caught in the stormy waters of Lake Michigan on June 8, 1854, he expected trouble.

With the lake level rising and the storm gaining in strength, Slyfield knew the ship was on its way to crashing into the breakers on the island's shore.

Slyfield held up a bottle and signaled for the crew to send him a line. They soon figured out what he was up to and fastened a line to a buoy, sending it overboard.

The buoy drifted ashore and Slyfield wrote a note, stuffed it into the bottle, and signaled for the crew to retrieve their line.

The note said: "Can I render you any assistance? If so, send word by bottle."

Sure enough, the crew wanted assistance. "Our big chain has parted, and the small one will not hold us long. Look out for us ashore," they wrote. About an hour later the brig swung broadside and the crew sent a pole out of the boat, making a ramp to the shallow water.

One of the crew slid down first and was helped ashore by Slyfield, followed by four ladies. The rest of the crew followed.

Slyfield returned to the lighthouse to discover that in his absence his wife had given birth to an eight-pound, blue-eyed boy.

June 8, 1953
Deadly tornado strikes Flint

It was sunset on June 8, 1953 when, without warning, a series of tornados swept through the Midwest.

The deadliest twister set down in the Beecher metropolitan district, a heavily populated residential area just north of Flint.

By the following day, state police had recovered 113 bodies from the area. Hundreds of people were injured.

Others were killed elsewhere in the state and in Ohio where a string of tornadoes ravaged cities and small towns but the devastation was by far the worst in Flint.

Governor G. Mennen Williams temporarily moved the state capital to Flint to oversee recovery efforts.

What, perhaps, made the tornados so deadly was that they appeared to come from nowhere. There was no heavy rain or hail that typically alerted people to take cover, although earlier in the day the U.S. Weather Service had asked radio broadcasters to warn listeners of approaching severe thunderstorms and high winds.

A woman in Flint, who identified herself as Elizabeth Croteau to a United Press reporter, said her six-month-old baby was torn from her arms and flung 50 feet when the tornado struck. Remarkably, the child suffered only bruises.

As the homeless made their way to shelters and the injured waited for space to open in hospitals, the death and destruction stunned the state.

June 9, 1913
Road "Bee" Day

Even after Detroit had established itself as a mass producer of automobiles, Michigan roads were in a sorry state.

Especially in out-of-the-way hamlets like Alpena, where the roads leading to and from other cities were little more than muddy and dangerous trails through the woods.

The conditions were bad enough that better roads became a celebrated civic movement in the early 20th century.

The *Alpena Argus-Pioneer* called June 9, 1913 "the biggest day in the recent history" of northeastern Michigan.

It was the day the Lake Huron Good Roads Association led an enormous effort to improve roads. Thousands of volunteers spent the day working on a gravel highway from Bay City to the Straits of Mackinac that was suitable for automobiles. That day 5,000 men worked together on the massive road construction project.

They laid gravel down along the highway, which had previously been a corduroy road, meaning it was made of logs, sand, dirt or swamp.

Women and children prepared meals and served refreshments along the road.

The road meant that the journey between Bay City and Alpena had been cut from days to as little as seven or eight hours.

June 10, 1916
Hemingway departs for northern Michigan

Writer Ernest Hemingway first came to northern Michigan in the summer of 1899, when he was an infant.

His family continued to bring Hemingway from their Oak Park, Illinois home to northern Michigan each summer and Hemingway's love of the region grew.

The family owned a cottage on Walloon Lake they called Windemere.

Hemingway returned to Michigan throughout his youth and travelled to the family's cottage after his tour as an ambulance driver in World War I. Although by 1920 Hemingway opted to travel and live in other parts of the world, he returned to northern Michigan in his fiction whenever he wrote about his alter-ego, Nick Adams.

Hemingway embarked on one of the trips to Michigan that influenced the Nick Adams stories on June 10, 1916.

Hemingway and a friend, Lew Clarahan, boarded a lake steamer from Chicago en route to Frankfort.

They planned to fish the Bear Creek in Manistee County, the Boardman River near Traverse City and the Rapid River near Kalkaska.

The outing formed the basis of two Nick Adams stories, "The Battler" and "The Light of the World."

Hemingway also remarked in a diary that he believed the trout fishing near Kalkaska was the best he had experienced.

June 11, 1805
Great fire levels Detroit

The morning dawned clear on June 11, 1805.

It was a Catholic feast day as well as a market day, so French farmers had come to town to attend Mass at St. Anne's before setting up to sell their produce.

John Harvey, a baker, needed to replenish his supply of flour and as he was leaving his shop, he tapped his pipe onto his boot. A live coal in the tobacco fell onto straw, igniting a fire.

Soon, Harvey's barn was engulfed and the fire spread to nearby buildings.

The call of "fire!" was heard and residents formed a bucket brigade from the river. The town had acquired a fire engine by then, but the rudimentary pump failed because the suction hose was put into a water tank next to a haberdasher's shop and became clogged with felt.

Soldiers rushed from the fort to help. Even British loyalist John Askin, who saw the black smoke rise from Detroit from his home in Windsor, gathered his sons and servants, loaded into a boat and paddled over to help.

The fire burned for three hours. When it was out, all that was left of Detroit was the fort, a warehouse near the river, a block-house and several blackened chimneys. People pitched tents and collections of food were made.

Father Gabriel Richard, a beloved Catholic priest who had been at St. Anne's since 1798, organized a makeshift relief organization for the homeless.

Richard was heard to remark: "Speramus meliora; resurget cineribus." ("We hope for better things; it will arise from the ashes.")

Those words were later incorporated into Detroit's official seal and became the city's motto.

At the time of the fire, Michigan had just been recognized as a territory. President Thomas Jefferson had selected William Hull, a 52-year-old New Englander and Revolutionary War veteran, to become the territory's first governor.

Hull arrived just in time to find the destroyed town.

But his administration drew up plans to rebuild Detroit, led by Judge Augustus B. Woodward. Woodward adapted a hub-and-spoke plan for city streets based on the layout of Washington D.C.

It called for two-hundred-foot-wide avenues and circular parks leading away from the city center. A remnant of Woodward's vision can be found in the center of Detroit around the southern end of the avenue that bears the judge's name.

Later planners, however, scrapped Woodward's design in favor of narrow streets intersecting at right angles.

June 12, 1957
Timothy Busfield born

B usfield was born in Lansing, graduated from East Lansing High School and attended college in Tennessee. The average-looking guy carved out an impressive career for himself in Hollywood, where he became a successful character actor.

He started off playing a geek in *The Revenge of the Nerds* and then moved to television where he played roles in *thirtysomething*, *Trapper John, M.D.*, and *The West Wing*.

June 12, 1878
James Oliver Curwood born in Owosso

James Oliver Curwood may be little known today, but in his time he turned out novels faster than Stephen King and saw many of them made into popular movies. The Owosso native wrote 32 novels and an autobiography between 1908 and 1931. Eighteen movies were made based on his stories – melodramatic tales of adventure that celebrated the wilderness of the north.

According to the Curwood Castle Museum in Owosso, Curwood was born on June 12, 1878, was expelled from high school, studied journalism at the University of Michigan and worked for the *Detroit News-Tribune*.

Much of the inspiration for his fiction came from a trip he took in 1909 to the Canadian northwest.

Once he made money writing fiction, Curwood returned again and again to the Yukon and Alaska for inspiration.

His writing eventually brought him wealth and enabled him to fulfill a childhood fantasy of living in a castle. He built the castle on the Shiawassee River in his hometown in the style of an 18th Century French chateau. The house now is the Curwood Castle Museum.

Curwood also owned an Upper Peninsula camp in the Huron Mountains and was an early environmentalist who was appointed to serve on the Michigan Conservation Commission in 1926.

Curwood died in 1927 after suffering a spider bite in Florida that apparently led to blood poisoning.

Owosso holds a Curwood festival each first full weekend in June.

June 13, 1910
The Alpena Flyer is born

Daniel Hanover incorporated the Alpena Motor Car Company on June 13, 1910 and within a month a construction company won a contract to build the factory in Alpena to produce the Alpena Flyer.

Production of the car began that October in the plant that had a capacity to build 2,500 cars per year.

Priced at $1,450, the automobile was light and inexpensive, with water-cooled four-cylinder engines and three-speed transmissions.

Initially, the car was a success. At the 1912 New York auto show, the Alpena Flyer was listed as one of the top 10 cars in the world.

Although the company received many orders, it could not keep up with demand. It also faced stiff competition from vehicles produced in Detroit.

The company faced another complication: they were ordered

to pay $400,000 after a patent-holder sued over the three-point suspension used in the gearboxes of the cars.

The Alpena Motor Car Company declared bankruptcy in 1914. The company produced 480 cars between 1910 and 1914.

June 13, 1953
Tim Allen born

Allen was born Timothy Alan Dick in Denver, Colorado, but it was Michigan where he formed his comedic sensibility and where he set the sitcom that made him a star. At age 11, Allen moved with his family to Birmingham after his father died in a car accident.

In 1978, Allen was arrested on drug charges and spent two years in prison. He has said he honed his comedy in prison and found he could avoid fights by cracking jokes.

Allen kicked off his comedy career performing standup at the Comedy Castle in Detroit, where he decided to change his last name. In 1991, he starred in his own television comedy, *Home Improvement*, a show that enjoyed years of success and made him a household name. He followed that up with a successful run of film comedies.

June 14, 1969
Calder sculpture in Grand Rapids dedicated

Anyone who has ever been lost on the confusing one-way streets of Grand Rapids has driven by a strange reddish-orange sculpture adorning a concrete plaza in the government building section of the city.

The name of the artist is Alexander Calder, known for the creation of mobiles and their lesser-known opposite, stabiles.

The work Calder designed for Grand Rapids was the first to be funded by the National Endowment for the Arts' Works of Art in Public Places program.

Called *La Grand Vitesse*, meaning the "big speed" or the "grand rapids," the work was dedicated to the City of Grand Rapids on June 14, 1969 and soon became the city's symbol.

The sculpture weighs 42 tons and is 54 feet long, 43 feet high and 30 feet wide.

June 14, 1908
Buster Keaton survives Muskegon vaudeville colony

Actors Joe Keaton and Paul Lucier, along with agent Lew Earl, wanted a place to create and perform their work. They picked Muskegon.

It was there on June 13, 1908 they launched the Artist's Colony Club, later to be known as the Actors' Colony.

The actors specialized in vaudeville-style performance. The colony was located in what was known as the Bluffton area of Muskegon and it drew hundreds of vaudeville performers each summer. It was a place where performers could take a break from their rigorous touring schedules and relax on the beach.

Keaton's wife and son, Joseph Frank, nicknamed "Buster," were billed as "The Three Keatons."

The act involved Keaton's father throwing his young son around the stage and into the audience for comic effect and it raised allegations of child abuse.

By the 1920s, the colony declined as movies replaced vaudeville to entertain the masses.

"Buster" Keaton adjusted.

He took his act from Muskegon to Hollywood where he became a pioneer of silent film comedy.

June 15, 1948
First night baseball game in Detroit

A baseball game played after sunset proved to be an amazing spectacle for the residents of Detroit.

"It takes a lot to awe Detroiters – but the new Briggs Stadium lights did just that Tuesday night," the *Detroit Free Press* reported. "So thrilled were the fans that they were momentarily speechless when the eight giant lighting standards, generating 182,000,000 candlepower, were turned on at 9:29 p.m."

The lights loomed 150 feet overhead and caused the playing field to glow green.

The lights cost $400,000 but the fans thought they were worth every penny.

They watched the Tigers beat the Philadelphia A's 4-1.

June 16, 1856
King Strang assassinated

James Jesse Strang, born in New York, converted to Mormonism after he met that religion's founder, Joseph Smith.

After Smith was murdered, Brigham Young and Strang feuded over who would succeed Smith. Young headed to Utah with the lion's share of followers. Strang took a splinter group of Mormons to Beaver Island in 1848 because of its isolation.

Strang, who claimed to be a prophet and a seer of God, considered himself ruler of the island and he settled in to lead a life that included multiple wives. He eventually had 12 children with five wives and he mandated polygamy among his followers.

In July, 1850, Strang made his position official when he declared himself to be "King of the Kingdom of God on Earth." (See the July 8 entry.)

By then, the number of his adherents on the island had almost doubled and Strang was developing a bad reputation on Michigan's mainland, where residents around Charlevoix complained that his followers often ambushed them, stealing food and goods.

Strang also began collecting "tithes" from the gentile, or non-Mormon, population on the island, mainly fishermen who had lived there much longer than he. Those who refused to pay were said to have been taken into the woods and flogged.

Strang's hostility to the non-Mormons and his disruption of the flow of whiskey on the island, soon caused most of the gentiles to leave. Later, the few families who stayed were forced to convert to his religion or leave the island.

However, it was not gentiles who would be Strang's downfall.

His authoritarianism grated on some of his followers, who could find themselves out of favor and whipped if they transgressed Strang's law.

The seed of Strang's downfall may have been an edict to the women on the island that they wear bloomers instead of long skirts.

Strang was ambushed and shot on June 16, 1856 by a follower Strang had severely punished for infidelity. The leader died on July 8, ironically the same day he had created as a holiday for himself.

June 17, 1873
Birth of Clara Ward

In the late 19th century, a wealthy socialite heiress from Michigan titillated newspaper readers with her misbehavior and escapades around the world.

Clara Ward, a native Detroiter, was the daughter of shipbuilding magnate Eber Brock Ward.

The elder Ward was reported to have said his offspring made his life difficult by not being a son, because a male would be expected to take over his enormous fleet of Great Lakes ships on his 21st birthday. Despite the gender issue, the father fully intended for his daughter to fulfill that role.

But that was not to be Clara's fate. Her father died when she was a toddler.

And as Clara grew up, she had the spunk her father admired, but not the desire to run the family business.

She reportedly had trouble in one school after another and her mother finally sent Clara to, depending on various reports, either "a school for young ladies" or a convent in England. The mother wanted to tame Clara's wildness.

Apparently the move to Europe had the opposite effect.

As a young woman, Clara's wealth and beauty attracted attention in newspapers and from royalty, namely Prince Joseph de Caraman-Chimay of Belgium – who married Clara Ward even though she was 15 years his junior.

Several years later, in 1896, she left the prince for a poor Gypsy violinist whom she met at a restaurant.

An enormous scandal in the U.S. and Europe ensued. When the couple traveled to Hungary to meet her beau's poor family, they were mobbed by gawkers and sometimes needed police protection.

The couple lived for a time in a castle in Egypt until she left the violinist for a Spaniard.

By the time she died in 1916, she had married four times and had become famous for her exploits.

An obituary that ran in newspapers around the country described her this way: "She was born in mystery. For two decades, she was the flame of Europe, friend of king and clown."

June 18, 1859
Wild case of self-defense

Seul Choix Point, a peninsula that juts into Lake Michigan about 15 miles from Manistique, was the unlikely scene of a murder leading to a trial and a court precedent that would be cited for decades.

Seul Choix Point was a place for Mackinac Island residents to fish during the summer. They lived in meager shacks and net houses set up in rows along the shore.

The murder case, eventually known as Pond v. People, began when three men who lived in the fishing village began bullying and terrorizing a resident they did not like.

Augustus Pond lived on the peninsula with his wife, three young children and two hired men. The family stayed in a one-room shanty and the hired men stayed in a room at the back of the net house.

In 1859, Isaac Blanchard, David Plant and Joseph Robillard spent the summer picking fights with Pond and terrorizing his family.

In the days leading up to the murder, the men and approximately 15 other inhabitants of the scrappy fishing village visited the shack where Pond lived and threatened him.

They messed with his property, harassed Pond's hired men and frightened his wife and children.

Finally Pond borrowed a shotgun from his brother-in-law.

Early one June morning, Pond heard the men tearing down the roof of his net house. He emerged with his weapon and announced that he would shoot if the men did not leave.

In response he heard another section of roof being torn from the building.

He said: "Leave or I'll shoot" before he fired, killing Blanchard with a load of pigeon shot.

Pond turned himself in and eventually was tried for murder on Mackinac Island, 75 miles away, then the seat of the Upper Peninsula's only judicial district.

At his trial, Pond was found guilty of manslaughter but attorneys appealed his case, arguing that the killing was justifiable homicide under common law.

In April, 1860, the Michigan Supreme Court heard the appeal, reversed the conviction and ordered a new trial. The decision established a standard for self-defense of property, and set guidelines for determining the use of deadly force to protect property when it lies within close proximity to one's dwelling.

The decision became well-known in legal circles.

U.S. Senator Prentiss M. Brown said "the case of the People versus Pond... has been said to be the most widely quoted Michigan case on the principles of law governing self-defense in a murder case of any Michigan Supreme Court decision. It has been quoted throughout the English-speaking world – wherever the English common law is in effect."

The family of Blanchard did not agree with the verdict.

Blanchard's gravestone stands in the Gros Cap Cemetery in St. Ignace and reads "Isaac Blanchard – Murdered June 18th, 1859."

June 18, 1855
First ships pass through the Soo Locks

The first ship to make its way into Lake Superior was the steamer *Illinois*, which passed through the locks in the canal at Sault Ste. Marie on June 18, 1855.

The first down-bound ship was the *Baltimore*.

The locks had officially opened the previous month. (See the entry for May 31.)

June 19, 1920
The case of the giant beaver

Workers toiled at the Michigan Central Railroad yards, digging a sewer a mile and a half east of Niles, when they unearthed an unexpected find – the skull of a giant beaver.

The discovery was made on June 19, 1920.

The giant beaver was a prehistoric beast that roamed North America along with mammoths and mastodons.

That area of Michigan must have appealed to Ice Age animals

as the bones of at least 28 mammoths were found in Berrien County.

The giant beaver, or *Castoroides ohioensis*, was a huge and presumably terrifying rodent that could grow to approximately eight feet in length and weigh nearly a quarter of a ton.

The giant beaver lived during the Pleistocene epoch and became extinct during the last Ice Age 10,000 years ago, possibly soon after humans moved into its habitat.

June 20, 1943
Wartime tension sparks Detroit race riot

Detroit had established itself as a world center of industry, and both blacks and whites had come to the city in the previous decade looking for work.

Many of the whites came from the south and they brought with them the Ku Klux Klan, which established a foothold in Detroit's factories.

Tensions between the races escalated during World War II as Detroit revamped its factories for wartime production.

Some whites from the south were uneducated and racist. The black population in Detroit was forcibly segregated and suffered institutional racism. On a sweltering day in June, tension between whites and blacks peaked.

Time magazine put it this way: "On Detroit's lush, leafy Belle Isle, thousands of Negroes and whites nervously held their Sunday picnics under the trees. They had reason for nerves: rumors of race trouble poisoned the June air, the same rumors that have stirred the city for months. As the sweltering thousands jammed the bridge to the mainland on the way home, they were ripe for explosion."

As folks from diverse backgrounds crowded off the island that evening, a fight between a white and a black broke out and the violence spread, growing out of control.

Much of the fighting took place on the Belle Isle bridge, where as many as 5,000 people were involved.

Police officers were able to contain the violence and, for a time, it appeared that the worst had passed.

The following day, however, a black man rushed into a nightclub in Paradise Valley, Detroit's segregated black community, to report that whites had killed a black woman and her baby by throwing them into the Detroit River.

Meanwhile gangs of whites moved into the city to respond to reports that white women were being attacked by blacks on the island.

Both reports were false but it was enough to reignite the smoldering violence from the night before. It threw Detroit into a full-scale riot.

178

White businesses around Paradise Valley were sacked and looted. Black people were attacked by white mobs along Woodward Avenue.

The 24-hours of shooting, knifing and looting that followed left 35 dead and 700 injured.

When it became clear that local and state police could not quell the violence, federal troops were brought in to restore order.

June 21, 1861
Soldiers muster in Adrian

After the outbreak of the Civil War and President Lincoln's call for the states to provide troops, the trustees of Adrian College voted to transform their campus into a military training center.

The city of Adrian funded the construction of a mess and dining hall.

For a time Adrian College became known as Camp Williams and it was home to the 4th Michigan Volunteer Infantry.

More than 1,000 soldiers came to Adrian from southeastern Michigan to train.

On June 21, 1861, 30,000 people assembled to see the soldiers off to war.

The 4th was assigned to the Army of the Potomac and would go on to fight in 41 battles, including Gaines Mills, Fredericksburg, Chancellorsville, Petersburg, Gettysburg and Wilderness.

June 22, 1938
Joe Louis knocks out Max Schmeling

Adolf Hitler almost certainly listened on the radio along with the rest of the Third Reich as Joe Louis, the "Brown Bomber" from Detroit, pummeled Max Schmeling.

The fight, which took place at Yankee Stadium, was scheduled to go 15 rounds but lasted only two minutes and four seconds.

The fight was a rematch. Schmeling, known as the "Black Uhlan from the Rhine," beat Louis the first time the fighters met.

The fight was more than a mere sporting contest. Hitler touted Arian supremacy and for a black man to prove himself superior to the best the Reich had to offer proved embarrassing for Hitler.

People packed into Yankee Stadium to see the fight. Anyone who arrived late or busied themselves lighting a cigar missed the action. Even though the fight was short and the ticket prices were astronomical for the period, the match was exhilarating. Those who didn't attend Yankee Stadium could hear the fight broadcast on radio. The coverage was done in English, German, Spanish and Portuguese for fight fans across the globe.

"As far as the length of the battle was concerned, the investment in seats, which ran to $30 each, was a poor one. But for excitement, for drama, for pulse-throbs, those who came from near and far felt themselves well repaid because they saw a fight that, though it was one of the shortest heavyweight championships on records, was surpassed by few for thrills."

"All Germany, clustered around its short-wave radio sets in the early morning hours, was thunderstruck and almost unbelieving at the unexpected news that 'Unser Max' Schmeling had failed in his heavyweight comeback try, and failed by the knockout route," the Associated Press reported. "All over the Reich they had clustered in homes, restaurants and cafes to hear the fight they hoped would bring the world's championship to Germany. It was said Adolf Hitler at his Bavarian mountain retreat heard the disheartening news."

In Detroit, black residents of their segregated neighborhood, "Paradise Valley", danced in cordoned-off streets to celebrate the victory.

Louis gave away most of his boxing career fortune and wound up working as a greeter in a Las Vegas hotel.

Schmeling, who refused to become a Nazi and turned down the "Dagger of Honor" from Hitler, became friends with Louis and helped him later in life when Louis was destitute and in poor health.

Louis, who was born in Alabama, moved to Detroit when he was 12.

June 23, 1963
King's "I have a dream" speech unveiled

The throng of marchers, numbering up to 125,000 persons, stretched out for a mile as they marched down Woodward Avenue to Cobo Hall.

They sang "We Shall Overcome" and "Battle Hymm of the Republic" as they marched for civil rights in what was at the time the largest such march in the nation's history.

The march concluded at Cobo Hall where Martin Luther King Jr. spoke to a crowd of 25,000. King urged support of President John F. Kennedy's civil rights bill and he pleaded for nonviolent support of his cause.

It was the first time he used the phrase "I have a dream" in a speech, a phrase that would become famous when he used it at the civil rights march in Washington later that year.

King's call for nonviolence was heeded remarkably – despite the enormous size of the crowd, no incidents of violence occurred during the demonstration march or at the rally.

June 24, 1960
Trouble on the eve of the opening of
the Houghton-Hancock Bridge

The planners of Houghton and Hancock opted for a different kind of bridge to cross Portage Lake and still allow large ships to pass through the canal. Instead of a drawbridge, they built a vertical lift bridge, the only one of its kind in Michigan and at the time the world's heaviest lift bridge. The entire center span raises and lowers to allow lake traffic to pass.

The bridge replaced a steel swing bridge constructed there in 1905 that could carry automobiles and trains.

The new bridge, designed by engineers in Chicago at a cost of $11 million, featured two levels – both levels could carry automobiles while the lower level could also carry trains. When the lower section was raised to allow boats to pass underneath, traffic could still flow across the bridge's upper section.

The bridge opened to autos in December, 1959, before it was entirely completed.

The bridge was to be formally dedicated with marching bands and jet flyovers but a day before the celebration, on June 24, 1960, a steamship captain wanted to pass under the bridge.

The captain of the *J.F. Schoellkopf* sounded his whistle but the bridge did not open and the steamer almost collided with the structure. The captain ordered the ship's engines reversed and the crew dropped anchor.

The anchor became entangled in the telephone lines on the bottom of the channel and cut two of six Michigan Bell cables, cutting off service to 1,000 customers in Hancock.

June 24, 1873
Elk Rapids Iron Company produces first blast of iron

Elk Rapids was once one of the nation's greatest producers of iron.

The Elk Rapids furnace, which stood 47 feet tall and 12 feet in diameter, was constructed in 1872 and produced its first blast of iron on June 24, 1873.

The logging firm of Dexter and Noble selected Elk Rapids for its furnace because of vast stands of hardwood timber that sat ready for the taking.

They turned the hardwood into charcoal used to fire the furnace. The company received shipments of iron ore from the Upper Peninsula and smelted it near the shore of Grand Traverse Bay.

The company was the town's major employer until around World War I, when the hardwood forests had been depleted.

June 25, 1891
Murderer becomes deputy sheriff in Seney

Dan Dunn, who moved from Roscommon to start a saloon in the Upper Peninsula lumber camp town of Seney, had been in a dispute with Tom, Luke, Bill, Steve, Dick and Jim Harcourt, also from Roscommon.

The feud climaxed on June 25, 1891, when Dunn shot and killed 20-year-old Steve who had come into his bar to buy a friend a drink.

A newspaper reported the murder with a disapproving slight to Seney: "The lumber town of Seney, about seventy miles southeast of here, had its weekly murder Saturday."

The report described Dunn as the proprietor of a "pinery dive" and said Harcourt was shot in the wrist, jaw, and abdomen and though while still alive, was expected to die.

Harcourt did die, and Dunn was tried on murder charges. Dunn claimed self-defense and was acquitted.

The Harcourt boys decided to settle the score.

A short while later, Jim Harcourt shot and killed Dunn at a saloon in Trout Lake. Harcourt was sentenced to seven years in prison in Marquette but was released after three for good behavior.

The people of Seney had petitioned the governor for early release, saying Harcourt had done the town a favor because Dunn was such a menace.

Harcourt returned to be elected township supervisor for nine terms. He later became a deputy sheriff and conservation officer.

June 26, 1922
Founding of ill-fated Fordson

The Village of Springwells opened its first municipal building on June 26, 1922, but the village did not last long.

Springwells became a city two years later.

The figure of Henry Ford loomed large over the city and within a year Ford's hometown was renamed Fordson, after Henry and his son, Edsel.

Fordson was not to last long, either.

The city consolidated with Dearborn in 1929.

The name lives on at Fordson High School in Dearborn and on the nameplates of Fordson tractors.

June 26, 1974
Derek Jeter born

Derek Jeter was born in New Jersey but when he was a youngster his family moved to Kalamazoo, where Jeter began playing T-ball at age five. Despite growing up in Michigan Jeter rooted for the Yankees, not the Detroit Tigers, on account of a grandmother in New York who took him to Yankees games.

In high school in Kalamazoo, Jeter's talents for baseball began to really show.

Jeter hit over .500 in his junior and senior years, and he reached base nearly two-thirds of the time. Just as his senior year ended in 1992, Jeter was drafted by the Yankees. Two years later Jeter was named minor league player of the year. In 1995, he began his major league career with the Yankees. The following year, the first year he started at shortstop for the Yankees, the team won their first World Series since the 1970s and Jeter went on to become a player beloved by New York fans.

June 27, 1875
First tornado bears down on Detroit

Sidewalks were uprooted and buildings were obliterated when a tornado tore through Detroit on June 27, 1875.

Mayhem followed in the streets of Detroit. Two days later, the *Detroit Free Press* called the tornado one of the worst things that ever happened to the city: "One of the most startling and terrible calamities known in the history of Detroit befell the city Sunday afternoon, resulting in a serious loss of life and the wounding of nearly fifty persons, besides tremendous destruction of property."

According to records from the National Weather service, two people died in the storm.

To the residents of Detroit, the aftermath of the early evening storm looked like a wasteland that certainly should have claimed more than two lives.

"Shortly after six o'clock rumors were heard down town that a tornado had swept over a portion of the city, demolishing houses, barns, stores, etc. and killing scores of men, women, children and animals," a *Detroit Free Press* reporter observed. According to a 2003 Detroit *Free Press* article, this was the first recorded tornado in the history of the city.

The War Department's Signal Corps began collecting weather data in Detroit in 1870.

June 28, 1900
Dedication of the Dewey Cannon

A unique Spanish-American War cannon had been captured during the war by Admiral George Dewey, who became famous after his victory at the Battle of Manila Bay.

The cannon was looking for a home at the turn of the century, and it was up to communities to raise money to house the war-time souvenir.

The citizens of Three Oaks, in a patriotic frenzy after the war, raised $1,400 to build a memorial to the men of the U.S.S. Maine. Nearly 300 sailors died after the ship exploded near Havana, causing America to go to war even though it was unclear what caused the explosion.

Nonetheless, the money raised by the citizens of Three Oaks was the largest amount, per capita, in the nation.

A local newspaper announced this under the headline: "Three Oaks Against the World."

President William McKinley dedicated the park and the cannon was later dedicated on June 28, 1900 in front of thousands who turned out for the ceremony.

June 28, 1836
First combine patented

Hirum Moore and Cyrus McCormick were in a race to improve the way grain was harvested from fields.

Both wanted a machine that could handle a portion or all of the task, making the labor intensive job more profitable for farmers.

McCormick gets credit for inventing the reaper, or harvester, and his name is recorded in history textbooks near other great inventors such as Eli Whitney or Thomas Edison.

Moore lost the race, but it may have been because he was so far ahead of McCormick that no one could see the genius of his invention.

Moore attempted to combine the reaper and the thresher into one big machine – a combine – that could clear fields of wheat and process the stalks along the way.

Moore's reaper-thresher promised to do the work of dozens of workers.

He also believed McCormick stole his ideas, used his blue-prints, and received fame and fortune from his invention. Moore spent much of his later embroiled in patent lawsuits.

Moore won a patent for a combine on June 28, 1836.

Although Moore was the first to patent a combine, it took decades for his idea to catch on.

June 29, 1864
The "Mystery Ship" sinks

The *Alvin Clark* was built in Detroit in 1847. It was 105 feet long, had a beam of 25 feet and two masts.

Captain William M. Higgie, of Racine, Wisconsin, sailed the lumber schooner with a small crew and an empty cargo hold on June 29, 1864 when a summer squall suddenly battered the ship and forced it underwater, almost entirely intact, near Chambers Island in Green Bay.

Higgie, a passenger and a crew member were lost. Two crew members survived and were picked up by a passing ship.

The sinking of the ship would not attract much attention. It became one of thousands of Great Lakes shipwrecks to be lost and the *Alvin Clark* would sit quietly on the floor of Lake Michigan for more than 100 years until it snagged a fisherman's nets.

He asked a diver, Frank Hoffman, to unhook the nets. Hoffman was amazed that the nets were snagged on an old wooden schooner on the lake bottom.

Hoffman and other divers would spend several years raising the ship, at first in secret and, then, once salvage rights were acquired, amid a lot of media attention. Items were brought up from the ship, souvenirs of an extinct way of life on the lakes – a captain's writing desk, three pennies, a brass locket, a wallet, a water pitcher, a crock of cheese and an old oil lamp.

The ship finally was raised from a depth of approximately 110 feet and towed to shore. Thousands of spectators looked on as the ship was brought to the surface in July, 1969.

Amid the salvage operation, the origin of the ship was a mystery – and was dubbed "Mystery Ship" – until one of the divers came across an article from the *Green Bay Advocate*. The June, 1864 article offered a clue – it described the loss of the *Alvin Clark*, which seemed to match in location and ship description the "Mystery Ship." Further research proved that to be the identity of the ship.

The salvagers attempted to find money to preserve the ship and a place where it could be put on public display.

The ship was taken to Menominee where it moored at the "Mystery Ship Seaport." There, the ship and its artifacts became a tourist attraction.

But the attraction didn't make enough in ticket sales to pay for the salvage or maintenance of the *Alvin Clark*.

As Hoffman struggled and failed to raise money, he wondered how so many resources could be put into the construction of replica schooners while an authentic schooner wasted away.

The Great Lakes Maritime Institute called the ship the oldest wooden schooner in the nation.

Hoffman sold the ship in 1987 to a group of investors who also failed to find a way to keep the ship and it wasted away further.

The ship was preserved after 105 years at the bottom of Lake Michigan but once the ship was out of that deep, cold water, it began to rapidly deteriorate.

The remnants of the ship were demolished with a bulldozer in May, 1994.

June 30, 1805
First governor of the Territory of Michigan

Although the British lost the Revolutionary War and the fledgling country was handed over to the upstart Americans, the British hung onto Detroit and Mackinac Island for 13 years.

It was not until 1796 when conflicts between the British and the French in Europe persuaded the British to relinquish the Michigan forts.

The territory was turned over to the Americans by September 1796.

Michigan became part of the Northwest Territory, the region established by Congress in 1787 north of the Ohio River and west of Pennsylvania.

The name of Michigan was first attached to the region in 1805, although as a political unit it looked somewhat different than it does today, containing more land in the south and very little of the Upper Peninsula.

William Hull, a Massachusetts native, was appointed governor and on June 30, 1805, he and the territory's other appointed officials set out to govern from the new capital in Detroit.

**Harriet Quimby,
First Lady of Flight**

Arcadia Historical Society

**Queen's Float at the Traverse City
Cherry Festival Parade,
circa mid-1900s**

SAM

**Hartwick Pines State Park,
largest state park
in the lower peninsula**

CHL

**Lewis Cass,
appointed governor of
Michigan Territory in 1813**

CHL

**U.S.S Wolverine,
oldest iron ore ship
in the world**
CHL

**1955 Lincoln Futura,
aka Batmobile**
CHL

**Early vacationers on porch
of Grand Hotel, built in 1887**
CHL

An amazing device
CHL

**Hollanders at the Tulip
Festival**
SAM

**Michigan's only four-term governor,
G. Mennen Williams and his wife, Nancy**
CHL

**Long-time friends,
Henry Ford
and Thomas Edison**

REO Motor Company
CHL

The Edmund Fitzgerald
CHL

**Batter up!
House of David
baseball players**
CHL

**Huson
Motor
Company in
business
from 1909
to 1954**
CHL

**Mackinac Bridge, world's longest suspension
bridge at its opening Nov. 1, 1957**
CHL

Governor William G. Milliken,
Michigan's longest-serving
governor

Isle Royale National Park
-- Benjamin Franklin
negotiated its inclusion
in the new American

CHL

Pioneer family
in late 1800s

SAM

"Sunday Best" dress code
at Bob-Lo's merry-go-round
in 1915

SAM

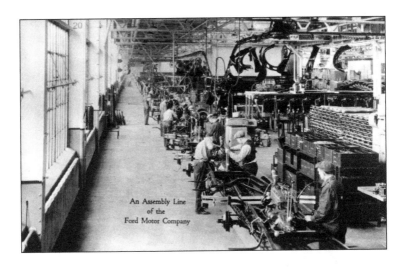

**Ford Motor Company
assembly line**
CHL

**The state capitol,
completed in 1873**
CHL

**Portrait of
Governor Kim Sigler
in front of his plane**
CHL

**French Missioary
Father Marquette,
founder of
Michigan's first
European settlement
at Sault Ste. Marie**

CHL

**Fort Brady
at Sault Ste. Marie,
site of last British flag
flown over
American soil**

CHL

**Detroit Tigers, 1909, with Ty Cobb,
Triple Crown Winner**

CHL

**The circus
comes
to Cheboygan
in 1908**
SAM

The Soo Locks
CHL

Calumet labor dispute in 1913
CHL

**Governor George Romney and
1968 candidate
for the presidency**
CHL

**Ford Rotunda --
once the fifth-leading
tourist destination
in the U.S.**
CHL

**Finnish weaver at work
in the Uppper Peninsula**
SAM

Woodward Avenue at turn of the 20th century
CHL

**President Gerald Ford
and First Lady Betty Ford
in Grand Rapids**
CHL

**The old Mormon print
shop on Beaver Island**
CHL

**Vacationland Ferry in the Straits of Mackinac
before construction of "Big Mac"**
CHL

197

**Michigan
Civil War soldiers
march in Detroit**
CHL

Ann Arbor Railroad Ferry
CHL

**Interior of Briggs Stadium,
renamed Tiger Stadium in 1960**
CHL

**Belle Isle,
largest island park
in the U.S.**
CHL

**Governor Jennifer Granholm,
Michigan's first
female governor**

**An outing on Mackinac
Island,
late 1800s**
SAM

Early Jefferson Avenue
CHL

Calumet miners
CHL

**Mining Camp
at Iron Cliffs**
CHL

Michigan Avenue Bridge in Lansing, 1870
CHL

Governor Hazen S. Pingree,
present at Appomattox
for surrender of
Robert E. Lee
CHL

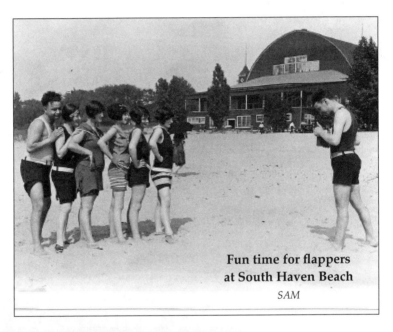

**Fun time for flappers
at South Haven Beach**
SAM

**Women at Swedish
Festival in Cadillac**
SAM

201

President Theodore Roosevelt --
in Marquette to testify
about his drinking habits
CHL

Northern Michigan
lumberjacks
CHL

Michigan Mining School in Houghton,
founded in 1885, now Michigan Technological University
CHL

July

July 1, 1959
Anatomy of a Murder Premiers

*A*natomy of a Murder, the film based on the work of an Upper Peninsula outdoorsman and lawyer who became a Michigan State Supreme Court Justice, premiered at the United Artists Theater in Detroit on July 1, 1959.

The movie, directed by Otto Preminger, starred James Stewart, Lee Remick and George C. Scott.

The courtroom drama tells the story of a defendant charged with murder who claimed insanity because the victim had raped his wife. The story was filmed in Big Bay and Marquette.

John D. Voelker, the author, wrote under the pen name Robert Traver. Voelker's life is described in the March 19 entry.

July 2, 1954
The "accidental" Daisy Air Rifle

The Plymouth Iron Windmill Company, located in the Michigan city that bears its name, began to produce and sell windmills for farmers around 1882.

The organizers discovered their product was not as popular as they had hoped and by 1888 the company was close to bankruptcy. The board of directors failed by one vote to liquidate the company.

An incentive was needed for farmers to buy the windmills.

A Plymouth watch repairman and inventor came to see the company's general manager, Lewis Cass Hough, with an idea.

Clarence Hamilton had invented an air rifle made of metal. Another air rifle had been manufactured out of wood – that rifle was also manufactured in Plymouth – but a metal air rifle was a novelty.

Hough fired the gun at an old shingle and liked the product immediately. He exclaimed, in the slang of the time, "Boy, that's a daisy!"

Hough convinced the board of directors that the Daisy Air Rifle could be used as a premium item to sell windmills.

The popularity of the air rifle soon eclipsed the windmills, according to the Daisy Airgun Museum. By 1890, the company's 25 employees produced 50,000 guns.

The company abandoned the manufacture of windmills in 1889.

By the end of the century, the company was the dominant manufacturer of air rifles and had seen 30 competitors come and go.

Hough died in January, 1902 and C.H. "Uncle Charlie" Bennett took his place, with Hough's son working as secretary and treasurer of the company.

The following year they introduced Daisy's flagship product, the No. 3 – a nickel-plated, 1,000-shot lever-action repeater rifle.

In the coming years, Bennett traveled the world, finding markets for the guns in countries as far away as China.

The company's most iconic gun, the Model 40 Red Ryder Western Carbine, was introduced in the 1940s. The Red Ryder became the obsessive focus of the main character, Ralphie, in the classic movie *A Christmas Story*.

Plymouth became the "air gun capital of the world" but that would end in 1958. The company closed its Plymouth plant that year and moved to Rogers, Arkansas. All that remains of Daisy in Plymouth is the Daisy Air Rifle exhibit at the Plymouth Historical Museum.

July 3, 1897
"Holocaust at Lake Ann"

Whoever wrote the headline for *The Morning Record*, a newspaper in Traverse City, was a bit melodramatic when he came up with "Holocaust at Lake Ann" to announce a fire that burned the village on July 3, 1897.

The fire wiped out the 50 buildings that comprised Lake Ann's downtown and left 75 families homeless. The estimated damage, in 1897 dollars, was placed at $100,000.

The newspaper reported one fatality – an 80-year-old woman who had escaped her home but returned to recover some valuables.

Until the fire, the residents of Lake Ann considered themselves rivals of Traverse City in a race to become the business center of northern lower Michigan.

The fire broke out mysteriously at William Habbler's sawmill about 1:30 p.m. The mill was idle as residents prepared for the following day's celebrations.

It was speculated that a spark from a tugboat ignited the blaze.

Traverse City residents rushed to fight the fire and offer aid. Firefighters arrived from Traverse City aboard a special train, making the journey to Lake Ann in 54 minutes.

Residents worked in the following days to make sure Lake Ann inhabitants were clothed, fed and sheltered. In addition, the mayor of Traverse City issued a proclamation asking for aid.

Lake Ann never became a business center to rival Traverse City, although it remains a charming village that attracts many summer residents who come for peace and quiet on a small lake.

July 4, 1832
Cholera arrives in Detroit

Cholera came to Michigan after the Black Hawk War in 1832. It arrived, along with a streamer – the Henry Clay – filled with troops on July 4 that year.

Some of the troops were stricken with cholera, an intestinal infection spread by contaminated water or food. When a soldier died of the disease, the steamer was ordered to leave the port the following day.

It was too late. There were 58 cases of cholera and 28 deaths within two weeks. Among the dead was the beloved priest, Father Gabriel Richard, who died later in the year, weakened from his work caring for the sick.

Towns outside Detroit set up road-blocks to prevent spread of the disease. Despite the measures, cholera spread inland and 11 persons died in Marshall.

This was the first of three cholera epidemics that would strike Detroit. The most severe broke out two years later and claimed seven percent of the city's population.

July 4, 1907
When the cat's away, the mice will play

It used to be illegal to sell alcohol on an official holiday, even a holiday like the Fourth of July, which had become associated with picnicking and merriment.

It may have been illegal to serve and drink alcohol, but the law was largely ignored.

However, not everyone was willing to sit by and let the scofflaws drink. The temperance movement was growing in influence, especially in conservative communities.

There was growing pressure to enforce the law. A major crackdown occurred on Independence Day, 1899, when 145 liquor dealers in Grand Rapids were arrested.

Eight years later, as July 4, 1907 approached, Prosecutor John S. McDonald announced that the law would be enforced in Grand Rapids again and citizens should expect no liquor sold on the holiday.

As the sun rose over that summer day, saloons remained shuttered and bottles corked.

McDonald, apparently satisfied that the citizens had adhered to his decree, boarded a train to spend the day on Lake Macatawa in Holland.

The train barely made it out of the station before the bars in Grand Rapids opened and the liquor flowed.

The city's afternoon newspaper carried an article about the city being awash in alcohol.

When McDonald learned of the imbibing he returned to Grand Rapids where he and members of the Anti-Saloon League toured the city, taking notes of the happenings inside the city's bars.

Approximately 50 people were arrested.

July 5, 2002
Cussing canoeist's conviction unconstitutional

One August day in 1998, Timothy Boomer of Roseville was canoeing on the Rifle River in Arenac County. He discovered despite the high thermometer reading, flowing river water is extremely cold.

Boomer fell out of his canoe and let loose with a string of profanities as he slapped the water to register his displeasure.

Michael Smith, his wife and their two children were canoeing about 40 yards behind Boomer that day. A county sheriff deputy patrolling the river also heard the commotion and the foul language. He was a quarter mile away.

Smith and the deputy objected to Boomer's profane rants.

The case made it to the office of a county prosecutor, who charged Boomer with a 105-year-old law that makes it a misdemeanor to curse in front of women and children.

Boomer contested the charges but he ultimately was convicted and sentenced to three days in jail and four days of community service.

The case drew international attention and the American Civil Liberties Union took over the defense of Boomer's case. ACLU lawyers argued that his speech, though it may have been vulgar, was protected under the First Amendment of the U.S. Constitution.

Boomer appealed to the Michigan Court of Appeals on the grounds that the law was unconstitutional. The court agreed and reversed his conviction.

In the court's opinion, released on July 5, 2002, Judge William B. Murphy wrote: "Allowing a prosecution where one utters 'insulting' language could possibly subject a vast percentage of the populace to a misdemeanor conviction."

July 6, 1854
Birth of the Republican Party

The Republican Party was formed when neither the Democrats nor the Whigs would take a solid stand against slavery.

The passage of the Kansas-Nebraska Act opened western territories to slavery and enraged many Midwesterners, who wanted at the very least an end to the spread of slavery.

Men opposed to the act convened in Jackson on this date to rally against slavery.

They met outside, "under the oaks," because the city had no hall large enough for all who wanted to attend. This was where the term "Republican" was first used to describe the fledgling party.

Jackson's claim to being the birthplace of the Republican Party was bolstered in 1910 when President William Howard Taft drove in a parade through the city as part of a celebration that dedicated a plaque at Second and West Franklin streets that declares "here … was born the Republican Party."

July 6, 1931
Della Reese born

Born Deloreese Patricia Early in Detroit, she began singing in her family's church at age six, and she toured with gospel singer Mahalia Jackson as a teenager. At age 18, she formed the Meditation Singers, the first group to break into Las Vegas with a gospel act. In the meantime, she also attended Wayne State University, but had to leave school before receiving a degree because of a family illness. Reese scored her first hit in 1957 with "And That Reminds Me." Her best-known single, "Don't You Know," was released two years later. In 1970 she became the first black woman to appear on *The Tonight Show with Johnny Carson*. After a string of minor television and film roles throughout the '70s and '80s, she played Tess on *Touched by an Angel* from 1994 to 2003.

July 7, 1948
Girl killed by bear

Three-year-old Carol Ann Pomranky lived with her family in a remote fire tower cabin in the eastern Upper Peninsula. Her father, who worked for the U.S. Forest Service, was away from home as Carol played outside the cabin at approximately 2:30 p.m. on July 7, 1948.

Inside the cabin, the girl's mother watched in horror as a black bear appeared, grabbed her daughter and dragged her into the woods.

The girl screamed for help and was attempting to crawl away from the bear as her mother reached the back door. Before the mother could scare the bear, the creature gripped the girl and went off into the woods.

Alex Van Luven, a woodsman from Brimley, located the girl's body with a tracking dog. Wayne Weston, a commercial fisherman, guarded the body as Van Luven went in search of the bear. Soon after Van Luven left, the 125-pound bear returned. Weston shot and killed it.

Even though bears primarily survive on the nuts and acorns they forage, they are opportunistic predators and even a small bear can kill a child or a fawn.

July 7, 1865
Michigan soldier hangs conspirators
in Lincoln assassination

Christian Rath, of Jackson, served in the 17th Michigan Infantry, was wounded at Antietam and twice found himself a prisoner of war.

Just days before Lincoln's death, Rath was promoted to brevet major and it fell to him to supervise the hanging of the conspirators in Lincoln's assassination.

Rath sewed the hoods and clapped three times when the hangman's door was to open.

The four conspirators sentenced to death for aiding John Wilkes Booth's assassination of Lincoln were hanged in Washington on July 7, 1865.

After that solemn event, Rath returned to Jackson but was haunted by the deed for the rest of his life.

In particular he was plagued by the hanging of Mary Ann Surratt, whom many believed was innocent.

Rath was convinced he was doomed to hell and became a Christian Scientist with the hope of saving his soul.

July 8, 1850
James Jesse Strang crowned King of Beaver

It didn't take long for James Jesse Strang and his flock of Mormon believers to decide that, even though they were latecomers to Beaver Island, they owned the place.

The fishermen and Indians who already lived there became wary when Strang appeared with a few followers – and even more wary when a few years later the Mormon population exploded.

Yet they didn't chase Strang and his people away when they first arrived. Rather, they hired his followers as workers, enabling the self-proclaimed prophet to get a foothold on the island.

Strang first visited the island in 1845, looking for a place to move his flock of Mormons who had splintered from the church led by Brigham Young. Strang and his people had first settled in Voree, Wisconsin, but he wanted someplace further away from disapproving non-Mormons, or gentiles.

In the spring of 1849, Mormons arrived on the island in large numbers.

The gentiles watched as the sect built cabins, erected mills and constructed a dock that threatened their ability to trade with the steamship traffic between Chicago and the Straits.

As their numbers grew, Strang and his followers asserted more power. Strang made it known that he would banish whiskey from the island. It was also clear to the non-Mormons he wanted them gone, too.

Also in 1849, as Strang worked to increase the size of his flock, Strang reconsidered his position against polygamy. He claimed he had a vision from God, allowing polygamy. The first order of business for Strang, age 36, was to take an 18-year-old woman as his second wife.

The following year, Strang would claim another vision from God that would make his power on the island absolute.

On July 8, 1850, Strang crowned himself King of Beaver Island in a ceremony held outside in the town he named for himself, St. James.

July 9, 1822
Henry Rowe Schoolcraft's
first council with Indians

Colonel Hugh Brady led the 250 men of the Second U. S. Regiment as the unit made camp in a wilderness outpost in Sault Ste. Marie during the onset of winter, 1821. One of the first efforts was to restore a complex of dilapidated buildings used in the past by fur traders.

The Indians looked on in disdain, thinking the new development could not be good for their dominion over the wilderness.

On July 9, 1822, Henry Rowe Schoolcraft, appointed by the federal government to be Michigan's superintendant for Indian affairs, sat down for his first diplomatic effort with Indians around Sault Ste. Marie.

When he addressed the Indians that day, Schoolcraft said it seemed to be well received.

Well received by everyone, that is, except Chippewa Indian chief Sassaba.

Sassaba came to council dressed in the scarlet uniform of a British soldier, unlike the other chiefs, who arrived in their native dress. Sassaba resented the Americans because they had killed his brother in a battle.

Sassaba responded to Schoolcraft's speech with a hostile outburst. Brady interceded, explaining to Sassaba that the Americans were going to build a fort. He added that the Americans would respect ground considered sacred by the Indians and avoid that land when constructing the fort.

Sassaba suspected that the arrival of Americans was different from the camps of the French and English, who wanted furs but did not want to settle – the Americans planned to stay and cut down the forest, ruining the land for the Indian way of life.

In his memoir, Schoolcraft recorded the death of Sassaba just over a month after his meeting with him.

"This chief, who has from the day of our first landing here, rendered himself noted for his sentiments of opposition to the Americans, met with a melancholy fate yesterday," Schoolcraft wrote.

Schoolcraft added that Sassaba would go on drinking benders for several days and had been on one of those sprees when he last saw him, walking through the village wearing only a wolf skin pulled over his body.

He was drunk when he attempted to head down the St. Mary's River in a canoe and was unable to pull to shore before he reached the rapids. That was the last that anyone saw of Sassaba.

July 9, 1975
Jack White born

Born John Anthony Gillis to a large, musical Catholic family in Detroit, White began playing drums, guitar and piano at an early age. As a young man, White considered becoming a priest but was drawn to music instead.

He played in numerous bands around Detroit while working as an upholsterer. White found his sound after he met and married his first wife, Meg White. He took her name and the couple later claimed they were siblings. The band, the White Stripes, was formed after Meg tried out a drum kit and Jack liked the sound.

The two-person band, known for appearing only in the colors red, black and white, attracted a large following for their strange, energetic sound and they released six albums in 10 years. The couple found their biggest success after they divorced and released *White Blood Cells*. Jack White later remarried and has since moved to Nashville. He also appeared in the film *Cold Mountain*.

July 10, 1887
Grand Hotel opens

A century that opened with Mackinac Island as one of North America's most strategically important military posts came to an end with the island having found a completely different identity.

In the late 1800s, Mackinac Island grew into one of the most popular resorts in the country. Operators of railroads and steamships recognized the burgeoning tourist industry could keep them in business even if all the state's trees had been cut down.

The Michigan Central Railroad, the Grand Rapids & Indiana Railroad and the Detroit & Cleveland Steamship Navigation Company came together to build an enormous hotel – the Grand Hotel – on the island, one that would become a destination in and of itself. It was a majestic building that would keep passengers paying fares to ride trains and steamships.

Steamships arrived from Chicago, Detroit, Cleveland, Buffalo, Montreal and elsewhere with vacationers after it opened on July 10, 1887.

212

The first year rates were between $3 and $5 per night.

The hotel features what is commonly cited as the longest wooden hotel front porch in the world at 660 feet and has hosted five U.S. presidents – Harry S Truman, John F. Kennedy, Gerald Ford, George H.W. Bush and Bill Clinton.

July 11, 1796
Americans take Detroit

A long time passed between the American victory in the Revolutionary War and the day when Americans finally took Detroit from the British.

Captain Moses Porter and 65 troops arrived to claim Detroit for the Americans on July 11, 1796, giving Porter credit for raising the first American flag over Detroit.

Even though the British had signed away Michigan to the Americans in the Treaty of Paris 13 years earlier, Britain stubbornly claimed the region and maintained the forts that protected fur-trading routes.

The Americans had a tough time convincing the British to abandon the valuable fur-trading route. The British hoped the American colonies would squabble among themselves over ownership of the Great Lakes region, making it possible for them take much of the territory for themselves.

They also hoped conflicts with Indian tribes would stem the Americans' resolve and the British incited the Indians against the Americans.

Over the years, Britain became distracted by disputes with Spain and France, the fur trade declined, American settlers flooded into the West, and the British foothold in Michigan began to slip.

Still, they were reluctant to give up the Upper Great Lakes.

When John Jay went to London as a special minister to negotiate a settlement of the western boundaries for Canada and the United States, the British at first refused to turn over Michigan.

Then came news of the victory of American General Anthony Wayne at the Battle of the Fallen Timbers against Indians loyal to the English.

Finally the British were ready to honor the boundaries hammered out 13 years earlier.

With the Jay Treaty of 1794, England agreed to cede Detroit and Michilimackinac to the Americans.

July 11, 1846
First newspaper published in the U.P.

The first Upper Peninsula newspaper was published in Copper Harbor, dated July 11, 1846.

Publisher E.D. Burr and Editor John N. Ingersoll published the weekly until winter arrived and the newspaper discontinued for the season.

The following year the paper reappeared in Sault Ste. Marie. The four-page weekly was called the *Lake Superior News and Miner's Journal*. The paper would later change hands and move to Marquette where it would become the *Marquette Mining Journal*.

July 12, 1901
A golden crucifix discovered in Frankfort: artifact or hoax?

The construction of a new hotel in Frankfort led to a curious discovery by diggers: a golden crucifix. The townspeople thought the cross, which was 11 inches tall and 5 inches across with gold plating, was the property of Father Jacques Marquette and had been buried for 225 years.

Marquette may have died in Frankfort in 1675, although residents of Ludington have a pretty good argument that he died in their city that year.

It is also commonly accepted that a year or so after his death, Marquette's remains were exhumed by Indians and reburied in St. Ignace.

But over the years, Frankfort and Ludington have fought over their claim to the famous missionary.

The newspaper article says the crucifix, which appeared to be of French origin, was in the possession of the hotel contractor and that he planned to give it to the Kent County Historical Museum in Grand Rapids.

It's possible the discovery of the cross was a hoax perpetrated by the hotel owners to drum up business.

July 12, 1982
The end of the Checker Cab

The final Checker Cab rolled off the company's production line in Kalamazoo on July 12, 1982.

It was hailed in newspapers as the end of an era; however, Checker Cabs continued to prowl American streets for years to come.

In Kalamazoo, it also meant the loss of a major employer.

The company laid off approximately 200 employees when the plant closed. Checker Cab began in Chicago around 1922 and later merged with another Chicago cab manufacturer. The company later acquired the Dort Automobile factory in Kalamazoo and moved its operations there.

Checker competed with Yellow Cab – competition that escalated into violence in the 1920s when the home of Checker's owner was firebombed.

In its heyday Checker Cabs were synonymous with large cities, with 5,000 registered in New York City.

In 1997, the *New York Times* reported that only one Checker Cab remained licensed in the city.

July 13, 1951
Death of Michigan's last Civil War veteran

Orland LeValley died in April 1948, leaving Michigan without any surviving Civil War veterans.

That changed about five months later, when Joseph Clovese moved from Louisiana to Pontiac to live with friends. He was 104 years old.

Born January 30, 1844, Clovese was a slave until age 17, when he ran off to join a group of Union soldiers.

He served as a drummer boy in the battle of Vicksburg and later enlisted in a regiment of "colored troops."

After the war, Clovese worked on Mississippi steamboats and on a crew that strung telegraph wires through the South.

It took some time after Clovese moved to Michigan before people realized the state was again home to a Civil War veteran.

Clovese called the *Pontiac Press* to ask where he could find the nearest Grand Army of the Republic Post, an organization for Civil War veterans. He learned there were none – the last closed upon the death of LeValley.

Nonetheless, Clovese stayed active among the remaining veterans around the country. He attended the last National Encampment of the G.A.R. in Indianapolis in 1949. Of 12 veterans who were alive at that time, Clovese was one of six to attend.

Pontiac adopted Clovese as one of its own and held celebrations for the old soldier for his next three birthdays, including his final one when he turned 107, according to the Michigan department of the Sons of Union Veterans of the Civil War.

Clovese died on July 13, 1951 at a veteran's hospital in Dearborn.

July 14, 1863
Michigan soldier captures enemy flag;
wins Congressional Medal of Honor

Years after they happened, Charles M. Holton described the events of a day when he and other Michigan soldiers played

215

a pivotal role in determining the outcome of the Civil War.

Holton, then a 25-year-old soldier from Battle Creek, served in the Michigan Cavalry Brigade when he found himself at Falling Waters, Virginia on the morning of July 14, 1863.

General George Armstrong Custer led the Michigan Brigade into enemy territory where one Union brigade from Michigan found itself face-to-face with four enemy brigades.

A division of General Robert E. Lee's army had failed to cross the Potomac. The Michigan soldiers found the Confederate fighters dug in and supported by artillery.

Despite a hail of bullets that met them as they entered the enemy's territory, Holton said the fighters cut their way through the Confederate stronghold.

"Seeing the color-sergeant of the 55th Virginia fall wounded, I sprang from my horse and seized the colors," Holton recalled. "As I remounted, I heard the wounded color-bearer say, 'You Yanks have been after that old flag for a long time, but you never got it before.' While we were forming up to charge them again from the rear, the Confederates threw down their arms, and we marched 400 prisoners from the field."

Years later, Holton would be awarded the Congressional Medal of Honor for taking the enemy's flag.

Holton was one of 70 soldiers from Michigan to receive that award for action in the Civil War.

Taking the enemy's flag from the battlefield was considered a critical turning point in a Civil War battle; an enormous moral victory for the takers and a disheartening blow for the losers.

July 15, 1940
If you seek giant shoes, look about you

In the window of Snyder's Shoes, an enormous pair of shoes beckons strollers down River Street in Manistee.

The shop doesn't specialize in gigantic shoes; its proprietors sell a variety of normal-sized footwear.

The shoes are there because on July 15, 1940, Robert Pershing Wadlow, the world's tallest man, died during a visit to Manistee and left his shoes behind.

Wadlow reached the incredible height of 8 feet, 11 inches tall. He weighed 490 pounds. His out-of-control growth was due to an overactive pituitary gland, a condition that could be treated today.

Wadlow was born in Alton, Illinois in 1918 and as an infant he was below average size.

That changed as he grew, quickly overtaking his four siblings who grew at a normal rate.

By age 13, Wadlow stood over 7 feet tall and became the world's tallest Boy Scout.

At 18, he had grown to over 8 feet tall and weighed nearly 400 pounds. He wore size 37 shoes that had to be specially made and cost $100 per pair.

Because of his odd podiatric needs, Wadlow signed a contract at age 20 with the International Shoe Company. He was to receive free shoes in exchange for going on a promotional tour.

He travelled around the country but he didn't plan on making a life of being a circus sideshow act. Wadlow planned to attend college and become a lawyer.

Early in his 20s, however, his enormous frame began to take a toll on his health.

He needed braces in order to walk and he began to lose feeling in his feet.

In early July, 1940, Wadlow was on a tour stop in Manistee when one of his leg braces dug into his leg and caused a blister, leading to an infection.

Doctors did what they could, performing blood transfusions and surgery but Wadlow's condition worsened. He died in his sleep in a Manistee hotel room on July 15.

Wadlow left behind some curious artifacts of his towering existence. His likeness is preserved in statues on display in Ripley's Believe it or Not! museums.

His hometown in Illinois erected a statue in his honor in 1984.

And, although his family destroyed his belongings after his death so they would not become morbid collectors' items, a pair of Wadlow's shoes remains in Manistee.

July 16, 1812
War of 1812 breaks out in Michigan

Despite treaties and peace agreements, tension between the Americans and the British in Canada never really settled down in the first decades of the United States.

The British had long incited Indians into violence against Americans, who had a ceaseless hunger to settle further west.

In 1811, after the defeat of Shawnee Chief Tecumseh at Tippecanoe, the discovery of so many British-manufactured weapons in the hands of the Indians served as a warning of what was to come.

Elsewhere in America, the British broke treaty agreements, captured French ships in U.S. waters and treated the American government with contempt.

Finally, President James Madison declared war on the British in 1812. In Michigan, however, British forces appear to have been better prepared for war than their American opponents.

The War of 1812 began in Michigan when British troops in Canada left their fort on St. Joseph Island on the St. Mary's River and set out for Mackinac Island late on July 16, 1812.

Mackinac Commander Lieutenant Porter Hanks was unaware that war had been declared. He led a post that consisted of 57 men, including officers.

Captain Charles Roberts, commander of the British forces, devised an ingenious plan to overwhelm the American forces on Mackinac.

The fort on Mackinac Island had been built part way up on a hill. That left higher ground.

When Roberts arrived on the island he and his men hastily crossed into the interior and marched to the top of the hill behind the fort, setting up a six-pound cannon, and positioning his company to either take the fort outright or take it in an overwhelming slaughter.

This account is continued in the following entry.

July 17, 1812
The surrender of Fort Mackinac

Early in the morning of July 17, 1812, Porter Hanks, lieutenant of artillery and commander of the fort on the island, looked up the hill behind Fort Mackinac.

There he saw enemy troops that greatly outnumbered his own and an "iron six pounder" aimed at his position. All Porter could do was to raise a white flag.

Hanks wrote to Governor William Hull weeks later to explain the surrender. Hull could probably empathize with Hanks. He would soon surrender the fort in Detroit to the British.

Hanks learned from a trusted Indian interpreter a day before the attack that Indians from several tribes were gathering en masse with British forces north of the island.

Hanks sent a scout to spy on the British who was soon captured, taken prisoner and sent back with a message – surrender.

The British told him any civilians who sought refuge in the fort would be slaughtered by Indians. Inhabitants of the island were to be taken to the west side and quietly put under British guard.

The decision to surrender was a fortunate one for Hanks.

Hanks and his men were allowed to leave the island and retreat to Detroit, where they were stationed when that fort was surrendered a month later.

July 17, 1824
No more Hurons

Politicians in Michigan decided that too many rivers and places in the territory had been named after the Huron Indian tribe, causing confusion.

The Legislative Council of the Michigan Territory passed a resolution on July 17, 1824 stripping the Huron name from all but two of the rivers which bore that name.

The name Huron comes from the French term, "Quelles hures," which means "What unkept heads." Legend has it that was the French reaction to the wild and strangely-dyed hair of the band of Indians they encountered upon arriving in the Upper Great Lakes.

The resolution, however, did not stop the organization of Huron County, in the thumb which happened in 1859.

July 18, 1938
Ferry service between Detroit and Windsor ends

For decades, residents of Detroit and Windsor depended on ferries to shuttle them across the half-mile expanse of the Detroit River.

Ferry service hung on even after the Ambassador Bridge opened in 1929 and the Detroit-Windsor Tunnel a year later.

But within several years, the business no longer made sense and the owners of the ferries *LaSalle* and *Cadillac* ceased operation.

On the final day the service was offered, July 18, 1938, thousands of passengers showed up for one last leisurely ride across the river.

July 19, 1838
Michigan celebrates construction of a canal

Michigan had just become a state when it smartly eyed the new and successful Erie Canal, which stretched across New York.

It seemed that a canal that eased transportation across the young nation could bring an economic boom. Any option that made the Detroit to Chicago route faster was studied.

Early Michiganders decided that instead of making the long trip around the Lower Peninsula through the Straits of Mackinac, ships could travel across the bottom of the state, if only there were a canal.

Plans called for the use of the Clinton River from the long-since abandoned village of Belvidere to Mt. Clemens. Digging was to begin in the village of Frederick toward Utica, Rochester and Pontiac.

The muli-million dollar canal would then cross Michigan to the Kalamazoo River, making the connection to Lake Michigan.

In 1837, the state appropriated $40,000 to begin the canal's first leg.

On July 19, 1838, the *Detroit Free Press* announced the festivities that were planned to celebrate the beginning of the project.

The city of Mt. Clemens was awakened by the firing of a signal gun, followed by speeches and plenty of food and drink.

Governor Stevens T. Mason turned the first shovel of dirt.

Michigan Every Day

Actual work on the canal began the following day. The work was parceled into one-mile increments from Frederick toward Utica. Laborers filled the region, jabbing shovels into the ground and carrying wheelbarrows of earth from the canal. Locks and an aqueduct were constructed.

But in 1843, the Morris Canal and Banking Company, the company that financed the project, went bankrupt. Workers went unpaid and walked away from the project.

Meanwhile, railroads were spreading around the country. By 1846, the state government acknowledged the canal project was a failure. People realized railroads would make better transporters of goods and people across the country than canals.

Segments of the doomed canal are still apparent in parts of Shelby Township in Macomb County.

They can be seen along the 2.5-mile nature trail in River Bends Park and a segment of the canal crosses 22 Mile Road just west of Shelby. There is a state historical marker at Bloomer State Park where John R Road ends.

July 20, 1831
Michigan's first tourist

When Alexis de Tocqueville embarked on a nine-month fact-finding tour of the United States for the French government, the notable author spent some of his time in Michigan.

Tocqueville was busy composing his book, *Democracy in America*, which would go on to become a staple in the study of American government.

In other writings, Tocqueville mused specifically about his time in Michigan.

The philosopher expected to find primitive people in Michigan but he concluded the state's inhabitants had formed a modern society, even if their world was dour and humorless.

Tocqueville was particularly struck by the wilderness in Michigan. In his account, *Quinze Jours au De'sert*, Tocqueville wrote, "Everything there is abrupt and unexpected; everywhere, extreme civilization borders and in one sense confronts nature left to run riot."

He reached Detroit on the afternoon of July 20. "Detroit is a little town of two or three thousand souls, founded by the Jesuits in the middle of the forest in 1710, and still having a great number of French families."

He found the inhabitants unwilling to accept or understand that he was there on a sightseeing mission. The notion that someone would come to Michigan as a tourist was inconceivable.

"To break through almost impenetrable forests, to cross deep rivers, to brave pestilential marshes, to sleep out in the damp woods, those are exertions that the American readily contemplates if it is a question of earning a guinea; for that is the point. But that one should do such things from curiosity is more than his mind can take in.

"Besides, living in the wilds, he only appreciates the work of man. He will gladly send you off to see a road, a bridge, or a fine village. But that one should appreciate great trees and the beauties of solitude, that possibility completely passes him by."

After a few days in Detroit, Tocqueville moved up toward Pontiac and Saginaw.

When he arrived at a small settlement of cabins on the Flint River, Tocqueville wrote that he was greeted by a black bear used as a watchdog by the settlers. Tocqueville reached Saginaw, a settlement located further into Michigan's wilderness than any other, where he was attacked by massive numbers of mosquitoes and spent time with the Indians and white settlers of the region.

Tocqueville spent two weeks in Michigan, part of a nine-month expedition he undertook to learn about the United States for the French government.

July 21, 1865
Birth of Fred Warner, cheese factory owner and governor

Fred Malthy Warner was born July 21, 1865 in Nottinghamshire, England and brought by his family to Michigan.

At three months of age, he was orphaned and adopted by the family of P.D. Warner, who served as a state senator and a representative.

He grew up in Farmington and attended Michigan Agricultural College.

Warner worked at his adoptive father's general store and started a cheese factory in 1889. He went on to open 12 more.

The Fred M. Warner Cheese Company made Warner wealthy and, at its height, the factories manufactured two million pounds of cheese per year.

Warner began life in politics at age 25 when he was elected to the Farmington Village board of trustees, where he served for nine years.

He then became a state senator and from 1901 to 1904 he was Michigan's secretary of state under Governor Aaron T. Bliss.

He became governor in 1904 as a Republican and served three terms through 1910.

He was considered a progressive, advocating regulation of the railroad and insurance industries, conservation and women's suffrage.

He also promoted highway construction and a law that created government inspections of factories.

Warner died at age 57 of kidney failure.

July 22, 1930
Mayor Charles Bowles recalled

Mayor Charles Bowles came to power in Detroit at a bad time.

He was elected in 1930 on a platform that promised cuts to the city's budget.

Once in office, he had to confront the Great Depression.

The unemployed lined the streets looking for help from the government just as Bowles was supposed to be cutting city departments.

When citizens marched on city hall to call for relief, Bowles ordered the city's mounted police to disperse the crowd.

His proposal caused immediate ire from the people and he was recalled in a special election within seven months of taking office.

One of Bowles' fiercest opponents was murdered hours after the recall. See the entry for July 23.

July 22, 1968
Gruesome murders discovered in Good Hart

On July 22, 1968, a caretaker visited the cottage owned by Richard Robison near Good Hart, a village overlooking Lake Michigan between Harbor Springs and Cross Village. Before the man reached the door of the cabin, he was repelled by the stench of death. He left and called police.

When police arrived, under a wave of flies they discovered the bodies of Richard Robison, 42, and his family: Shirley, his 40-year-old wife; sons, Richard Jr., 19, and Randall, 12; and daughter, Susan, 8.

The bodies were riddled with bullets. Police said a .25-caliber handgun had been used to shoot each victim in the head. Susan Robison may have been sexually assaulted.

Police determined the mass killing had taken place about a month earlier and at first they suspected it had to be the work of more than one killer.

Decades later the case remains unsolved, but police have said evidence pointed to Joseph Scolaro, who was a partner with Robison in a Detroit-area advertising business.

Scolaro was never charged, despite circumstantial evidence that tied him to the crime. He committed suicide five years after the murders and left a note in which he maintained his innocence.

Scolaro owned guns that police believed were the kind used in the murders, he had no alibi for almost half of the day of the killings, and he had had an argument on the telephone with Robison on the day of the slayings.

Police built a case against Scolaro based on ballistics but the county prosecutor never brought charges. The prosecutor apparently believed the crime could not have been committed by one person and he wanted evidence that linked the crime to accomplices before bringing a case.

The case was revived in 2003 when Emmet County Sheriff Peter Wallin found a box of evidence shortly after taking office.

The box was discovered in the back of a closet in the sheriff's office.

Detectives pored through hundreds of pages of documents in the box, as well as the dusty case file.

Police sought new avenues for a lead in the case through DNA and ballistics but they eventually closed the case.

They believed Scolaro committed the murders and that he acted alone.

July 23, 1872
The "Real McCoy" product patented

Elijah McCoy became a great success in a time when most black people in America struggled to survive.

Born in 1844 in Ontario, Canada to fugitive slaves, McCoy became a mechanical engineer and an inventor.

His inventions may be long forgotten but he gave Americans the expression "The Real McCoy."

When McCoy was young, his family returned to the United States and settled in Ypsilanti, where McCoy developed an interest in machinery.

After finishing school, McCoy traveled to Edinburgh, Scotland, where he completed an apprenticeship in mechanical engineering.

Back in America, McCoy faced racism and instead of practicing in his chosen field he was forced to work as a fireman for the Michigan Central Railroad.

His job duties at the railroad included oiling the engines. McCoy did not merely oil the engines, however. He considered the process and, drawing on his training, came up with a better method to do the job.

Trains previously had to be stopped while a worker laboriously oiled the moving parts. McCoy invented a "lubricating cup," which automatically oiled the engine as it ran.

McCoy patented his first invention, the automatic lubricator, on July 23, 1872.

It proved so effective that it became known as "The Real McCoy," to distinguish it from inferior pretenders.

At the time of his death, McCoy's company, the Detroit Lubricator Company, had patented 78 inventions. Most of McCoy's work had to do with lubrication of trains but he also patented an ironing board and a lawn sprinkler.

July 23, 1913
Strike in copper country

Changes were coming to the boom region of the Keweenaw, where for 40 years there had been prosperity and peace between copper mine companies and miners. In the early 20th century, the amount of copper in the rock began to diminish while the price of the metal fell. As a result, copper companies looked for ways to cut costs.

To spend less on labor, the companies introduced a technical innovation – the one-man drill.

Until this time, it was a job done by two men. The one-man drill meant less work was available for miners. It also made the work more dangerous because miners had to venture into the caverns alone.

The tensions created an opening for the Western Federation of Miners, a union that sought to represent the Keweenaw's workforce.

The mine bosses considered the Western Federation a radical, Marxist organization to be broken at all costs. As the union grew more powerful, a showdown became inevitable.

It began when a strike was called on July 23, 1913 and violence broke out.

Governor Woodbridge N. Ferris received a telegram from the Michigan National Guard that day informing him of the initial chaos.

Striking workers used violence to prevent anyone from working. Miners who emerged from the shafts that day were beaten.

The workers demanded an eight-hour day, higher wages and the prohibition of the one-man drill.

The Houghton County Sheriff brought in strike-breaking thugs and Ferris called in the National Guard.

Violence continued on the Keweenaw throughout the year, culminating with the Italian Hall disaster (see Dec. 24).

The strike ended the following April. The workers won an eight-hour day and higher wages but they were forced to live with the one-man drill.

July 23, 1930
Jerry Buckley assassinated

For weeks, Gerald E. "Jerry" Buckley ranted on his radio show against Charles Bowles, the mayor of Detroit.

He spent the evening of July 22, 1930 broadcasting the results of the recall election. The results were favorable from Buckley's perspective – he could take a lot of the credit for ousting the man who *Time* magazine called "the big, bluff Charles Bowles" from the mayor's office.

At approximately 1 a.m., Buckley finished his radio show, which broadcast from the La Salle Hotel in Detroit. He was in the hotel's lobby reading a late edition newspaper about the election results.

Suddenly three men entered the lobby and walked straight for Buckley. A barrage of bullets was fired and the men were gone as quickly as they had come. Buckley was dead, riddled by 11 bullets.

Mayor Bowles was recalled partly due to of a bad economy but also because he was thought to have connections with gangsters. Detroit residents could not help but whisper their suspicions.

Governor Fred Warren Green flew from Holland to Detroit to calm a city terrified over the murder of a popular broadcaster.

Green threatened to order martial law unless the city's crime wave abated. Buckley was the 11th homicide in the city in less than three weeks.

Approximately 100,000 residents lined up to view Buckley's casket. His brother Paul, a former prosecutor, said he believed his brother's murder was retaliation for the campaign he waged against Bowles.

The police commissioner, who was appointed by Bowles, countered with a dubious charge that Buckley was an extortionist and racketeer. He maintained that Buckley was killed because of the company he kept. Meanwhile the governor oversaw the murder investigation and made sure that it was conducted independently of the Detroit police department. Three men were indicted for Buckley's death.

They were tried the following April and found not guilty.

Time magazine summed up the case this way: "Still unanswered was Detroit's question – 'Who killed Jerry Buckley and why?'"

July 24, 1701
Detroit: Oldest continuously inhabited community in Michigan

A side from the Jesuit priests who came to Michigan because they wanted to save the souls of Indians, Europeans who ventured into the Upper Great Lakes were driven by one item – beaver pelts.

The French had already settled in Sault Ste. Marie and St. Ignace before they looked to Lower Michigan.

Antoine Laumet de la Mothe, sieur de Cadillac, fresh from a stint in command at the Sault, recognized the strategic importance of the river that connected Lake St. Clair and Lake Erie and petitioned the French government for permission to establish a fur trading settlement there.

Cadillac received the approval. On July 24, 1701, on a schooner loaded with barrels of brandy, Cadillac and approximately 200 fellow Frenchmen and Indians landed on the bank of the Detroit River and founded the City of Detroit, which took its name from the French expression for "the strait."

King Louis XIV granted the first tract of land, 15 acres, to Cadillac.

The French had not landed in Detroit earlier because the Iroquois Indians prevented them from settling so far south. Until the 18th century, the French made do with their outpost at Michilimackinac.

By the time Cadillac arrived in Detroit, the French had decided to ignore the threat of the Iroquois: they were more concerned with British advances into the region.

In addition, they had cultivated good relations with other Indian tribes in the region and those Indians were growing dependent on trade with the French. Huron, Ottawa and Potawatomi Indians had accepted Cadillac's offer to live near the new settlement and conduct trade.

Cadillac built Fort Pontchartrain in Detroit, near the present-day intersection of Jefferson Avenue and Shelby Street.

It should be noted that Cadillac established the first European settlement of Detroit. That area of wilderness was known to be home to a village called Teuchsa Grondie, settled by Indians around 1620.

Earlier settlements, such as the Sault, St. Ignace or Niles, were founded by missionaries but abandoned before they were settled again. In contrast, the settlers of Detroit brought their wives and families and planted roots.

Since that day in July of 1701, Detroit held on and has been a fort, a village or a city ever since.

July 25, 1812
First Americans killed in the War of 1812

The Fort on Mackinac Island had been taken by the British in the War of 1812.

From Detroit, American Commander William Hull moved his forces to Sandwich, now a neighborhood in Windsor. He issued a proclamation to the Canadians, telling them to stay in their homes because America had been "driven to arms" against Great Britain. Hull urged the Canadians to choose the American side: "I come to find enemies, not to make them. I come to protect, not to injure you," Hull said.

When Hull was absent during his trips to Detroit every few days, Colonel Duncan McArthur took command of American forces in Canada.

On July 22, McArthur decided to send forces to attack Fort Malden, which was located in what is now Amherstburg, Ontario.

The plan stalled as the American forces were unable to find a way to get their artillery through the swamps.

Two days later, McArthur learned that a party of Indians had been spotted near Turkey Creek. He sent a militia of some 120 men to fend them off.

The militia found the Indians the next day, on July 25, 1812. A battle ensued, but the band of Indians had been reinforced and they broke the American soldiers' line. Confusion and retreat ensued.

Six American soldiers died in the skirmishes, becoming the first U.S. casualties in the War of 1812

July 25, 1817
Detroit's first regularly published newspaper

Technically, Detroit's first newspaper, *Michigan Essay or, the Impartial Observer*, was first published on Aug. 31, 1809.

However, only one issue hit the streets and there is no record that a second edition ever was published.

The *Detroit Gazette* is credited as the city's first regularly published newspaper.

Its first issue, published July 25, 1817, was followed by subsequent issues until 1830, when fire destroyed its plant on Atwater Street near Wayne.

July 26, 1701
Founding of Michigan's oldest church, Ste. Anne de Detroit

Just two days after the French landed in Michigan and founded Detroit they began building a Catholic church. Just west of where Jefferson Avenue and Griswald Street are today, construction of the structure began on July 26, 1701, Ste. Anne's Day. That first church was destroyed in a fire a little more than a year later.

For a while services were held in a make-shift building inside Fort Pontchartrain.

The church's eighth (and present) home is at 1000 Ste. Anne Street near the Ambassador Bridge.

Ste. Anne's has been continuously holding services longer than any other church in Michigan.

July 27, 1876
Founder of Holland dies

Albertus Christian van Raalte, a Reformed Church pastor, wanted a place where he could lead his band of Dutch immigrants.

Van Raalte's flock of 53 members followed him across the Atlantic to New York and onto the shores of Lake Michigan where they founded Holland and, later, Hope College.

227

Michigan Every Day

The group of Calvinist separatists had been persecuted in the Netherlands. The location of Holland, fairly cut off from other developments in the state, suited them.

The land also was promising because of the Black River, which led into Lake Michigan and Lake Macatawa.

However, there was a hitch – the land already was inhabited by Ottawa Indians. The Indians and the stern Dutch clashed but, as in other locations, the white settlers won and the Indians were forced to relocate. The Ottawa moved to Northport, not far from where their descendants are today, in Peshawbestown on the Leelanau Peninsula.

Van Raalte envisioned Holland as a Christian community, but division and strife among the settlers – and presumably the U.S. Constitution – prevented a church-state from truly forming on the shores of Lake Michigan.

Holland is known today for its Tulip Time Festival, which takes place in early May. Holland also is known as the "City of Churches." It has 170 of them, and lays claim to kicking off the "What would Jesus do?" plastic bracelet fad.

Holland's founder died on July 27, 1876, five years after he saw his city destroyed by fire.

July 27, 1884
Loss of the steamer John M. Osborn

It was a warm evening and the fog was thick around Whitefish Point in Lake Superior.

The steam barge *John M. Osborn* left Marquette with a load of iron ore with two barges in tow, the *George W. Davis* and the *Thomas Gawn*.

The fog forced the captain to blow the ship's horn three times every two minutes, according to shipping regulations for such conditions.

But one blast of the horn brought an immediate answer from a ship bearing down out of the fog into the *Osborn*.

The steel prow of the Canadian Pacific steamer *Alberta* emerged from the fog, speedily heading for the *Osborn*.

The *Alberta* crashed into the *Osborn* near her boiler room. The ships became locked together, but it was the *Osborn* that was going down fast. Crew from that ship jumped onto the other. A passenger aboard the *Alberta* jumped aboard the *Osborn* to save one of her injured crew. Just as he reached the injured sailor, the ships separated and the *Osborn* rapidly sunk. Four men, including the *Alberta's* heroic passenger, went down with the ship.

The *Osborn* shipwreck lay undiscovered for a century until she was found in 1984 northwest of Whitefish Point at a depth of 170 feet.

The Michigan Department of Transportation considered the

Osborn to be significant in the story of Great Lakes shipping and funded research into her history.

July 28, 1967
Final day of Detroit Riots

For many Detroiters, the first signal that something was wrong in their city arrived during a Detroit Tigers game.

In the small screens of television sets across the area, pillars of black smoke could be seen rising from behind the stadium where the Tigers played the New York Yankees. As the teams played baseball, the city burned.

The violence was set off when police raided a party in a black neighborhood on July 23, 1967. The police made the bust on the grounds that the party was a "blind pig," a place where alcohol is sold without a license. To the residents of the neighborhood and the partygoers who had gathered to welcome home a black soldier from Vietnam, the police raid was an invitation to revolt.

Tensions between the black community and the largely white police force had been brewing for many years and black citizens insisted they had been mistreated by the police.

When 82 people were arrested at the party, pandemonium broke loose. Hundreds of persons rushed into the streets to protest.

U.S. Representative John Conyers Jr. appeared on the streets with a bullhorn, attempting to calm the crowd but was shouted down.

Mayor Jerome P. Cavanagh called hundreds of state police troopers into the city but the violence was already out of control.

A curfew to keep residents off the streets after 9 p.m. failed to quell the violence. Bars and theaters were ordered to close. President Lyndon Johnson sent thousands of National Guard troops into Detroit.

None of these measures stopped the violence that flowed through the streets of Detroit over several hot July days.

When the riots ended, the official tally counted at least 43 dead, more than 500 injured and over 7,000 arrested.

Three of those deaths happened at the Algiers Hotel on July 26 after a raid by Detroit police, there on a report of a sniper.

Police were on edge because they were the target of sniper fire and one officer lost his life to a sniper's bullet.

The Algiers Motel, which was located on Woodward Avenue and has since been demolished, was considered by police to be a haven for prostitutes and drug dealers. Eyebrows rose when a group of black teenage musicians checked into the hotel and they were visited by two white women.

When police raided the motel, violence broke out, although there was no evidence that anyone in the hotel put up a struggle upon the arrival of the police.

229

Three unarmed black teenagers were killed and nine others were beaten. The dead were: Auburey Pollard, Fred Temple, and Carl Cooper.

The officers and National Guard troops who were responsible for the violence first denied any knowledge of how the three teenagers were killed. However, an investigation determined Officers David Senak, Robert Paille and Ronald August fired the deadly shots.

Charges were brought but none of the officers was convicted of a crime.

Violence continued through July 28, when the riot was finally dampened.

July 29, 1826
Death of Chief Topenebee

It is odd that Americans honor the Indians whom they went to war with, killed or displaced.

Chief Pontiac, who devised a smart plan to take the fort at Detroit, had a city and a car named after him.

Tecumseh, who conspired with the British to rid North America of Americans, also was honored with cities and companies bearing his name.

Chief Topenebee, chief of the Potawatomi in southwest Michigan, was a war chief who fought alongside Tecumseh in the War of 1812.

After warring with the Americans and losing, Topenebee "buried the hatchet," in the Indian lexicon of the day. He later signed several treaties ceding land to the United States.

Perhaps he later regretted the surrender and the added insult of obtaining very little for the Indians while turning over so much to the Americans.

At any rate, Topenebee turned to liquor and became a well-known drunk in Michigan.

On one occasion he was admonished by Lewis Cass, territorial governor, to stay sober so he could look after members of his tribe.

Topenebee is reported to have replied, sarcastically: "Father, we care not for the land, or the money, or the goods; what we want is whiskey, give us whiskey."

Topenebee died on July 29, 1826, two days after a fall from a horse, just as Michigan's wilderness was being surveyed by its new American inhabitants.

Topenebee had a son who shared his name and would go on to sign more treaties with the Americans. That may explain why, in some sources, a much later date is listed for his death.

There is no explanation for one legacy Topenebee left behind, however.

At one time, there were more Boy Scout camps in America

named after him than any other individual.

July 30, 1975
Jimmy Hoffa last seen

One of the most famous missing person cases in American history unfolded in the parking lot of Machus Red Fox restaurant in Bloomfield Township.

That's where 62-year-old Jimmy Hoffa went to meet an old business associate on July 30, 1975. It was the last time anyone saw Hoffa.

Hoffa's 13-year prison sentence on bribery charges was commuted in 1971 by President Richard Nixon. When the labor leader left prison, he tangled with Frank Fitzsimmons, the man he had picked to lead the Teamsters while he was incarcerated.

However, the FBI settled on a suspect for Hoffa's presumed murder – Anthony "Tony Pro" Provenzano, the boss of the New Jersey Teamsters.

Hoffa and Tony Pro were old friends, but when they served time together in a federal prison, they squared off over union turf.

Tony Pro told Hoffa to back off and threatened to kill Hoffa. He reportedly said: "They won't find so much as a fingernail of yours."

There are numerous theories regarding what may have happened to Hoffa's body – he was put in 55-gallon steel drum and buried in a landfill in New Jersey; his body was taken and entombed in the concrete foundation of a building (Giants Stadium in New York or the public works garage in Cadillac are two candidates); or he was ground up in a meat processing plant and discarded in a swamp.

His body never has been found and no one has been charged with his murder. Authorities keep searching, however. The last search, based on a tip, was in 2006 when the FBI spent several days excavating portions of a farm in Oakland County's Milford Township. No evidence of Hoffa's body was discovered.

July 31, 1763
Chief Pontiac's victory at Bloody Run

During Chief Pontiac's siege on British-held Detroit, an officer at the fort convinced his commander to let him lead a raid on Pontiac's camp about two and a half miles north.

Major Henry Gladwin attempted to dissuade Captain James Dalzell from the idea, but Dalzell persisted and was finally granted permission, despite Gladwin's concern that Dalzell and his men would be no match for Pontiac.

Plans for the attack were not kept secret, however. Word of the plot leaked to French inhabitants, who shared the information with the Indians.

Pontiac had plenty of time to prepare and he planned an ambush of his own.

Dalzell and his men left the fort at around 2 a.m. on July 31, 1763 and were set upon as they marched toward Pontiac's camp.

Dalzell and two officers were killed, along with a sergeant and 18 soldiers. Dozens were injured. The Indians reported that they had lost five men.

The ambush happened at what is now Elmwood Cemetery in Detroit along a stream since known as Bloody Run.

The battle was a victory for Pontiac, but his siege came to an end in late October when he wrote to Major Henry Gladwin to request peace, having lost the support of the French and unable to cut off supplies coming to the fort via the river.

"All my young men have buried their hatchets. I think you will forget the bad things which have taken place for some time past. Likewise, I shall forget what you have done to me, in order to think nothing but the positive," Pontiac wrote in French, in a letter he addressed to "My Brother."

The siege of Detroit was the longest sustained military operation by Indians in American history.

July 31, 1924
State begins car ferry service at Straits of Mackinac

For 34 years, the Michigan State Department of Highways offered a way for motorists to bridge the gap between the Upper and Lower peninsulas.

The car ferry service began on July 31, 1924 and ceased when the Mackinac Bridge opened in 1957.

The only ferry service in the country offered by a state highway department, it came about amid public furor over the high prices and lack of reliability of ferry services operated by railroad companies.

August

Aug. 1, 1928
Detroit zoo opens; mayor saved from polar bear

Acting Detroit Mayor John C. Nagel was scheduled to speak at opening day festivities at the Detroit Zoo on Aug. 1, 1928. As he made his way to the bandstand, he was greeted by a polar bear that had managed to get loose by jumping a moat.

Nagel, unfamiliar with polar bears, did not know the peril of his situation. He attempted to be friendly with the bear, extending his hand to say hello.

The encounter could have been a disaster had not trainers intervened and forced the bear back.

The zoo's design enabled the encounter between the bear and the mayor but it also allowed people to view animals in a manner that was unfamiliar to Americans in the early 20th century.

Instead of featuring animals in cages, planners wanted exhibits that were as close to the natural habitat of the animals as was practical.

The Detroit Zoological Society commissioned Boston architect Arthur Shurtleff who based the design on the idea of a zoo without bars. The Detroit Zoo featured animals roaming outdoors, separated from the public by moats and walls built of concrete made to look like rocks.

That first year, the zoo was a huge hit with the public. Tens of thousands of people lined up to get a look at some of the zoo's most popular attractions, such as Paulina the elephant and a set of young lion cubs.

Aug. 1, 1963
Poet Thoedore Roethke dies

Thoedore Roethke, a Pulitzer Prize-winning poet was born in Saginaw May 25, 1908. He attended the University of Michigan and Harvard, although he was forced to abandon graduate studies for economic reasons. He taught at several universities, including Michigan State College (now Michigan State University). His best known poem is "Meditation at Oyster river." Historical markers are located at his boyhood home and burial place in Saginaw.

Aug. 2, 1964
Aerial performer killed

Edward Henry Knipscheild, better known as "Captain Eddie," performed his aerial act at Tiger Stadium before a crowd of thousands.

The 57-year-old was known for an act in which he would twirl by his mouth from a crossbar. He was on a crossbar on Aug. 2, 1964, when he fell 80 feet before a crowd of 22,000 people.

Police said Captain Eddie was putting his wrist through a leather loop when he lost his balance and fell to his death.

Aug. 3, 1795
Treaty of Greenville signed

After General "Mad" Anthony Wayne defeated the Indians at the Battle of Fallen Timbers, which is discussed in the Aug. 20 entry, the Treaty of Greenville called for peace between the Indians and Americans as well as the return of the prisoners on each side. In addition it gave Americans what they were very interested in – the land around Detroit and the area surrounding the Straits of Mackinac.

The treaty also ceded most of Ohio and a six-square mile swath of land where downtown Chicago is today to the United States.

The treaty was signed by Wayne and representatives from a dozen Indian tribes, including the Ottawa, Chippewa, and Potawatomi.

In exchange for all that land, the government agreed to deliver goods valuing $20,000 and "...henceforward every year forever the United States will deliver at some convenient place northward of the river Ohio, like useful goods, suited to the circumstances of the Indians, of the value of nine thousand five hundred dollars...."

Aug. 4, 1976
Library of Congress names first black Poet Laureate

Robert Hayden grew up in the Detroit ghetto known as "Paradise Valley." Hayden was raised in a troubled family as a foster child. Because his small stature and need for thick glasses caused him to be an outcast in the tough neighborhood, Hayden turned to literature as a refuge.

Hayden attended Detroit City College, later known as Wayne State University, but left in 1936 after he was accepted into the Federal Writers' Project where he studied black history and culture.

Hayden published his first volume of poetry, *Heart-Shape in the Dust*, in 1940 and the following year enrolled in the University of Michigan, where he earned a master's degree.

Hayden taught for several years in Michigan before he became a professor at Fisk University in Nashville, Tennessee. He returned to Michigan in 1968 and died in Ann Arbor in 1980 at the age of 66.

Hayden was named the first black Poet Laureate by the Library of Congress on Aug. 4, 1976. He served for two years.

Aug. 5, 1980
Nazi becomes Republican candidate for Congress

Gerald Carlson, a former member of the Ku Klux Klan, the John Birch Society and the American Nazi Party, surprised Democrats and horrified fellow Republicans when he appeared with the G.O.P. ticket for Congress on a one-issue platform: "to contain the black race."

The Dearborn Heights man won the primary election of Aug. 5, 1980 by a margin of 55 to 47 percent.

He defeated mainstream candidate James Caygill, who spent $30,000. Carlson raised $180.

Carlson promised to work on legislation that would ban blacks from white neighborhoods and said he dreamed of one day getting rid of black people in America altogether.

Carlson lost in the general election to Representative William D. Ford, a Democrat who had held the 15th Congressional District seat for 16 years.

It was a bad year for Republican candidates in Detroit. Alfred L. Patterson, who sought to unseat Representative William M. Brodhead in the 17th District, ran his campaign from a state mental hospital with $13 in funds.

The 25-year-old had been involuntarily committed by his father after he made threatening remarks about Senator Edward M. Kennedy of Massachusetts.

Aug. 6, 1845
First U-M graduation held in Ann Arbor

The University of Michigan was founded in Detroit in 1817, but the institution did not really take off until the State Legislature named Ann Arbor as the site for the school in 1837.

Classes began in the fall of 1841 when the school numbered seven students and two faculty members.

The first graduation took place on Aug. 6, 1845 at the First Presbyterian Church.

Graduation ceremonies were held in the building for 11 years until the university decided to construct a larger assembly hall.

Aug. 7, 2008
Yooperland treasure found: JFK ate here

On this day Carole Eberly discovered the stainless and glass block West Bay Diner in Grand Marais. She sat at the counter and drank one of their outstanding chocolate malts -- not to be missed -- as her mind wandered back to the 1950s.

The circular exerior is rare -- only nine such diners survive.

Michigan Every Day

Built by Paramount Diner Car Company in 1949 in New Jersey, Rick Guth and Ellen Airgood brought it across the Mackinac Bridge in November, 1997.

"The west end was almost completely gone -- only the booth, mostly rotted and home to skunks and raccoons remained" said Airgood. "It was eerie -- abandoned and full of promise."

The two entrepreneurs numbered nearly 200 interior stainless pieces and spent the winter of 1997 figuring out what went where without a blueprint or pictures. They scrubbed, polished, replaced and reinstalled in their space time.

After seven months, the diner opened in 1998.

FYI -- JFK ordered two cheeseburgers, with everything, to go on Sept. 24, 1963 when the diner was still in the Garden State.

Aug. 7, 1970
Goose Lake International Music Festival
leads to outrage

The long-haired hippies turned out to rock with Bob Seger, Jethro Tull, Iggy and the Stooges, Alice Cooper, Chicago and others at a three-day music festival on a 390-acre park in Jackson County.

On the opening day of the festival, Aug. 7, 1970, the press called it a long weekend of "love, drugs, and ear-splitting music."

By the time it was over, it was a statewide scandal.

Initially, police reported that the festival was peaceful, though they arrested approximately 50 persons that first day on drug charges outside the park.

Part of the problem was the size of the crowd, estimated at 200,000 young people from across the Midwest and Canada. The promoters expected only 60,000.

The bigger problem, perhaps, was that older residents of the state did not approve of what they read about the concert in their local newspapers.

The promoter attracted the large crowd with promises of low prices for refreshments, free food, "and time for 'right on' political speeches by local radicals."

The festival grounds were surrounded by a 12-foot electrified fence that featured barbed-wire "to keep out freeloaders" and to keep in the drunk and stoned hippies. While police stayed outside of the area to avoid sparking a riot, a private police force of approximately 400 patrolled inside the venue.

The young people were free to listen to rock and roll, parade around half-naked and consume drugs all weekend.

Unlike other rock festivals around the country, no violence broke out and there were only minor injuries.

By the time the festival was over, however, the absence of violence could do nothing to stop a tidal wave of opposition to the concert.

Governor William G. Milliken condemned the use of drugs at the concert.

After the concert, on orders from Milliken, police arrested more than one hundred participants on drug charges after undercover police attended the concert.

The following Sunday, Milliken made a statewide radio broadcast announcing he would prevent such concerts from taking place in the future.

Steve Seymour, who attended the concert and wrote about it decades later on his blog, Rock n Roll Graffiti, said he believes the concert was better than Woodstock but that the negative press caused the festival to virtually disappear from the public memory.

"The weekend was over. The bands played. There was no violence," Seymour wrote. "In the end, tens of thousands of rock music fans enjoyed themselves and only a tiny percentage were arrested on drug charges. Yet publicity at the time created a negative perception of Goose Lake in the public consciousness which continues to this day."

Aug. 8, 1878
Death of George A. Mitchell, founder of city of Cadillac

Cadillac had just been incorporated as a city when a year later the residents mourned its founder.

The main streets of Cadillac at the time were spotted with stumps where white pine had recently been cut, making travel hazardous.

George A. Mitchell was returning home from a shingle mill he owned on Pine Street and was thrown from his buggy. He struck his head on a stump, leaving him unconscious.

Three days later, on Aug. 8, 1878, he died of the head injury.

It was a blow to the community. Mitchell had donated land for churches and was an influential promoter of Cadillac.

Mitchell had been elected Cadillac's first mayor the year before. He wanted the Wexford County seat moved to his home town, but he died several years before that happened.

Aug. 9, 1924
Ku Klux Klan pays a visit to Traverse City

At 8 p.m., without any warning, burning crosses appeared in downtown Traverse City. Three explosions rocked buildings and blew out storefront windows along Front Street.

At the Lyric Theater, which was packed for a Saturday night show, the series of explosions caused panic.

239

Women fainted and a few minor injuries were suffered before a fire chief and manager calmed the crowd.

As firefighters raced to extinguish the burning crosses and the police department scrambled to figure out what was going on, some persons saw a spooky sight – a large sedan carrying four robed and hooded men carrying a lighted sign that read "K.K.K." The car spouted red flares as it crept down Front Street.

Copies of the Klan's newspaper, *The Fiery Cross*, were distributed through town.

Despite the brazenness of the attack, the *Traverse City Record-Eagle* reported the following Monday that no one knew the license plate number of the mysterious sedan. One pedestrian told a reporter that he approached the car and looked inside – the men were wearing hoods but no masks – but he didn't recognize the identity of the men.

Police Chief John Blacken offered a reward of $25 for information about the string of strange crimes.

Although the acts bore the signature of out-of-town instigators, police believed that some local people abetted the visiting Klansmen.

In the aftermath, the city council doubled the award to $50. But the Ku Klux Klan spokesman in Traverse City denied the Klan's involvement in the "tactics of terror" in a letter mailed to the police. The unnamed spokesman said, as proof, the Klan had a policy of not allowing burning crosses to blaze unattended.

Nonetheless, within a few days police had enough evidence to charge the local Klan leader, B.B. Carleton, with setting off the bombs.

Carleton, who skipped town, was arrested later in the month in Indiana and brought back to Traverse City to stand trial. He was acquitted of the charges.

Aug. 10, 1947
Michigan trembles as its largest earthquake strikes

Buildings rocked in Battle Creek, a theater crowd in Coldwater panicked, and furniture tumbled over in homes across southwest Michigan when an earthquake struck on Aug. 10, 1947.

The quake struck on a Sunday, causing the most severe damage in Branch County, where chimneys and windows were damaged.

No one was injured in what is believed to be the largest earthquake ever to hit Michigan.

The temblor was also felt in Detroit and four other states.

Aug. 11, 1884
Body of arctic explorer arrives in Kalamazoo

In the end, Edward Israel found himself in dire circumstances – a winter at a camp miles inside the Arctic Circle with little shelter and an exhausted food supply.

Israel started life in Kalamazoo. He was the son of Mannes Israel, the village's first Jewish resident.

Edward Israel attended the University of Michigan, studying astronomy. As Israel was about to graduate, a professor nominated him to become part of an Arctic expedition organized by the federal government. He accepted, becoming one of 25 members of the Lady Franklin Bay Expedition, named for the group's destination far above the Arctic Circle.

The expedition members traveled to Newfoundland and from there took a ship in June, 1881 to Lady Franklin Bay.

There, they built Fort Conger. They had plenty of food and were relatively comfortable. Israel would spend two years at the frozen outpost, taking astronomical measurements and studying the magnetism of the north pole.

In the summer of 1882, a ship scheduled to replenish the camp's food supply failed to arrive. This ominous event did not cause immediate alarm because the expedition had enough food for another year.

In 1883, summer returned once again, bringing some warmth and constant daylight, but no shipment of provisions. The expedition then set out for Cape Sabine in search of an emergency cache of supplies and rescue.

Israel was responsible for guiding the group from Fort Conger to Cape Sabine, using his astronomical measurements to navigate over constantly shifting ice.

At Cape Sabine, the expedition received bad news – the delivery ship had been crushed in the ice and sunk. Only a fraction of the provisions was saved. The group faced another winter in the Arctic, this time with little shelter and a rapidly dwindling food supply.

Nine months passed. All but six expedition members died of starvation or exposure, including Israel. The Kalamazoo man died in May 1884, just three weeks before a Navy ship managed to reach the cape and rescue the survivors.

Israel's body was returned to his hometown and thousands turned out to the railroad depot to greet the train. He was buried in the Jewish cemetery in Kalamazoo on Aug. 11, 1884.

Aug. 12, 1679
Discovery of Lake St. Clair

The first sailing vessel to navigate the Great Lakes was constructed near Niagara Falls and launched in the summer of 1679.

The *Griffin* was built by Rene-Robert Cavelier, sieur de La Salle, who wanted to explore the Upper Great Lakes in search of a water route to the West to seek his fortune in the fur trade.

La Salle and a party of 34 men, including Father Louis Hennepin, a Catholic priest, sailed across Lake Erie and reached the Detroit River in early August.

On Aug. 12, 1679, the *Griffin* arrived at Lake St. Clair. La Salle's party named the lake *Lac Sainte Clair* in honor of Sainte Claire of Assisi, whose feast day fell on that date.

The spelling was later changed by mapmakers or government officials to Saint Clair.

The fate of the La Salle expedition is described in the March 24 entry.

The party also named the strip of land at the mouth of the Milk River *Point a Guignolet*, after a grape-like berry the French fermented into brandy.

The area would later become the city of St. Clair Shores.

Aug. 13, 1873
Work starts on Crystal Lake canal

Some early Benzie County residents had big ideas for their out-of-the-way slice of real estate.

What if the big, beautiful Crystal Lake was connected to nearby Lake Michigan?

And so the debacle of draining Crystal Lake began.

Designers of the canal believed if they dredged a small canal from Crystal Lake to the Betsie River, outflow from the lake would erode a channel suitable for navigation into the lake from Lake Michigan.

Once that happened, people who owned land around Crystal Lake could start counting their money – much lumber stood uncut in the interior of the county, out of reach because it grew far away from a river or a railroad line.

At the time, the level of Crystal Lake was much higher than today and filled the bowl of land surrounding its present day shore.

In fact, the shoreline pressed against the forest, and in order to walk around the lake, a person had to swing from tree to tree.

When the dredging was completed in September, water from Crystal Lake rushed through the new channel.

As the water flowed out in the following weeks, the steamer *Onward* managed to navigate a course up the waterway from Frankfort to Crystal Lake, where the captain picked up passengers and returned to port.

But the channel was never navigable again after the water drained away.

The Crystal Lake water level had receded so much that it alarmed residents and, within several years, a dam was constructed to block the outflow and preserve the water level.

The upside to the fiasco was not apparent to the 1873 residents of Benzie County – they had exposed what would become some of the state's most valuable waterfront real estate.

Crystal Lake now has a beach and is a famous summer getaway.

The village of Beulah also owes its existence to the outflow. Had Crystal Lake not been lowered, much of the village that later became the county seat would be under water.

Aug. 14, 1969
Detroit Yacht Club accepts its first black member

The Detroit Yacht Club on Belle Isle had been threatened with eviction by the City of Detroit because of its long-standing whites-only policy.

Dr. Charles A. Murphy's application was sponsored by an attorney and supported by five other yacht club members, making Murphy the club's first black member

Kenneth Gunsolus, the yacht club's commodore, said Murphy's application was the first the club had received from a black man.

Aug. 15, 1885
Edna Ferber born in Kalamazoo,
"greatest American woman novelist of her day"

The author of such works as *Giant, Showboat* and *Cimarron,* Edna Ferber was born in Kalamazoo to a storekeeper and his wife. As a youngster she moved to Chicago and Iowa with her family, finally settling in Appleton, Wisconsin.

A prolific writer of short stories, plays and novels, Ferber won a Pulitzer Prize for her book *So Big* in 1924. She was a member of the Algonquin Roundtable, a group of smart and witty writers in New York City, her home when she died in 1968. Upon her death, the New York Times said literary critics of the 1920s and '30s did not hesitate to call her "the greatest American woman novelist of her day."

Aug. 16, 1958
Madonna born in Bay City

Madonna Louise Ciccone, born in Bay City, was raised in
Rochester Hills, where she grew up wanting to be a ballet
dancer. She attended the University of Michigan for two years before, with $35 in her pocket, she moved to New York City to pur-
sue her dream. Soon she shed her ballerina dreams and turned to
pop music. Her first album, *Madonna*, a collection of dance songs,
was released in 1983. Her follow-up album, *Like a Virgin*, became a
number one best-seller in the U.S.

Residents of Bay City have mixed feelings about their native
daughter. She once called Bay City "a stinky little town" in a national interview. However, a return visit to the town by Madonna
was cause for front-page news.

Madonna also has ties to Leelanau County, where her father,
Tony Ciccone, owns a winery near Suttons Bay. He released a special label, "Madonna Wine," in 2006.

In 2008, she headlined the Traverse City Film Festival, bringing
the national spotlight to the shores of Grand Traverse Bay.

Aug. 16, 1812
Commander of Detroit surrenders to British

At the outset of the War of 1812, the military forces in Detroit
outnumbered the British forces in Windsor. A series of bad
decisions by the commander of Detroit, General William Hull,
however, led to a part of Michigan once again in British hands.

After the war broke out, Hull, who commanded a superior
number of troops, hesitated when he had a chance to rout British
forces.

Hull's pause allowed the British to bring in reinforcements, led
by Sir Isaac Brock, a military commander with more experience
than Hull.

On Aug. 15, 1812, British and American forces traded fire from
cannons facing each other across the Detroit River.

By the following morning, the residents of Detroit huddled as
the cannon balls crashed and exploded into the fort. A court-martial hearing was taking place that morning over the surrender of
Fort Mackinac to the British the previous month. A shell exploded
in the courtroom; Lieutenant Porter Hanks, who surrendered
Mackinac, was killed, along with two others. Another shell exploded in the soldiers' barracks, killing two.

Hull had enough and he dispatched his son, who crossed the
river with a white flag.

Hull's decision to surrender led to a court-martial and a death
sentence once his misdeeds had been sorted out. That sentence
was set aside by President James Madison because of Hull's record

of heroism during the Revolutionary War.

Aug. 17, 1980
Detroit Tigers retire Al Kaline's number 6

Although Al Kaline was born in Baltimore, he was known as "Mr. Tiger." He devoted his entire 21-year playing career to the Tigers. Only he and Ty Cobb played for at least 20 years with the Detroit team.

The right-fielder appeared in more than a dozen All-Star games, won 10 Gold Glove awards and personified the team's excellence during the 1968 World Series when he hit .379.

Kaline finished his career in 1974 with 3007 hits and 399 home runs. He was elected to the Baseball Hall of Fame in 1980.

Since retiring, Kaline has remained active with the ball club, first as a television broadcaster and then as a consultant.

Aug. 18, 1926
President Coolidge eats giant Traverse City cherry pie

"PRESIDENT GETS TRAVERSE PIE," the *Traverse City Record-Eagle* headline shouted, in bold letters at the top of the page.

The newspaper's sub-head proudly read: "Coolidge well pleased to eat cherry pastry – Tribute to nation's executive to be served at dinner tonight."

The article described who would be eating the pie that evening in the summer White House in the Adirondacks – the president, the First Lady and some elder statesmen. It assured readers that the oversized pie, made from cherries grown at Frank Burkhart's farm, arrived "in excellent condition" after an automobile trip of 870 miles.

Traverse City resident Wallace Keep had been a college classmate of Calvin Coolidge and was able to set up the pie delivery.

The stunt provided great publicity for Traverse City and its cherry pies.

The following day's *Record-Eagle* featured a photograph of the gigantic pie that contained 5,000 cherries, weighed 46 pounds and measured nearly three feet across.

Aug. 19, 1922
FBI agents bust communists in southwest Michigan

Agents from the FBI Chicago office knew that there was a secret meeting of the Communist Party planned somewhere near St. Joseph. Among the attendees was thought to be Professor

Michigan Every Day

H. Valetski, a Russian agent who had been sent by Moscow to help organize the Communist Party, which had been forced underground, in the United States.

The Party chose Bridgeman, near St. Joseph, for its conference because a meeting had been held there successfully before. The site was a farm turned summer resort owned by Karl Wulfskeel. The meeting was set up under the guise of a week-long meeting of a singing club.

The communists took security measures by posting guards, forbidding members to leave during the convention and ordering attendees to refrain from speaking to strangers.

Details of the convention were so secret that delegates did not know where it was to be held until a few days before it began.

Unknown to them, however, the group had been infiltrated by FBI mole Francis A. Morrow, a delegate to the convention.

Acting on the information from Morrow, two agents arrived in St. Joseph on Aug. 19, 1922, two days after the convention began in search of its locale.

The agents learned from the Bridgeman postmaster that an unusual number of foreigners had drifted through town in the previous few days.

They traded in their suits for overalls and wandered through the woods during a rain-soaked night in search of the conventioneers.

The following morning, they were successful.

The men wandered into the camp and casually inquired about renting a cottage. One of the agents recognized William Z. Foster, a left-wing labor organizer who became a communist after a trip to Russia a year earlier.

Foster also recognized the FBI agent.

The agents were followed as they made their way through the woods back to Bridgeman to plan a raid. However, most of the communists fled before the agents returned, in order to protect the Russian agents among them who could be imprisoned.

By the time the FBI launched its raid, only 17 of the 80 party members remained. Morrow was nonetheless able to show the agents where party records were buried. The records included instructions from Moscow considered to be a plot against the United States. That plan brought national attention to Bridgeman.

Those arrested in the raid were charged with breaking laws created to fight communists in America. The state "criminal syndicalist" law made it a felony to use violence or other objectionable means to bring about political change. All the defendants were acquitted after a jury in St. Joseph failed to reach a verdict in 1923.

Aug. 19, 1951
Tigers pitch to midget

When Detroit Tigers pitcher Bob Cain took the mound in the second game of a double header against the St. Louis Browns on Aug. 19, 1951, he must have been stunned.

Between the games, the Browns, who were at home, unveiled a new player. Eddie Gaedel, at 3'7" and weighing 65 pounds, popped out of a paper mache cake that had been rolled out onto the field next to the Brown's dugout.

Gaedel wore a "1/8" on his jersey and sported a miniature bat. This would be no ordinary day at the ballpark.

Gaedel stepped up to the plate in the pinch hitter's spot. Gaedel's strike zone, Cain later said, was "about the size of a baby's bib."

Gaedel walked in four pitches.

The Tigers wound up winning the game 6-2, but it was Gaedel's walk that people talked about.

Major League Baseball quickly reacted with a rule that required players to be at least 4'8" tall.

Aug. 20, 1794
Battle of Fallen Timbers

The Indians and the British were frustrating American attempts to move West to settle Ohio and Michigan.

Several military commanders tried and failed to move into Ohio to protect the settlers.

President George Washington wanted the military advance accomplished, so be tapped General "Mad" Anthony Wayne, who had earned a reputation for fearlessness during the Revolutionary War.

Wayne agreed to lead an army West and was put in command of 2,500 men.

On Aug. 20, 1794, Wayne took his soldiers into battle where Americans had earlier been routed by Indian warriors who were supplied and encouraged by the British.

The battle took place about 10 miles south of Toledo on the banks of the Maumee River. The name Battle of Fallen Timbers came about from a tornado that had recently decimated the area, leaving trees uprooted and the landscape scarred.

The discipline and training Wayne brought to the men bore good results. This time the Americans routed the Indians.

The battle may have taken place in Ohio, but the day is significant in Michigan history because it opened Michigan to settlement by the Americans.

The battle caused the British to reconsider their position. They had been unwilling to give up Detroit and Mackinac, despite previously agreeing to do so, but Wayne's victory convinced the British it was time to retreat into Canada.

Wayne would visit Detroit two years later, when an American flag flew over its fort. He stayed briefly in Detroit until leaving for his home in Pennsylvania. He became ill on that journey and died at the age of 51.

Despite spending so little time in Michigan, Wayne was considered a great benefactor to the state, for without his actions it may have remained in British hands. In his honor, a county and a state university bear his name.

Aug. 21, 1960
Death of Mackinac Bridge's designer

Dr. David B. Steinman was not from Michigan, but he left a big mark here.

A lifelong resident of New York, Steinman, a civil engineer, devoted his life to the development of long-span suspension bridges.

It took that kind of bridge to connect the two peninsulas of Michigan by a highway. There had been earlier talk of building a bridge, most notably a plan to shorten the distance over water by constructing a series of bridges that would connect the peninsulas by way of islands around the straits, including Mackinac Island.

Steinman designed more than 400 bridges but he considered the Mackinac Bridge his crowning achievement. When the bridge was completed in 1957 it was the longest suspension bridge in the world. Today, it ranks as the 12th longest suspension bridge in the world and the third longest in the United States.

Steinman grew up in a large immigrant family and the Brooklyn Bridge loomed over his childhood.

When the Tacoma Narrows Bridge in the State of Washington, which Steinman did not work on, collapsed in 1940 in heavy winds, people questioned the soundness of suspension bridges.

However, when he planned the Mighty Mac, he developed a design capable of withstanding more than the highest winds northern Michigan could offer.

The bridge is five miles long and is suspended by 42,000 miles of steel cables.

Steinman died on Aug. 21, 1960, just three years after completion of his greatest achievement.

Aug. 22, 1902
Founding of the Cadillac Automobile Company

During the Civil War, Henry M. Leland, a young man of about 18 years, worked in a government armory, manufacturing tools used to make rifles.

After the war, Leland continued to toil as a machinist, working for a sewing machine company and manufacturing boat engines.

In Detroit in 1890, he and a partner started a machine shop called Leland Faulconer Manufacturing Company, which produced internal combustion engines.

The machinist had an excellent reputation as an engineer. At the beginning of the 20th century, Leland's company made engines for Oldsmobile, the first successful mass-production car in the world.

Leland bought one of those Oldsmobiles so he could tinker with the engine and improve its performance.

Oldsmobile owner Ransom E. Olds was uninterested in Leland's results. So when a group of investors who had tried but failed to start a car company with Henry Ford approached Leland, he jumped at the chance. The group formed the Cadillac Automobile Company on Aug. 22, 1902.

Leland is little known because he decided not to name the car after himself but rather after the Frenchman who founded Detroit, Antoine Laumet de le Mothe, sieur de Cadillac.

The company's first car was a one-cylinder model that quickly earned a reputation for quality. That was followed by a car with a four-cylinder engine.

Leland eventually sold the Cadillac company to General Motors in 1917. That same year, with World War I upon the country, Leland started a business building aircraft engines. After the war, that company turned to making cars. Leland named his new model after a former president – Lincoln, again passing up an opportunity to make his own name famous.

Around Detroit, however, Leland was considered a driving force in the city's automotive boom years.

Lincoln soon fell upon hard times, however, and was forced to declare bankruptcy. The Ford Motor Company purchased Lincoln in 1922 and added the nameplate to its stable.

Aug. 22, 1942
Aircraft carrier launched in Lake Michigan

The *U.S.S. Wolverine* and her sister ship, the *U.S.S. Sable*, were luxury vessels modified by the Navy to serve as training vessels for pilots and crew to learn how to take off and land at sea.

The *Wolverine* was launched on Aug. 22, 1942 and just three days later the first aircraft flew from its deck.

In October, an F4F-3 Wildcat crashed into Lake Michigan after a failed takeoff from the *Wolverine*. Neither the pilot nor the plane was ever found. Over the three years the ships trained pilots, the *Wolverine* and *Sable* left relics of World War II-era aircraft scattered across the floor of Lake Michigan.

One hundred twenty-two planes crashed and eight pilots were killed.

Michigan Every Day

In 2004, the Naval Historical Center's underwater archeology branch began an effort to map the lost vintage aircraft.

Aug. 23, 1873
First edition of the *Detroit News*

James E. Scripps had a revolutionary idea in newspaper publishing. Newspapers of his day were partisan and depended on support from the political parties to keep the presses running.

Scripps attempted to start a newspaper and run it like a business. Rather than depend on support from a party, he sought to boost circulation and make money selling ads.

Scripps' project launched on Aug. 23, 1873, when he published the first edition of *The Evening News*.

The Evening News distinguished itself from its competitors, such as the *Detroit Free Press*, by charging less per issue and by focusing on sensational news. The paper cost 2 cents while most other papers cost 5 cents.

Scripps instructed his reporters to write in a casual language.

Aug. 24, 1998
Detroit's gigantic stove restored, unveiled

Before automobiles transformed Detroit, the city was known as the stove capital of the world.

It was fitting, in 1893, that Detroit represented its heritage at the World's Columbian Exposition in Chicago with a giant stove.

The Michigan Stove Company set out to construct what it called a "Mammoth Garland" stove for its exhibit.

Built of wood, the stove weighed 15 tons and stood 25 feet tall.

After its display at the Manufacturers and Liberal Arts Building at the fair, the stove was broken down and reassembled next to the Michigan Stove factory at Adair and East Jefferson in Detroit.

The giant stove was moved up Jefferson Avenue just west of the Belle Isle Bridge in the 1920s. It was moved to the Michigan State Fairgrounds in 1965, where it was put in storage in 1974 because it was rotting.

In 1998, the state fair raised money to restore the stove and the refurbished one was unveiled on Aug. 24.

Aug. 25, 1933
Tom Skerritt born

Tom Skerritt was born in Detroit and attended Mackenzie High School and Wayne State University. He has appeared in over 40 films, including *Top Gun*, *M*A*S*H* and *The Dead Zone*.

He also starred in the television series *Picket Fences.*

Aug. 25, 1895
Notorious train robber shot down by posse

John Smalley, the "Whiskered Train Robber," did most of his dirty work in southern Michigan and northern Indiana, where he robbed trains of payroll.

Between jobs, he hid out with his common-law wife, Cora Brown, in an isolated cabin in southern Clare County. There, Brown worked as a prostitute and was known as "Black Diamond."

Smalley's first recorded brush with the law in northern Michigan took place in 1893, when he was arrested in Cadillac for a robbery he was suspected of staging in Indiana.

Although Smalley carried eight revolvers and $1,700 in cash, he was released for lack of evidence.

Smalley lived this way for about a decade, committing crimes in the south of the state and returning north to be with Cora Brown until the heat died off. This lasted until August of 1895 when a train robbery went awry.

Smalley and three men boarded a Chicago & West Michigan train south of Grand Rapids, took over the express coach and gagged the agent before making off with several thousand dollars.

Within two days, detectives working for the railroad were on Smalley's trail and had tracked him to a Grand Rapids & Indiana train, where he was confronted by Detective George Powers in the smoking car.

Powers should have been suspicious of Smalley's attire. Despite it being a very hot night, Smalley wore a large overcoat.

After the detective told Smalley that he was under arrest, Smalley pulled a revolver from his coat and shot Powers in the head. Smalley jumped from the train and made off into the woods.

Powers soon died of his wound and Smalley quickly became a wanted man.

He was spotted on Aug. 25 by a businessman in McBain who recognized him from a description he had read in a newspaper.

The sheriffs of Wexford, Missaukee and Kent counties gathered men and rushed to McBain as soon as they learned that the notorious thief and killer had been spotted.

Later that evening, the officers surrounded a home in McBain where Smalley was thought to be holed up with Brown and her family.

A sheriff announced himself and ordered Smalley to come out. Cora Brown doused the lights before she and her family crept out the back. The posse unloaded their rifles and pistols into the house.

There was silence for a few minutes before someone could find the courage to check inside the house. When two deputies finally entered, they found a dead Smalley sprawled upon the floor with a gun in each hand.

Smalley was said to have bragged that he had taken in more than $1 million as a robber but none of the money was ever found.

Aug. 26, 1889
Final stagecoach robbery in Michigan

Billed not only as the final stagecoach holdup in Michigan but the final one east of the Mississippi, Reimund Holzhey captured attention for a crime spree that lasted five months and ended with a stagecoach robbery in Gogebic County.

His final stagecoach stickup was a bold one. Just 22 years old, he stopped a coach that was carrying four prominent bankers on their way to vacation at Lake Gogebic. Holzhey demanded money and valuables from the passengers but one of the men would not cooperate. When the man reached into his coat as if he were reaching for his wallet, he pulled out a handgun.

A.G. Fleischbien, of Belleville, Illinois, drew his revolver and fired at the robber, but Holzhey stood his ground and returned fire.

The horses dashed away and Holzhey continued to fire. Fleischbien was struck by a bullet in the thigh, and he and another passenger were thrown from the coach.

Holzhey told them both he would kill them if they didn't hand over their money. They gave him $40 and he left, but Fleischbien later died.

He was arrested in Republic, tried and convicted of murder. Holzhey became a model inmate, however, and devoted himself to self-improvement and he was paroled well short of completing his life sentence.

Aug. 27, 1856
Abraham Lincoln speaks in Kalamazoo

Abraham Lincoln was relatively unknown the only time he delivered a speech in Michigan.

What little notoriety he did achieve among Michigan citizens with his speech was largely negative.

Lincoln had been invited to Kalamazoo by prominent local attorney and Republican Hezekiah G. Wells to speak in support of the presidential candidate John C. Fremont.

He spoke at a rally held in Bronson Park that drew people from across the state. Two tons of bread and four hundred hams were consumed. Nine bands played throughout the day. A train from Detroit brought 600 spectators.

While endorsing the candidate, Lincoln also defended the highly unpopular Fugitive Slave Act, which required Northern states to assist in the capture of escaped salves and he advocated compromise on the question of whether to allow slavery in new territories. Michigan residents were adamantly opposed to slavery.

The only press account of it was discovered years later in the files of a reporter from the *Detroit Advertiser* who took down Lincoln's speech in shorthand.

Fremont lost the election but he carried Michigan.

The negative reaction Lincoln received to his speech may explain why Lincoln never returned to speak in Michigan again. Lincoln was too moderate for the radical audience, who wanted to hear the leader take a bolder stand against slavery.

Aug. 28, 1978
Civil War historian dies in Frankfort

Bruce Catton was born in Petoskey in 1899 and raised in Benzonia where his father, a Congregational minister, struggled to run the Benzonia Academy.

His boyhood is recounted in his memoir, *Waiting for the Morning Train*, in which he describes a Benzie County virtually cut off from the rest of the world.

Catton described how early encounters with Civil War veterans spurred an interest in that war that would grow throughout his life.

Catton attended Oberlin College but left before he received a degree due to the outbreak of the World War I. Catton served in the Navy during the war, later becoming a reporter and working at newspapers around the country.

During World War II, Catton served as director of information for the War Production Board and later held similar posts at the Department of Commerce and Department of Interior.

He wrote his first book in 1948, *War Lords of Washington*. It was not a commercial success but the experience inspired Catton to become a full-time author.

Catton was also a founder and editor of *American Heritage* magazine.

He continued to turn out works on the Civil War and eventually became a well-known and well-paid author.

He won the Pulitzer Prize for *A Stillness at Appomattox*. His best-known works are *The Army of the Potomac* and *The Centennial History of the Civil War*.

Catton spent much of his professional life away from Michigan, but he always returned to the state and the county he loved. He wrote an excellent book about the state called *Michigan: A History*.

He died on Aug. 28, 1978, at Paul Oliver Hospital in Frankfort, where he spent his summers.

Aug. 29, 1862
The 24th Michigan marches out of Camp Burns

Michigan's 24th was organized in response to an embarrassing episode in Detroit during the Civil War. It would go on to suffer some of the worst casualties of any that fought in the war.

The regiment formed while the war was going badly in the North and President Abraham Lincoln called for 300,000 more volunteers.

Michigan Governor Austin Blair pledged six regiments to fulfill Michigan's commitment. In mid-July Detroit Mayor William C. Duncan held a rally at the intersection of Woodward and Michigan avenues in hopes of inspiring men to enlist.

But Confederate instigators in the crowd, believed to have arrived from Windsor, left the mob with the impression that a draft was being proposed and the rally turned into a riot.

Civic leaders were humiliated and attempted to redeem Detroit by organizing another regiment to add to the six formed to answer Lincoln's call.

By the time the 24th Michigan marched to war on Aug. 29, 1862, thousands of citizens packed balconies, roofs and sidewalks along Woodward and Jefferson avenues to cheer.

Near Washington, the regiment joined the Army of the Potomac and was assigned to the Iron Brigade. It took time for the Michigan soldiers to prove themselves and win acceptance from more seasoned troops, but after several dozen of them were killed or wounded in a skirmish leading up to the Battle of Fredericksburg, the Michigan soldiers gained respect and were issued the Iron Brigade's trademark black hats.

The regiment would meet great suffering and gain fame the following July, when it happened upon an army of Confederate soldiers near Gettysburg. Of the nearly 500 soldiers who went into that key battle, only 96 made it back to camp. The others were killed, injured or taken prisoner.

Aug. 29, 1925
Black gold found in Michigan

"Oil men optimistic," the *Saginaw News* reported on August 29, 1925.

Prospectors believed they had found the state's first oil field the previous week and they set out drilling into the earth at a site known as Deindorfer Woods.

The Saginaw Prospecting Company oversaw the operation, which found oil at 1,873 feet.

The well yielded 23 barrels per day.

Over the decades, oil wells spread across the state until there were thousands of oil and natural gas wells in operation.

Aug. 30, 1840
Birth of Hazen Pingree

Born Aug. 30, 1840 in Maine, Hazen Pingree made a name for himself as a soldier in the Civil War.

He fought in the battle of Spotsylvania and was captured by the enemy. He was confined for five months at the notorious Confederate prison Andersonville until he escaped by assuming the identity of a prisoner who was to be exchanged. Pingree then returned to the battlefield.

After the war, Pingree settled in Detroit where he worked at a shoe factory. He learned the business quickly and by 1866 he and a partner started their own shoe company called Pingree and Smith.

The company soon became one of the largest and best-known footwear manufacturers in the United States.

Pingree was elected mayor of Detroit in 1889 and governor of the state in 1897.

As mayor, Pingree worked to end corruption in the way the city awarded public works contracts. He attempted to end private utility monopolies, proposed the city should operate its own electric plant, and battled to lower streetcar fares.

Pingree became nationally famous during a depression that struck the nation as he was mayor of Detroit.

He turned vacant land in the city into gardens that could be used to grow food for the city's poor in what was dubbed the "potato patch plan."

As governor he advocated the eight-hour workday and the direct election of U.S. senators.

Despite his business and political acumen, he remained known for his military service.

The *Michigan Legislative Manual and Official Directory* for 1899-1900 states: "Governor Pingree has in his possession, at his Detroit residence, three old muskets, one of which was carried by his great-grandfather in the Revolutionary war; another by his grandfather in the War of 1812; and the other by himself through the war of the Rebellion."

Pingree died in 1901 while returning from an African safari with his son and then Vice President Theodore Roosevelt.

Aug. 31, 1809
First newspaper

Father Gabriel Richard, a Catholic priest from France, came to Detroit in 1798 to assume responsibility for the church in the

Upper Great Lakes region.

He was also interested in politics and culture, bringing one of the first printing presses to Michigan. With this press was published Michigan's first newspaper, edited by James M. Miller.

The newspaper was supposed to be a weekly, printed on Thursdays, but after its first edition, the *Michigan Essay: Or, the Impartial Observer,* ceased publication. A copy of the rare newspaper is located at the Burton Historical Collection of the Detroit Public Library.

Richard served the area until 1832 when he died of cholera, which he contracted while helping others during an epidemic that swept through Southeastern Michigan.

Aug. 31, 1967
Offhand remark derails governor's presidential hopes

George Romney was a rising star in the Republican party by the late 1960s. The successful businessman came to politics from the auto industry. As CEO of American Motors Corporation, Romney took on the Big Three auto makers with a slate of compact cars, including the Rambler, that turned around the company and made Romney a household name.

Romney was elected the state's governor in 1962. He set his sights on the Republican nomination for the presidential election of 1968. The good-looking, well-spoken moderate entered the campaign as the favorite.

Romney may have won the GOP nomination had it not been for a comment he made in an interview with Detroit's WKBD-TV on Aug. 31, 1967. Romney attempted to explain why he no longer supported the war in Vietnam. He said that his previous support for the war came after a trip to the country two years earlier when he met with American military commanders.

"When I came back from Vietnam, I just had the greatest brainwashing that anybody can get," he said. "I no longer believe that it was necessary for us to get involved in South Vietnam to stop Communist aggression in Southeast Asia"

Romney and his interviewer did not think much of the comment at the time, but by the next day reaction to a presidential candidate admitting he could be brainwashed turned into a firestorm. Romney's campaign faltered and, after a poor showing at a primary the following February, Romney withdrew from the race.

September

Sept. 1, 1914
Last passenger pigeon dies

Near the close of the 19th century, flocks of passenger pigeons darkened Michigan's skies as millions of the birds made the state their summer home.

Early settlers found the birds so tasty and easy to kill that Michigan's passenger pigeons went the way of the mastodon.

The last one died on Sept. 1, 1914, in captivity in the Cincinnati Zoological Gardens.

The passenger pigeons nested in hardwood forests near the Great Lakes in the summer and flew south for the winter.

As the forests disappeared and the birds sought nesting areas in and around farms, the birds came to be seen as a nuisance, often requiring an umbrella for protection.

But they were also a delicacy. They were killed at a rate of 50,000 per day and shipped to restaurants around the country.

Hunting passenger pigeons became a profession and they were taken in unlimited numbers.

A Michigan historical marker commemorates a massive slaughter of the birds near Petoskey in 1878.

In Oden, the marker explains that the passenger pigeon, once North America's most numerous bird, made its pathetic last stand against hunters in that area.

Bird hunters devised some not-so-sporting methods to flush them out and make them easier to kill.

They baited the birds with alcohol-soaked grain, which slowed them down. They also set fires to smoke them out of their nests.

One particularly gruesome method involved sewing a captured bird's eyes shut so it could be used as a decoy. Tied to a stool that could be raised into the air with a lever, the bird would flutter its wings as it fell and attract other birds that could be caught in nets.

Thus, the term stool pigeon.

Sept. 1, 1939
Lily Tomlin born

Tomlin was born in Detroit and grew up in a working class neighborhood. She attended Wayne State University to study medicine, but after taking several theater classes her life changed course. She began to appear in coffee houses around Detroit developing her comedy act.

She moved to New York City in 1965 and further honed her comedy chops. She became a star after she joined the cast of *Laugh-In* and she starred in six comedy specials throughout the 1970s and early 80s.

Tomlin was also successful on Broadway, where she starred in *The Search for Intelligent Life in the Universe*, a play that was such a hit it toured the country for four years after its first year in New York. She also appeared in dozens of movies (*Nine to Five, All of Me, Short Cuts* and *The Incredible Shrinking Woman*) and television shows (*The X-Files, Sesame Street, Will & Grace* and *The West Wing*).

Sept. 2, 1902
First traffic fatality

B efore highways stretched across Michigan and cars crowd- ed its cities, the automobile recorded its first official fatality in the state.

The fatal accident did not play out in the familiar scenario often seen now involving speed and a car crashing into another or a tree.

Rather, the accident could be viewed as a collision between two eras.

George W. Bissell, a wealthy lumberman, was driving his horse and buggy on the morning of Sept. 2, 1902. An automobile, trav- eling at a fast clip for the period, passed by and either crashed into Bissell's carriage or came close enough to spook the horses, causing them to jump.

Bissell's buggy lost a wheel and turned over where he struck his head on Brooklyn Street in Detroit. The 81-year-old did not survive.

Sept. 2, 1922
The odor of alcohol cause for dismissal at Ford

P rohibition was the law of the land and Henry Ford was dis- turbed that many citizens, including his employees, contin- ued to drink.

"This has got to stop, and we're going to end it in short order," Ford told reporters. "Starting Monday it will cost a man his job without any excuse or appeal being considered."

Ford posted a notice for workers on Sept. 2, 1922 that anyone coming to work smelling of beer, wine or liquor would be fired on the spot. Anyone caught with alcohol in their possession or at their home would also lose their job.

Ford said: "The Eighteenth Amendment to the Constitution is a part of the fundamental law of this country. It was meant to be en- forced. Politics has interfered with enforcement of this law, but, so far as our organization is concerned, it is going to be enforced to the letter. I have always been opposed to all forms of intoxicants. Beer, wine and liquor never did anybody any good – and they have caused incalculable suffering and misery in the world."

Sept. 3, 1783
Treaty of Paris signed; America obtains Isle Royale

The Revolutionary War treaty brought the territory that would become Michigan into the United States. However, it would be another 13 years before the British abandoned its posts in Detroit and Mackinac, giving up its hold on the fur trade.

In addition to cementing the future state's place in the Union, the treaty also caused the international boundary running through Lake Superior to swing awkwardly north to capture Isle Royale for the Americans.

While negotiating the treaty in Paris, Benjamin Franklin stubbornly maintained that an odd boundary line through the northernmost Great Lake should separate the United States and Canada.

Instead of being drawn down the middle of the lake, as it is through Ontario, Erie, and Huron, the line through Superior would start at the center but would rise north and west toward present day Thunder Bay, Ontario, including Isle Royale on the American side. It would then return to the center to separate the United States and Canada at what is now the border between Ontario and Minnesota.

Franklin knew about Isle Royale and the legend of its spirit-haunted copper mines and he wanted that natural resource for the new country.

According to accounts, several American businessmen brought three Chippewa Indians and an interpreter to Paris to tell Franklin about copper on Isle Royale.

The island was the only one mentioned by name in the treaty.

Franklin's haggling over the island irked the British officials into surrender, according to lore.

Britain's prime minister, Lord Rockingham, tired of two years of argument reportedly said: "Mr. Franklin, I don't give a damn if that island is solid copper. If the treaty conference had lasted another week, you Yankees would have insisted on running your infernal boundary line around Ireland."

Sept. 4, 1838
Potawatomi forced from state;
Indian "trail of death"

General John Tipton rounded up 859 Potawatomi Indians, including approximately 150 from Michigan, for a forced move to prairie land west of the Mississippi.

The fertile land around the Great Lakes was coveted by white settlers most of whom wanted the Indians removed. In response, Congress passed the Indian Removal Act in 1830.

But the Potawatomi did not want to abandon land so rich in

fish, game and sugar-producing maple trees.

Tipton tricked many of them, including Chiefs Menominee, Black Wolf and Peepehawah, by calling them in to council. He then surrounded them with troops.

The march west, prodded by soldiers' bayonets, began Sept. 4, 1838.

Father Benjamin Marie Petit, a French priest who followed, called the relocation a "trail of death."

Although records differ about the march's death rate, one estimate puts the dead at one in five.

The disaster prompted many Potawatomi who managed to remain in Michigan to migrate to Canada. Others fled to Northern Michigan to blend in with bands of Ottawa or Chippewa, or hid in denser forest in the south of the state.

Governor William Woodbridge, the state's second governor, appealed to the federal government for troops to root out the remaining Indians. Eventually the federal and state governments shifted their position, allowing the remaining Indians to stay.

Sept. 4 1957
The birth of a huge flop

In a strange twist, the Ford Motor Company gave away ponies to sell cars.

It started after the automaker declared Sept. 4, 1957 to be "E-Day," when the world would see the much-anticipated new Edsel.

The car generated a lot of excitement as Ford went to new lengths to generate buzz about the car line.

The Edsel featured an oval grill, a rolling dome speedometer and a push button transmission in the middle of the steering wheel, where the horn normally went.

The style of the car, kept under wraps until its well-publicized launch, evoked a strong reaction from the American public. It was not the reaction for which Ford executives had hoped.

The car soon became a joke. As the models sat in showrooms and went unsold, and the ones that hit the road suffered from numerous defects, the car's name became a punch line – "Every Day Something Else Leaks."

Some observers believe that beyond its unattractiveness and unreliability, the Edsel failed because it was designed through market research.

Executives dreamed up the Edsel as a model that would appeal to a nation brimming in post-war prosperity. Marketers researched a list of names for the car – Mars, Jupiter, Rover, Arrow, Dart, Ovation. None of those caused a sensation. The name Edsel is credited to Ernest Breech, then chairman of the board, who suggested naming the car after Henry Ford's son.

In a panic over the car's failure, Ford's PR department came up with an idea – every Edsel dealer would hold a drawing to give away a pony – or test-drivers could take $200 in cash.

A thousand ponies were shipped to Edsel dealers. This lured customers into showrooms for test drives, but most of the winners opted for $200 in cash, leaving Ford with a surplus of ponies. The company was not equipped to feed and shelter the animals, compounding the Edsel problem.

The company hoped to sell 200,000 cars in that first year. It sold less than a third of that, and sales fell off in the second year. When the third year's models hit showrooms, Ford only sold a few thousand and the company killed the brand.

Sept. 5, 1881
Fire burns Michigan's thumb

After loggers slashed their way through the forest, they left behind stumps, wood scraps, sawdust and branches to dry under the sun.

Farmers who wanted to clear the land of this debris found the simplest method was to set fires and attempt to contain them. This method proved disastrous on Sept. 5, 1881, when conditions were too dry and strong southwesterly winds spread fires across the thumb.

Many survivors reported that the entire region was so overcome by smoke that it was difficult to breathe. The fire made refugees out of the thumb residents, who hastily retreated to the safety of Lake Huron.

The fires raged on for three days until they were doused by a heavy rain.

They claimed anywhere from 125 to nearly 300 lives and burned more than a million acres of land in Huron and Sanilac counties. The bodies of a family of seven were found suffocated in a well where they had sought refuge.

Newspapers reported that the villages of Anderson, Carson, Tyre, Richmondville, Charleston and Sanilac were destroyed.

When news of the destruction reached the East Coast, Clara Barton, famous for her humanitarian work during the Civil War, organized an aid campaign for the 15,000 people left homeless. They became the first people helped by a fledgling organization, the American Red Cross.

Sept. 6, 1901
Detroit native assassinates McKinley

President William McKinley, on a visit to the Pan American Exhibition in Buffalo, New York, held a reception for the public at the Temple of Music at 4 p.m.

As a stream of folks pressed into the hall and a line formed to greet the president, a normal-looking, average-sized man in a black suit approached. He appeared to have a bandage or a handkerchief wrapped around one of his hands.

As he neared McKinley, he raised his hand and fired two shots into the president, shooting through the cloth that concealed the revolver.

Two government agents and a bystander jumped on the assassin, wresting the revolver from him and subduing the man.

Panic followed shocked silence in the crowded hall.

McKinley did not die immediately. He appeared stunned after being shot and then walked to a chair to sit, removing his hat and resting his head in his hands.

One of the bullets struck him in the chest and was easily removed by surgeons. The other bullet hit McKinley in the stomach and posed more serious trouble for the president. McKinley died eight days later.

That day investigators had a signed confession from Leon F. Czolgosz, a Michigan native who most recently lived in Cleveland.

Czolgosz, an anarchist, believed killing the president would put an end to the American government.

Sources vary on Czolgosz's early life. Some newspaper accounts say he was born in Alpena; others Detroit. It is also said he lived for awhile in the Upper Peninsula lumber town of Seney, a place of notorious violence and debauchery. Some accounts said he was run out of town over his promotion of socialism or anarchy. Other accounts have it that Czolgosz only became interested in radical politics shortly before the assassination.

In his confession, Czolgosz described a pathetic life that led him on a path to becoming an anarchist and assassin: "Yes, I know I was bitter," he wrote in his confession. "I never had much luck at anything, and this preyed upon me. It made me morose and envious, but what started the craze to kill was a lecture I heard some little time ago by (socialist) Emma Goldman. She was in Cleveland and I and other anarchists went to hear her. She set me on fire."

Sept. 7, 1808
Uriah Upjohn born: son creates dissolvable pill

Before there were pills as we know them, doctors relied on liquid medicine or hard pills that may – or may not – have broken down in the body.

William Erastus Upjohn, the son of a physician, was born in 1853, worked in a pharmacy, graduated from medical school and had a medical practice in Hastings. But at home in his attic, he tackled two problems facing doctors – how to deliver medicine that would dissolve in the body and how to ensure the precise amount of an active ingredient in a medical dose.

Upjohn solved both problems when he developed a method for turning doses of medicine into dissolvable pills. He received a patent for his process in 1885.

Upjohn was also a natural when it came to marketing. He created demonstration kits for doctors around the country, showing how easily the new pills crushed into a pine board compared to the typical hard ones.

In the meantime, Upjohn began working on a machine to mass produce the pills. With his brother Henry, the Upjohn Pill & Granule Company, was created. Eventually, two other Upjohn brothers joined the operation.

In its first year in Kalamazoo, the company had a dozen employees and manufactured pills from nearly 200 different formulas.

In 1995, the Upjohn Company merged with Pharmacia. It is now owned by Pfizer.

Upjohn was the son of Uriah Upjohn, born in Great Britain on Sept. 7, 1808. At the age of 20 he moved his family to the United States.

After studying medicine and becoming a doctor, he moved to Michigan about the time the territory became a state.

Uriah bought some land in Richland, between Kalamazoo and Battle Creek, and built a cabin. He began a medical practice there and for two decades roamed five counties on horseback, making house calls at a time when the rudimentary science of medicine offered little more than the distribution of quinine to fight malaria and offers of condolence to the dying.

Upjohn developed a reputation as a dedicated doctor who would go to great lengths to aid the sick.

He married Maria Mills and the couple had 12 children, 11 of whom survived. Two daughters were among the first women to study at the University of Michigan. Two sons attended that university's medical school, including Upjohn's best-known offspring, William.

Sept. 8, 1925
Clarence Darrow: a man's home is his castle

Ossian Sweet worked hard to move his black family out of the ghetto.

He put himself through college, medical school and did postgraduate work in Europe to become Ossian Sweet, M.D. But amid Detroit's turbulent racism, the violence and the tumult of the ghetto followed Sweet to the good side of town.

Sweet and his wife Gladys bought a home on the corner of Charlevoix Avenue and Garland Street on the city's east side.

Michigan Every Day

Trouble began on Sept. 8, 1925, the day the family moved into the house and started receiving threatening phone calls.

But Sweet was determined and resourceful.

The following day, the Sweets took their two-year-old daughter to relatives and asked Ossian's brothers and seven friends to come to the house for protection. The men armed themselves, prepared to defend the home.

As the day progressed a mob of whites congregated outside the house. Police arrived, but they made no attempt to prevent the crowd from bombarding the house with rocks.

Increasingly, the people inside Sweet's home felt under attack and the evening climaxed in a flurry of bullets shot from inside the darkened house.

When the firing was over, Leon Breiner, a white man who had been smoking on a porch across the street, was killed. Police arrested eleven people inside the house, including Sweet and his wife, and charged them with first-degree murder.

At first the case garnered little attention and the Sweets and their friends' prospects of obtaining justice seemed dim in a city angry over the killing of a white man by a black defendant.

However, the defendants' outlook improved when famous attorney Clarence Darrow agreed to take the case.

Police, prosecutors, and white witnesses insisted there was no mob outside the home and the shooting was entirely unprovoked, the product of a conspiracy to commit first-degree murder.

During the trial, Darrow systematically poked holes in this version of events until a truer picture of what happened that day emerged.

Darrow based his defense on a case precedent in Michigan law, *People v. Augustus Pond* (see June 18), that recognized an individual's right to defend himself if he were under attack in his own home.

It was fortunate for Darrow that he was able to argue his case before Judge Frank Murphy, who would go on to become mayor of Detroit, governor, United States attorney general and a justice of the United States Supreme Court. Murphy was a champion of human rights.

A mistrial was declared after an all-white jury could not reach a verdict. Prosecutors attempted to convict Henry Sweet, Ossian's 21-year-old brother, but the jury found the defendant not guilty, putting an end to the case.

"The verdict meant simply that the doctrine that a man's home is his castle applied to the black man as well as to the white man," Darrow wrote of the trial.

Sweet would go on to found the Good Samaritan Hospital in Detroit and live in his house until 1944.

Sept. 9, 1910
Pere Marquette 18 sinks; 29 crew and passengers die

The *Pere Marquette 18* was considered one of the finest car ferries in the world. It was also one of the most expensive.

The ship had spent the summer carrying passengers from Chicago on excursions to Waukegan for the Chicago Navigation Company. On Sept. 9, 1910, the vessel returned to its regular route, carrying passengers and train cars across Lake Michigan between Ludington and Milwaukee.

A day earlier, the ferry was inspected by government officials and found to be in fine condition.

The *Pere Marquette* set out early from Ludington. But en route to Wisconsin and the 350-foot ship began to take on water around 4:30 a.m.

Captain Peter Kilty was warned that the pumps could not keep up with the flow pouring into the ship's hull. Kilty picked up steam in an effort to make it to Wisconsin as soon as possible.

The captain and his crew knew the situation was dire and they needed to throw the railroad cars overboard. With great difficulty they managed to remove nine cars from the hold but the loss of freight did not lighten the load enough to prevent the ship from going under.

At approximately 5 a.m., news of the disaster reached shore.

A wireless operator sent a simple message – "Car Ferry No. 18 sinking – Help."

The operator sent the message repeatedly for an hour. The operator is believed to have stayed at his post as the ship sunk into Lake Michigan.

The *Pere Marquette 17* was sent out immediately to aid its sister ship.

No. 17 reached its destination in time to witness the final minute of *Pere Marquette 18*.

The ship's enormous bow lifted into the air as the crew of *No. 17* looked on, horrified. As the bow rose, the stern swung underwater and the ship crashed rapidly into the water.

The surface was littered with debris and people. Witnesses looked on as some passengers were sucked into the vortex of turbulent water left by the *Pere Marquette 18*.

The crew of the *No. 17* launched lifeboats to collect survivors.

One life boat was lowered into the lake just as a large wave crashed into the side of the ferry. Two of the crew were lost.

In all, 29 crew and passengers on board the *No. 18* drowned. Thirty-three were saved.

What caused the ship to take on water and sink remains a mystery.

Sept. 10, 1913
"Big Annie" Clemenc arrested in Calumet

Ana Clemenc, over six-feet tall and a striking-looking woman, was the heart and soul of a long miner's strike in Calumet.

Clemenc, married to a miner, supported the workers after most joined the Western Federation of Miners who went on strike for better wages and working conditions in 1913.

She carried an enormous flag, leading daily parades held by the miners

While strikers used violence to prevent strikebreakers from entering the mines, Clemenc used speeches and persuasion, urging workers to honor the picket lines. Clemenc and other sympathizers, however, were known to snatch the lunch pails of workers heading into the mines or brush them with a broom that had been dipped in sewage.

Although Clemenc watched the stream of men file into the mines, at times she was able to persuade a few to turn back.

This led to confrontations with strikebreakers hired by the mining companies.

There are various accounts of numerous police arrests of Clemenc.

One incident occurred on Sept. 10, 1913, when she successfully stopped a man from entering the mines. She was ordered off the street by police.

Her response: "No, I'm not going. I have a right to stand here and quietly ask the scabs not to go to work."

Several officers then grabbed her as she resisted and forced her into a car that took her directly to jail. She was convicted of assault and was sentenced to pay a fine and spend time in jail.

Clemenc became nationally famous after a confrontation in Calumet between police and a union parade when soldiers and strikers fought. Clemenc draped herself in an American flag, taunting the soldiers to harm her. Newspapers around the country began to follow the exploits of "Big Annie."

Clemenc also helped organize a Christmas pageant that year. She and other women realized the holiday was bound to be gloomy for families of the striking miners.

This event turned tragic and is the subject of the Dec. 24 entry.

After the strike and following her jail sentences, Clemenc divorced her husband and married one of the newspapermen who had come to Calumet to cover the strike. She moved to Chicago and had a daughter. She died in 1956.

Sept. 11, 1889
Exclusive hunting club rejects Henry Ford

Prominent citizens of Marquette joined with wealthy Chicagoans and Detroiters to purchase a vast tract of land in the Huron Mountains to preserve it from logging and make it their own private hunting and fishing club. The beautiful old-growth forest is located adjacent to Lake Superior, north of Marquette and southeast of the Keweenaw Peninsula.

The club's articles of association, which were drawn up and signed on Sept. 11, 1889, limited the number of members who could build cabins on the 24,000 acre tract to 50.

Today the club remains secretive and ultra-exclusive. It is patrolled by a private security force and visitors are not welcome.

Approximately 100 years ago, when the club was equally exclusive, Henry Ford wanted to join.

Ford loved the Upper Peninsula, where he bought huge tracts of land. He owned logging operations to supply wood for his downstate auto factories and also vacationed in the U.P. with friends such as Thomas Edison and Harvey Firestone.

But when Ford, considered one of the most powerful men in the world applied for membership, the club turned him down. The 50-cabin limit was strict and Ford would have to wait for someone to die or want to sell. That was unlikely.

Ford, however, was someone who got what he wanted.

As the magnate applied for membership and was rebuffed, another development posed a danger to the club. In 1919, the state highway department planned construction of a highway through the Huron Mountains that would run from Marquette to Big Bay, through the private club to Skanee and around to L'Anse. The highway was to be called M-35.

Ford purchased land adjacent to the Huron property and the proposed highway.

M-35 was constructed in segments to the east and west of the club, but construction was never completed through the Huron Mountains.

Somehow Ford was able to derail the project and, in exchange, was granted membership to the Huron Mountain Club, where he lived up to his reputation and hired famous architect Albert Kahn to build a cabin for him that would outdo all others in the club.

The cabin was constructed in 1929.

Sept. 12, 1887
Alma College opens

Nearly a hundred students attended classes at Alma College on its opening day on Sept. 12, 1887.

The college was founded by Presbyterians who received a gift of 30 acres of land from an Alma resident and $50,000 from a Bay City man.

It received a charter from the state in April of that year and opened with a faculty of nine.

Although the college holds on to its Presbyterian roots, the school is open to students from all backgrounds.

That said, Alma takes much of its identity from its Scottish heritage.

Its band wears kilts and, in addition to traditional marching band instruments, includes a bagpipe section. The school has a registered tartan, or plaid pattern, used to make kilts that distinguish the school as a unique Scottish clan. On Memorial Day each year, the college hosts the city of Alma's Highland Festival, featuring traditional Scottish games, music and sports.

Sept. 13, 1832
First priest in Congress dies in Detroit

Father Gabriel Richard was born in France and was 31 years old when he arrived in Detroit to serve as pastor at St. Anne's Church.

In the years he spent in Detroit, Richard left his fingerprints over almost all of the significant events in the city after Michigan became a territory of the United States.

He started the city's first-known news service, a town crier who read the news of the country and the world in a town square. He established the city's first library. He published the city's first newspaper, the ill-fated *Michigan Essay or The Impartial Observer*. (See the Aug. 31 entry.) He brought the first church organ to Michigan. He helped establish a road between Detroit and Chicago. He founded what became the University of Michigan. He gave Detroit its motto after the city was ravaged by a fire in 1805, "Speramus meliora; resurget cineribus," which means, "We hope for better things; it will arise from the ashes." And he was the first priest to serve in the United States Congress.

No wonder he has been called the "second founder of Detroit," after the French explorer, Antoine Laumet de la Mothe, sieur de Cadillac.

During the War of 1812, after the British took Detroit, Richard refused to pledge allegiance to the British, saying he already had sworn an oath to the United States. He was held in British custody until he was released at the demand of Shawnee Chief Tecumseh, who recognized Richard's devotion to the spiritual lives of Indians.

Richard was a beloved figure in Detroit and was elected to Congress as a non-voting member when Michigan was a territory. His campaign got a boost from the large French population of Detroit.

In the national capital, Richard was a figure of curiosity who enthralled the nation's leaders with stories of life with the Indians. He cut an odd figure, dressed in knee breeches, silk stockings, a long black coat with a gaping collar and a skirt that reached to his ankles.

While serving in Congress, Richard had some trouble at home. He excommunicated a parishioner who had divorced his wife and remarried. The act hurt the man's business and he sued, winning damages of just over $1,000. Richard could not pay and was jailed, winning release only after friends posted bail. Word of the incident reached Rome and probably cost Richard the seat of Bishop in the church.

Richard died of cholera on Sept. 13, 1832, after he spent months caring for Detroit residents stricken with the disease. (See the July 4 entry.)

Sept. 14, 1862
Battle at Middleton, Maryland

When the 17th Michigan Volunteer Infantry Regiment marched out of Detroit in August, 1862 under the command of William H. Withington, it consisted of inexperienced soldiers.

The men came straight from farms or workshops, were suited up for military service, given some rudimentary training and shipped off for battle.

And the soldiers were young: one company in the regiment was almost entirely made up of students from the Ypsilanti Normal School (later Eastern Michigan University).

They passed through Washington D.C. in early September on the way to Maryland, where they saw their first action on Sept. 14, 1862 at the Battle at Middleton.

A Michigan historical marker is located at the Maryland spot where the ragtag Michigan troops got their first taste of the Civil War.

The regiment, which served under General Ambrose E. Burnside's 9th Army Corps, found the enemy at around 9 a.m. that day.

The 17th held their position against the Confederate troops for several hours.

Later in the afternoon, the southern soldiers were ordered into an all-out attack on the Union line.

At approximately 4 p.m., the Confederate and Michigan soldiers met in a field and the northerners pushed their enemy back. The southern soldiers took positions behind stone walls.

The Michigan soldiers steadily advanced and captured the walls, earning 17th the nickname, "Stonewall Regiment."

The battle was costly. Of 500 men who fought, 27 were killed outright and 114 suffered fatal wounds.

Sept. 15, 1997
Domain name Google registered

Larry Page grew up in East Lansing, the son of Dr. Carl Victor Page, a computer science professor at Michigan State University.

Page attended the University of Michigan, where he earned a bachelor's degree in engineering, before moving to California to attend Stanford University, where he studied computer science and went on leave before earning a Ph.D.

Page grew up with an interest in computers. While at Michigan, he built a laser printer out of Lego bricks. At Stanford, Page stumbled on how to create a search engine after he took an interest in how websites were linked to one another.

Page teamed up with Sergey Brin, a math genius and native of Moscow who also was at Stanford.

They developed an algorithm that ranked websites based on the quantity and quality of the sites that linked to them, a method that returned better search results than existing search engines.

Inspired by its possibilities, they named their company Google, after googol, the term for the numeral 1 followed by 100 zeros.

Page registered what would become the most valuable real estate on the web on Sept. 15, 1997.

Page may have left his hometown for California but he didn't turn his back on Michigan.

In 2007, the company opened an office in Ann Arbor, home to its AdWords division that was to employ as many as 1,000 people.

Sept. 15, 1878
First phone book published

Not long after phones were installed in houses around Detroit, someone figured it would be handy to make a list of the people who had phones.

The first phone book, published on Sept. 15, 1878, listed 124 customers in Detroit who had signed up for "the speaking telephone."

The device had been introduced to the world just two years earlier at the Centennial Exposition in Philadelphia.

The phone book was titled "List of Subscribers."

Sept. 16, 1931
The Purple Gang's Collingwood Massacre

Just as Detroit's location made it a center of beaver pelt trade when the Great Lakes economy was driven by fur, Detroit became a trade center for booze during Prohibition.

The reason was simple – liquor was not banned in Canada and police had trouble tracking motor boats as they crossed the Detroit River under the cover of darkness.

As Detroit became a center for illicit booze, organized crime soon followed.

The most notorious criminals of the Detroit underworld were known as the Purple Gang.

The leaders of the Purple Gang were four brothers – Abe, Joe, Raymond and Izzy Bernstein.

They made their money by hijacking shipments of liquor brought in by older, more established gangs.

Since criminals don't report crime, this tactic had advantages.

But stunning brutality was necessary to make a living stealing from mobsters and the Purple Gang earned its reputation in blood. When a load of liquor landed on the Detroit shore, its owner had to be prepared to fight to the death to protect it from these gangsters.

The gang prospered for years under this business model. But, despite a growing list of enemies, the gang's downfall came from the inside.

A group of gang members brought to Detroit to work as enforcers decided to branch out on their own. They worked outside of the territory they had been allotted, double crossed business associates and lost bets they couldn't cover.

Their moves were seen as a prelude to breaking from the gang to become an underworld power in their own right.

Three members of the gang, Hymie Paul, Joe Sutker and Joe Lebowitz, were called to an apartment on Collingwood Avenue on Sept. 16, 1931, ostensibly to work out a deal for peace.

The men arrived unarmed for a meeting with Purple Gang leaders.

They were shot down and killed in what would come to be known as the Collingwood Massacre.

Their driver, Sol Levine, was spared due to his friendship with Ray Bernstein.

Levine soon was captured by police and convinced to testify.

That prosecutors had a living witness to the massacre simplified their task. Ray Bernstein, Irving Milberg and Harry Keywell were convicted of first-degree murder and sentenced to life in prison.

Sept. 16, 1908
General Motors founded

William Durant, the grandson of former Michigan Governor Henry Crapo, was born in 1861 and by age 30, despite dropping out of school, became a success selling horse-drawn carriages in Flint.

In 1904, Durant, by then a multi-millionaire, applied his knowledge of vehicles to the auto industry and became general manager of the Buick Motor Company.

On Sept. 16, 1908, Durant incorporated General Motors, which acquired Oldsmobile, Pontiac, Cadillac, and several parts manufacturers.

Durant was forced out of his company two years later when it found itself in financial trouble and needed the help of east coast banks. However, he returned to the car business, teaming up with Louis Chevrolet to manufacture affordable cars that could compete with Ford's Model T. He made enough money to buy himself back into General Motors, becoming president in 1916. But he was forced out again several years later.

Durant attempted and failed to start another car company and lost his fortune in the stock market crash of 1929. For a while, he ran a bowling alley in Flint. He died in New York City where he was supported by old business associates from General Motors, including Alfred P. Sloan, his successor as GM president.

Sept. 17, 1929
Mysterious Kalamazoo fires

For several years, suspicious fires plagued Kalamazoo. The first inferno struck the city in December, 1925, when the First Congregational Church burned.

A month later, an entire block burned at Rose and West Michigan Avenue, with losses estimated at $92,000.

In March, the First Methodist Church was destroyed and two firefighters were killed. In April a fire took the Moose Temple on Portage Street. In July, the Presbyterian Church was set ablaze. There were two more large fires that December.

The frequency of the fires convinced residents that an arsonist was at work. Despite all of the probable crime scenes, investigators had no luck finding any clues and things quieted down for the city's fire department for a few years.

Then a spectacular fire broke out on Sept. 17, 1929 at the National Refining Company on Lincoln Avenue.

Fifty families were forced to flee their homes after seven 19,000-gallon gasoline storage tanks exploded.

Shortly after, another fire struck, this one at the Regent Theater.

Police arrested a youth after that blaze. He admitted to all the fires, however the boy's mental state cast doubt on the validity of the confession.

Sept. 18, 1869
Body washes ashore; spawns Manistee murder case

Two young men, George Vanderpool and Herbert Field arrived in Manistee in the fall of 1868 and became partners in a small bank.

After church on a Sunday afternoon in September, the men met at their office. They were prominent members of the thriving logging town and, by all appearances, their business partnership was amicable. However, prosecutors would later argue that they drew up papers on this Sunday to dissolve their business.

It was the last time anyone ever saw Field alive.

The disappearance of a prominent citizen caused a stir in the town and Vanderpool became a suspect as residents became convinced Field met with foul play.

Field resurfaced almost two weeks later, on Sept. 18, 1869, when his body washed ashore near Frankfort, his skull crushed in two places and a rope tied around his waist, apparently to connect him to a weight that would keep his corpse submerged in Lake Michigan.

Vanderpool was accused of murder. Investigators believed he crept up behind his partner and struck him on the head before disposing of his body into the water.

The mood in Manistee was fervently against Vanderpool. His trial took two months with the evidence against him all circumstantial. However, he was found guilty of first-degree murder and sent to the state prison at Jackson for life in solitary confinement.

By the time of his conviction, the case had become national news and many Michigan residents believed Vanderpool was railroaded by authorities in Manistee.

The case hinged around a red stain found in the partners' office and expert witnesses argued over what it meant.

One doctor claimed, without a doubt, that medical science proved the stain was the blood of a human being. Another doctor, with just as much certainty, maintained that science offered no method to determine whether the stain was human or animal blood.

In addition, Field, who was in his early 20s at the time of his death, was known as a restless adventurer who repeatedly put his life at risk.

As more people became uncertain of Vanderpool's guilt, money was raised from around Michigan to fund his appeal.

Eventually, Vanderpool's supporters secured a new trial, this one held in Kalamazoo. This time the jury could not reach a verdict. Seven on the jury believed Vanderpool to be guilty. Five voted for acquittal.

A third trial in Kalamazoo ended in Vanderpool's favor. He walked away a free man and there is no record that anyone paid for the murder of Field.

Sept. 19, 1968
Denny McLain personifies 1968 Detroit Tigers

The Detroit Tigers were on their way to not only the American League pennant but to win the World Series in 1968. Tiger fever was high and a song belted out on local airways proclaimed, "We're all behind our basement team – go get 'em Tigers." At the forefront of that effort was pitcher Denny McLain, who had a spectacular season.

The Tigers were up against the New York Yankees on Sept. 19, 1968 when McLain pitched his 31st win of the season, a remarkable feat. He became the first pitcher to surpass Dizzy Dean's 30-win year in 1934. McLain finished the year with 31 wins and six shutouts, an obvious choice for that year's prestigious Cy Young Award for pitching.

Detroit bested the St. Louis Cardinals in a series that went the full seven games, ending with a victory at Tiger Stadium on Oct. 10, 1968. McLain had only one victory in the World Series. Mickey Lolich pitched three of the winning games and earned the Most Valuable Pitcher for the series.

Sept. 19, 1844
Iron discovered in the U.P.

Surveyor William A. Burt had spent years mapping northern Michigan. He and his sons worked their way across the rugged Upper Peninsula to mark township and section lines for the State of Michigan.

On the morning of Sept. 19, 1844, he set out near the site of what is now Negaunee near Teal Lake.

Burt soon noticed his compass was not behaving properly. At times, when Burt had a sense of which direction was north, the compass pointed south. Elsewhere Burt watched the needle bounce erratically.

Burt had invented the solar compass, which he patented in 1836, after previous surveying efforts were hampered by the slight effects of ground minerals on magnetic compasses.

He was accustomed to minor variations. But the spinning compass needle Burt watched on that day made him realize he was sitting on something significant.

The party looked around and discovered specimens of iron ore in the area.

The discovery of the mineral caused some immediate trouble for Burt and his men.

By the next day they were out of food and overcast skies rendered their solar compass useless. They also could not depend on the magnetic compass.

The expedition had left a cache of provisions stored on their route but they feared that without a compass the search for the food would be futile. That evening they chopped down a tree and cooked two porcupines for dinner. The following day the weather cleared and they were able to find their stored food with the solar compass.

Thus, the Marquette Range was the first of three iron ranges to be discovered in the Upper Peninsula. Later explorers discovered the Menominee and the Gogebic iron ranges.

In 1847, the Jackson Mining Company began hauling loads of iron out of the Upper Peninsula. At first, iron extraction was limited to iron ore outcroppings at the surface. The first shafts were sunk after the Civil War.

Within 50 years, the vast supply of iron in the Upper Peninsula would feed a burgeoning auto industry.

Sept. 20, 1873
First glow from St. Helena Island Lighthouse

Situated in Lake Michigan, just west of the Straits of Mackinac, St. Helena Island had long been a stopover on the trade route between Lake Michigan and Lake Huron.

While the island was an inviting place to take refuge from storms and to stock up on supplies, dangerous shoals in the path to the island also made navigation perilous.

After several ships wrecked on the shoals, Congress authorized funds to pay for a lighthouse on the island.

Work was completed in the summer of 1873 and, upon the arrival of a Fresnel lens specially ordered from France, the beacon was lit on Sept. 20, 1873.

Over the years the number of people who made their living on the island dwindled and the light was automated in 1922. The lighthouse then fell into disrepair.

The property was restored by the Great Lakes Lighthouse Keepers Association and in 2001 the entire island was purchased by the Little Traverse Conservancy.

Sept. 21, 1903
Automotive pioneer
Preston Thomas Tucker born in Capac

Preston Thomas Tucker's obsession with automobiles began at an early age but he took a roundabout route to founding a car company.

Although his venture into the automobile industry ultimately failed, perhaps due to the meddling of established car companies, he was the first to introduce many innovations that are standard on cars today.

Tucker was born in Capac, between Flint and Port Huron, and worked a wide variety of jobs before he developed his first car. Tucker managed a brewery, worked at a Cadillac dealership and was a police officer in Lincoln Park.

Tucker's desire to become a police officer may have been motivated by the fast cars officers drove, but Tucker put himself in the thick of law enforcement, taking a job in the Detroit area during Prohibition.

However, Tucker's love of cars won out over his police career and he was drawn to the Indianapolis 500, where he developed a relationship with race car designer Harry Miller.

By 1941, Tucker worked with his mother at an Ypsilanti business. Ypsilanti Machine, that attempted to sell an armored car to the government for use in World War II. The military was only impressed with the vehicle's gun turret, however, which it appropriated for use in the Navy.

Although Tucker's attempts to run a successful wartime company met with little success, after the war Tucker was ready to start a car company. And he had a lot of good ideas.

Tucker drew up plans for the Tucker Torpedo, a radical vehicle for its time. The vehicle, which Tucker called "the car of tomorrow," would include a padded dash, a pop-out safety windshield and a center headlight that would turn with the car.

Tucker found a factory in Chicago to manufacture his car. He raised approximately $17 million through a stock sale and in June, 1947, unveiled a prototype of his 1948 model to great public fanfare. Orders for the car poured in and dealerships were organized.

But building a successful car company in the shadow of the Big Three automakers was not so simple. Tucker openly complained that the auto industry used its political power to harass his business at every turn, sent spies into his company, bribed his employees and prevented him from securing needed materials.

Whatever chance the company had was lost when the Securities and Exchange Commission launched an investigation into the company and word was leaked to the press.

By the time of his trial in 1949 on charges related to the sale of stock, it was clear that the government case was weak and Tucker was acquitted. But by then, irreparable damage had been done to the company.

Only 51 Tucker sedans were ever built and Tucker died in 1956 of pneumonia in Ypsilanti.

Sept. 21, 1945
Jerry Bruckheimer born

Jerry Bruckheimer was born in Detroit to Jewish immigrants from Germany. At home, he spoke German and English, and he attended Mumford High School in Detroit before moving to

Arizona for college, where he studied psychology and mathematics.

All along, however, Bruckheimer loved movies. He moved to Los Angeles from New York, where he worked in advertising after college, before learning of an opportunity to produce a film. That was the early 1970s and since then he has produced more than 30 films and television shows, including *Flashdance*, *Top Gun*, and *The Pirates of the Caribbean* series. He also produced the television show *CSI: Crime Scene Investigation*.

Sept. 22, 1989
Yugo plunges over Mackinac Bridge

The Yugo, a Yugoslavian-made car, was appealing to some American drivers in the 1980s because it delivered great mileage, due to its light weight and aerodynamic design.

Those facts, combined with high winds, created a tragic situation for a motorist crossing the Mackinac Bridge on Sept. 22, 1989.

On that day a bridge worker called the U.S. Coast Guard in St. Ignace at around 6:45 p.m. to report something terrifying he had witnessed. It appeared that a small car attempting to cross the bridge was battered by high winds and was finally swept off, plunging 170 feet to the water below.

A cold front from Canada was blamed for the howling winds, which also stirred up the water around the Straits of Mackinac so that an immediate rescue attempt was cancelled.

Leslie Pluhar, a 31-year-old waitress from Royal Oak, was alone and headed north in her blue 1987 Yugo when it flipped over the outer guardrail.

It took police and rescuers days to figure out who went over the bridge and recover the vehicle.

She en route to the Upper Peninsula to meet her boyfriend and investigators said they believed her car struck an inner guardrail before spinning and flipping over the outer guardrail.

Pluhar's family sued the state, arguing that the guardrail, at just over three feet tall, was too short to prevent a car from plummeting off of the bridge.

The lawsuit was settled in 1994.

In 1997, a second vehicle plummeted from the bridge.

Richard Alan Daraban, 25, of Macomb County's Shelby Township, died after he lost control of his Ford Bronco while passing a truck. The Bronco skidded along the guardrail, spun over the side of the bridge and into the frozen straits below.

At the time, the Michigan Department of Transportation assured the public that there was no cause for alarm. While two vehicles had been lost from the bridge in its 40-year history, the odds of getting across safely were pretty good -- 94 million vehicles had crossed the bridge since it opened in 1957.

Many motorists approach the Big Mac with trepidation. Because of this, the bridge authority offers drivers for people who are afraid to drive across the bridge themselves. On days of extreme wind, drivers only are allowed to cross with escorts -- large trucks that drive on the outside lane to act as wind breakers for cars on the inside lane.

Sept. 23, 1967
Lake Michigan fishing frenzy tragedy

By the mid-1960s, tinkering with the Great Lakes ecosystem by humans had caused some serious problems.

The opening of the Erie Canal and the Welland Canal in the 19th century brought the invasive sea lamprey into the Great Lakes. These monster-like creatures latch onto and suck the life out of native species such as lake trout and whitefish.

It took decades for the sea lamprey to make its way into the lakes and establish themselves. But without natural predators, they flourished.

By the 1960s, the numbers of lake trout and whitefish dwindled while alewives flourished.

The alewife population exploded to the point that they were washing up and rotting on beaches by the millions, the stench turning away would-be beach goers.

Michigan wildlife officials responded in two ways – they stepped up control measures for the sea lamprey and they looked for a fish species that would eat alewives.

They decided Pacific salmon would be the ideal predator for the small fish that were stinking up the beaches while offering a unique sports fishing opportunity.

It turned out that the scheme worked. The salmon were planted and survived. By the fall of 1967, Lake Michigan was bursting with the first class of planted Coho salmon.

Suddenly, anyone with a boat headed out to the big lake to fish for an easy dinner.

So excited were the fishermen than many failed to heed a small craft advisory on the morning of Sept. 23, 1967.

The storm brought high winds that produced eight-foot waves.

The small vessels used by many fishermen were no match for the turbulent lake waters, which swamped and overturned many boats. As a result, seven people drowned.

Sept. 23, 1879
Detroit buys Belle Isle

Detroit's first residents knew Belle Isle as Hog Island, because of a herd of the animals that roamed its terrain.

The island got its later and more fortunate name from Lewis Cass, territorial governor. The island was named after his daughter, Isabella.

Later residents of Detroit decided the island would make a good park and the city bought the island on Sept. 23, 1879 for $200,000.

Frederick Law Olmsted, designer of New York's Central Park, was consulted, and the city's parks department developed the island as a public place that covers 981 acres.

Today the island is home to the Dossin Great Lakes Museum, the Ann Scripps Whitcomb Conservatory, nature trails, a beach, the Remick Music Shell, and the Detroit Yacht Club.

Sept. 24, 1830
Beginning of end to death penalty in Michigan

Stephen Gifford Simmons, a 50-year-old tavern keeper and farmer, had been convicted of murdering his wife, Levana, in a jealous, drunken rage.

The murder caused a furor among residents, who wanted to see Simmons pay. But by the time his body slumped dead in the hangman's rope, Simmons may have single-handedly ended the death penalty in Michigan for good.

The government of Michigan was the first in the English-speaking world to bar the death penalty, in 1847.

Simmons was a massive, good-looking man. He was well-educated but he became obnoxious and prone to starting fights when he drank. This habit had, over the years, spawned many enemies.

Simmons murdered his wife on a night he had been drinking. He arrived home and demanded that she drink with him. She took a few sips of whiskey but refused anymore. He flew into a rage. He struck her so hard with his fist that she suffered a fatal head injury.

The assault was witnessed by Simmons' two daughters.

It took a lot of work by lawyers to seat a jury of citizens who were not convinced that Simmons should hang.

Once a jury was seated, the trial was almost a formality. His daughters were called to the witness stand. Each described how their father killed their mother. Case closed.

Simmons was sentenced to hang on Sept. 24, 1830.

Since executions were a spectator sport, hundreds turned out to witness Simmons die.

A regimental band was on hand to make the social event even more grand.

But when Simmons emerged from the jailhouse and was walked to the scaffolds, his demeanor startled the crowd.

He sat patiently, watching the crowd, as the death warrant was read.

281

Then he rose to speak, delivering a moving address. He admitted his faults. He pleaded with the crowd to avoid too much drink, to avoid making his kind of mistake. He said he yet hoped for mercy from the court or from the governor but ended his speech with a popular hymn, sung in a beautiful baritone, that asked forgiveness from God.

This was not the scoundrel the crowd had come to watch die.

The mood of the crowd changed. Instead of a thirst for blood, the throng now wanted mercy.

But the mechanism had been set in motion and nothing could stop the hanging.

After Simmons was killed, the crowds met in taverns and discussed what had happened. People questioned their support of hanging as a means to punish murderers. It would take 17 years and much political maneuvering before the state would outlaw the death penalty.

But it is the death of Simmons that is credited for prohibiting capital punishment in Michigan.

Sept. 25, 1854
"Son" of Lord Byron sent to state prison

The residents of Adrian must have had a hard time figuring out what to make of Augustus Stuart Byron McDonald when he arrived in their town in the early 1850s, claiming to be the son of famous poet Lord Byron. Could this be true? Apparently is was enough to get him a job as a printer at an Adrian newspaper, the *Michigan Exposition*. It was later reported that his work habits were irregular and he was often out late at night.

Soon Byron injected himself into the mystery of a series of crimes that plagued the railroad near Adrian, threatening to undermine the public's confidence in train travel and nearly causing the death of railroad engineer T.T. Parker.

A band of hoodlums were placing obstructions along railroad lines, hoping to derail trains. They would then take the money from the mail shipments.

In one of these attempts, the locomotive of a mail train was thrown from the tracks near Adrian, seriously injuring the engineer. The only evidence investigators found at the scene was a print from a boot.

That same day, the railroad superintendant received a letter. The writer said he knew of a gang intent on murderous mischievousness. The writer signed himself A. Stuart (i.e. Byron).

A meeting was arranged where Byron claimed he had the proof needed to arrest the gang. He offered to provide it for a reasonable fee.

He was suspected trying a con, but since his was the only lead, the railroad engaged Byron's services.

About the same time, a detective was hired by the U.S. Postal Service. He was Allan Pinkerton of Chicago, who quietly began an investigation of train derailments.

Byron made frequent reports to the railroad superintendant, but failed to provide evidence against the gang. The railroad grew suspicious of Byron, who seemed to be collecting more information about the railroad than he offered about the gang. It was also apparent that the gang had an inside source at the post office because attempted derailments invariably happened to trains carrying large amounts of money.

During one of his visits with Byron, the superintendant laid down some dirt outside of his office to take an impression of Byron's boot print. They matched, but it was not enough proof for a court case.

While on a visit to Chicago, Byron was arrested at Pinkerton's direction. Byron spent a month in a jail cell with an undercover police officer from Milwaukee who posed as a thief.

Byron pleaded with the inmate to testify in Adrian on his behalf. Byron asked the man to tell the court that he, not Byron, was at the scene of the derailment. In return, Byron would set the man up in a lucrative position with the gang.

Byron demanded a trial in Adrian, saying he would be exonerated. Perhaps, Byron wrote, the people of Adrian would give him a financial reward for protecting them from train bandits.

Byron was returned to Adrian and tried for the attempted murder of Michigan Southern Railroad engineer T.T. Parker.

He was shocked when the witness he expected to call for his defense appeared for the prosecution. Testimony from the Milwaukee police officer sealed Byron's fate.

On Sept. 25, 1854, Byron was sent to the state prison in Jackson for life.

Sept. 25, 1926
The Red Wings come to Detroit

The Detroit Red Wings trace their roots back to Victoria, British Columbia, where the Victoria Cougars played in the Western Hockey League until the rights to their players were purchased by a group of Detroit businessmen on Sept. 25, 1926 who moved the team to Michigan.

First known as the Detroit Cougars and later the Detroit Falcons, the team became the Detroit Red Wings in 1932 and almost immediately began winning Stanley Cups.

In their first seasons, the team played at an arena in Windsor because there was no suitable rink in Detroit. In 1927, the team moved into the new Olympia Stadium, where they would play until 1979.

The team became the Red Wings after they were purchased by grain millionaire and shipping magnate James Norris, who turned the franchise around after a few years of poor performance on the ice and in the ledger books.

The Wings won Stanley Cups in 1936 and 1937. In their first Stanley Cup victory, the team beat the Toronto Maple Leafs three games-to-one. The following year, they defeated the New York Rangers three games-to-two.

The team would go on to win 11 Stanley Cups through 2008, including four championship titles in the 1950s and back-to-back victories in the 1997 and 1998. Their most recent victory came at the expense of the Pittsburgh Penguins, who lost to the Wings in six games.

The back-to-back wins in the late '90s ended a major Cup drought in the franchise's history when the team's lackluster performance on the ice earned them the moniker "Dead Wings" from frustrated fans. The team made up for the miserable seasons in the 1970s and 1980s by reaching the playoffs in 17 consecutive seasons by 2008.

Sept. 26, 1963
Elephant rampages through Lansing

When brothers Asa and Merlin Schiedel heard loud noises outside their home and looked outside, the men were greeted with a preposterous surprise.

A circus elephant charged through their backyard and onto the driveway. As 67-year-old Asa attempted to get away, he inadvertently stepped into the elephant's path. The animal knocked Asa down before butting him and trampling over him.

A neighbor who yelled at the elephant to shoo him away was credited with saving the man's life.

The elephant, known as Rajje, had been part of the King Shows and Circus, which was performing at a local shopping center. Rajje apparently became irritated at a certain point in the performance and rebelled against her trainer. The trainer said the elephant just walked away and then became confused.

One of the elephant's first stops was at Arlan's Department Store, where the elephant burst inside and terrorized crowded shoppers as she marauded down the aisles toward the men's and sporting goods departments.

The elephant spent about 15 minutes rampaging through the store, smashing windows and merchandise and causing thousands of dollars in damage, before leaving by a back exit. Amazingly, no one was injured.

Rajje led police on a two-mile chase through Lansing, as the berserk elephant attempted to throw a car out of his way.

Rajje, a 13-year-old who weighed 3,000 pounds, was finally put down in a barrage of gunfire from police.

Sept. 26, 1987
Anglers find giant slab of copper near White Pine

The most famous chunk of native float copper found in the 19th century (see Oct. 11), may be in the possession of the Smithsonian Institution in Washington D.C., but two fishermen discovered an even larger heap of nearly pure copper while fishing near a ravine in the western Upper Peninsula.

The copper boulder was tucked away far enough into the wilderness that it survived well over a century of copper hunting in the U.P. It was found on land where mineral rights belonged to the Copper Range Company.

The company paid the fishermen, Bill and Erick Yrjana, $500 to lead them to the find and then put the 5,950-pound slab of copper on display in Calumet.

The copper boulder is 82 inches long, 64 inches wide and about six feet thick. It was estimated to be worth, based on 1987 copper prices, $6,000. The Ontonagon boulder, on the other hand, weighed a mere 3,750 pounds.

Sept. 27, 1962
Nuclear plant opens in Charlevoix

The first nuclear plant in Michigan opened without much fanfare on Sept. 27, 1962.

Consumers Power Company officials said at 2:35 p.m. that day they had achieved a controlled nuclear reaction -- seven fuel bundles were lowered into a reactor.

The plant took 30 months and $27 million to build and would at first produce enough electricity to power a community with a population of 65,000.

Although the plant closed in 1997, a decade later debate still lingered about what should be done with the site. At the time of its closing, it was the oldest nuclear plant in the country.

The Little Traverse Bay Conservancy wanted to buy a large portion of the property with the help of state funds to make it a nature preserve. It said the land was habitat for deer, bear, porcupine and bald eagles. It is a rare chunk of Lake Michigan property in an area where most of the lakeshore is privately owned and developed.

A coalition of environmental groups opposed the plan because of radioactivity at the site and the possibility that the state could spend millions of dollars to assume liability for ruined land and dangerous groundwater.

Sept. 27, 1999
Final game at Tiger Stadium

The stadium at the corner of Michigan and Trumbull had hosted more than a century of baseball games. Opened in 1912 as Navin Field, the park was renamed Briggs Stadium in 1938. That name was in place until 1960 when the historic structure was renamed Tiger Stadium. The home of the Detroit Tigers baseball club and former home of the Detroit Lions, the majestic structure was filled to capacity in 1999 when it saw its last major league game before it was shuttered.

The final game ended with a Detroit Tiger victory over the Kansas City Royals 8-2.

The game also featured an address by Al Kaline, who said that at age 18, in 1953, when he first came to Tiger Stadium, that it looked like a fortress or a battleship from the outside but from the inside felt welcoming with green grass and cheering fans.

The stadium closed when the Detroit Tigers moved to Comerica Park, near the center of the city's downtown.

Sept. 28, 1912
Muskegon 216, Hastings 0

It was the best day in Michigan high school football -- or the worst.

That depended upon where one sat at Hackley Field, still home of the Muskegon Big Reds, who still lead Michigan high schools in all-time victories.

One of those came that Saturday afternoon, Sept. 28, 1912, when Hastings High School came to town and left with a 216-0 drubbing by the home team. The daily Muskegon News Chronicle headline gloated: "Muskegon High Sets World Record for High School Game with Hastings; Team's Weak Point Seems Eliminated; Visitors Totally Helpless."

Nearly a hundred years later the game remains the most lopsided in Michigan high school history.

Muskegon player Fred Jacobs scored 54 points for the Big Reds with nine of the team's 32 touchdowns. But most of the News Chronicle story focused on the shortcomings of the Hastings team.

"Although the world's records fell in the game," the story reported, "it is not anything to be particularly proud of, for such an aggregation termed a football team as Hastings had gathered could not be found again in a long search. The visitors had three men that know a football from an egg and those three could not make the Muskegon second team."

The story also focused on the differences between the towns themselves and why the outcome of the game could have been predicted before it began.

While the big city daily boasted about its town's gridiron glory, the weekly in Hastings, The Hastings Banner, handled the loss with some grace and understatement.

That week's report of the game appeared on page 13 in a column labeled "Items From the City Schools." One had to sort threw the week's school news, such as "The ninth grade English class has been making short oral reports of interviews on various subjects," to finally find news of the football game, under the headline "Defeat at Muskegon Taken Cheerfully."

The report on the game explained the varying level of seriousness each town took in the game. The Hastings writer declared: "We are glad to say that Hastings played in the football game that was, for Muskegon, the World's Championship."

There was no mention of the score but the article did note that some Hastings fans attended the game.

That left the front page of the Hastings paper open for more important news -- "A Drunken Stranger Makes Dire Threats;" "Runaway Horse Leaps Clean Over a Buggy."

But the story lingered until the following week's edition. A Banner writer attempted to put the stunning loss in perspective, noting that another team, fielded by the Ferris Institute, bowed to Muskegon in a 165-0 loss. "So we are not the only ones who have been beaten by Muskegon."

Sept. 29, 1813
Americans retake Detroit

There was no resistance this day in 1813 when the Americans took Detroit back from the British. The soldiers arrived to find that the British had abandoned the village and the fort it held for just over a year.

There were two bloody encounters that led the British to retreat and their Indian allies to lose heart.

The first happened in May, when Henry Proctor, the British commander, decided to attack a small American stockade in Sandusky County, Ohio.

In command of the American post was Major George Croghan, a 21-year-old Kentuckian.

Croghan did not stand much of a chance against Proctor's superior numbers and firepower. Croghan commanded only a small post -- its artillery amounted to one six-pound cannon.

Proctor demanded that Croghan surrender. In exchange he promised to protect the Americans from the Indians, a promise that must have been hard to swallow given the River Raisin massacre earlier that year.

Croghan replied: "When the fort shall be taken, there will be none to massacre. It will not be given up while a man is able to resist."

A battle followed and the Americans fought with tenacity. One soldier was killed and seven were wounded. The British lost 50 men, including two officers.

The other significant battle that brought Detroit back into American hands happened on Lake Erie in early September.

The Americans sought control of Detroit's water route to prevent movement of British reinforcements and to cut off their food supplies.

The task of taking Lake Erie fell to American Lieutenant Oliver Hazard Perry. The British fleet was commanded by Commodore Robert H. Barclay. When the armadas met, the Americans had more ships but the British had superior firepower.

On the morning of Sept. 10, Perry hoisted the battle flag on his ship, the *Lawrence*, and steered his fleet toward Barclay's. Fighting ensued for hours until ships on both sides were battered and many lives were lost. When the *Lawrence* lost its last gun, Perry escaped in a boat and made it to his second ship, the *Niagara*, which was unharmed. Perry took that ship into battle. By now the enemy ships were in such bad shape, Perry was able to wipe out the British fleet.

Barclay surrendered and Perry wrote a message to his commander, William Henry Harrison: "Dear General -- We have met the enemy, and they are ours."

The victory left no alternative for the British but to abandon Detroit.

When the Americans returned, on Sept. 29, 1813, they found that much of the city had been burned, but they met no resistance.

Sept. 30, 1980
Thousands greet oceanographer
Jacques Cousteau in Detroit

Famous French oceanographer Jacques Cousteau arrived in Detroit aboard his research ship, *Calypso*, where 5,000 people greeted him at Hart Plaza on Sept. 30, 1980.

Cousteau made the stop on a trip back from Lake Superior, where he had been filming a series of television specials for the National Film Board of Canada.

The visit highlighted some serious concerns Cousteau and other researchers had about the Great Lakes. Cousteau told reporters that he was baffled by the lack of life in the lakes.

Cousteau said he believed over-fishing, pollution and invasive species were to blame. He hoped science and research could one day turn around the health of the lakes.

October

Oct. 1, 1908
First Model T produced

The Ford Model T, the car that would revolutionize the auto industry and secure Detroit's claim to being the Motor City, was produced at the Ford Motor Company's Piquette Avenue plant in Detroit. The first Model T drove out of the plant on Oct. 1, 1908.

The car would become the staple of the company for 19 years as 15 million automobiles were produced.

The Model T's best feature was its price. For the first time, ownership of an automobile was within reach of regular folks. It also was reliable and able to navigate the poor roads of the era.

The car could travel up to 45 miles per hour and got 13 to 21 miles per gallon.

Oct. 1, 1920
Aviatrix lost over Empire

Senorita Deborah DeCostello came to the village of Empire billed by the Tinney Flyers Corporation as the "world's most daring aviatrix" who would perform the "most spectacular and daring act in the world," according to a poster printed for the Leelanau County Fair.

It turned out the advertisement touting the daredevil act was not exaggerated.

DeCostello's stunt – she would jump from an airplane at 5,000 feet and dangle from the plane by a rope until she would land safely on the ground with the assistance of a parachute – turned out to be fatal.

High winds delayed the act, scheduled for late September. On Oct. 1, 1920, despite persistent winds, the barnstormer made her death-defying leap.

As the 26-year-old leaped, the rope that connected her to the airplane broke and winds pushed her out over Lake Michigan. Rescue boats were dispatched but there was no sign of the woman until her body washed ashore several days later.

DeCostello did not have any family or loved ones to retrieve her body. She is buried in St. Philip's cemetery in Empire.

Oct. 2, 1919
Orchestra Hall opens in Detroit

It took just four months and 23 days to build Orchestra Hall, home of the Detroit Symphony Orchestra.

Workers speedily constructed the building because the orchestra's recently-appointed music director, Russian pianist Ossip

Gabrilowitsch, insisted that the orchestra have a suitable home.

The hall was completed on Oct. 2, 1919, and the first concert at the Woodward Ave. venue was held later that month.

Under Gabrilowitsch, the Detroit Symphony saw a golden age for two decades as the world's most famous musicians, composers and conductors made Detroit a stop on their tours.

The Great Depression brought trouble for the orchestra and it moved to the Masonic Temple Theater in 1939 to save money.

Orchestra Hall reopened two years later as the Paradise Theatre and the venue became a magnet for the country's most famous jazz musicians such as Ella Fitzgerald, Billie Holiday, Count Basie and Duke Ellington.

In the 10 years of its existence, the Paradise rivaled the Apollo Theater in Harlem.

Like so many old buildings in Detroit, the theater fell into disrepair. After the Paradise closed in 1951, the building rotted away and by 1970 the city planned to demolish Orchestra Hall. However, a group of citizens emerged to lead a fight to save the theater.

Led by orchestra bassoonist Paul Ganson, the group marched near the theater and held sidewalk performances that managed to turn away the wrecking ball. The building was added to the National Register of Historic Sites in 1971.

Restoration of the building took place for another two decades. Millions of dollars were raised as the decorative plasterwork was replaced, the theater's original box seating was restored, and a new stage and lighting were added.

As restrooms and backstage facilities were modernized, the original decorative paintings were replicated to restore the grandeur of the theater's golden age.

The Detroit Symphony Orchestra moved back into its historic home in 1989 as restoration continued. The hall celebrated the completion of another wave of restorations in 2003.

Oct. 2, 1873
Construction of new state capitol commences

It was a welcome sign of progress that the state soon would have an impressive, new granite capitol building in Lansing.

The cornerstone for the capitol was laid amid great fanfare on Oct. 2, 1873.

Special trains brought a crowd of 20,000 to the capital for the ceremony. Any fraternal club in Michigan that had a marching band showed up for the hoopla.

Construction already had started on the building and, although the ceremony took place in late 1873, the cornerstone reads: "A.D. 1872."

Construction was completed in 1879 and cost $1.2 million. The building replaced a wooden structure.

Oct. 3, 1980
Somewhere in Time opens

Christopher Reeve played a contemporary young play-wright. Jane Seymour starred as a great American theater star of 1912.

Reeve's character sees a photo of the beautiful young starlet, wills himself back in time, and the stars fall in love.

Vincent Canby reviewed the film in the *New York Times*, saying the movie did "for time travel what the Hindenburg did for dirigibles."

The film may have been campy and, for some viewers, unintentionally comedic, but it was special for Michigan residents. It wasn't merely shot in the state; it was filmed at the Grand Hotel on Mackinac Island.

Canby gave a better review to the location: "The film's principal setting is Mackinac Island, Mich., and its Grand Hotel, which is one of the last, great 19th-century American resorts sill in tip-top shape. The hotel and Mackinac are spectacularly lovely, but fail to give substance to this ephemeral endeavor."

Despite the lackluster reviews that greeted the film's release on Oct. 3, 1980, the movie would go on to become a cult classic and spawn a fan club of devoted followers, some of whom believe *Somewhere in Time* ranks among the best films ever made.

On the west side of the island, there is a monument dedicating the spot where a famous line from the film, "Is it you?" was uttered by Reeve.

An extra on the film, Jo Addie, runs a website devoted to articles about *Somewhere in Time*, memorabilia from the film, and thousands of pages of anecdotes about the movie.

Beginning in 1990, fans of the film have been able to attend a *Somewhere in Time* weekend at the Grand Hotel each October.

The Mackinac Island State Park Commission began renting the *Somewhere in Time* gazebo on the island for weddings beginning in 2006. For $500, a couple can get married in the actual gazebo seen in the film.

Oct. 4, 1641
First Europeans come to Michigan

The first Caucasians who ventured into the land that would become Michigan arrived in birch bark canoes.

French priests left the Penetanguishene, which is on the Georgian Bay in Ontario, paddling north toward Manitoulin Island.

It took 17 days to arrive at their destination but on Oct. 4, 1641, Father Isaac Jogues and Father Charles Raymbault arrived at the falls of St. Mary's River, where they found thousands of Chippewa Indians.

The Europeans and their religion were unknown to the Indians but they warmly welcomed the newcomers.

The priests discovered the attraction the area held for the Indians – the river teemed with whitefish and wildlife abounded in the thick woods that surrounded the settlement.

The Chippewa told their guests about a great body of water to the west which they called Gitchi Gomee, or great water. This would later be named Lake Superior.

Beyond that were lands filled with deer and buffalo, although they Indians warned the priests about traveling too far west to land inhabited by Sioux Indians, who would accord a much less friendly welcome.

The priests were encouraged that the Chippewa would be receptive to a permanent mission at the Sault.

Although the Chippewa invited the men to stay for the winter, the priests decided to make their way back to Canada, a decision that would prove fatal for Raymbault.

Raymbault attempted to return to a village of Algonquins near Lake Nippissing but the weather slowed his journey He spent the winter on the shore of Lake Huron, sickened with tuberculosis that would kill him the following year.

Jogues also would run into bad luck that would prevent him from returning to the Sault.

He returned to what is now Canada to live with a tribe of Huron Indians but was captured by a marauding band of Mohawk Indians.

Jogues' Huron Indian friends were burned at the stake and Jogues was tortured. He eventually was ransomed to the Dutch and he returned to France. He came back to North America in 1646 and again was captured by Mohawk Indians and this time was tortured to death.

Oct. 5, 1833
Detroit makes ecclesiastical history

Many Roman Catholics were a part of the early days of Detroit. But while their significance was great, their numbers were not. Detroit did not become a diocese of the Catholic Church until Oct. 6, 1833. The diocese needed its own bishop and Pope Gregory XVI named Frederick John Conrad Rese to serve in that venerable position.

Bishop Rese was born in Germany and ordained there in 1823. He arrived in Detroit to fill a void created by the death of beloved Father Gabriel Richard, who died in 1828. St. Anne Church, which remains in operation today, was the first church to serve as the city's cathedral.

When Michigan first was settled, it fell under the jurisdiction of the diocese of Bardstown, Kentucky until 1821 when the Michigan Territory became part of the new Diocese of Cincinnati.

The new diocese had 30 priests and approximately 24,000 Catholics, mainly those who had immigrated from France, England, Ireland and Germany. There also were some parishioners who were American born and approximately 3,000 Native Americans who had converted to Catholicism.

Oct. 5, 1813
Death of Chief Tecumseh

For Americans settling in the Michigan frontier, Chief Tecumseh, an ally of the British and a sworn enemy of the American's westward advancement, posed almost as much trouble as Chief Pontiac had when he made his siege on Detroit 50 years earlier.

Tecumseh was more problematic for the Americans than any single British officer during the War of 1812, which had its culmination in the Midwest at the Battle of the Thames.

While the battle did not take place in Michigan, it was a decisive American victory that ensured the Michigan Territory would one day be part of the United States rather than part of Canada.

The events leading up to Tecumseh's death began after the Americans reclaimed Detroit from the British in late September of 1813. The action prompted British General Henry Proctor to flee Fort Malden, in what is today Amherstburg, Ontario, because he feared that the Americans had cut off his supply lines.

General William Henry Harrison, commander of the American forces in the West, left Detroit to chase Proctor and his men into Canada.

Harrison commanded more than 3,000 soldiers, while Proctor had around 800 at his side, plus approximately a thousand Indian warriors led by Tecumseh.

Proctor's weaker numbers were only part of his problem. Not only were his soldiers demoralized and on the run, but they faced the possibility that Tecumseh, angered by Proctor's refusal to stay and fight, would rebel.

For Tecumseh, the British abandonment of Detroit was a betrayal.

On their way to meet the British, the Americans captured British stragglers and supplies until they reached the Thames River, where one of the decisive battles of the War of 1812 would take place.

On Oct. 5, 1813, Proctor decided to stop the retreat and dig in at Moraviantown, near present-day Chatham, Ontario, approximately 55 miles east of Windsor.

Proctor planned to trap the Americans at a point on the Thames River. Proctor would force the Americans into a swamp where Tecumseh and his men would be waiting.

But when the Americans approached the British line, the British cannons failed to fire and the Americans broke through. The British soldiers fled or surrendered.

If the battle against the British had been an easy victory, the Americans were in for a much different kind of fight against Tecumseh, however.

A cavalry led by Colonel Richard Johnson was sent to meet Tecumseh's forces and a furious battle ensued.

In the fighting, Johnson was severely wounded and several Americans were killed.

The battle turned, however, after one of the Americans killed Tecumseh.

Tecumseh's death meant the Indians had not just lost a brilliant and brave military leader, but they had lost the heart of their opposition to fight the Americans.

After the battle, the Americans burned Moraviantown and returned to Detroit. Had Harrison stayed put, southwest Ontario might now be part of Michigan.

Nonetheless, Harrison earned immense popularity for his leadership and would go on to be elected a U.S. senator from Ohio and then president of the United States.

Oct. 6, 1991
Ernie Harwell calls his "final" ballgame

The Detroit Tigers traveled to Baltimore to play the final game of the regular season. For the beloved broadcaster Ernie Harwell, it appeared the game would be his last as a Tigers announcer.

What made Harwell's supposed final game on Oct. 6, 1991 so notable was that the play-by-play man was not leaving on his own terms. In a move inexplicable to fans and the baseball world, Harwell had been fired.

Harwell was a Detroit institution. Tiger's fans thought of him as part of their family whose arrival each year into their homes through their radios signaled the start of spring.

He was considered one of the greatest baseball broadcasters ever and had been inducted into the Baseball Hall of Fame.

Harwell, determined to leave gracefully, did not make a fuss about his firing.

"My main reaction has been one of puzzlement," he told reporters. "I've had so much support from people, and that's been very gratifying. I can't allow myself to be bitter. We all have to move along."

At the time, Harwell was not sure whether he would retire or take a job with another team and, therefore refused to make that season a farewell tour.

"I don't want to be one of those guys who says goodbye and

296

then comes back next month," he said. "That's kind of embarrassing."

A month after he left the Detroit airwaves, there was talk he would take a job calling games for the New York Yankees. Harwell began his career in the major leagues as the announcer for the Brooklyn Dodgers in 1948, after he was traded from a minor league team and became the only broadcaster ever traded for a player.

Harwell's contract with both the Tigers and its broadcasting station, WJR Radio, would not be renewed for the 1992 season. A Tigers vice president said Harwell was let go because his broadcasting skills had diminished over the previous few years.

The move caused a furious backlash against team owner Thomas Monahan and team president Bo Schembechler, the former U-M football coach.

Bumper stickers appeared around Detroit exclaiming, "Say it ain't so, Bo." Newspaper columnists seethed. Fans threatened to boycott Tiger games and Monahan's other business, Domino's Pizza.

Harwell returned in the 1993 season after the team was sold to Mike Ilitch. He retired on his own terms in 2002 after 42 seasons broadcasting Tiger games.

Oct. 7, 1935
Detroit Tigers win first World Series

The Tigers began playing major league baseball in 1901 but the team was unable to win a world championship in three and a half decades. This despite employing baseball luminaries such as Ty Cobb, who led the Tigers to World Series appearances three years in a row – in 1907, 1908, and 1909.

That changed in 1935, when the Tigers won their division's pennant by winning their division by three games during the regular season. They faced the Chicago Cubs, who took the first game of the World Series 3-0 in Detroit.

Detroit came back resoundingly in the next game, winning 8-3. The Cubs won just one more game as the Tigers went on to win the World Series title in six games.

The Tigers won the World Series again in 1945, 1968 and 1984.

Oct. 7, 1916
The "Human Fly" climbs building in Detroit

In an era before climbing tall buildings was outlawed after horrified crowds watched daredevils plunge to their deaths, the *Detroit News* brought attention to a new classified ad office by hiring the "Human Fly" to climb one of Detroit's tallest buildings, the 14-story Majestic Building, on Oct. 7, 1916.

A day prior to the climb, the newspaper promoted the stunt shamelessly, announcing to readers that they could see the man President Grover Cleveland had dubbed the "Human Fly" at just past noon the following day.

"You watch him tomorrow," the paper reported. "He will come from the door of the News downtown office dressed in a white duck suit and hat, with a Detroit News bag thrown over his shoulder and several copies of the latest edition in it."

At the time of the stunt, approximately 150,000 people crowded into Woodward and Michigan Avenues to gawk.

The climber, Harry Gardiner, calmly approached the building, made the sign of the cross and started to climb.

Apparently the only special equipment Gardiner used was a pair of athletic shoes.

He made his way up the building, grasping at crevices in the brick and lifting himself onto ledges.

The crowd was mostly quiet as Gardiner pressed on. The most thrilling part of the climb came at the 12th floor, where Gardiner made his way horizontally across the building to avoid a huge arch.

Gardiner straddled the arch support and swung over it to reach the opposite ledge, a feat it took the climber four tries to accomplish.

When Gardiner reached a rope set out for him so he could pull himself onto the building's roof, the crowd burst into cheers.

Gardiner had climbed 211 feet in 37 minutes, and the event was such a success the newspaper planned to offer a second show the following Saturday. That event was cancelled, presumably at the behest of police or city officials.

The Majestic Building was demolished in the 1960s and replaced by the First Federal Building.

Oct. 8, 1871
Fire ravages Michigan

The summer had been hot and dry. Wilted leaves fell onto sawdust, wood scraps and brush. For weeks, fires had burned out of control across the state. Residents of Detroit were used to a smoky haze that obscured their view of the sky. The scent of fire hung over the state from burning forests.

However, the real crisis did not appear until Oct. 8, 1871, when hurricane-like winds pounded the state, stirring up the fires and spreading them with fury across the landscape.

That horrific day in Michigan might be better known had it not been the same day as the Great Chicago Fire.

Nonetheless, estimates of the dead in Michigan reached into the hundreds. Thousands or tens of thousands were left homeless.

298

So many fires consumed the state that day that a full catalog is impossible to recount in a short space.

In the Upper Peninsula, flames from the Peshtigo fire in Wisconsin, which killed more than a thousand in that state, jumped the Menominee River into Michigan, turning the sky red, wiping out forests and towns and killing anything in its way.

Lumber camp towns were especially vulnerable, due to the excess sawdust and scraps of wood.

Manistee was devastated by fire that day. Holland was struck by a firestorm. The fires in those towns swept across the state to Lake Huron.

Separate fires broke out in the Thumb and burned thousands of acres.

Students and faculty at the Michigan Agricultural College, the precursor to Michigan State, formed bucket brigades to save their campus.

Contemporary accounts of the fire blame the drought, the strong winds, and the condition of the land after it had been clear-cut by loggers.

Oct. 9, 1975
KISS descends on Cadillac

On most days in most years, the City of Cadillac attracts campers and fishermen to its parks and lakes.

But one day in 1975, Cadillac looked like a much different place. It was the day the rock band KISS came to town for a parade and concert. The event saw Cadillac's most prominent citizens sporting the band's trademark black and white face paint.

The publicity stunt was just goofy enough to work. It received attention from newspapers across the country. The story was covered in *Rolling Stone* and *Billboard* magazines.

Cadillac High School English teacher and assistant football coach Jim Neff inadvertently caused the whole thing to happen.

Neff wanted to motivate his Cadillac Vikings football squad when he nicknamed the defense "KISS," which he said stood for "keep it simple stupid."

The team had just followed up an undefeated season with losses in their first two games.

Neff decided to play KISS records before and after practice to motivate the team. It must have worked because the team won its next seven games.

Word that their songs inspired the team made its way to the band. One thing led to another and arrangements were made for a KISS homecoming concert the following season.

For 24 hours, on Oct. 9, 1975, Cadillac became a city of rock 'n' roll.

The band arrived in town at noon and retreated to Bill Oliver's

Caberfae Motor Lodge, where the members put on their famous makeup.

The group went downtown, where police and firefighters acted as official escorts to Cadillac High School, where students lined the school's entrance to welcome the band.

Students showed KISS members a film they had made about the band. The group also met with the football team and the marching band.

Some members of the community had been wary about the Satanic-looking rock band coming to their town visiting their school, and playing for their children.

But the band members behaved and left a favorable impression. The band was even willing to remove references to alcohol from their work and to refrain from fake blood-spitting during the concert.

Students and faculty, Cadillac residents young and old, were united in an unlikely way.

The following day, band members had breakfast with civic leaders, who wore face paint like the band. A parade through town was held before they returned to the high school to say goodbye.

KISS maintained it came to Cadillac not for publicity but because it loved football and appreciated that the music had inspired the team.

Bassist Gene Simmons told a reporter: "We were the ones who left Cadillac inspired. That concert, the parade and everything else from our time there will go down as one of the most important moments in our band's history. We have performed hundreds of concerts in lots of cities all over the world and the Cadillac performance will never be forgotten by any of us."

Throughout the rest of the football season, KISS called Neff each Friday night to see how the team had done.

Oct. 10, 1901
Ford wins race

Henry Ford had a promising career as chief engineer at Detroit's Edison Illuminating Company but his first love was tinkering with automobiles.

He had tried and failed the previous two years to develop an auto manufacturing business. He had wealthy backers and attempted to get the Detroit Auto Company off the ground but it was not to be.

So, on Oct. 10, 1901, Ford took one of his contraptions to the Grosse Pointe Race Track, where he entered a race against Alexander Winton, a Cleveland auto manufacturer considered one of the greatest racers of the day.

It took Ford some time to discover how to make the turns at a high speed but once he got the hang of it, Ford overtook Winton, whose car suffered mechanical problems.

Ford won the race and much positive publicity.

The win helped him recruit backers who put up money to form the Henry Ford Motor Company, a precursor to the corporation that would make Ford one of the world's wealthiest men.

Oct. 10, 1938
Blue Water Bridge opens

The long process to build a bridge that connects the United States and Canada between Port Huron and Sarnia actually began in the 1920s.

Construction of the bridge was complicated because it needed approval not just from the cities but also from the U.S. Congress and the Canadian government.

In May 1928, the residents of Sarnia held a celebration after President Calvin Coolidge signed the St. Clair Transit Bill and the Canadian government passed a similar measure.

They assumed construction of a bridge was imminent but the countries soon tumbled into the Depression and the project was canceled.

In 1936, after the project had faltered several times, it was taken over by the Michigan Bridge Commission. Financing was arranged and construction began the next year. The bridge cost $3.6 million, which is nearly $54 million in present-day dollars.

A second Blue Water Bridge opened in 1997 next to the original bridge. The original bridge carries westbound traffic, and the newer bridge carries travelers heading to Canada.

Oct. 11, 1843
Legendary copper boulder arrives in Detroit

Early settlers learned from French fur traders of a great mass of copper located in the wilds of the western Upper Peninsula. Later, geologist Henry Rowe Schoolcraft attempted to devise a way to remove it, only to give up in the face of what seemed like a futile endeavor.

For decades, no one thought the massive rock could be moved from its perch along the Ontonagon River.

Still, the Americans wanted it. When the federal government negotiated a treaty with the Indians to secure lands in the area, Americans demanded mineral rights that would include the copper boulder. The United States won, despite the fact that the Ontonagon boulder was considered sacred to the Indians.

Somehow, the boulder became an obsession for a Detroit hardware store owner. Julius Eldred had read Schoolcraft's report on copper in Michigan and caught copper fever. He was determined to own it.

When Eldred arrived in Ontonagon in 1841, he bought the boulder for $150 from Chief Okondokon, whose tribe resided at the mouth of the river. Eldred thought the Indians still owned the boulder and Okondokon apparently was happy to indulge his delusion.

Eldred returned to Detroit before traveling again to the Upper Peninsula in 1843, ready to set his plan in motion. Upon his return, Eldred discovered that his party was one of several that had arrived in Copper Country that summer to stake its claim.

When he arrived at the boulder with approximately 20 men and moving equipment, Eldred found the boulder guarded by a larger group of men who had secured a permit from the U. S. War Department. The group claimed ownership of the boulder.

However, Eldred was determined. He negotiated to buy the 3,700-pound copper rock again.

This time he paid $1,365.

Eldred's men, with a specially constructed cart, rope, and pulleys, inched the rock through the wilderness. Railroad track was laid and the rock pushed forward. The track was then pulled up and hauled in front of the boulder to be laid again.

Amazingly, Eldred managed to get the boulder over hills and through thick woods to the shore of Lake Superior.

But by the time the boulder was out of the wilderness, Eldred received some bad news – ownership of the rock now was claimed by the federal government. He met a military official who had orders to confiscate the rock.

Eldred was furious and dumbfounded. He put great effort and expense into the project and had nothing to show for it.

Eventually, the military officials agreed that the $700 the War Department had agreed to pay for the rock's removal from the wilderness was not fair compensation and Eldred should be allowed to take the rock to Detroit.

Eldred arrived in Detroit with the natural curiosity on Oct. 11, 1843.

A tent was set up on Jefferson Avenue where Eldred charged gawkers 25 cents for a peak at his massive chunk of copper.

Still, many people believed the boulder belonged in Washington D.C. as a national exhibit.

Orders finally came from the U.S. District Attorney. The boulder was confiscated by soldiers and taken to Washington.

Eldred followed the boulder to Washington and continued his fight. After three years of negotiations, Congress authorized a settlement. The government paid Eldred and his sons $5,664.98 for their trouble.

The boulder remains at the Smithsonian Institution, although it is not currently on display.

In the 1990s, the Keweenaw Bay Indian Community petitioned

the federal government to have the boulder returned to the Upper Peninsula on the grounds that it is a sacred object to the tribe. The request was denied.

Oct. 12, 1973
Nixon picks Gerald R. Ford for vice president

For 24 years, Gerald Ford had been attending the Red Flannel Festival in Cedar Springs, a small town north of Grand Rapids that billed itself as the red flannel underwear manufacturing capital of the world.

This year would be no exception, although Ford, a member of the U.S. House of Representatives for decades, now was flanked by a cadre of Secret Service agents and many more reporters as he marched in a parade, sporting a red flannel vest and walking alongside a high school marching band.

"I'm a little overwhelmed, to be quite frank and a little thrilled and pleased," Ford said at a stop at Jordan College. "As soon as we go to work next week, I'm sure some of this overnight glamour will wear off."

Ford was swept into the national spotlight a day earlier, when, in an announcement that surprised many in politics, President Richard M. Nixon named Ford as his new vice president on Oct. 12, 1973.

Ford, then House Minority Leader, stepped out of a safe congressional career into a presidential administration embroiled in controversy.

Ford replaced Spiro T. Agnew, who resigned as vice president a few days earlier after he pled guilty to income tax evasion.

Ford was a popular pick. In more than two decades in Congress, the Republican – known for his integrity and openness – had friends on both sides of the aisle.

After Nixon resigned and Ford became president on August 9, 1974, he gave up any chance of winning the presidential election in 1976 when he pardoned Nixon.

In addition to being the only president from Michigan, Ford is also the only president to have never won a national election.

Ford attended the University of Michigan on a football scholarship where he was a star center. On Oct. 15, 1948, he married Elizabeth " Betty" Anne Bloomer, a dancer who studied under Martha Graham. Mrs. Ford was known for her candor and as an outspoken advocate for women's rights.

He died Dec. 26, 2006 at the age of 93. His presidential museum is in Grand Rapids, on the shores of the Grand River.

Oct. 13, 1845
Douglass Houghton drowns in Lake Superior

There is perhaps no one who did so much to discover the wealth of Michigan for so little in return.

Douglass Houghton was the first to hold the title of state geologist of Michigan and he took his job seriously.

He traveled the Upper Peninsula where he painstakingly surveyed its mineral riches.

Houghton was paid a meager salary while other men made fortunes from what he learned about the copper and iron in the wilderness.

He received no wealth from the copper mining district of the Keweenaw, which grew upon his painstaking scientific work and eventually paid out $332,000,000 in dividends to mine company shareholders.

Perhaps if Houghton had lived longer than 36 years, he would have seen a profit from his endeavors.

Houghton was born in Troy, New York in 1809, studied medicine and settled in Detroit to practice medicine and dentistry. Houghton was a member of Henry Rowe Schoolcraft's expedition to the Upper Peninsula, where he established a reputation as a great scientist after he published reports about copper deposits and botany.

On Oct. 13, 1845, as Houghton was preparing to leave the Keweenaw region for the lower peninsula after a summer of work, he set out in a small boat to join to a geological surveying party about 10 miles away.

As he and four rowers left Eagle River late in the day, a large storm swept in just as their destination was in view.

An enormous wave capsized the boat and all of the men fell into the water. One of them attempted to save Houghton, but he insisted he could make it to shore without any aid and told his men to save themselves. All but Houghton and one other man made it to shore alive.

Houghton's body remained in the icy water until the following spring.

There is a monument to Houghton in Eagle River and the largest city in the copper district is named after him.

Oct. 14, 1960
President Kennedy proposes the Peace Corps

Presidential candidate John F. Kennedy harkened back to an earlier and almost extinct era in American politics in the campaign of 1960. While his opponent Richard M. Nixon hopped from one place to the next in a jet, Kennedy led a one-day whistle-stop tour of Michigan by train.

Kennedy was after the state's 20 electoral votes, then the seventh most of any state. His stop in Michigan began in Ann Arbor, where he arrived after his plane landed at Willow Run Airport.

A few hours earlier the candidates had tangled in their third nationally televised debate in New York City. When Kennedy arrived in Ann Arbor at 2 a.m. on Oct. 14, 1960, he expected to get some sleep in a room at the Michigan Union .

But when Kennedy arrived, he found throngs of students waiting for him at the entrance.

Kennedy did not have a speech prepared but he decided to address the crowd nonetheless.

He could have resorted to a standard stump speech or merely asked for their votes, but instead he spoke extemporaneously, asking the students if they were willing to make a sacrifice for their country.

While Kennedy did not name or describe the Peace Corps, Kennedy's improvised talk about the need for young people to give something to their country through work in the Foreign Service is credited with giving life to the notion of the organization he would go on to create.

Kennedy said: "How many of you who are going to be doctors, are willing to spend your days in Ghana? Technicians or engineers, how many of you are willing to work in the Foreign Service and spend your lives traveling around the world? On your willingness to do that, not merely to serve one year or two years in the service, but on your willingness to contribute part of your life to this country, I think will depend the answer whether a free society can compete."

While history marks the moment as significant and the university memorializes it with a marker at the spot where Kennedy spoke, Kennedy's words generated little buzz at the time.

In fact, in its article on Kennedy's tour of Michigan, the *New York Times* does not even mention the proposal.

Rather, that newspaper's report on what happened in Ann Arbor focused on whether Kennedy had said "hell" into a microphone while speaking to an aid about technical difficulties during a speech made the next morning.

Such an utterance could have been scandalous because Nixon had recently singled out such language as dangerous to children.

Kennedy's train later made stops in Jackson, Albion, Marshall, Battle Creek, Kalamazoo, Grand Rapids, Lansing and Saginaw.

Kennedy carried Michigan on his way to victory that November.

Oct. 15, 1880
Steamer *Alpena* lost off Holland

When the steamship *Alpena* left port in Grand Haven carrying up to 100 passengers and crew along with several railroad cars filled with apples, the evening was fair and the lake was calm.

The barometer was falling but the weather was beautiful and warm. There was likely little about Oct. 15, 1880, to concern passengers as they embarked on their short sail to Chicago.

However, with little warning, a storm churned up the lake and battered the cities and villages on the Lake Michigan coast.

In Muskegon, residents clung to lamp posts to stay erect in the face of gale force winds. Smoke stacks toppled while billboards and road planks were flung through the air.

If conditions were so severe on land, those aboard the *Alpena* found themselves in worse circumstances with no place of refuge.

Exactly what happened to the *Alpena* and its passengers is not known. For weeks after she disappeared, evidence of her fate littered Lake Michigan.

A ladder and a pail that bore the markings of the ship washed up on a beach near Holland.

Two lifeboats also were found on shore, their oars tied down, indicating that the passengers had not been able to launch them before they were swept from the ship.

Several messages also were found. A bottle that washed ashore contained the insurance papers of two passengers. On the bottom of a basket someone had written a description of the *Alpena's* final moments – the ship was being torn to pieces and its passengers knew they were doomed.

A similar message, written by the captain, was found on a shingle.

Perhaps the most eerie evidence of what happened were the apples bobbing in the waters near Holland the following weeks.

Only a small number of bodies were recovered.

The captain of the *Alpena* was not the only captain on the Great Lakes that day to ignore the falling barometer. As many as 90 other ships were lost in that storm, which lasted for two days.

Oct. 15, 1908
The Metz fire

Newspapers around the country reported about the 75-mile-long wall of flame that tore through northeast Michigan.

In a state that saw so many deadly fires, this fire stands out because of the horror it brought to the residents to the tiny town of Metz, near Alpena, and the magnitude of the flames that swept through logging towns.

In Metz, on Oct. 15, 1908, residents hastily hopped aboard a Detroit & Mackinac Railroad train hoping to outrun the flames.

The train was rushed to the village with three empty freight cars and two coal gondolas to help residents escape. The train, filled with men, women and children along with whatever possessions the townsfolk could carry, hastily steamed out of town to the south.

After two miles, the conductor noted that the train was headed toward large cedar post piles on each side of the track that were ablaze. The conductor opened the throttle and attempted to race through the fire but the heat had twisted the rails. Just as the train reached the fire it derailed and burst into flames.

Sixteen people aboard died, many of them women and children, and dozens were badly burned.

Oct. 15, 1951
First international television broadcast

WWJ-TV sent an announcer, Bud Lynch, across the Detroit River to the Government Dock in Windsor.

Lynch hosted a live broadcast that featured coverage of an informal reception given for Prince Philip, Duke of Edinburgh, and Princess Elizabeth of Great Britain, who four months later would become Queen of England.

This was the first live international television broadcast.

Oct. 16, 1986
Joe Louis fist sculpture dedicated

As a boxer, Joe Louis united a nation in the lead-up to World War II when he defeated German boxer Max Schmeling for the heavyweight title of the world.

The city of Detroit honored its hometown hero with a symbol of his strength – an extended fist, similar to his boxing jab. Artist Robert Graham's sculpture to honor Louis was commissioned by Time Inc. and dedicated on October 16, 1986.

The 24-foot long black arm and fist is suspended from a pyramid support in the median on Jefferson Avenue across from the downtown's Hart Plaza. The sculpture weighs approximately 8,000 pounds.

A life-sized statue of "The Brown Bomber" is found inside Cobo Hall, near the fist statue.

Oct. 17, 1926
The "Radio Priest" delivers first sermon in Detroit

It was unlikely anyone predicted that Catholic priest Father Charles Coughlin, who took the pulpit for the first time in suburban Detroit on Oct. 17, 1926 would become one of the most influential men in American politics, hosting a national radio show that spewed his anti-Semitic views.

The same year that he started preaching, Coughlin appeared on radio to reach a wider audience.

Coughlin turned to radio after Detroit's bishop asked Coughlin to open a church in Royal Oak in 1926. Coughlin needed to raise money, and he noted that no other priest had taken to the airwaves. He convinced a Catholic manager at WJR to give him a radio show.

Coughlin proved adept at raising money over the airwaves.

His fundraising paid for his church, the National Shrine of the Little Flower, a landmark on Woodward Avenue in Royal Oak.

At first, Coughlin talked about religion on his show but soon branched into politics as his popularity grew. His message attracted millions of listeners. At the height of his heyday, one in three people in the country tuned in to the weekly broadcast of the Radio Priest. He founded a newspaper, *Social Justice*, to further spread his views.

A new post office had to be built in Royal Oak to handle the 80,000 letters he received each week.

His views were complicated – he staunchly opposed communism but he also opposed wealthy industrialists who controlled the means of production, and he was an ardent supporter of unions.

He was one of Franklin D. Roosevelt's staunchest supporters. However, Coughlin decided Roosevelt's reforms did not go far enough and that Roosevelt was not committed to driving "the money changers from the temple." Then Coughlin became one of Roosevelt's loudest detractors.

Although he claimed he was not an anti-Semite, Coughlin remained consistent in his anti-Jewish views.

He cloaked his hatred for Jews in code language, referring to "international bankers" and blaming Communism on "Karl Marx, a Hebrew." He defended the actions of the Nazis as necessary to stop the spread of Communism and attempted to use his clout to prevent the U.S. from entering World War II.

Perhaps the war took the wind out of Coughlin's demagoguery or perhaps he was silenced by the Catholic Church. The Roosevelt administration took steps to remove Coughlin from the air and prevent the distribution of his publication through the mail.

Coughlin ceased broadcasting in 1942. He remained a priest until his retirement in 1966 and died in 1979 at the age of 88.

Oct. 18, 1919
The case of the missing nun cracks open

Sister Mary Johns had a troubled life. She moved into a convent at age 9 when she was orphaned. At age 18, she took vows to become a nun. In her early 30s, she became ill and it was thought that Sister Mary Johns should move from Detroit to Isadore, a tiny spot in Leelanau County, where the northern Michigan climate might improve her condition.

In Isadore she joined a small church community that was led by Father Bieniawski, his sister and two nuns. Also in Isadore were the priest's Polish housekeeper and her daughter.

At first, it looked as though the change of scenery was good for the sister. She liked her new surroundings and loved to spend time outdoors picking flowers.

Sister Mary Johns was on one of those walks when she was last seen in August 1907.

Father Bieniawski returned from fishing on Lake Leelanau to learn Sister Mary Johns had disappeared. He made a quick search through the grounds and the buildings but found no trace of the nun.

The sheriff was called and hundreds of parishioners searched the area for weeks. Those who knew her were certain she would not have merely have run off. Bloodhounds were brought in, psychics offered their services and the search continued.

Some thought Sister Mary Johns may have wandered into a large cedar swamp at the base of Lake Leelanau.

The mystery deepened when an unsigned letter arrived claiming that Sister Mary Johns had run away and should be left alone. The letter had a Chicago postmark.

Months passed. Then years. And the case of the missing nun faded away.

Eight years later there was another lead. A woman confessed to a priest in Milwaukee that she had murdered a nun and buried her underneath a pile of lumber in the basement of a church in Isadore.

Oddly, no action was taken and more years passed.

The crime was finally uncovered during a botched effort to cover it up in 1918.

A new church was planned for Isadore and Father Edward Podlesweski, who had replaced Father Bieniawski, removed bones from the basement of the church and buried them in the cemetery. He wanted to avoid the embarrassment the discovery of the body would have caused.

But Father Podlesweski was having an affair with a 19-year-old girl. When the affair was discovered by the girl's father, the girl told what she knew about the bones found in the basement.

Warrants were issued for the arrest of Father Bieniawski and his housekeeper, who were living in Manistee.

As the investigation unfolded, it was determined the priest knew nothing of the murder of Sister Mary Johns and that the housekeeper, Stanislawa Lypszynska, had acted alone.

Authorities said Lypszynska confessed in jail to a woman who spoke Polish, planted in an adjacent cell to pose as a fellow inmate with a sympathetic ear.

The housekeeper later denied giving the confession.

The housekeeper was convicted on Oct. 18, 1919. Apparently she killed the sister out of jealousy; Sister Mary Johns spent too much time with the priest.

Oct. 19, 1918
No church on Sunday

In newspapers across Michigan, tucked away amid headlines about World War I deaths and news of the German Kaiser, residents learned that starting this Sunday, by order of the state government, all meeting places would be closed.

The order went into effect on Oct. 19, 1918, just after midnight, and was to remain in force until further notice.

The front page of the *Traverse City Record-Eagle* made no mention of the reason for the ban because people already knew why.

In an editorial in the same edition, the newspaper bemoaned a lack of willingness among citizens to contain contagious diseases like Spanish influenza, which was ravaging Michigan that fall.

"When scarlet fever is prevalent, there are plenty of people who will send their children to school when they have enough of the disease to give it to other pupils," an editor wrote. "They dislike so much to be quarantined that they will conceal the suspicious symptoms until someone is really very sick and they get scared."

The editorial concluded that if only people were willing to stay out of work or away from school when they got sick, thousands of lives could be saved.

The day following that churchless Sunday, the newspaper described the city as a ghost town: "Yesterday was, perhaps, the quietest Sunday in the history of the city. Churches and theaters remained closed. Few people were on the street. But for the fact that the gasoline ban had been raised, permitting the use of motor cars, the streets would have been deserted."

Oct. 19, 1903
Western Michigan founded

The support for a state school in Kalamazoo was overwhelming. When voters went to the polls on Oct. 19, 1903, the residents voted 8 to 1 in favor of a measure to fund construction of the Western State Normal School, later known as Western Michigan University.

Kalamazoo was selected as the site because of its central location in southwest Michigan. It also won the college because its residents agreed to raise $120,000 in a bond sale to pay for 20 acres of land, improvements, roads and building construction.

Oct. 20, 2001
"Gateway to Freedom" installed at Detroit River

Detroit played a critical role in the Underground Railroad in the early 19th century. It was the last stop for slaves headed to freedom in Canada and many brave Detroiters, as well as other Michiganders, aided the fleeing slaves.

To commemorate this history, the development group Detroit 300 commissioned two sculptures, one installed in Detroit, the other in Windsor. They were dedicated on Oct. 20, 2001.

The Detroit sculpture features nine slaves led by an Underground Railroad conductor, framed by two pillars. The "conductor" points toward freedom in Canada.

The conductor in the statue is a likeness of George deBaptiste, a former steward of President William Henry Harrison. DeBaptiste worked as a caterer during the day and helped escaping slaves by night. To cross the river, deBaptiste was forced to hire a white steamship captain because blacks were not issued pilot licenses.

In Windsor, the commemoration features a 22-foot tall granite "Freedom Tower," with statues of a male slave showing thanks, a female slave holding a baby and a female Underground Railroad operator welcoming them.

Oct. 21, 1970
Sleeping Bear Dunes National Lakeshore authorized

A national park along the Lake Michigan shore in Leelanau and Benzie counties first was proposed in 1961 by U.S. Senator Philip Hart.

The natural beauty of the steep bluffs, sandy beaches and pristine lakes and streams that ran through the property was ideal for preservation.

But the proposal not was met with resounding approval.

Many property owners in the proposed park district feared the government would confiscate their land.

Proposals were put forward and compromises offered. Landowners grew distrustful of politicians. Local newspapers took sides.

Congress finally authorized a park on Oct. 21, 1970 that would include 35 miles of shoreline on the mainland as well as North and South Manitou Islands. The park included dunes, forests, beaches, a lighthouse dating back to 1871, three former life-saving service stations and a restored farming district.

The homeowners' fears were not misplaced. Much of the land was acquired by the federal government. Some residents believed they were bullied into selling their land.

It was 1976 before the park opened. The process of acquiring land for the park proved complicated and bitterness over the park among people who were displaced still lingers.

Oct. 21, 1929
The Edison Institute founded

The date for the occasion was the 50th anniversary of the invention of the incandescent light bulb by Thomas Edison, Henry Ford's friend.

President Herbert Hoover visited Dearborn on Oct. 21, 1929 to dedicate the Edison Institute, which consisted of Greenfield Village, the Henry Ford Institute and the Greenfield Village Schools. Edison also had a prominent role at the grand opening.

Edison and Ford had done more than anyone else to change the way Americans lived. Ford's transformation of the auto industry put an end to rural life as Ford knew it as a boy. Yet, Ford regretted how the world had changed and he sought to preserve what he could in his collection of artifacts from 19th century American life.

Greenfield Village was America's first outdoor museum and it contains more than a hundred historic buildings brought there from around America. The museum complex is less than a mile from Ford's home, Fair Lane.

The Henry Ford Institute contains Ford's collection of Americana, which he began to acquire in 1906.

Oct, 22, 1898
First flight or big hoax?

According to his own account, Augustus Moore Herring of Benton Harbor achieved what was thought impossible on Oct. 22, 1898 – he lifted off the ground in a flying contraption and briefly soared through the air using mechanical power.

Herring forgot one crucial ingredient in his quest to be the first man to fly, however – there was no photographer on hand to document the flight.

Absent that, instead of accolades, all Herring found was skepticism.

There was a reporter on hand for the flight, that was supposed to have taken place at Silver Beach in St. Joseph and there was a report about it in the *Benton Harbor Evening News*.

Others maintain that Herring was doomed to obscurity not for lack of proof but because his machine was not very good.

The compressed air engine could only keep the plane aloft for seconds and there was no way to steer the plane. What Herring had was little more than a noisy glider. Newspapers reported that he remained aloft for 8 to 10 seconds.

However, Herring was the first to receive a patent in aviation.

He applied for a patent for his man-supporting, heavier-than-air flying machine in 1896.

Herring failed to become a household name and five years later Orville and Wilbur Wright took off in their airplane, photographer on hand, and flew into the history books.

Oct. 23, 1959
Sam Raimi born in Royal Oak

Sam Raimi used his love of the Three Stooges and an 8mm camera to launch a career that would make him one of the most successful directors in Hollywood.

Born in Royal Oak on Oct. 23, 1959, Raimi began making movies at an early age with good friends Bruce Campbell, who would go on to become an actor, and Robert Tapert, who would become a producer, writer and director.

Raimi left Michigan State University to make *Evil Dead*, produced after he and his friends made a short film that raised approximately $350,000 for the feature length movie.

Evil Dead did not interest U.S. distributors until Raimi took the film to Europe, where the low-budget horror film was a hit. When the movie finally was released in the U.S. to good reviews and strong box office sales, Raimi was on his way.

The Three Stooges influence was evident in the follow up/remake of *Evil Dead, Evil Dead II,* which featured more dark humor, slapstick comedy and basically told the same story as the first movie with a larger budget.

Raimi went on to direct *Darkman* and *Army of Darkness*, a sequel in the *Evil Dead* series that was more fantasy than horror and went on to become a cult film.

Raimi strayed from his trademark horror films in the middle 1990s, becoming a mainstream Hollywood director, making the western *The Quick and the Dead*, a thriller called *A Simple Plan* and *For the Love of the Game*, a baseball movie.

In 2002, he released *Spider-Man*, followed by two more films in the franchise, which cemented Raimi's name among directors who made blockbuster Hollywood movies.

Oct. 24, 1901
Michigan teacher first over Niagra in a barrel

Niagara Falls had been discovered. Barrels had been invented. It was only a matter of time before someone would put the two together.

The unlikely person to first do this was a 63-year-old school teacher from Bay City.

Annie Taylor hoped to give a spark to her life and earn some money on the lecture circuit after accomplishing the feat. She was a widow and had failed in an effort to start a dance school in Bay City. Her life was near financial ruin.

Taylor chose the Canadian Horseshoe Falls for her stunt and hired a Bay City cooper to build her a barrel.

She was carried by boat into the Niagara River on Oct. 24, 1901 and lowered herself into her barrel. A bicycle pump was used to pressurize the barrel. Then it was dropped into the water and she floated down the river toward the falls as hundreds of spectators gathered to watch what promised to be a tragedy.

In the darkness of the barrel, Taylor waited as the water pulled her rapidly toward the falls. The entire journey took 18 minutes.

Gawkers watched the barrel reach the crest of the falls and plunge with the rushing water. The barrel disappeared in the foam and the mist for a moment before it popped up intact in the pool below the falls.

A rescuer on a boat who was waiting to recover Taylor shouted, "My God, she's alive!" as he opened the barrel. Taylor, it turned out, had suffered only minor injuries.

Among Taylor's first words after freeing herself from the barrel were: "Nobody ought ever to do that again."

The stunt was not the boon to Taylor's life for which she hoped.

She was unable cash in on her fame as a circus performer as did Charles Blondin when 50 years earlier he became rich and famous after walking over the falls on a tightrope.

Taylor thought the new medium of film was beneath her and she refused to appear at dime museums.

Her life ended in poverty and she spent her last years autographing postcards at Niagara Falls.

Oct. 25, 1825
Erie Canal opens

In its early years, few people lived in Michigan and land was inexpensive.

To reach Michigan by land meant scaling mountains thick with forest and negotiating dangerous swamps.

Travel from the east was easier with the opening of the Erie Canal, on Oct. 25, 1825.

The journey from New York to Detroit could be measured in days rather than in weeks.

With the opening of the canal, a tidal wave of settlers from New England moved to Michigan, taking advantage of the cheap, fertile land.

Also, the cost of shipping goods from Michigan to the east became about a quarter of what it had been before.

Oct. 25, 1902
Sault Ste. Marie power canal opens

For years residents who lived around Sault Ste. Marie dreamed of harnessing the flow of the Saint Mary's River to generate power. In a power canal, electricity is generated as water descends level to level. Electric generators are powered by water wheel-driven shafting.

In 1898, Francis Clergies, an industrialist who lived in Sault Ste. Marie, Ontario, organized the Michigan Lake Superior Power Company to build a canal on the American route where several previous fortunes had been lost in such an endeavor.

After four years of excavation, a canal 200 feet wide, 24 feet deep and more than two miles long was completed.

It opened on Oct. 25, 1902 amid a great celebration.

Clergue spent $50,000 for fireworks, bands and food. People came from cities across the country to celebrate its opening.

Nonetheless, Clergue's business failed. But the canal opened new opportunities for industry in the region.

The first enterprise to take advantage of the power canal was Union Carbide Company, which later moved from Sault Ste. Marie to West Virginia and Texas and became a multinational corporation.

Oct. 26, 1854
Birth of Charles W. Post

Charles W. Post was born in Illinois on Oct. 26, 1854. Although he would go on to become a wealthy man, it took Post a while to find his way in life.

At the age of 38, Post sought treatment for poor health at the Seventh Day Adventists' Battle Creek Sanitarium, a place that promoted good diet, rest and exercise as a cure. It also scared people off stimulating beverages such as coffee.

Post was almost penniless and his wife sold suspenders door-to-door to pay for his treatment. At the sanitarium, he took a liking to the cereal and cereal beverages that had been developed by Dr. John Harvey Kellogg.

After his treatment, Post spent $69 to start a company that produced a cereal drink, Postum, a beverage similar to one developed by Kellogg called Caramel-Cereal.

An early advertisement for Postum featured a face that somewhat resembled Santa Claus and read, "No! I don't drink coffee. It does not agree with my health. The crank is the man who persists in drink that slowly ruins his stomach and nerves. I drink Postum Food Coffee."

Post is believed to be the first to offer coupons for products in print advertising.

He went on to produce another product, Grape-Nuts, a cereal also similar to food Kellogg served at his sanitarium. Post mimicked several other Kellogg products and eventually amassed a vast fortune.

Post's health remained a problem and he moved to California seeking a better climate. He died in California in 1914. His company went on to become General Foods Corporation.

Forty-two companies sprang up in Battle Creek in the early 20th century to cash in on the cereal frenzy.

John Kellogg's brother, W. K. Kellogg, hoping to get on the success in 1906, formed the Battle Creek Toasted Corn Flakes Company, which went on to become Kellogg Company.

Oct. 27, 1879
First telephone

The first phone installed in a Michigan town was not in Detroit or Grand Rapids or Ann Arbor but in Rockland, a town of a few hundred residents in the Upper Peninsula's Ontonagon County.

The people of Rockland laughed when Linus Stannard installed a "box" in his home so he could talk over a wire with neighbors; neighbors who had no telephones of their own.

Stannard had visited the Centennial Exposition in Philadelphia in 1876 and listened to a lecture by Alexander Graham Bell.

Stannard often walked miles to a neighbor's house to deliver a message or discuss business, so Bell's invention that enabled its user to speak over long distances interested Stannard.

When Stannard arrived home, he discovered his fellow townsfolk unimpressed

But Stannard convinced five nearby friends to start a company and construct a private line.

Eighteen miles of wires strung on cedar poles were stretched from Greenland to Ontonagon through Rockland, a job that took two weeks and was completed in March of 1877.

Once up and going, the five men had a party line and almost every night they demonstrated the strange device.

At first skeptics believed they were being hoaxed and that the singing or talking they heard was not coming from miles away but from an adjacent room. Eventually these people became convinced the telephone was real and on Oct. 27, 1879 the partners formed the Ontonagon County Telephone Company.

Oct. 28, 1929
Opening of famous Detroit restaurant

The building on Gratiot Avenue in Detroit was built around 1880. It had been a grocery store. Later it was a cigar factory. In 1929, Joe Muer, who had run the cigar manufacturing business at the site with his father for more than 20 years, decided to turn the building into a restaurant. It opened on Oct. 28.

The following day, markets on Wall Street crashed, signaling the start of the worst economic period the country had ever seen, the Great Depression.

A restaurant that opened on the eve of the world's most horrific economic collapse did not have much of a chance for survival as fortunes were lost and people tightened their belts.

Nonetheless, Muer's Oyster House, later known as Joe Muer's, would go on to become one of the city's greatest and best-known restaurants. The family would go on to reign over a restaurant empire.

In 1993, Muer's grandson, Charles Muer, disappeared with his family in a storm while they were sailing on a 40-foot yacht in the Bahamas.

Joe Muer's closed in 1998 after the company filed for bankruptcy.

Oct. 29, 1927
Death of James Vernor

Perhaps more than automobiles or the Motown sound, nothing is so uniquely Detroit as that strange and imposing fizzle that accompanies a gulp of Vernor's Ginger Ale.

James Vernor invented what would become known as "Detroit's Drink" at a pharmacy in downtown Detroit just after the Civil War.

Vernor had worked in the pharmacy at 235 Woodward Avenue before the war and took it over in 1865 upon his return from service in the 4th Michigan Calvary.

Accounts vary on how Vernor came up with his fiery ginger ale.

He may have simply stumbled upon a blend of ingredients while experimenting after his return from the war.

A more interesting version of the story has it that Vernor experimented with concoctions for a beverage flavored with ginger root before he left to become a soldier at age 19. Upon his return four years later, he discovered that his ginger ale formula was perfected as it aged in wooden casks.

Either way, the strange tasting beverage was a hit.

Vernor eventually closed his drug store so he could focus his energies on the soft drink. He opened a bottling plant a few blocks away.

In the company's heyday, a huge illuminated Vernor's sign could be seen from Detroit or Windsor. Visitors could see the beverage being bottled and buy a large glass for a nickel.

Vernor's son took over the business after Vernor died in 1927 at age 84.

Asked when the elder Vernor retired from the business, his family is said to have responded: "a few hours before he died."

In the 1950s, when part of the company went public after the death of James Vernor II, the beverage's name changed from Vernor's to Vernors.

Many Michiganders remember being given Vernors as children as a tonic for various childhood ailments.

Oct. 30, 1956
Elvis emulators give up their hairstyles, but what about those Blue Suede Shoes?

High school boys in Romeo, located in northern Macomb County, really thought Elvis Presley was great and emulated him in the early days of rock and roll.

Most notably, they wore the sideburns and duck-tail haircuts favored by Presley. In 1956, Elvis was just gaining national attention for his unique style, both in music and attire.

Administrators at Romeo Community High School would have none of it. Teachers complained that the new look spawned defiant behavior – and they wanted it stopped. Superintendent T.C. Filppila took immediate action, telling the 52 boys if they did not get haircuts by Oct. 30, 1956 they were not to attend school the next day.

Two local barbers offered free haircuts to the boys who could not afford them. All boys complied and went to school the next day.

Oct. 31, 1926
Halloween takes Houdini

Of all the days for the escape artist and magician Harry Houdini to die, he couldn't have picked a better one than Halloween.

Houdini died just over a week after he was attacked by a fan in Montreal.

The fan wanted to test Houdini's purported invincibility in his belly region – Houdini boasted that he could sustain multiple blows from a fist to his abdomen.

However when McGill University student J. Gordon White-head confronted Houdini as he rested after a performance, Houdini was not prepared for the blows.

Houdini endured the pain and attempted to shrug off the attack, continuing his performances despite his weakened condition.

The magic tour took Houdini to Detroit, where he was urged to go to a hospital rather than perform. However, Houdini declined. He collapsed after a performance – his final one – at Detroit's Garrick Theater.

Doctors at Grace Hospital determined Houdini had a gangrenous appendix and it was removed. But the poison already had taken hold.

Seconds before he died, on Oct. 31, 1926, Houdini is reported to have told his brother: "I'm tired of fighting... I guess this thing is going to get me."

His insurance company determined the death was due to the punches Houdini sustained in his dressing room.

This account of Houdini's death is disputed, however.

Houdini may have died merely of appendicitis, a condition that was aggravated, but not caused, by the repeated blows.

Others have surmised that Houdini was poisoned.

Houdini was a controversial figure because of his work to debunk a group of psychics known as the "Spiritualists."

When he lost his mother, Houdini desperately wanted to speak to the dead, but as a magician, he knew the tricks others used to present an illusion. His quest to speak to the dead led him to a campaign against performers who conned people into believing they could speak to ghosts.

Houdini had a standing offer of $10,000 for anyone who could prove true psychic ability, but no one collected the prize.

Oct. 31, 1962
International Bridge opens

The bridge that carries traffic on I-75 from the far reaches of northern Michigan into Sault Ste. Marie, Canada opened on Oct. 31, 1962.

Construction of the steel truss arch bridge began in 1960. The bridge consists of two separate spans – one that carries traffic over the American locks and another over the water on the Canadian side.

There had long been a call for a bridge to join the American and Canadian cities of Sault Ste. Marie.

President Franklin D. Roosevelt signed an act authorizing a bridge in 1940 but World War II interceded. Later, President Dwight D. Eisenhower signed legislation that revived the act in 1953.

November

Nov. 1, 1957
Mackinac Bridge opens to traffic

Five miles of open water between Mackinaw City and St. Ignace meant the two peninsulas were united only in theory. In reality, they were separate lands.

Then, on Nov. 1, 1957, an astonishing feat of engineering was completed – the Mackinac Bridge became the world's longest suspension bridge.

The first passengers actually crossed a day earlier when busloads of students from St. Ignace traveled to Mackinaw City so they could be part of the opening day ceremony.

A formal, official opening day ceremony also had to wait until the following spring, when organizers believed they would have a better chance at good weather. That turned out to be a bad bet. The following June 25th, the grand opening was marred by rain and cold. But on Nov. 1, 1957, unseasonably warm and sunny weather greeted the hundreds who turned out to be the first paying customers of the Mackinac Bridge. (Michigan weather! Go figure.)

The first to pay the toll heading north was the state's governor, G. Mennen Williams.

The link between the state's peninsulas was one of the most important days in the state's history. It put an end to talk of Wisconsin taking the Upper Peninsula, or statehood for the remote, and cut-off, region of Michigan. It also meant that traffic would no longer have to back up for miles from Mackinaw City during hunting season, when thousands of vehicles waited to board ferries.

Talk of connecting the peninsulas had been going on for decades. Horatio Earl, the state's first highway commissioner, proposed a floating tunnel across the straits. Others thought a bridge between Mackinaw City and St. Ignace impossible, so they proposed a series of bridges that would hop traffic from one island to the next – from Cheboygan to Bois Blanc Island to Round Island to Mackinac Island and finally to St. Ignace.

It wasn't until the 1950s that serious work began on the bridge, led by Senator Prentiss Brown and Governor Williams. The massive project was studied tirelessly before construction began. It took 2,500 workers, 85,000 pages of blueprints, 71,000 tons of steel, 466,000 cubic yards of concrete and 41,000 miles of cable wire to build the five-mile-long bridge.

Remarkably, the massive construction project only claimed the lives of five workers.

The bridge took 42 months and nearly $100 million to complete.

Nov. 2, 1976
Voters approve the 10-cent deposit law

Conservation groups long sought a way to stop bottles and cans from littering Michigan's highways.

The solution – a 10-cent deposit on most bottles and cans sold in the state as an incentive for people to pick up their trash. A simple solution but not one quickly embraced.

Beverage manufacturers and retailers furiously fought the proposal. They managed to kill bills introduced in the state legislature, but things were slowly changing – the nation celebrated its first Earth Day in 1970, and Michigan welcomed a Republican governor who espoused conservation and environmental causes. Governor William G. Milliken sided with the conservationists over business interests and became the first to sign a citizens' group petition to enact the 10-cent bottle deposit law.

Milliken's wife, Helen, led a grassroots campaign for the measure and raised money for the drive from garden clubs across the state.

On Nov. 2, 1976, voters approved the law by a 2-to-1 margin, becoming the only state in the nation to have such a large deposit. (Remember the *Seinfeld* episode with Kramer and Newman?)

Nov. 3, 1930
First underwater roadway tunnel to foreign country

A first effort to connect Detroit and Windsor with a railway tunnel failed in 1871 when workers struck a pocket of sulfurous gas and became deathly ill. They refused to return and the project was abandoned.

Later in the decade, a tunnel from Grosse Isle into Canada was scrapped when workers struck limestone.

A Michigan Central Railway tunnel linking Detroit to Windsor was finally completed in 1910, just as Detroiters feared that international traffic would move to Port Huron, which also had a railroad tunnel.

But just as the railway tunnel opened, automobile traffic picked up in Detroit. A tunnel for car traffic was proposed and gained popularity but it was apparent that politics would interfere with the project. There was too much opposition from the backers of the 1929 Ambassador Bridge.

A group of private business interests organized to back the project, sparked by Fred W. Martin, a Windsor Salvation Army captain who brought together architects and engineers from New York and bankers from around the country.

Work on the tunnel began in 1928. Crews on each side of the river dug approach tunnels to the river's edge. A crew working from a barge dug a trench across the river bottom from Windsor to Detroit. Enormous steel and concrete tubes were sunk into the trench. Nine sections were lowered into the river and divers bolted them together.

Ventilation towers constantly pump fresh air into each end of the tunnel so that travelers do not suffocate or inhale carbon monoxide. The private company that operates the American side of the tunnel claims the air is cleaner in the tunnel than on the street.

The mile-long tunnel was completed at a cost of $22 million and opened to toll-paying traffic on Nov. 3, 1930.

The tunnel remains the only international, underwater tunnel that carries automobile traffic.

Nov. 3, 1948
Truman defeats Dewey

The nation and, famously, the nation's media, expected Thomas Dewey would defeat Harry S Truman in the presidential election of 1948.

Dewey was the governor of New York but, because he was a native of Owosso, people in his hometown followed the election results closely.

Dewey was born over his father's general store and one of his teachers in Owosso remembered Dewey as "the most cantankerous little devil that she ever encountered." He went to the University of Michigan and Columbia University before he became famous for fighting the Mafia as a prosecutor in New York.

By the time he ran for president, his hometown in Shiawassee County was ready for its place in the national spotlight. Citizens printed fliers with Dewey's mustachioed face that beamed "Welcome Home" and civic leaders planned a victory celebration downtown.

Such preparations were not as embarrassing to the town as the *Chicago Tribune* headline "DEWEY DEFEATS TRUMAN" was to that newspaper. But it was not to be for Owosso when the votes of Nov. 3, 1948 were tallied.

Nov. 3, 1926
State's most deadly mine disaster

Keeping water out of mines was constant work in the Upper Peninsula mining country.

The Barnes-Hecker mine in Marquette was particularly prone to flooding. Late in the morning of Nov. 3, 1926, water rushed into the 1,000-foot shaft, killing 51 miners. Water poured into the shaft so quickly only one person escaped. The disaster left 132 children without fathers.

The mine shaft never reopened after it became the site of the worst mining disaster in Michigan's history.

Nov. 4, 1952
First black woman in the state senate

Cora Brown was born in Alabama and moved to Detroit with her family when she was a child. She graduated from high school in Detroit and later, after working as a social worker and a police officer, earned a law degree from Wayne State University.

She attempted a run for the state senate in 1950 and lost.

When she was elected state senator from Detroit in 1952, she was the first woman of color to be elected to the upper house of a state legislature.

Nov. 4, 1975
Upper Peninsula not to be 51st state

Almost since the Upper Peninsula was populated, there has been talk of secession from Michigan.

Proposals have ranged from statehood for the sparsely populated, mineral rich land, to union with Wisconsin.

Although rhetoric for independence may have run high at times over the years (proponents even gave the new state a name: Superior), residents in two Upper Peninsula communities had their say in the voting booth on Nov, 4, 1975. The proposal to break from Michigan was soundly rejected.

In an advisory election, residents in Marquette voted 1,841-770 against the idea, while in Iron Mountain the measure went down 1,601-745.

Nov. 4, 1907
Faygo founded

Russian immigrant brothers Ben and Perry Feigenson founded a pop brand after the bakers experimented with cake frosting recipes to come up with flavors for carbonated soft drinks.

The beverage started out as Feigenson but was shortened to Faygo because the original name did not fit on a pop bottle.

The first flavors the company introduced after its founding on Nov. 4, 1907 were fruit punch, strawberry and grape.

The company's market spread from Detroit to the rest of the state in the 1960s as the soft drink was advertised during Detroit Tigers games.

Later the drink expanded to markets beyond Michigan and is now sold in 32 states, mostly east of the Mississippi.

Faygo has remained a Detroit drink, however. Its home since 1935 has been at 3579 Gratiot Avenue on the city's east side. Approximately 400 workers are employed there today.

(Editor's Note: For those non-native to Michigan: "pop" is what much of the rest of the country calls "soda.")

Nov. 5, 1975
Upper Peninsula rejects Project Seafarer

It was supposed to be a massive underground grid that would enable the military to communicate with submarines far under the sea in the event of a nuclear attack against the United States.

The U.S. Navy needed a way to communicate with its nuclear submarines, which were designed to remain submerged for weeks or months at a time, because radio transmissions cannot penetrate seawater.

The solution it came up with was an "extremely low frequency" transmitter that could be used to communicate with subs around the world, even if they were deep in the ocean. A section of land in the Upper Peninsula was deemed a suitable site for the enormous transmitter and the government set about plans to construct it.

Yoopers, however, wanted a say in the matter.

In an advisory election on Nov. 5, 1975, voters in four communities around the U.P. voiced their opposition in margins of up to 8 to 1.

The negative public reaction prompted Governor William G. Milliken to take a stand against the project. The following year he received promises from President Gerald Ford and challenger Jimmy Carter that Michigan could veto the project. After Carter's victory, Milliken received a letter from the military that the views of Michigan residents would be given "very great weight" in the decision of where to locate the project. That might have been a nice gesture, but it was far from the veto that had been promised.

Milliken became a louder opponent to Seafarer, which could have made the Upper Peninsula a far different place than it is today.

Initially, it was to involve thousands of miles of cable buried under an area of 1,200 square miles. The project would require construction of more than a thousand miles of 25-foot-wide roads cut through forests in an area up to a quarter of the peninsula.

The billion-dollar project would have brought jobs to the U.P., but there were concerns about what the low frequencies would have meant for plant growth, wildlife and human health.

Backlash over the proposal caused the military to scale back the project, which was renamed Project ELF. It was built in a less disruptive fashion and in a much smaller area in the western U.P.

and Wisconsin. It operated between 1985 and 2004.

Nov. 6, 1973
Coleman Young elected first black mayor of Detroit

Coleman Young, a state senator, and John F. Nichols, former police commissioner, faced off in a race for the mayor's office when Detroit was evenly split between black and white residents.

Both candidates kept race out of the political contest and Young narrowly defeated Nichols in the Nov. 6, 1973 election. Young received 231,798 votes to Nichols' 217,479.

Although accepted into the University of Michigan, the future mayor could not afford to attend. Instead, Young was drafted into service in World War II, where he served with the all-black Tuskegee Airmen. After the war, Young worked as a cab driver, painter, salesman and dry cleaner, frequently getting into trouble at his jobs over his efforts to organize workers. He was fired from a job at the post office after attempting to start a union.

Young helped organize the Negro Labor Council, an organization dedicated to finding better opportunities for black workers.

Labor organization brought Young to politics but he lost his first bid to become a state representative from Detroit's Black Bottom District in 1959.

Young persisted and was elected state senator in 1963.

As mayor, Young attempted to bring reconciliation to a city that had been bitterly divided since the 1967 riots.

He attempted to save downtown with the Renaissance Center and he helped General Motors build a plant in Poletown. Young also devoted his time in office to increasing the minority-owned contracts awarded by the city.

Nov. 7, 1707
First execution in French Detroit

Not long after the settlement of Detroit, its founder, Antoine Laumet de la Mothe, sieur de Cadillac, was called back to Montreal.

In Cadillac's absence, Etienne Venyard, sieur de Bourgmont was placed in charge. His administration proved to be a disaster. (See the June 6 entry). Bourgmont mismanaged the city so badly that he feared rebellion and retribution. He subsequently fled.

Cadillac investigated the matter upon his return. He sent an officer and 15 men to hunt down Bourgmont and his fellow deserters to arrest them for disobeying military orders.

Bourgmont was thought to be engaged in a scandalous affair with a woman at a small settlement on Lake Erie where the deserters had fled, but when Cadillac's officer attempted to arrest

Bourgmont and the others, only one man was found – an associate of Bourgmont named Bartellemy Pichon dit La Roze.

La Roze was tried before a tribunal that included Cadillac and was found guilty of desertion.

His punishment was to be "a avoir la teste cassée jusque a se que mort sensitive," or death by hanging.

La Roze's execution was carried out on Nov. 7, 1707, the first execution to take place in Detroit.

Nov. 8, 2002
8 Mile debuts

Marshall Bruce Mathers III, better known as rap star Eminem, took the stories of his rough upbringing in the tough streets of Detroit, put them to music with lyrics that disturbed some and delighted others, and won fame and fortune.

Eminem's rapping style over an accessible hip-hop beat, bookended with catchy and melodic choruses, turned him into one of the most successful artists of the early 21st century.

Born in Kansas in 1972, Mathers' father left when the boy was an infant and his impoverished teenage mother shuffled the young family back-and-forth between Kansas City and metro Detroit.

As a white kid attending mostly black schools, Mathers turned to freestyle rap as a means to fit in and make a name for himself. He started rapping in his early teens and eventually took his talents to "rap battles" where performers could compete before an audience that would determine who was superior.

This was a tough path for a white kid in Detroit. And because of his race, Mathers was mostly rejected by the city's black hip-hop community.

Mathers, though, fed on the rejection and his words became sharper. Despite the anger in his music, Mathers' work often exposed his vulnerability, shortcomings and dark sense of humor.

Mathers was employed by the family restaurant Gilbert's Lodge in St. Clair Shores when his big break came in 1998.

He had managed to release a record, the *Slim Shady EP*, and legendary hip-hop artist and producer Dr. Dre heard a recording of Eminem taking part in a rap contest in Los Angeles. The unlikely underground rap star was soon signed to a label.

Eminem's first album, the *Slim Shady LP*, reached No. 2 on the Billboard charts within weeks of its release.

That breakthrough came in 1999 when, despite the dark and violent subject matter of his work, his angry wit and incredible ability to spatter words in complex rhythms attracted a mainstream following. Some believe that Eminem was able to be one of the most successful crossover rap stars because he is white.

Eminem's second album solidified his fame. The *Marshall*

Mathers LP sold more than eight million copies in the U.S.

Mather's life story, in the form of fiction, was told in the film *8 Mile*, which was released on Nov. 8, 2002.

Eminem starred as rapper Jimmy "B. Rabbit" Smith Jr., a Detroit artist who overcomes hardship and racism to succeed in Detroit's hip-hop scene.

Nov. 9, 1913
Great Lakes' worst storm

All indications showed that a severe storm was about to strike the Great Lakes and there was plenty of warning for ships to take cover.

Nonetheless, ships across the lakes failed to heed the advice. Almost as soon as the storm struck, on Nov. 9, 1913, so did the reports of lost ships and boats that were battered and washed up on shore. Rescuers waited 16 hours for the hurricane force winds to die.

In all, 40 were ships sunk, 235 lost their lives to the lakes and broken vessels littered the shore of Lakes Huron and Superior.

Nov. 10, 1975
Edmund Fitzgerald sinks in Lake Superior

The Great Lakes have claimed so many ships and so many lives. The best known are the 29 men who went down aboard the 587-foot *Edmund Fitzgerald*, which sunk during a pounding storm on Nov. 10, 1975.

Its celebrity is due in part to the song by Canadian folk singer Gordon Lightfoot, "The Wreck of the *Edmund Fitzgerald*," which he wrote after reading of the 29 tolls of the bell rung at Mariners' Church of Detroit soon after the tragedy.

The wreck remained fascinating for another reason – no one knows with certainty why the *Edmund Fitzgerald* sank.

An early theory, put forth by the U.S. Coast Guard, proposed that the *Fitzgerald* sank after it broke in two when thrust out of the water by two large waves simultaneously. That theory was debunked in the early 1990s when a film crew reached the wreckage and found evidence that the ship was intact when it sank and broke into three pieces when it reached the lake bottom, 535 feet below the surface.

Another theory claimed the ship sank after she filled with water that poured in through improperly secured hatch covers.

Yet another proposition maintained that the hatches were secured but structural failure claimed the ship.

Despite efforts by loved ones of the lost crew to have the shipwreck designated a burial site to keep away divers, the wreck has been visited numerous times by submarines.

The ship's bell was salvaged and put on display at the Great Lakes Shipwreck Museum at Whitefish Point.

Nov. 11, 1929
Opening of Ambassador Bridge

For decades, steamship owners were able to block attempts to build a bridge across the Detroit River. They argued that a bridge would be a hazard to navigation. It also happened that a bridge threatened their hold on commerce crossing between Detroit and Windsor.

In the boom times of the 1920s, however, it was clear that the river needed to be crossed by something other than ferries. Two projects emerged – the Ambassador Bridge and the Detroit Windsor Tunnel – and they raced to become the first to cross over or under the river.

Despite a flaw in the steel wires of the bridge that caused a delay, the bridge opened nine month ahead of schedule and a year before the tunnel (See Nov. 3).

On the day the bridge opened, Nov. 11, 1929, it caused excitement on both sides of the river.

Approximately 60,000 people showed up to mark the opening of the bridge, which was dedicated by Governor Fred W. Green.

The stock market had crashed just a couple of weeks earlier, sending a panic and a dark cloud over the nation but the people of Detroit and Windsor were ready to celebrate when the bridge opened.

At the time, it was the longest suspension span in the world.

The man who put together the private deal to build the bridge, Joseph Bower, rejected two names for the bridge (the Detroit River Bridge or the Bower Bridge) in favor of the Ambassador Bridge, a name that symbolized the friendship between the two nations the span connected.

Nov. 12, 1912
Liquor sellers derail women's suffrage

On this day in November that included a presidential election and a state amendment to give women the right to vote, it appeared the suffrage amendment would pass with a solid majority.

Still, it was a big election that brought record turnout, partly because of a three-way race for president that saw Democrat Woodrow Wilson defeat Republican incumbent William Taft and Theodore Roosevelt, who ran on his splinter Bull Moose Party ticket.

But across the state, it appeared that a majority of voters came out in favor of a woman's right to vote.

Days after the election, the tally of those in favor of the amendment led by well over 10,000 votes.

The following week however, in counties throughout the state, liquor interests began making appeals to boards of canvassers.

On Nov. 12, 1912, they called for returns in counties across the state to be thrown out because of faulty ballots. In some cases the suffrage amendment was only partially printed on ballots. In other cases, it appeared alongside another issue on a ballot.

In Detroit, there were irregularities reported in precincts across the city. Pro-suffrage leaders expressed alarm that votes in favor of the amendment had mysteriously disappeared.

The Detroit News Tribune chronicled the dispute over the vote count and reported that it was "the saloon men" who were fighting against the amendment at every turn.

The newspaper did not delve into what motivated the liquor distributors and tavern keepers to fight so vehemently against the women's vote, but readers at the time understood the issue very well.

They knew that many woman voters would align with the temperance movement to outlaw alcohol in the United States.

It took 10 more days before "all" of the votes were tallied. The final count put those against the suffrage amendment ahead by 723 votes in an election that saw approximately 435,000 Michiganders cast ballots.

Two weeks later, the State Association of Farmers' Clubs passed a resolution calling for statewide prohibition of alcohol because of what saloon-keepers had allegedly done to thwart the women's vote.

Voters in Michigan gave women the right to vote in state elections in 1918 and women's suffrage was guaranteed nationwide when the 19th Amendment to the Constitution was enacted in 1920.

Nov. 13, 1972
Governor buys state's first lottery ticket

Whatever reasons the state had when its founding fathers outlawed lotteries in the first state constitution drafted in 1835 were long forgotten by the 1970s when Michigan looked for new revenue sources.

Lotteries looked like a good bet to raise money, the constitution was amended, and Governor William G. Milliken bought the first lottery ticket sold in the state on Nov. 13, 1972. The ticket, a loser, was donated to the Michigan Historical Commission.

In the days leading up to the lottery, the state-sponsored gambling caused a mild hysteria among residents. Newspaper writers swooned about what was dubbed "the chance of a lifetime."

In Dearborn, which was one of four municipalities given a license to sell lottery tickets, the city voted to let its employees buy the 50-cent lottery tickets through payroll deductions.

The measure passed unanimously with Dearborn Mayor Orville Hubbard saying the idea came to him in "a flash of inspiration – like a girl on first sight."

When sales of lottery tickets kicked off, more than 7,000 establishments across the state were licensed to sell and lines formed with customers ready to buy a ticket or five.

There would be nearly 4,000 winners each week who would take home $25. Winning the $25 would enter the ticket-holder into a drawing for $1 million, which the state promised to hold after it sold 30 million tickets.

Lottery money at first was directed into the state's general fund. In 1981, the money was devoted to education, but that did not result in a windfall for schools since legislators allocated less from the general fund for education.

Nov. 14, 1857
First gas light in Grand Rapids

When natural gas came to Grand Rapids, it came with a fury. The Grand Rapids Gas Light Company, a local concern, beat out-of-towners in a race to lay gas lines through the city to bring this novel energy into homes and businesses.

Gas lines were first laid at Ottawa Avenue and Ferry Street that August. Soon four miles of gas mains had been laid.

The novelty of artificial light illuminating the darkness caused a crowd to gather at Canal and Pearl Streets, where, on Nov. 14, 1857, Francis B. Gilbert, president of the power company, lit Grand Rapids' first gaslight.

Soon, shops, inns and a number of private residences, invariably owned by the city's wealthiest citizens, signed up for the service.

In its first year, the Grand Rapids Gas Light Company sold a million cubic feet of gas to a hundred customers.

Like other methods of illumination, candles and oil lamps, natural gas carried a risk of fire. However, it provided a reliable source of light.

But by 1880, the gas company had reason to fear a new technology that had the potential to wipe out its business – electricity.

At first, electricity seemed a threat but the gas company carried on, hedging its position by offering a new service – gas hookups for stoves.

By 1882, there were about a dozen electric lights in the city, but gaslight still dominated.

Across the city thoroughfares were lit up at night with gaslights.

On the outskirts of the city, where neither gas lines nor electric wires yet reached, oil lamps remained the source of light.

Natural gas became more affordable in the early 20th century as advances in its delivery system were developed. But by the 1920s, the industry faced a new problem.

During Prohibition, moonshiners tapped into the lines with garden hoses to steal the gas for powering their stills. The moonshiners often were able to move on before the company caught on to a line breach.

Nonetheless, the Grand Rapids Gas Light Company survived electricity and moonshiners. It went on to merge with other companies and become part of Michigan Consolidated Gas Company.

Nov. 14, 1828
Last British post in Michigan surrendered

The British were slow to turn over their Michigan posts after Americans won the Revolutionary War and that stubbornness continued after their loss in the War of 1812.

The last British-held military post in Michigan was on Drummond Island, and they held it for years after the war, unwilling to give up what was once a critical region for trade and military dominance.

The British were forced to leave Mackinac Island after they signed the treaty that ended the war in 1815 but they didn't move far. The soldiers reached Drummond Island, unpacked and built a new fort, which they argued was in Canadian territory.

In 1822, a British-American survey determined that Drummond Island, in fact, was within the boundaries of the United States.

It took the British several more years, but they finally relented and abandoned Fort Drummond on Nov. 14, 1828.

The dispute had its origins in the Treaty of Paris that ended the Revolutionary War.

The description of the border between the two countries did not mention the islands in northern Lake Huron; it merely separated the countries by a line that ran through the Great Lakes.

The 1822 survey determined that Drummond Island belonged to the Americans and Manitoulin Island, the world's largest fresh water island, belonged to Canada.

The British soldiers and the island's civilians set off for Canada and became the original settlers of Penetanguishene, Ontario, near the Georgian Bay. They left behind 20 government buildings on the island.

Nov. 15, 1883
Michigan town makes reputation with corsets

The Warren Featherbone Company may not be well-known today but in its heyday it was a household name.

Behind the company was Edward K. Warren, a dry goods store owner who spent several years looking for a substitute material to make corsets. Whalebone was the most common product used to make corsets firm and flexible but it was getting more expensive as whales were becoming scarce.

Warren happened upon an idea – quills from turkey feathers could be processed as a less expensive replacement. He could use cheap quills discarded by feather duster companies in Chicago as his raw material.

He patented the concept and opened a factory to produce his product on Nov. 15, 1883. Eight workers were employed by the Three Oaks-based manufacturer.

It took years to develop a product that was considered suitable by dressmakers. Warren hired women to travel the country and to Europe to promote the product and gradually made inroads.

Warren, who was raised in Three Oaks, soon became a wealthy man and his product put the Berrien County town on the map.

Warren's company was able to adapt his product as fashion changed in the decades between the 1880s and the 1920s. The company, which sold corsets worldwide, survived for more than 120 years.

Today, Warren probably is better known for conservation than for corsets. Warren purchased 300 acres of virgin beech and maple forest in Berrien County to preserve it from development. The land is known today as Warren Woods. He also bought for preservation a section of Lake Michigan Dunes, land that was at the time thought to be worthless. It later became the Warren Dunes State Park.

After his death, the fashion world revolted against the corset as women wanted naturally fitting and more comfortable clothes.

The company gradually put less emphasis on featherbone and invested in synthetic materials, selling diapers called Feathertex baby pants in the 1930s and supplying raincoats for the war effort in the 1940s.

The company moved to Georgia in 1956 and concentrated on producing clothes for children.

Nov. 16, 1965
Death of Harry Blackstone

Harry Blackstone was born in Chicago in 1885 and kindled a love for magic at age eight when he received a magic set as a gift.

Blackstone would go on to become a world famous magician on the level of Harry Houdini. But he would also leave his mark on Colon, a small Michigan town in St. Joseph County that he first visited in 1926.

Blackstone ultimately would help make Colon the "Magic Capital of the World."

Born Harry Bouton, Blackstone rose to prominence as a magician in the 1920s and 1930s as he toured the country with his Vaudeville-style act that wowed audiences with a disappearing bird-cage trick and a woman sawed in half only to emerge unscathed.

In the summer of 1926, when he and his wife were looking for a place to retool their equipment and rest for the season, they happened upon Colon and discovered an island on Sturgeon Lake that was for sale.

The island perfectly fit Blackstone's needs, offering a farmhouse, cottages for his staff and a barn for his livestock.

The residents of Colon immediately took to the world famous magician who performed a show at an afternoon garden party. The out-of-the-way farming town was glad for the excitement in their midst and the townsfolk became instant fans of magic.

Blackstone liked to fish in the lake but he also awed his neighbors by performing a death-defying underwater escape from the lake before 2,000 people. If there was any doubt, the town's residents now believed that their neighbor was truly the greatest magician in the world.

Blackstone invited Australian magician Percy Abbott to Colon in the summer of 1927. Abbott and Blackstone ran a magic company together for 18 months but a business dispute led to a falling out and Colon's two famous magicians spent the rest of their lives not speaking to one another.

Abbott wound up spending the remainder of his days in Colon, marrying a local girl, raising four children and starting a company that would become the largest magic trick manufacturer in the world, the Abbott Magic Novelty Company. Abbott and a partner also established the annual Abbott Get-Together, a weekend of magic shows for magicians that attracted performers from around the country and later from around the world.

Blackstone remained a world famous magician and also remained in Colon, though he did not attend the Get-Togethers until after Abbott's death. Late in life, Blackstone moved to California for health reasons but he maintained that he preferred Colon to anywhere in the world.

Blackstone had a son, Harry Blackstone Jr., who would go on to become a famous magician in his own right.

Colon renamed its Main Street to Blackstone Avenue in the 1960s. Blackstone was buried at Lakeside Cemetery in Colon following his death on Nov. 16, 1965.

Nov. 17, 1807
Treaty of Detroit signed

William Hull, governor of the Michigan Territory and superintendant of Indian affairs, held a council at the fort in Detroit with the chiefs of the Chippewa, Ottawa, Potawatomi, and Wyandot tribes.

The Indians signed away their claims to southeast Michigan in the Treaty of Detroit, which was executed on Nov. 17, 1807.

In the treaty, the Indians gave up their claims to the lower eastern quarter of the Lower Peninsula and a section of Ohio north of the Maumee River.

In exchange, the Americans paid the Indians $10,000 in money, goods and animals.

The money was split into thirds with the Chippewa and Ottawa each to receive one share and the remaining share to be divided equally among Potawatomi and Wyandot tribes. In addition, the tribes were to receive "forever" an annual payment of $2,400, distributed under the same formula.

Nov. 18, 1958
Carl D. Bradley sinks

An early winter storm swept the nation, stranding motorists and taking lives across the western states before it arrived with a fury in the Great Lakes.

When the storm struck, the *Carl D. Bradley* was in the wrong place – a region of Lake Michigan north of Charlevoix long known as the "graveyard of ships," due to the treacherous shoals and the distance between safe harbors.

The cargo ship broke in two on Nov. 18, 1958.

Two crewmen somehow survived: First mate Elmer Fleming and deck watchman Frank Mayes, both residents of Rogers City.

The men managed to climb into a life raft just as the *Bradley* snapped and they survived 14 frigid hours on the lake before being rescued by a U.S. Coast Guard cutter.

The 615-foot *Bradley* sunk at a time when many people thought the days of tragic shipwrecks on the Great Lakes were a thing of the past because of improvements in shipbuilding, weather forecasting and communication.

The day following the wreck, ships and Coast Guard airplanes crisscrossed the lake in the area of the loss. Later, rescuers searched the islands around northern Lake Michigan in a futile attempt to find survivors – all they could do was collect bodies from the water. In all, 33 sailors were dead.

The town of Rogers City, where 25 of the crew had lived, mourned the loss more than anywhere else.

After the rescue, Fleming told reporters he heard a thud and the ship began to list and then sink. Before he left the ship as other crew members scrambled to find life vests, Fleming attempted to make a distress call over the radio.

As Fleming made the frantic "Mayday" call at 5:31 p.m., he feared no one received the call. But the distress signal was picked up by a radio operator in Charlevoix, who could hear the chaos on the ship as crew members panicked.

Fleming and Mayes were lucky. Fleming was inspecting a life raft as the ship was thrown to its side, tossing Fleming and the raft into the lake.

Mayes also was flung into the water, close enough to the raft to pull himself out of the lake.

Nov. 18, 1899
Boat pile-up at the Sault

The steamer *Siemens* was towing the barge *Alexander Henry* through the Soo Locks when it lost power in the 300-foot channel in the upper end of course two in the Little Rapids Cut.

First, the steamer *Holly* struck the *Siemens*. Behind the *Siemens*, the *North Star* was forced to change course and run aground to avoid a collision between the ships.

The boat pile-up caused traffic though the canal to grind to a halt for five days.

This was the second time that season that a boat pile-up had stopped traffic through the Soo.

In September, the locks closed for five days after the *Douglass Houghton*, with the barge *John Fritz* in tow, lost power and drifted broadside to the canal, blocking traffic and causing the barge to sink.

While the boat pile-ups were an expensive nuisance for shipping companies on tight schedules, they were a bonanza for the people of Sault Ste. Marie.

Local farmers peddled fresh milk and cream, butter, eggs and freshly slaughtered lamb, veal and chicken to the stranded sailors as they waited for the canal to reopen.

Nov. 19, 1966
MSU vs. Notre Dame in "Game of the Century"

When the two football powerhouse teams met for what was dubbed the "Game of the Century," Michigan State University and Notre Dame played for the national championship.

Even though that title was on the line, the rules allowed the football game to end in a tie.

The Nov. 19, 1966 game ended with a score of 10-10 at Spartan Stadium before an overflow crowd of more than 80,000 fans.

For MSU loyalists, the game became controversial.

Some noted some problems with the game, discovered after careful examination of game tape: In one instance, a Spartan defenseman was ruled offside by a referee. That call negated a fumble recovery by MSU and allowed the Irish to kick the tying field goal.

Also, officials overturned another fumble recovery in the final seconds of the game that would have given the Spartans good field position and a chance to win the game.

Finally, Notre Dame won the national championship through the UPI coaches poll, even though Ara Parseghian, the team's coach, did not go for the win but instead let the clock wind down when his team had the ball in the final seconds of the game.

Spartan Bubba Smith, who would go on to become a star in the NFL, called Notre Dame "a bunch of sissies."

Notre Dame went on to the Rose Bowl despite the tie. MSU had played in the Rose Bowl the year before but at the time the Big Ten had a rule that barred teams from playing in the title game for two consecutive years. Notre Dame beat the University of Southern California for the championship.

Nonetheless, the MSU-Notre Dame contest made the cover of *Sports Illustrated* in the lead-up to the game because both schools were undefeated. It was also a diversion from the war in Vietnam and the social unrest affecting the country.

The game was part of a golden age of Spartan football, which in the decades that followed faltered from its one-time perch of national prominence.

Nov. 20, 1951
First personal ad?

Margaret Ealy was apparently fed up enough in her search for a new husband that she took the novel approach of going to the local newspaper in an era before personal ads.

She told the *Traverse City Record-Eagle*, "I want a husband who will be a good father to Jamie."

That was all it took to get the newspaper interested. The search was on. In its Nov. 20, 1951 edition, the *Record-Eagle* published a large photo of the 39-year-old Ealy and her five-year-old son Jamie under the headline "She Seeks a Husband" on its front page.

A large caption explained that the divorcee was seeking a man of any age, preferably a Protestant college graduate. Also, the candidate for marriage must like children.

"Age is not a factor, she said, and there would be no housing problem as she has her own home," the newspaper explained.

Ealy had been a department store employee until she was stricken with pneumonia five months earlier and her illness made it difficult to raise her son alone.

The following day, the newspaper followed up the story, and the flurry of attention it received, in an article headlined: "Whole Nation Interested in Husband Hunt."

The article said that Ealy, "a comely 39-year-old divorcee," had received three calls from suitors by the following morning and she expected to meet each of them that day.

"Meanwhile the story of her appeal for a husband snowballed across Michigan as press wire services and metropolitan papers built up detailed stories on Mrs. Ealy's quest for a mate. The resultant flood of publicity was expected to bring a multitude of offers by phone, wire and mail," the newspaper reported.

It turns out the novel approach to find a love connection in a time before personal ads may have worked.

Grand Traverse County records indicate one Margaret I. Ealy married William Colteson in 1952.

Nov. 21, 1945
UAW strikes GM

Workers at General Motors, along with workers across the country involved in labor disputes, wanted better wages and working conditions.

On Nov. 21, 1945, 180,000 GM workers left their jobs in an historic strike.

Approximately 350,000 workers were left idle because of work stopped at the GM plants.

In the days leading up to the strike, it became clear there would be no common ground between the union and the auto industry.

Ground zero for the strike was Detroit but it would affect plants across the nation.

At the outset, the UAW wanted a 30 percent increase in wages and demanded arbitration to force GM to open its books at public hearings to determine the feasibility of a wage increase. The UAW also wanted GM and other car companies to pledge that vehicle prices would remain the same.

The union message was simple: "Show us you can't pay 30 per cent and still not raise prices and we'll scale down our demand."

The corporation was unwilling to open its books or agree to those terms.

The UAW released a statement that described its impasse with the company – "General Motors' reply to our arbitration proposal is a stall, pure and simple. It does not contain even a hint that the corporation accepts the principle of arbitration."

The strike was called at a specific hour across time zones so that work would cease at the same minute everywhere in the country. Work stopped in Detroit at 11 a.m.

The UAW wanted the country to see the largest industrial machine the world had ever seen come to a sudden halt.

The union strategy, according to then-UAW vice president Walter Reuther, was to "divide and conquer" the big three automakers.

As GM was struck, the union negotiated with Ford and Chrysler. More importantly, to get leverage against GM, the union made sure Ford and Chrysler plants hummed along smoothly as GM plants sat idle.

The strike could not have come at a worse time for GM, as auto companies shifted from war-time to peace-time production and the country had a huge appetite for new cars. Additionally, the strikers were in a better financial position than during the 1937 UAW strike because many had bought war bonds and saved money during World War II.

The strike would last 119 days and end after the union and GM agreed to a pay increase of 18.5 cents per hour.

Nov. 22, 1912
"Captain Santa" lost in Lake Michigan storm

Captain Herman Schuenemann worked for decades on and around the Great Lakes. He sailed schooners in the warmer months and ran a saloon in the winter. But it was one trip each year that made Schuenemann a local celebrity. In late November, he would load up a schooner with Christmas trees chopped from the Upper Peninsula and deliver them to Chicago, selling the trees from a port on the Chicago River.

In Chicago, newspapers dubbed Schuenemann "Captain Santa" because he gave trees to needy families. Schuenemann apparently liked the notoriety and he saved the news clippings in an oilskin wallet.

Taking Christmas trees from the Upper Peninsula to Chicago never made Schuenemann rich. It was a dangerous business because the trees, in order to be fresh when they reached their market, had to be transported as late in the season as possible. Late November can be a difficult time to be in a boat on Lake Michigan.

So it was when Schuenemann departed on what would be his final Christmas tree journey on Nov. 22, 1912. He launched from Thompson, near Manistique, on the schooner *Rouse Simmons*, so laden with Christmas trees stuffed into its hold and strapped onto its deck that it appeared to be a floating forest as it sailed off for Chicago that Friday.

Just as the *Rouse Simmons* left port, a treacherous winter storm swept over the lake. The *Rouse Simmons* had once been a sturdy and sleek schooner, but by 1912 she was 44 years old and showing her age.

It is unknown what happened to the Christmas Tree Ship over the next few days. It was spotted the following day, foundering off the shore of Wisconsin, about a hundred miles into its journey. Help was sent after her but she was not found.

The ship likely became weighed down from ice the storm deposited on its deck and in the trees. The added weight may have made the ship unstable and forced her underwater.

There were no survivors and accounts vary as to the number lost in the shipwreck from 12 to 25.

For years, Lake Michigan fishermen brought up nets containing Christmas trees. Several years afterward a fisherman brought up Schuenemann's wallet – complete with the news clippings that featured "Captain Santa" – and returned it to his family.

The year following the shipwreck, Schuenemann's widow, Barbara, arrived at the Clark Street Bridge in a schooner filled with Christmas trees, a labor she and her daughters remarkably carried on for years.

Perhaps it was the image of "Captain Santa" and the attention the shipwreck received in newspapers, or perhaps it was the memory kept alive by the captain's widow carrying on the family tradition, but this shipwreck fascinates more than most other Great Lake wrecks. Four histories, two documentaries, a children's book and several plays and musicals have been produced about the loss.

Each year a U.S. Coast Guard cutter takes a load of Christmas trees on the *Rouse Simmons'* route and delivers them to less fortunate families in Chicago in memory of the work of Captain Schuenemann.

Nov. 22, 1853
First steamer on Lake Superior blows up

It was no small task to get a ship such as the *Independence* into Lake Superior before the Soo Locks were constructed.

Along the St. Mary's River, which connects Lakes Huron and Superior, there was a mile-long stretch of furious rapids.

At the end of the summer of 1845, the *Independence* was one of four ships to enter the mouth of the St. Mary's with the intention of becoming the first steamship to sail on Lake Superior.

Although the *Independence* was the last of the ships that made the journey overland, when she pulled abreast of two ships in the lead, her captain was able to push his crew to ensure the *Independence* arrived at Lake Superior first.

She was taken around the St. Mary's River over seven weeks, rolled over logs on land around the rapids, and deposited into the lake in 1845, just in time to start hauling metal and supplies for the fledgling copper mining enterprises in the Upper Peninsula.

The *Independence* was constructed of wood to carry passengers and freight on the Great Lakes. As a steamer, she was considered to be a "bastard ship" because she was originally built as a schooner that would use sails rather than engines.

The Independence was constructed in 1843 by a Chicago ship-builder and the 119-foot ship weighed 262 tons.

The ship exploded on Nov. 22, 1853 near Sault Ste. Marie when its boiler blew.

Four to seven people are said to have died in the explosion. One account claimed that a crew member survived the explosion even after he was blown 200 to 300 feet into the air.

Additional loss was felt in Ontonagon, where residents awaited a shipment of winter supplies from the *Independence*. Instead, they had to survive the long winter with only salt pork and dried whitefish to eat.

Pieces of the *Independence* were littered around Sault Ste. Marie. For years they were recovered and sold as souvenirs.

Nov. 23, 1953
Fighter investigates UFO over Lake Superior; disappears

Late on Nov. 23, 1953, the radar at the Kinross Air Force Base detected something over Lake Superior.

The military outpost, constructed during World War II to protect the Soo Locks and reactivated during the Cold War as a component of North American Air Defense, or NORAD, scrambled a fighter jet to check out the unidentified flying object.

Back at the base, the ground personnel watched as the radar images of the F-89 jet fighter and the unknown object converged. The blips met and then both disappeared.

What happened to the jet and the UFO remains a mystery – or a secret. Pilot Felix Moncla and radar operator Robert Wilson have never been seen since.

At the time of the disappearance, officials said the incident was classified and refused to provide any information.

More than 50 years later, internet rumors and media reported that the fighter jet may finally have been discovered by a diving company working at the bottom of Lake Superior 40 miles off of the tip of the Keweenaw Peninsula.

The Great Lakes Dive Company, working late in the year, claimed it discovered the shell of an F-89 fighter with its canopy intact, indicating that Moncla and Wilson did not bail out before the crash.

The company was able to verify the tail number and observed that a wing had been sheered off.

Internet reports also claimed the divers found a half-buried metallic object next to the downed plane that resembled what could be the bubble in the center of the archetypical flying saucer.

These claims led to a backlash.

Respected Great Lakes shipwreck researcher Brendon Baillod said he investigated and determined it was "a moderately elaborate hoax."

He argued it was very unlikely that the Great Lakes Dive Company, an outfit no one had heard of until the F-89 fighter story emerged, could afford the equipment for a deep-water search. For one, the side scan sonar necessary for such a search costs more than $100,000.

Moreover, the secretiveness of the dive company's spokesman and the company's refusal to release details of its supposed find bolstered the widely held belief that the claim was a hoax.

Not long after the story broke, the Great Lakes Dive Company's website disappeared from the internet, giving further ammunition to their detractors.

The fate of that scrambled fighter jet and the identity of what it found over Lake Superior in 1953 remains a mystery.

Nov. 24, 1971
Plans for Renaissance Center unveiled

Downtown Detroit had been in decline for years.
Henry Ford II, the grandson of Ford Motor Company founder Henry Ford, proposed a complex of buildings he believed could return Detroit's civic and cultural center to the status of its illustrious, early 20th century past.

On Nov. 24, 1971, Ford posed for photographs with Detroit Mayor Roman S. Gribbs before a model of the ambitious development. It was to be the most expensive privately financed project in the world.

The projected cost of what was to be known as the Renaissance Center was $500 million and it would take a decade to construct.

The model unveiled at the news conference showed a hotel tower surrounded by smaller towers atop a shopping center.

Ford, then chairman of the Ford Motor Company, organized an effort to bring together other businesses to invest in the project.

For more than a decade businesses had abandoned downtown Detroit for the suburbs, and vacant buildings and crumbling lots dotted the cityscape.

The Renaissance Center would be built on a 28.5 acre lot at the center of the city on the shores of the Detroit River.

Ford was fighting an uphill battle, however. Even as he announced his plans, his brother, William Clay Ford, was planning to move his football team, the Detroit Lions, to Pontiac.

Plans, nonetheless, went forward and an architect was selected, John Portman, the planner of a similar development in downtown Atlanta called the Peachtree Center.

The first phase of the project opened in 1977 and the central tower became Michigan's tallest building.

Despite its origin as a pet project of Henry Ford's grandson, the RenCen, as it is known, was made General Motors world headquarters in 1996. General Motors and Chrysler Corporation, along with Ford, were among the original investors in the project.

The Detroit Lions did return to the city in 2002, with the opening of Ford Field on Woodward Avenue, just a half-mile from the Renaissance Center.

Nov. 24, 1892
Lake Michigan's first car ferry sails

The first car ferry to cross Lake Michigan loaded with railway cars embarked from Elberta on Nov. 24, 1892.

The ferry was laden with four carloads of coal. The *Ann Arbor No. 1* headed to Kewaunee, Wisconsin, where it ran aground upon its arrival.

The vessel was freed and towed to port, where repairs were made and the ship was loaded with 22 cars that contained flour.

The ship was notable for another reason. Designed by Frank Kirby, she featured two screws in the rear and one in the bow to break ice, making it the first triple-screw ship registered in America.

The 267-foot *Ann Arbor No. 1* had an oak hull sheathed in steel up to four feet above the water line.

Car ferries running from Ludington and Muskegon followed.

Nov. 25, 1981
First atoms smashed in Michigan

The superconducting cyclotron smashed its first atom in a test run at Michigan State University, marking the first time such an experiment was performed anywhere in the world.

That cyclotron would bring prestige to the university's physics department.

Although scientists were optimistic about what they could learn by studying atom smashing, they had no idea where they were headed when the project began.

"I can't stand here today and say what it is exactly that society is going to get from this but you can be sure it will be of some benefit," mused Henry Blosser, who then was the director of the National Superconducting Cyclotron Laboratory.

Scientists from around the world lined up to bring experiments to the $30 million cyclotron, which was funded by the university and the National Science Foundation.

In the decades since it opened, the laboratory has studied radiation treatments for cancer patients and health risks faced by astronauts.

The fundamental purpose of the laboratory is to attempt to unravel mysteries surrounding atoms.

The center remains one of the leading rare isotope research facilities in the country and enables MSU to boast a graduate program in nuclear physics second only to MIT.

Nov. 26, 1883
Sojourner Truth dies in Battle Creek

B orn into slavery in 1797 as Isabella Baumfree, Sojourner Truth toiled as a slave in New York state in the first decades of her life, sold from one slave owner to another, until she escaped to a Quaker family.

Baumfree became a free woman a year before New York abolished slavery.

She withstood the cruelties of slavery and sexism to go on to become the most influential black woman of her time.

As a free woman, Baumfree moved throughout the Northern states, finally working as a maid in New York City. In 1843, she changed her name to Sojourner Truth and traveled the country as a preacher fighting for equal rights.

She could not read nor write, but an admirer helped her write her life story, *The Narrative of Sojourner Truth, a Northern Slave, Emancipated from Bodily Servitude by the State of New York in 1828*.

It was through speeches that the women's rights and anti-slavery crusader made her greatest in-roads. Her style was informal, forceful and blunt.

Her most famous speech, delivered in Akron, Ohio in 1851, known as "Ain't I a Woman?" convinced white members of the women's rights movement that the cause of anti-slavery belonged alongside their own.

A crude transcript of the speech shows its raw power: "Dat man ober dar say dat womin needs to be helped over carriages, and lifted ober ditches, and to have de best place everwhar. Nobody eber helps me into carriages, or ober mudpuddles, or bigs me any best place. And ain't I a woman?"

Truth would go on to meet two presidents and to fight unsuccessfully for land grants to be given as reparation to freed slaves.

Truth first visited Battle Creek in 1855. During the Civil War, she helped enlist black recruits to fight in the Union Army. She later moved to Battle Creek, where she remained active into her 80s, traveling the state and the country to deliver speeches focusing on the rights of blacks and women.

In 1878, Truth spoke in 36 towns in Michigan.

She died at her Battle Creek home on Nov. 26, 1883. More than a thousand people came to her funeral service. She was buried in Battle Creek's Oak Hill Cemetery.

Nov. 27, 1872
Whitefish Point wreck

Lake Superior's "graveyard" – the 80-mile stretch of water around Whitefish Point – is home to countless shipwrecks. Today, the region is designated an "underwater preserve."

The area of Lake Superior is feared by sailors because it is exposed to the most punishing conditions Lake Superior can offer. There is no safe harbor between Grand Island and Whitefish Point. Ships that attempt to huddle in too close to land might break up on rocky shoals.

In 1847, *New York Tribune* editor Horace Greely, on a visit to the Upper Peninsula, wrote an editorial that criticized the lack of a lighthouse at Whitefish Point, writing that "every month's delay is virtual manslaughter."

Within two years a lighthouse had been constructed but the navigation aid did not put an end to shipping disasters.

The *Jupiter*, a wooden schooner barge en route from Marquette with a load of iron ore bound for Wyandotte, and the *Saturn*, another wooden schooner loaded with iron ore, found themselves in a severe storm on Nov. 27, 1872 as they rounded the point.

The barges were being towed by the *General Dix* when their tow line broke in the storm and the barges were swept into the shallows, away from rescue. Both ships had recently been built and were on the water for only a few weeks before they were lost.

All hands on board the barges, as many as 15 sailors and their loved ones, were lost.

The *Jupiter* and the *Saturn* were owned by shipping magnate Captain Eber Ward of Detroit.

In the wake of the disaster, Ward and others saw to it that four lifesaving stations were constructed along the coast between Grand Marais and Whitefish Point.

The shipwrecks were only recently located in the Whitefish Point Underwater Preserve. The *Saturn* wreck was discovered in 2006 and the *Jupiter* the following year, both located near Vermillion Point.

Nov. 28, 1906
Maiden voyage of the unlucky *Ann Arbor No. 4*

Of the many vessels to sail the Great Lakes and develop a reputation for bad luck, the *Ann Arbor No. 4* car ferry could rival the worst of them.

The fourth ship constructed for service out of Elberta, it was the product of 14 years of tinkering and redesign that should have capitalized on the mistakes of earlier car ferry designs.

The *No. 4*, constructed by Globe Iron Works of Cleveland, set off on its maiden voyage on Thanksgiving Day, Nov. 28, 1906, making it to Elberta in December. In her first two years of service the *No. 4* would get off to an inauspicious start.

The ferry ran aground in January on the rocky shores of Point Aux Barques en route to Manistique. The captain sent his son, who was first mate, and another crew member ashore in a smaller boat to call for help. The pair made their way to Thompson over an ice-covered beach.

They made it to a telephone and called for help, then sauntered into a nearby bar for drinks. When they made the return walk along the beach they arrived to find the *No. 4* gone. The wind had changed and the *No. 4*'s crew managed to free the vessel while the hands were gone. The two built a fire and camped in the hulk of an old beached schooner, catching up with their ship in Manistique.

A few months later, the *No. 4* capsized while being loaded with iron ore in Manistique. The boat tipped because too much of the heavy load had been placed on one side of the cargo hold. It took about 10 minutes for the ship to turn over, providing the crew and others on board enough time to get out alive.

The boat was righted and repaired at a dry dock in Milwaukee and returned to service the following September.

But the follies continued. In 1910, *No. 4* became ensnared in ice for two months in Lake Michigan near Manistique. Later that year she ran ashore in Green Bay. A month afterward the boat ran aground again near Manistique and the starboard shaft and screw were sheared off. Over the next several years, *No. 4* ran aground three more times and had other mechanical problems.

In February, 1923, a big storm struck Lake Michigan as *No. 4* was preparing to pull away from its dock in Elberta filled with 19 coal-laden railroad cars, automobiles and salt. Late that evening, the *No. 4* found herself in 30-foot waves whipped up by 80-mile-per-hour winds. In the rough seas some of the railroad cars in the cargo hold came loose.

The car loaded with automobiles broke free and plunged into the lake, taking the sea gate at the stern of the ship with it. Two coal cars slid off the stern and hung overboard. The crew opened other cars filled with coal and dumped it onto the deck in an effort to construct a temporary sea wall.

Early the next morning, the captain made the dangerous but brave decision to turn the boat around and head for Elberta. The ship survived her turn into broadside seas and then away from the wind. She managed to make it back to port despite the waves that crashed upon the unprotected stern. However, the ship was badly damaged and riding low in the water. The captain nearly made it around the pier and into calm water but the wind and waves pushed the *No. 4* into the break wall.

The ship was repaired again and her unlucky reputation continued – she twice more ran aground until she was sold in 1937 and renamed the City of Cheboygan, outfitted to take passengers and cars across the Straits of Mackinac until that business ended in 1957.

Later the ship's engines were removed and it was used as a barge for potato processing in Wisconsin. In 1975 it was sold for scrap in Italy.

Remarkably, despite its terrible track record, no one died or was seriously injured in any of the calamities that befell the *No. 4*.

Nov. 29, 1760
French surrender Michigan to British

The last French commander of the fort at Detroit, Captain Francoise-Marie Picote, Sieur de Bellestre, turned Fort Pon-chartrain and Michigan over to the British on Nov. 29, 1760.

It would be the last day the sun would rise over Michigan under the French flag.

Early historians of Michigan bemoaned the change, charging that the English brought a detestable attitude and stinginess to the region, ruining whatever good relations had been built up between the Europeans and the Native Americans.

The responsibility for the loss of Detroit cannot be placed on Bellestre, who fought bravely against the British for 30 years, including during the French and Indian War.

When English Major Robert Rogers arrived in Detroit to demand surrender, the French residents of Detroit were unaware of events that transpired to the east.

Rogers arrived with a large force, hoping his great number of military men would convince Bellestre of the comparative states of the English and the French military in North America.

Rogers first sent a courier to Bellestre to inform him that Canada had been taken by the British.

Bellestre suspected a bluff and requested time to consider the demand of surrender.

While he thought, he had a pole erected in the fort that featured an effigy of a crow picking at a human head. He wanted to communicate what would happen to the British if they attacked.

Rogers sent another courier to Bellestre but this time he also included a message from the governor of New France that laid out the state of affairs for Bellestre.

Bellestre may also have been persuaded by the generous terms offered by the English – the French would be allowed to keep their property, even the soldiers, as long as they made arrangements for safekeeping or sold them before they were taken as war prisoners.

Nov. 30, 1926
Chryslers end up in Lake Superior

The steamer *City of Bangor,* en route to Duluth, Minnesota with a cargo of 248 brand-new Chryslers, found herself headed directly into a fierce winter storm as it made the turn around the tip of the Keweenaw Peninsula.

The crew made it only halfway to Eagle Harbor when they determined they made a mistake by not seeking refuge from the storm. Their best chance would be to get to the lee side of the peninsula, where they might be able to wait out the storm in calmer water.

But the steam-powered steering gear broke, the ship was tossed around in 25-foot troughs and she wound up battered into the shallows two miles west of Keweenaw Point. The ship was torn open in the ice of Lake Superior on Nov. 30, 1926.

The men on the ship were lucky. The ship provided a barrier against the waves and they were able to launch lifeboats into the calmer water toward the beach.

On shore, where the story should end, the men's luck ran out. They found themselves on land but far from shelter.

The men spent the first night before roaring fires and the officers forced the crew to keep moving so they would not succumb to the cold. They expected to be rescued in the morning but the storm was too severe and prevented help from arriving. The storm also brought large amounts of snow and the seamen could not make the six-mile walk to Copper Harbor in the cold and knee-deep snow drifts with their low-cut footwear.

The Eagle Harbor Coast Guard crew saw the five officers and 24 crew members trudging through the snow on the second day of their ordeal. They were eventually picked up.

With the crew of the *City of Bangor* safely in Copper Harbor, attention turned to the automobiles.

During the storm, 18 cars were flung from the deck of the ship to a resting place on Lake Superior's floor.

The remaining vehicles were encased in ice soon after the ship went aground. During some mild weather in December the remaining automobiles were chopped from the ice and winched off the *Bangor.*

Teams cleared a road over the ice to Copper Harbor and the cars were driven to a field where they waited for spring when the roads would be drivable. The cars were driven back to the Chrysler plant and refurbished.

Nov. 30, 1885
Traverse City State Hospital opens

The sprawling campus of Victorian brick buildings southwest of Traverse City was first known as the Northern Michigan Asylum. Later it was called the Traverse City Regional Psychiatric Hospital. The locals called it the state hospital.

It opened in Nov. 30, 1885 and housed 43 residents, overseen by Dr. J.D. Munson, the facility's superintendent for its first 39 years.

Some early treatments at the hospital would be considered barbaric by modern standards. In addition to the use of opiates to calm patients, insulin shock, lobotomies and electric shock were also administered.

The facility had grown to 1.4 million square feet by the 1950s and housed nearly 3,000 residents.

The hospital operated a farm of more than a thousand acres and a factory that made the facility almost self-sufficient.

But changes in the way society treated and categorized those with mental conditions led to the decline of the state hospital.

By the mid 1980s, the facility cared for only 150 patients, those considered to have the most acute psychiatric cases.

The hospital closed in 1989.

In the 1990s, there was a community-wide debate over whether the buildings should be razed or saved. Conservation won out, and in the early 21st century the facility is slowly being transformed into a multi-use development that features high-end condominiums, shopping, restaurants and office space.

December

Dec. 1, 1892
Trial for Baron Albert von Molitor's
murderers begins in Alpena

Mystery shrouded Rogers City resident Baron Albert von Molitor.

The prosperous lumberman reputedly was the illegitimate son of King William of Wurttemberg of Germany and had been forced to flee his homeland for America.

When Molitor arrived in America he fought for the North during the Civil War.

He later helped survey Lake Huron. It was this task that led to his fortune.

While surveying the western shore of the lake, he discovered a valuable stand of pine that he purchased in 1871 with William E. Rogers. Rogers City one day would be located on that tract of land.

Rogers returned to New York City, however, and left the development of Rogers City to Molitor and an associate, Frederick Denny-Larke.

They exploited the lumber and promoted the region in German newspapers, enticing a large number of German and Polish immigrants to settle in Rogers City.

As time wore on though, Molitor's brand of dictatorial rule became unpopular with the townsfolk.

Molitor controlled every aspect of local government and questions were raised about increases in taxes. When confronted by an angry mob that wanted to inspect the county finances, Molitor arrogantly refused.

The settlers' frustration was expressed most acutely in August 1875 when a group of settlers gathered outside Molitor's offices and fired through the window, killing the Baron and his clerk.

The murder was investigated but the authorities either found nothing or looked the other way, perhaps influenced by the shared dislike of the town founder.

The assassination was soon forgotten.

But 15 years later, one of the assailants unexpectedly confessed to his part in the slaying and named many fellow citizens as accomplices. Because the remaining defendants in the crime were all prominent citizens of Rogers City, the trial was moved to Alpena to find an impartial jury.

The trial of five men tied to the assassination plot began on Dec. 1, 1892. They were convicted of Molitor's murder and sentenced to life in prison.

By 1904, all had been pardoned.

Dec. 2, 1925
Birth of Julie Harris

Actress Julie Harris won great acclaim for her performances on Broadway and in Hollywood but also showed a sterling character, battling back after breast cancer and a stroke.

The actress was born on Dec. 2, 1925 in Grosse Pointe, the daughter of an investment broker and a nurse. Her parents took her to see live stage plays when she was a child, sparking an interest in acting. After graduating from Grosse Pointe Country Day School (now University Liggett School), she headed for New York.

She made her Broadway debut at 20 in a comedy called, "It's A Gift." The play didn't last long but she received the attention she needed to be placed in other productions.

Harris is the most honored Broadway performer in Tony Award history, with 10 nominations and five wins. She also appeared in a number of movies, including *East of Eden* and *Requiem for a Heavyweight*. On television, she fared just as well – winning three Emmy Awards out of 11 nominations.

Perhaps her most poignant role came in a made-for-television movie called *The Way Back Home*, in which she played a grandmother affected by stroke.

After suffering her stroke in May 2001, she went to the University of Michigan Aphasia Program for rehabilitation. In 2007, that program honored her at its annual fundraiser.

Harris has received a number of honors in addition to her Tony and Emmy awards. She was awarded the National Medal of the Arts in 1994 by the National Endowment of the Arts and was the recipient of the 2005 Kennedy Center Honors.

Dec. 3, 1867
First sheriff killed in line of duty

Kalamazoo County Sheriff Benjamin F. Orcutt amassed plenty of experience as a soldier and officer of the law.

Orcutt was born in Vermont in 1815 and moved to Detroit at the age of 19 and settled in Kalamazoo in his early 20s. Within five years, he was elected town constable.

Orcutt later became a deputy U.S. marshal, served in the Mexican War in 1847, was elected sheriff in 1854 and enlisted in the 25th Michigan Infantry at the outbreak of the Civil War.

When he returned to Kalamazoo after the war, he was elected sheriff again.

Devoted to a job that could call upon him at any time, day or night, Orcutt lived in a house attached to the county jail. If there was a ruckus, he would be right there.

Early on Dec. 3, 1867, Orcutt heard a commotion coming from the jail.

He had reason to be on his toes – two of his guests were desperate burglars from a Chicago gang.

Orcutt leapt from bed and discovered the prisoners beneath one of the jail windows in the act of escaping.

The pair fled and Orcutt followed, yelling at the men to stop. Orcutt fired as the men ran across Michigan Avenue and separated.

One of the fugitives ran north and the other hid behind an oak tree in an alley between Rose and Burdick Streets.

Orcutt approached and shots rang out. Orcutt was struck during the exchange and fell to the ground.

The gunfire awakened neighbors who ran out and attempted to help the sheriff. Orcutt managed to get to his feet and back to secure the jail before he sought medical attention.

His wife Emily asked him whether he thought he had killed either of the bandits, not knowing that her husband had been hit, and he replied, "No, but I think he has killed me."

One of the bullets struck near his right collar bone and grazed a major artery. There was nothing doctors could do for the Civil War veteran.

He died later that month.

When the sun rose after Orcutt's shooting, residents discovered a stash behind the oak tree that included a jack screw, tarred rope and a kit of burglar tools. They also found specks of blood that indicated one fugitive had been wounded.

The trail of the killer and his accomplice went cold but in the months that followed, Kalamazoo officials hired private detectives in Chicago. They tracked down one of the escapees, Hugh Darraugh, and determined that he was not the man who shot Orcutt.

He was tried, convicted and sentenced to six years at the Southern Michigan Prison in Jackson, where he died.

Authorities in Kalamazoo were still not satisfied. They wanted to find the man who had killed their sheriff.

Eighteen months after Orcutt's death, another detective agency was hired, this one founded by Allan Pinkerton.

Wanted posters were placed around New York, describing the wanted man: "He is very dressy and proud, usually wears a high silk hat. Stephen Boyle is well known in New York City as a pickpocket, burglar and sneak thief; has travelled in almost every state, and is well known by all thieves as Stephe the Stage Busser (underworld slang for a thief) of New York; is an escaped convict from Sing Sing, New York and Joliet, Illinois; will probably stop at some private boarding house; will be found with Eastern thieves."

The shooter, Stephen Boyle, was tracked down in New York City. The detectives followed Boyle for three months before catching him in the act of burglary.

Michigan authorities wanted to extradite him, but Boyle had too much time to serve in New York, where he was sentenced to 40 years.

Historians cite Orcutt as the first sheriff in Michigan to be killed in the line of duty.

Dec. 4, 1838
The Battle of Windsor

The prospect of war between Canada and the United States may be fodder for a punch line in the 21st century, but early in the state's history the threat seemed very real.

Irish residents of Canada resented British rule over Ontario, charging that Canada was less prosperous than her neighbor due to differences between the American and British governments.

Several skirmishes in Michigan's first years of statehood led to Michigan becoming home to many of the Irish refugees from Canada.

These refugees, who recruited some Irish-Americans to their cause, called themselves Patriots. They were responsible for the "Patriot War" that lasted from 1837 until December 1838.

The Patriots gathered secretly in Michigan in places along the border with Canada in Detroit, Port Huron and Gibraltar. Their object was to take over southwestern Ontario.

They raided militia barracks and stole weapons, hijacked schooners and made several attacks on Canada that were quickly repelled by Canadian forces.

In Windsor, there was talk of an attack on Detroit, which was seen as a haven for the rebels.

In the United States, there were neutrality laws that barred citizens from aiding the rebellion against Canada. However, in many cases when rebels were caught stealing arms from American forts, the offenders were let off easily.

Eventually federal troops were brought in and Governor Stevens T. Mason aided them in attempting to thwart the Irish rebels.

The Patriot War culminated in the Battle of Windsor, which took place in the early morning of Dec. 4, 1838.

A battalion of over one hundred Patriots crossed the Detroit River on a hijacked steamboat and landed a few miles north of Windsor.

The men marched to Windsor at around 2 a. m. and set fire to the barracks, the guardhouse and a British steamer moored on the Detroit River.

The marauding quickly captured the attention of a strong British force. In a battle that ensued, the Patriots didn't fare well. Twenty-one were killed and four were captured before the invading force retreated. The four rebels who were captured were summarily shot.

Dec. 5, 1858
Death of Chief Okemos

Like most Indians of early Michigan history, the details of the life of Chief John Okemos are spotty.

Some say he was born in Shiawassee County circa 1775, somewhere along the Looking Glass River. Some say he was the nephew of – and a scout for – the great Indian warrior Chief Pontiac, who led the siege of Detroit.

If Okemos had Pontiac's blood in his veins, evidence started to show in 1796 when Okemos enlisted with the British in their attempt to expel the Americans from the upper Great Lakes.

During the Battle of Sandusky, Okemos served with a group of Indians who were ambushed by Americans. Okemos received scars to his forehead and suffered a slash to his back from a saber, a wound that never healed and would identify him throughout his life.

Okemos' recovery and his bravery in the battle brought him respect among his tribe, which named him chief, even though Okemos reportedly stood only five feet tall.

Okemos decided to retire from his fight against the Americans in 1814 when he met with the commanding officer at Fort Wayne in Detroit to announce that he would bury his hatchet.

In 1819, as chief of the Red Cedar Band of Shiawassee Chippewa Indians, Okemos signed the Treaty of Saginaw with Lewis Cass, the first territorial governor of Michigan.

Despite his short stature, Okemos had a memorable look. He was known for wearing a blanket coat with a belt, a turban-style cloth over his head, leggings and moccasins. He wore face paint on his cheeks and over his eyes. He carried an English hunting knife, a tomahawk and a steel pipe hatchet. As he wandered he was sometimes known to have played a flute.

He lived near Portland, northwest of Lansing, where he was said to have four wives.

Okemos often appeared at temperance picnics with as many as 12 children and he became a well-known character on Lansing streets.

In the 1830s, Okemos survived when much of his tribe was taken by outbreaks of smallpox and cholera brought by white settlers.

In the 1850s, Okemos remained in Michigan after many of his tribe members were removed from the state by the federal government.

Okemos died on Dec. 5, 1858. It is believed that Okemos was buried near Portland in the Indian village of Shimnecon on the Grand River.

Dec. 6, 1932
Detroit arson swindle foiled

The *Detroit Free Press* called it a case of "double-crossing, double-dealing and of dishonor among thieves."

When the steamships *Dover* and *Keystone* burned earlier that year, foul play was not suspected. Captain William Nicholson, owner of the boats, collected $285,000 from an insurance company.

After the captain was paid, a blackmail plot unfolded in Detroit's underworld and soon police uncovered what was touted as one of the boldest arson plots in the country's history.

Nicholson was a seasoned Great Lakes skipper who had owned boats for nearly two decades, but at age 68, he was almost broke.

Police later discovered that on the day the ships burned, Nicholson had $4 in the bank and an insurance payment due in two days.

What unfolded next could come from the pages of an Elmore Leonard novel.

Nicholson asked his nephew, Charles Nicholson, to see to it that both of his boats were destroyed in a fire. It was critical, the uncle told the nephew, that the fire not look suspicious. For this, the younger Nicholson would receive $5,000 in 90 days, as well as $5,000 with which to pay the arsonists.

The nephew found two men willing to accept the money for setting the boats ablaze.

Peter Mendis and Reuben Merrithew later told police they tied the boats together at the Detroit River docks where the steamships sat idle. They decided a fire had to start on one of the boats and spread to the other or the blaze would look suspicious.

They waited until a night when a strong wind blew in a favorable direction, boarded the *Dover*, and spread oil throughout the decks.

The boats burned and the insurance company agreed to pay. But it took only days for the plot to unravel.

Mendis did not want to wait 90 days for his share of the money. However, Captain Nicholson had not yet received his insurance payout.

Mendis contacted a hoodlum, Sam Palazzolo from Wyandotte, to pressure Charles Nicholson.

Nicholson, fearing he would be "taken for a ride" if he didn't produce the money, went to his uncle. The captain scraped together $5,000 for the accomplices. The nephew didn't tell his uncle that he, too, would get a cut of the $5,000 payout.

Soon, Palazzolo was back and he demanded a larger share of the insurance money. The two men who Charles Nicholson originally asked to set the fire also came back into the picture, demanding hush money.

Others also had heard of the arson plot. Three men whom Charles Nicholson had never seen before appeared at his Port Huron home and demanded shares of the money.

Perhaps the only thing that prevented the lowlifes of the Detroit underworld from bleeding Nicholson dry was that police caught on and investigators for Wayne County Prosecutor Harry S. Toy followed up on the arson and the blackmail.

Toy announced the arrests of the Nicholsons and charges against as many as eight other men on Dec. 6, 1932.

Dec. 7, 1945
Upper Peninsula island proposed as U.N. world headquarters

At the close of World War II, former Michigan Governor Chase S. Osborn thought Michigan would be a great location for a newly proposed international organization to promote world peace.

Sugar Island, at the eastern tip of the Upper Peninsula, should become home of the United Nations.

Osborn believed that this out-of-the-way locale would be ideal for the peace-making body because the island sits on a border between two countries that extends 4,000 miles and had been unfortified for almost 130 years.

Both Michigan senators and all house members, save one, joined in the cause. The Great Lakes Historical Society of Cleveland, the Algonquin Club of Detroit and the Detroit Marine History Society all threw their support behind the proposal.

On Dec. 7, 1945, the Michigan delegation sent a cable to London, England to request that Sugar Island be considered as the site for the United Nations.

The bid to become a world capital failed and instead another, more populated island – Manhattan – was chosen as its home.

Sugar Island, now a resort community and bird sanctuary for snowy and great gray owls, is accessible from the mainland by ferry.

Dec. 8, 1861
Birth of William Durant

William Durant, the grandson of former Michigan Governor Henry Crapo, was born Dec. 8, 1861 and by age 30, despite dropping out of school, became a success by selling horse drawn carriages in Flint.

In 1904, Durant, by then a multi-millionaire, applied his knowledge of vehicles to the auto industry and became general manager of the Buick Motor Company.

Four years later, Durant incorporated General Motors, which sold stock so that it could acquire Oldsmobile, Pontiac, Cadillac and several automobile parts manufacturers.

Durant was forced out of his company two years later when he was blamed for financial trouble that left General Motors vulnerable and in need of a bail-out from East Coast banks.

Durant soon got back into the car business, though. He teamed up with Louis Chevrolet, and eventually gained control of the company they started. Durant turned Chevrolet into a company that sold affordable cars that could compete with Ford's Model T. He made enough money to buy himself back into General Motors, becoming its president in 1916.

Durant was forced out again several years later.

Durant attempted and failed to start another car company and lost his fortune in the stock market crash in 1929. For a while he ran a bowling alley in Flint. He ended life in New York City where he was supported by old business associates from General Motors, including Alfred P. Sloan.

Dec. 8, 1956
Dedication of Central Michigan University's
Clarke Historical Library

A library dedicated to the State of Michigan was opened at Central Michigan University on Dec. 8, 1956.

The collection at the Clarke Historical Library focuses on first-hand accounts of life in pioneer Michigan and the Old Northwest Territory, the industrialization of the state, rural life and the history of Indian tribes in the state.

The library is named in honor of Dr. Norman E. Clarke, Sr., who donated his collection of rare and valuable books to form the nucleus of Clarke's holdings.

The library also collects newspapers from across the state to provide a catalog of day-to-day life.

An unusual feature offered by the Clarke Historical Library is a collection of children's books that date from the 18th century.

Dec. 9, 1923
Disappearance solved by a dream

At first it looked like merely a sordid abduction of a young girl by an older man.

Harry B. Proctor, a successful 31-year-old real estate salesman who was a husband and father, appeared at 14-year-old Edna Rhineberger Fullager's house. He asked her mother if he could take her along on several sales calls. He said they would be back in 30 minutes.

Fullager's mother reluctantly consented, even though, she said later, her daughter was reluctant to go.

But 30 minutes passed and neither returned.

The girl's mother went to the sheriff the next day to report the disappearance. She was told to wait a day or two to see if the girl would return on her own. Fullager was not satisfied and she went straight to the prosecutor.

A warrant for abduction was issued against Proctor.

The case immediately became the talk of Grand Haven, where both the man and the girl lived. Some believed Proctor, who until that time was considered a model citizen, had abducted the child and was holding her against her will.

Proctor's wife refused to believe her husband could be behind something so horrible.

The mystery dragged on for a month as police across the Midwest were on the lookout for Proctor and Fullager. It began to appear that the mystery might not be solved.

Then George E. Snyder, a neighbor of the Proctors, approached Mrs. Proctor with some strange news – for two nights in a row, Snyder dreamed that he watched a coupe like the one Proctor owned drive off of a dock in Spring Lake and into the Grand River.

Within several days police were dredging the river in that area, looking for a body, as thousands of residents looked on.

On Dec. 9, 1923, sheriff's deputies first found Proctor's car and then the two bodies.

It appeared that the car had been driven off the dock by accident in the darkness just a few minutes after the two had left the Fullager home a month earlier.

There was evidence that the pair struggled to free themselves from the submerged vehicle, using a wrench to smash the windshield, but that by the time they were free from the car it was too late.

Dec. 10, 1903
Kalkaska poisoner convicted

People whose lives intersected too closely with Kalkaska County nurse Mary McKnight often had the misfortune of winding up dead.

It took a while, but eventually the authorities came to suspect something other than coincidence.

Things began to unravel for the nurse when McKnight's brother and sister-in-law came to stay with her at her Fife Lake home around the turn of the century.

Soon the couple's three-month-old daughter, who Mary McKnight had been caring for, was dead.

The baby's father, John McKnight, consoled his wife before purchasing a coffin. When he returned, his wife was dead, too.

Mary McKnight used her medical training to determine a cause of death. She told her brother that his bride, Gertrude, died from an epileptic fit.

If John McKnight was suspicious, he couldn't have been suspicious for long – five days later he was dead, too.

The suspicion of the authorities in Kalkaska County, however, had yet to be aroused.

Mary McKnight went on about her business.

One day she went to the county clerk's office. She produced a document to show that she was owed $300 against 40 acres of land that had been owned by her brother, money she said she lent her brother to build a house.

The clerk only became suspicious went she looked at the paper and could plainly see that someone had sloppily doctored the document, changing $200 to $300.

It was this discovery that caused the sheriff and the prosecutor to take a closer look at the people left dead in Mary McKnight's wake.

Once the authorities had a court order to exhume her brother's body, Mary McKnight rushed by train to Traverse City to get a court order to stop them.

By the time she returned to Kalkaska the body had already been removed from its grave.

Samples were sent to Ann Arbor for testing, where it was determined that John Murphy had been poisoned by strychnine.

McKnight was taken to jail where, after she fasted for several days, she confessed, although not entirely.

She claimed she had given strychnine to her family members for their own good, to ease their suffering.

McKnight was convicted of murdering her brother on Dec. 10, 1903.

Investigators determined that the nurse probably committed many more murders, over the years poisoning two husbands, two nieces, a sister-in-law, her sister and several other people who had been in her care.

The woman profited from some of the murders, but this was apparently not her motive.

She was thought of as a friendly, gregarious person. One relative recalled that McKnight enjoyed attending funerals.

She spent 18 years in prison and died several years after her parole.

Dec. 11, 1934
Kerns Hotel fire

Legislators from across the state were in Lansing for a special session to address a recount of the November election for secretary of state and attorney general.

Some of the politicians stayed at a swanky, expensive hotel, but most of them stayed at the Kerns Hotel, a four-story, 211-room brick hotel that offered little in the way of frills but had rooms for $1.50 per night. Plus it offered the chance to spend the evening circulating from one room to the next, playing cards, telling jokes and making deals.

Twenty-six of the legislators were registered at the Kerns for the night of Dec. 10, 1934, and many of them were in no hurry to get home.

When one senator in that special session proposed postponing a vote on a resolution offering condolences to a colleague who was ill, Senator John Leidlein of Saginaw, sponsor of the resolution, moaned: "I may be dead tomorrow."

Unfortunately for the senator, his words proved prophetic.

Leidlein perished in a hotel fire that night along with State Representatives T. Henry Hewlett, Charles D. Parker, Vern Voorhees, John W. Goodwine, Don E. Sias and D. Knox Hanna. At least 25 other guests of the hotel also died.

Once the fire began about 5:30 a.m. on Dec. 11, 1934, it spread rapidly through the wooden interior of the old hotel, consuming the structure.

Some of the victims died when they jumped from an upper story window onto the icy sidewalk below or onto the ice of the Grand River behind the hotel.

Forty-four people were injured, including 14 of the 72 firefighters who arrived to battle the blaze. Many of the hotel's 215 registered guests survived by jumping into nets laid by firefighters below.

Surviving legislators, horrified by the fire, passed a bill to establish building codes for hotels. The law later was struck down by the Michigan Supreme Court.

There was no trace of Senator Leidlein in the charred remains of the Kerns but his key ring was found among the ashes.

Dec. 12, 1979
Joe Louis Arena, home of Detroit Red Wings, opens

The hockey arena was constructed over two years at a cost of $57 million and can hold up to 20,000 fans. But when it opened, it was nicknamed the "Joe Louis Warehouse" because it looked so drab inside.

When Mike and Marian Ilitch purchased the Red Wings in 1982, a major renovation was completed to improve the building's interior.

The building so closely associated with hockey – it is the center of the section of Detroit known as "Hockeytown" – started life hosting a basketball game.

The first event at the Joe saw teams from the University of Michigan and the University of Detroit take the court on Dec. 12, 1979. The Red Wings played their first game at the arena that Dec.

27 against the St. Louis Blues.

Dec. 13, 1862
Death of a Civil War soldier; birth of a Ford legacy?

As the Civil War dragged on, the Union Army had a harder time finding new recruits to replace the dead, maimed or retired in its ranks.

The situation became so dire that President Abraham Lincoln signed into law the country's first military draft.

To make the draft more palatable, there was a sweetener: for $300, a draftee could buy himself out of that year's draft. If he were to be drafted again, he could pay $300 more and receive another stay from service.

Michigan residents who could afford it spent a collective $594,000 under the provision.

The downside of this policy was that every time someone paid, someone who did not have the money was conscripted in his place.

To be permanently removed from the draft rolls, a person had to sign up someone else in their place.

The market for men willing to go to war in the place of another eventually settled on a cost of around $1,000 per person.

That's what Andrew Threadgould paid John Litogot to take his place.

Threadgould, a middle-aged man, left behind no historical record of what he did for a living or what happened to him during his life.

Litogot apparently did not mind taking his place in the war. The men posed together for a photo as Litogot enlisted in the 24th Michigan Infantry in August 1862.

On Dec. 13, 1862, Litogot died in battle at Fredericksburg.

His younger brother, Barney, was wounded in the same battle. His sister, Mary Litogot Ford, was carrying her first child at the time, a boy, Henry Ford, who would be born the following July in a Dearborn farmhouse. This young boy would grow up to be the international known founder of the Ford Motor Company.

Later in life, Ford believed that he was the reincarnation of his uncle, the Civil War soldier who died on the battlefield.

The family's experience in the war may have influenced Ford's pacifist leanings in later life.

Dec. 14, 1920
Death of "the Gipper"

George "the gipper" Gipp was born in what was then the copper boom town of Larium in 1895.

An exceptional athlete, he attended Notre Dame on a baseball scholarship but after he was recruited to play football by coach Knute Rockne, Gipp's exploits with the pigskin overshadowed his baseball ability. Gipp played quarterback, halfback defensive back and punter and went on to become the first player in Irish history to be named an All-American.

Gipp was complicated fellow. He was a poor student who was more than once expelled from school, only to return after administrators considered his athletic ability. He was a well-known gambler and pool hustler in South Bend and may have extended his interest in betting on Notre Dame football games, but he was generous with his winnings and became a beloved figure in the college town.

As his senior season wound down, Gipp developed pneumonia, possibly after insisting he be allowed to play in a game despite poor health. Complications from the illness led to his death on Dec. 14, 1920, but not before a perhaps legendary hospital meeting with Rockne, who later quoted the dying player as having beseeched his team to "win one for the Gipper."

Gipp is supposed to have said, "I've got to go, Rock. It's all right. I'm not afraid. Some time, Rock, when the team is up against it, when things are wrong and the breaks are beating the boys -- tell them to go in there with all they've got and win just one for the Gipper. I don't know where I'll be then, Rock. But I'll know about it, and I'll be happy."

Rockne is supposed to have used the line to inspire his team eight years later when the Irish faced an undefeated Army team at Yankee Stadium. Notre Dame won the game. The fame of the line was further amplified through its use in the movie *Knute Rockne, All American* when it was recited by actor Ronald Reagan. Reagan went on to use the line in political speeches.

Dec. 14, 1836
End of the Toledo War

Conflict with Ohio over the "Toledo Strip" had been brewing for a year.

The disputed narrow slice of land between Michigan and Ohio that includes the present-day city of Toledo was thought to be a valuable port.

President Andrew Jackson, in need of Ohio's vote for Martin Van Buren in the upcoming presidential election, sided with Ohio.

The dispute originated 30 years earlier because of poor map-making and conflicting descriptions of where the boundary lines should be. Ohio's northern boundary was supposed to stop at a line extending east from the southern tip of Lake Michigan, according to the Northwest Ordinance.

At the time, surveyors believed this would give Ohio the mouth of the Maumee River and a considerable amount of Lake Erie shoreline. In fact, once carefully measured, Ohio would lose Toledo, according to the letter of the law.

By the time President Jackson made his demands, there had already been several skirmishes between militias from Michigan and Ohio, Michigan's territorial governor Stevens T. Mason had been removed by Jackson and Michigan residents believed they were getting a raw deal.

Finally, Jackson signed a bill that would enable Michigan to become a state as long as it conceded the strip. In exchange, Michigan was granted the western three quarters of the Upper Peninsula, a concession thought worthless at the time.

Michigan was in a financial crisis, in part because of funds spent for a militia to defend the disputed territory. Its leaders realized Michigan needed to become a state soon in order to qualify for federal aid.

In what became known as the "Frostbitten Convention," on Dec. 14, 1836, delegates gathered in Ann Arbor and voted to accept Jackson's trade of Toledo for the Upper Peninsula (see April 26).

In the following election, Jackson was able to win the presidency for Van Buren, but he did it without the help of the Ohioans whose cause he had aided.

Their vote went to the Whig party candidate, William Henry Harrison.

Dec. 15, 1929
Eulogy for the grayling

The city was first known as Crawford, but once people began arriving in the 1870s the northern Lower Peninsula town's name would change.

Rube Babbitt, one of a group of legendary early Au Sable River guides, arrived in Crawford in the early 1870s.

He discovered a fish in that river like no other. It was a great sports fish. It was delicious. It was beautiful.

In the early days, there was a railroad camp and a few pioneer families living in the area.

At the time, Babbitt and his father had to walk to Bay City when they needed supplies.

On one of those trips they took the fish to Bay City to see if anyone could identify the species.

No one could.

Babbitt's father sent a fish to Washington D.C. for identification. They learned it was called a grayling, or *Thymallus tricolor*, and that the species was a culinary prize in Europe.

The Babbitts brought this news back to Crawford and it wasn't long before the town had a new name – Grayling.

"We were very much pleased with the discovery and resolved

to benefit from it commercially," Babbitt told the *Detroit News* on Dec. 15, 1929. Babbitt mourned the short time when the fish were so easy to catch from the Au Sable River.

"The grayling lay like cordwood in the Au Sable, and it was no trick to catch them on a fly tied with the feathers of a blue jay or high-holder, or a squirrel tail. From 1875 to 1881 father and I shipped out catches to a Chicago restaurant, which paid us the unheard-of price of 25 cents a pound."

People were drawn to the Au Sable because of this extraordinary fish and Babbitt showed them how to catch them.

Anglers came from around the world to fish for the grayling. Artists visited to paint them.

But the grayling's fate was sealed once logging camps were set up along the banks of the river.

The grayling today leaves only its name in Michigan. Logging of white pine in the region caused erosion into the Au Sable and changed the stream's ecosystem, killing off the grayling. The fish needed pure water kept at near-freezing temperatures by the shade of the trees to survive.

The grayling, a species related to trout and salmon, is extinct in Michigan but can be found in Montana, Europe and the Arctic.

Dec. 15, 1935
Detroit Lions win first championship

Detroit was abuzz in sports fan frenzy.

Just two months earlier, the Detroit Tigers had won their first World Series and hometown hero Joe Louis was tearing up the boxing world.

Now, the Detroit Lions were favored to win the National Football League championship in a game against the New York Giants.

The Lions, who were the Western Division champions, played the Giants at the University of Detroit Stadium before a crowd of 15,000.

The Giants were the defending champions, having defeated the Chicago Bears the year before in the title game. The Lions were favored, however, because they faced a tougher schedule than the Giants to get to the game.

Rain and snow caused thousands of spectators to stay away from the game; those who did brave the gale saw the Lions pummel the Giants 26 to 7.

Coach Potsy Clark surprised the Giants when he called a passing play on the first down of the game. The Lions were known for smash-mouth rushing and that's how they scored touchdowns.

For all of their hard work, the Lions players shared $7,207 while the Giants collectively split $4,804. Those were the players' shares of the gate receipts for the game, which the NFL said amounted to $33,477.

Dec. 16, 1982
Death of Orville Hubbard, Dearborn's "screwball mayor"

Orville Hubbard may have been one of the most divisive politicians in Michigan history. He may also be one of the most divisive mayors in American history.

Hubbard was born in 1903 on a farm in Union City, a rural town in Branch County. He served in the Marines, studied law, moved to Dearborn and in his early life made a career out of running for public office.

Finally in 1941, the people of Dearborn opted for a change and they elected the 225-pound "Little Orvie" mayor.

Hubbard would serve as mayor for 36 years, become famous for his racist rants and would be credited with the "accomplishment" of keeping Dearborn almost entirely white during his tenure.

For the record, Hubbard maintained he was no racist and there is little evidence he was a white supremacist. But his claim that he was not a racist was tenuous and perhaps a matter of word play.

Hubbard managed Dearborn under the slogan "Keep Dearborn Clean." Many believed that was a thinly-veiled directive to "Keep Dearborn White." And indeed, only a handful of black families lived in the city of 90,000 by the time Hubbard left office in 1978.

Hubbard ordered the police department to shoot looters on sight during the 1967 Detroit riots. He was interviewed by an Alabama newspaper in the 1950s, bragging about the lack of a black population in Dearborn, saying "I am for complete segregation, one million percent, on all levels." For that, *Time* magazine labeled him "screwball mayor."

In 1965, when Hubbard was acquitted in a federal civil rights conspiracy case, he took the jurors out for a steak dinner, inviting more criticism.

He also did well by the citizens he governed.

He is credited with the purchase of the Dearborn Towers, an 88-unit apartment complex in Clearwater, Florida, that is available for Dearborn retirees and he founded Camp Dearborn in Milford Township, a 626-acre recreational area for Dearborn residents. He was able to spend so lavishly because of the taxes brought in from the Ford Motor Company, headquartered in Dearborn.

Hubbard died four years after he retired, on Dec. 16, 1982.

Later that decade, a citizen group raised funds and erected a statue of Orville Hubbard outside city hall.

In 2006, a musical based on Hubbard's life called "Orvie!" premiered, written by former *Detroit News* reporter and Hubbard biographer David L. Good.

Dec. 17, 1918
Airfield named after pilot who averted
an Armistice Day disaster

Lieutenant Clifford Morrow got an airport named after him the hard way.

In November, 1918, World War I came to an end and the residents of Detroit were ecstatic.

More than 100,000 people rushed into the streets for a celebration that began at 5 a.m. after the news broke.

Acting Mayor Jacob Outhard declared a holiday in the city and government offices were closed. Work stopped at many factories. A parade, musical performances, speeches and fireworks were staged almost spontaneously to celebrate Armistice Day.

An air show also was planned, using aircraft and pilots from the army base at Acceptance Field. Among the four pilots who performed an aerial show after the 3 p.m. parade was Morrow, a Pennsylvania native who was stationed in Springwells Township (now a part of Dearborn) as a flight instructor.

Morrow piloted a bi-winged JN-4 Jenny plane, designed by Curtiss Aeroplane and Motor Corporation with an engine from Packard Liberty. The Jenny was powerful and agile, well suited for training pilots or performing stunts to amuse a crowd.

On Armistice Day, Morrow and his fellow pilots stunned the crowd with corkscrew maneuvers, loops and tailspins.

Morrow, caught up in the thrill of the crowd, performed at lower and lower altitudes, weaving around downtown buildings. His recklessness riveted the crowd.

Morrow took a 90-degree turn around the spire of Central Methodist Church, turned over the Detroit River and grazed the treetops over Grand Circus Park before turning into a steep climb to avoid the Fyfe Building.

Morrow left too little room for error in the stunt and a wing clipped a flagpole as he attempted to soar over the building, sending his plane into a turn and on a collision course with the crowd.

Some in the crowd could tell Morrow was fighting for control of his plane as he hurtled toward the onlookers. He managed to turn the errant plane from its path and into a neighborhood instead.

The plane crashed into a two-story home on Montcalm Street, two blocks away. The owner and tenants of the home were among the celebrating crowd, so although Morrow was killed, no one else was injured.

The Detroit City Council, recognizing that while Morrow could not save himself, his actions in the final seconds of his flight certainly saved countless others, petitioned the army to rename Acceptance Field after the aviator.

The airfield was officially renamed Morrow Field on Dec. 17, 1918.

Although the airfield was closed several years later, the pilot's name remains in the Detroit area, on Morrow Circle in Dearborn.

Dec. 18, 1927
First no passing zone

Automobiles had been driving on roads for decades before someone realized that cars should be prevented from passing each other in certain areas, such as on hills or around curves.

Michigan was the first state where something was done about it.

Michigan workers first painted yellow lines on roads to indicate where cars could not pass on Dec. 18, 1927.

The new highway markings came along just as roads in Michigan were being paved. The following year, the state highway department posted signs to alert drivers to stretches of road where they were allowed to pass and when they were entering a no-passing zone.

The signs were necessary so drivers would know what the lines on the pavement meant.

Henry Hart, a judge from Midland, is credited with pushing the notion of no-passing zones.

He promoted the familiar yellow triangular signs, warning drivers of no-passing zones that are credited with saving thousands of lives in the state.

Michigan also was a leader in other developments that led to safer roads.

The first center line laid down on a road was painted on a Michigan road in 1911.

The first-ever stop sign appeared in Detroit in 1915.

And the first three-colored traffic signal was installed at the intersection of Woodward and Michigan Avenues, the center of downtown Detroit, in 1920.

Dec. 18, 1886
Ty Cobb born

Georgia may lay claim to its native son Ty Cobb, but it was in Michigan, playing for the Detroit Tigers, where Cobb spent a career that earned him the reputation as one of the greatest baseball players ever.

Cobb received the most votes in the inaugural Hall of Fame ballot in 1936 when he was inducted along with Babe Ruth and Honus Wagner. Cobb played baseball in an era known for low scoring games and few home runs. His ability to hit and steal bases, made him the most potent offensive player until Babe Ruth came along.

The only season Cobb hit under .300 was his first. He went on to complete 23 seasons batting above that mark, a Major League

record that has withstood the decades since Cobb left the game.
Cobb died on July 17, 1961.

Dec. 19, 1856
The legend of Kalamazoo celery

Kalamazoo's most prominent citizens showed up at the Burdick Hotel's Grand Ballroom on the evening of Dec. 19, 1856 for a banquet to honor the city's firefighters.

In addition to the finest food frontier Michigan could offer, those assembled also tasted a culinary curiosity.

The green, crunchy and stringy vegetable bewildered and delighted the assembled epicureans. Celery had been introduced to Michigan.

As the story goes, the hotel received the exotic ingredient from farmer George Taylor, a Scottish immigrant who had brought celery seed from his native country and cultivated it in southwest Michigan.

He offered it to the hotel with the hope that he could develop interest in his crop and create a market.

By the late 19th century, celery had caught on.

Kalamazoo promoted itself as "Celery City" and was a hub for celery farmers.

It may have been Kalamazoo's desire to promote itself as a celery capital that led to the story of the dramatic introduction of the vegetable at the Grand Ballroom.

Although residents of southwest Michigan were mostly farmers in the 1850s, it is unlikely they had never heard of celery before Taylor arrived in the United States and served it to the well-to-do Kalamazooans.

Whether Taylor was the first celery farmer in Kalamazoo, or in the state or in the nation, the crop took hold in the farms around Kalamazoo and for a time the city's name was associated with celery.

Dec. 20, 1897
First door-to-door mail delivery in Traverse City

Before door-to-door mail delivery in Traverse City, people trekked to the post office daily to pick up their mail.

On Dec. 20, 1897, the local post office offered home delivery.

A force of five carriers hit the street that day and they had to repeatedly explain what they were doing, telling the same story at every home.

"You won't have to go to the post office anymore," one of the mailmen said. "We will bring you your mail."

Dec. 21, 1934
Filming begins in Hollywood
for northern Michigan police drama

Traverse City residents eagerly anticipated an upcoming movie about police work in their area.

As they learned in a front page article in the *Traverse City Record-Eagle*, shooting for the drama "Car 99" began on a Hollywood lot on Dec, 21, 1934, but much of the action would take place in their town.

"Thirty troopers of the Michigan State Police, in tailored uniforms which would be the envy of the crew at East Lansing, went into action this week on the Paramount lot here, as Director Charles Barton began the screening of 'Car 99,' the first picture based on the activities of Michigan troopers," the article explained.

With actual shooting set to begin, the film was supposed to take four to five weeks.

The movie was based on articles written in the *Saturday Evening Post* by Karl Detzer. Most of the action was set around Traverse City and a fictional village named Pine River.

The story also took some liberties with Michigan geography. There was a scene in which a trooper left East Lansing on a motorcycle and arrived in Houghton Lake thirty minutes later.

The cast of the movie included such stars as Fred MacMurray, Sir Guy Standing, Frank Craven, Nora Cecil, William Frawley, Ann Sheridan and Marina Schubert.

After the movie was quickly shot, edited and released, the *New York Times* published a review calling it one of the most thrilling films made in Hollywood.

The story centered on a manhunt for a sophisticated professor, who was also a bank robber.

"The chase scenes alone are enough to keep an average audience in a state of breathless excitement, but the picture possesses, also, a fund of comedy and sufficient heart interest to placate the feminine filmgoers," the reviewer wrote.

However, the movie was not destined to become a classic. Although it was based on articles about real police work, the plot featured illogical twists, such as when the mastermind professor disabled the Michigan State Police radios, requiring officers from Massachusetts to come to their aid.

Detzer, who also wrote the screenplay for the movie, kept his ties to northern Michigan.

Detzer bought the *Leelanau Enterprise* in 1948, which he owned briefly. He was buried in Leelanau County after his death in 1987.

Dec. 22, 1762
Fire at the Sault

After the French and Indian War, Alexander Henry became one of the first residents of Sault Ste. Marie.

Henry soon learned the challenge Michigan offered as a place to live, especially northern Michigan – and particularly in the winter.

He spent his first in Michilimackinac and his second at the Sault, where he befriended the French settlement's commandant, Jean Baptiste Cadotte, a prominent fur trader.

Cadotte had married the daughter of an influential Ojibwa chief and learned to speak the native language, an extremely useful skill in the fur trade.

Henry saw the advantages and wanted to learn the language, too. Following in his friend's footsteps, he settled into the Sault for the winter.

In preparation for winter, he set out and caught some 500 whitefish. They were frozen and strung up on a pole for drying.

But on the morning of Dec. 22, 1762, Henry awoke to find most of the buildings in the small settlement on fire.

Henry broke the bedroom window of Cadotte's house and saved the commandant. He also managed to save a small amount of gunpowder before the rest of the supply exploded in the fire, but the stores of food for the winter were destroyed.

To prevent starvation, an expedition quickly was organized to travel to Michilimackinac for help. Fortunately it was a mild December and the party was able to reach its destination by the end of the month.

The following day, the Straits froze and navigation became impossible. In Sault Ste. Marie, Cadotte, Henry and the remaining residents took shelter in one remaining building, hunting and fishing in order to survive.

Small game could be found in the woods and Henry learned the Indian art of spearing trout through the ice. The inhabitants survived into February when they determined the ice was solid enough to walk down the St. Mary's River to Michilimackinac.

Cadotte, Henry, two Indians and two voyageurs took a portion of what little food was left and made their way by snowshoe. After seven days the party made it to Detour, the halfway point, where, to their horror, they found Lake Huron remained unfrozen.

The party was stranded and the trip had been difficult for Cadotte. It was decided that the Indians and voyageurs, who could travel more quickly than Cadotte and Henry, would go back to the Sault for more supplies.

Cadotte and Henry hunkered down and waited four days for the Indians and voyageurs to make the trip to the Sault and back.

As the expedition progressed further toward Michilimackinac, Cadotte's feet became blistered by the snowshoes. Progress slowed and the threat of starvation returned.

Henry left Cadotte with one of the voyageurs and made his way to the fort at Michilimackinac in a day. The next day a contingent of soldiers made it to the spot where Cadotte lay immobile, arriving just in time to rescue him.

After a journey between the Sault and the Straits that had lasted nine days, Cadotte and Henry were finally safe.

Henry returned to the Sault later that winter to find the remaining settlers had survived on a diet of maple sugar.

Dec. 23, 1843
Alphadelphia founded

In 1843 a group of Americans led by Dr. Henry R. Schetterly arrived in Kalamazoo, intent upon establishing a Utopian commune.

They were interested in the philosophy of Plato and Thomas Moore and their views on the common ownership of property.

It was an idyllic vision – families would live together in harmony and share in collective prosperity through common work .

The Alphadelphia Association began in Jackson County, when 56 men convened to draft a constitution to govern a Utopian community. Days later, on Dec. 23, 1843, Schetterly and a committee arrived at a section of land that struck them as perfect for their enterprise.

The land encompassed a quarter of Comstock Township, in Kalamazoo County, and offered fertile farmland, stone and lumber for building materials, and the Kalamazoo River, which offered water and power.

The community founders set out first to build a headquarters for Alphadelphia, which means first brotherhood. The two-story building was completed in the fall of 1844 and measured 20 by 200 feet.

The constitution of the commune provided that no member would be forced to worship any particular religion, although most of the members were Universalists. It also required the community to take care of the sick and elderly.

Membership quickly exceeded 300 with families building their own homes on the vast stretch of land. Members agreed to contribute their own skills to the common effort, whether they were a farmer, a mechanic, a builder, a manufacturer, a printer, a tailor or a teamster. One member contributed a sawmill to the cause.

The Alphadelphians were also were successful in convincing many Kalamazoo County pioneers to join them.

The experiment lasted only four years.

An early 20th newspaper blamed the failure on the laziness of community members – many believed that once they were part of a commune they no longer needed to work hard to ensure his well-being.

Others believe the society foundered because of rifts among members who resented the contributions of others compared to their own.

The land was sold to Kalamazoo County in 1848 after the venture failed.

Schetterly remained committed to the notion of Utopianism and attempted to join two other communes after Alphadelphia failed.

He finally moved to Grand Traverse County, where he took charge of the Grand Traverse Bay lighthouse.

Dec. 24, 1913
The Italian Hall disaster

Tension was high in Calumet as Christmas approached in 1913.

A strike had been called in Copper Country that July and the strife between striking workers and mine managers had already turned violent.

Strike organizer Big Annie Clemenc was among the women who helped organize a children's Christmas pageant in a year that otherwise looked like it would offer little cheer over the holidays.

The party took place on Christmas Eve and saw several hundred striking miners and their families pack into the Italian Hall.

Sometime during the performance, someone yelled "fire!" inside the building, causing a stampede from the second floor to the hall's single exit.

Seventy-two people were crushed and killed in the stampede, most of them children.

The mystery of who yelled "fire!" has never been resolved, although the strikers believed it was an anti-union agitator working for the mine companies. According to accounts sympathetic to the mine companies, it was a striking worker who caused the disaster to generate support for the union.

Witnesses gave many conflicting accounts and many varying descriptions of the person who instigated the mad rush from the building.

The Western Federation of Miners, the striking union, blamed the Citizens Alliance, an organization founded by the mine bosses to oppose the strike.

After the disaster, which made headlines across the country, the Citizens Alliance offered financial aid to the grieving families, but it also wanted a statement from the Western Federation exonerating it of responsibility for the cataclysm.

Charles Moyer, the union boss, refused, instead ratcheting up his anti-mine rhetoric with charges that the companies were responsible.

While at his hotel in Hancock soon after the disaster, Moyer was shot, kidnapped, put on a train to Milwaukee and told never to return.

Some accounts claim it was the mine bosses who arranged the assault on Moyer because he inflamed the strikers' belief that they were responsible for the tragedy. Others claim Moyer was forced out of town by vigilantes enraged at Moyer's refusal to take aid from the Citizens Alliance.

The Italian Hall in Calumet was demolished in 1984, although a state historical marker was erected where the building once stood.

Dec. 25, 1911
Death of Chief David Shoppenagon

David Shoppenagon, by some estimates, was 103 when he died on Christmas Day, 1911.

A Chippewa Indian who was born in an Indian village in what became Saginaw, Shoppenagon defied the forces of the 19th century that put most of his tribe onto reservations, making them adapt to European customs.

In the mid-1800s, when most of his tribe moved onto a reservation in Isabella County, Shoppenagon remained in the Saginaw valley where he continued to hunt and fish for survival. His wife, Irene, earned extra income by weaving and selling artistic ash splint baskets. Shoppenagon used tribal skills handed down for generations to make finely crafted canoe paddles and snowshoes which he sold.

Shoppenagon also became a famous a guide for whites who wanted help hunting and fishing in the Michigan wilderness

The Indian and his family finally were forced to move after an explosion in the number of white settlers to Saginaw brought more industry and destroyed the wilderness that Shoppenagon depended on for his livelihood.

In 1876 he moved his family to a wigwam on the banks of the Au Sable River near Grayling.

Moving to the northern wilderness rather than to the reservation near Mt. Pleasant enabled Shoppenagon to continue living a life in the model of Indian traditions while avoiding government meddling.

Shoppenagon was able to continue his life as a hunting and fishing guide in Grayling where he was hired by many wealthy white sportsmen.

Shoppenagon's success in hunting bear made him a local celebrity whose exploits were frequently recounted on the front pages of the *Crawford Avalanche*.

Shoppenagon also profited from the northern Michigan lumber industry. He acted as a scout for a company and helped them find the most valuable stands of pine. In exchange, Shoppenagon earned a lifelong pension and was provided the lumber needed to build a wooden house on the banks of the Au Sable.

It is unclear that Shoppenagon was ever actually an Indian chief. He may have come to be thought of as a tribal chief through the marketing of the lumber company, which described their spokesman as a Chippewa chief.

Crawford County's weekly newspaper ran an obituary after Shoppenagon died that described the elderly man as a still active outdoorsman who had taken a hunting trip into the woods that lasted for weeks within two years of his death.

Dec. 26, 1900
New York Times disses Michigan in general, Benzie County in particular

A skull and other items of historical significance were supposedly discovered by Ann Arbor Railroad workers who were digging in Frankfort, in Benzie County.

The discovery of the skull was said to lend credibility to Frankfort's claim that Father Marquette died on its shore on his famous exploration through the Great Lakes.

Frankfort had been, and remains, in a long-time feud with Ludington over which Lake Michigan town can lay claim to the place where Marquette died.

That a skull was discovered in Frankfort around 1900 did not mesh with the well-established account of what happened to Marquette after his death.

It was believed that some time after his death his body was exhumed by Indians from its grave on the Lake Michigan shore and taken for burial to St. Ignace, where Marquette had founded a mission.

The controversy was enough for the *New York Times* to weigh in from the newspaper's faraway editorial offices.

The newspaper noted that the mystery of the location of his body was solved to some satisfaction in 1877 and that "real estate speculators" must be behind any attempt by Frankfort to reassert its claim to the famous French priest.

"While cordially sympathetic with their desire to make the metropolis of Benzie County interesting, and while thoroughly agreeing with what we take to be their belief that the grave of Pere Marquette would be about the most interesting possession a Michigan town can hope to have, we must confess to serious doubt as to the authenticity of their find," the *Times* editorial page said in Dec. 26, 1900.

The New York writers went on to dispute that Marquette was buried in Frankfort, contending he was buried in St. Ignace. (It is commonly believed that Marquette died in either Frankfort or Ludington, was buried near the shore of Lake Michigan, and his remains were later disinterred and moved to St. Ignace. See May 18.)

"Still, the Michigan Historical Society ought to know more about the subject than we do, and if, as reported, its members support the claims of Frankfort's antiquarians, of course that goes far toward upsetting received theories and establishing new ones."

The newspaper concluded its opinion piece saying that Marquette was too good a man to have his remains fought over for the purpose of boosting tourist revenue:

"Anyway," the account continued, "there should be no quarrel over Pere Marquette's bones. He was a man of peace, notable in his day and in many later days, because he helped instead of harmed the Indians, and neither killed them nor was killed by them. Explorers of that sort are rare."

Dec. 27, 1821
First executions in Michigan territory

Two Indians, Ketaukah and Kewaubis, were hanged in Detroit on Dec. 27, 1821, the first people to be executed in the territory of Michigan after American rule was established.

Ketaukah was accused of murdering Dr. William S. Madison and Kewaubis was accused of murdering Charles Ulrich.

When the courts discovered that a technicality would prevent the conviction of the men, the territorial legislature was convened by Detroit judges and the law was changed so that the trials could proceed to their desired conclusion. This *ex post facto* lawmaking is now unconstitutional.

The attorney for one of the defendants found it almost impossible to represent his client, who readily admitted to committing the murder.

Ketaukah, supposedly told his lawyer that he saw the doctor walking and thought he would like to shoot him.

The lawyer attempted to persuade the defendant to say something to mitigate his story, suggesting that perhaps he was aiming at something else and the shooting was an accident.

The Indian caught on and said that he was shooting at a bird.

When asked how far the bird was from the doctor, the Indian replied that the bird was about an inch from his head.

The lawyer is said to have then given up on mounting a serious defense for Ketaukah, who promptly was sentenced to death.

Michigan became first state to outlaw the death penalty in 1864.

Dec. 28, 1973
Mayor Coleman Young takes office early;
issues warning to suburbs

Detroit's first black mayor took the oath of office four days early amid only a handful of supporters, on Dec. 28, 1973.

The city charter required Coleman Young to be sworn in on Jan. 1, but Young did not want to bother with a ceremony on the holiday.

During the ceremony, Young set the tone for what would be a rocky relationship with Detroit's suburbs. He made a statement that was interpreted much differently inside Detroit versus outside Detroit.

The flamboyant and well-spoken mayor said, "I issue an open warning to all dope pushers, to rip-off artists, to all muggers. It is time to leave Detroit. Hit Eight Mile Road. And I don't give a damn if they are black or white, if they wear Superfly suits or blue uniforms with silver badges. Hit the road."

Detroiters took Young's comments merely to mean that the mayor would be tough on crime. Residents of the suburbs heard an invitation for criminals to practice their work in the suburbs.

Dec. 29, 1957
The curse of Bobby Layne

The Detroit Lions first played in Detroit in 1934, when professional football was not greatly popular.

Three other professional teams had tried and failed in Detroit by the time the Lions came along. Before the Lions there were the Detroit Heralds, the Detroit Panthers and the Detroit Wolverines.

The Lions formed from a National Football League franchise from Portsmouth, Ohio called the Spartans. It was purchased by a radio executive for just under $8,000, renamed and moved to Detroit, where the team played at the University of Detroit stadium for crowds that averaged around 16,000 people.

The Lions were hot from the start, winning their first championship in 1935. (See Dec. 15)

By the 1950s, the Lions dominated the NFL, winning four division titles and three championships. Under coach Buddy Parker, the Lions won back-to-back championships in 1952-53, beating Cleveland both times.

During its greatest period the team was led by quarterback Bobby Layne, who in addition to bringing championships to Detroit, also made the cover of *Time* magazine. He was credited with bringing greater popularity to the NFL, which for years had languished behind college football with fans.

Coach George Wilson brought the Lions their last title, which they won on Dec. 29, 1957.

The game was played in Briggs Stadium, before a crowd of 55,263 who watched the Lions beat the Cleveland Browns 59-14.

Star quarterback Bobby Layne missed the game due to a broken ankle. Tobin Rote took his place.

After that season the Lions traded Layne, thinking he was past his prime.

Layne was so upset about the trade he is supposed to have said, as he was leaving Detroit for Pittsburgh, "The Lions will not win for 50 years. "

If Bobby Layne did curse the Lions, it worked.

William Clay Ford bought the team in 1964 for $4.5 million and the team has won just one playoff game since. The team has not returned to a championship game in more than 50 seasons.

Dec. 29, 1902
The birth of professional hockey

The opening of the Amphidrome in Houghton marked a new era in hockey. The arena hosted its first game on Dec. 29, 1902, when Portage Lake beat the University of Toronto, 13-2.

Hockey took off in the Keweenaw and, by the following year, the Portage Lake Hockey Club became the first in the world to pay all of its players.

In 1904, the team beat the Montreal Wanderers on home ice for what was billed as the first world championship of hockey.

Later that same year, Houghton businessman James Dee and dentist John "Doc" Gibson, an Ontario native and former hockey player, organized the world's first professional hockey league.

The league was comprised of teams from Houghton, Calumet, Sault Ste. Marie, Michigan, Sault Ste. Marie, Ontario, and Pittsburgh.

The league only lasted three seasons. The National Hockey League was formed in 1917.

Dec. 30, 1934
Del Shannon born

Born Charles Weedon Westover in Grand Rapids, Del Shannon emerged to pop stardom in the early 1960s. He grew up in the small farming town of Coopersville between Grand Rapids and Muskegon. Shannon learned to play the ukulele from his mother as a child and played guitar at age 14.

After a stint in the army, Shannon moved to Battle Creek, where he sold carpet by day and attempted to make a name for himself in music under his stage name at night. After two years of performing in small-time clubs, Shannon was discovered by a deejay who helped him get a record contract. Soon Shannon recorded his song "The Runaway" and he had a smash hit.

In his first year he scored four Top 40 hits. Shannon's music was popular in Britain in the early 1960s and while on trip there he met the Beatles. He was impressed with one of their songs, "From Me to You," and he recorded it. It became a hit in the U.S., the first song to make the charts in America written by John Lennon and

Paul McCartney.

Shannon continued to record songs and perform until he committed suicide on Feb. 8, 1990.

Dec. 30, 1936
UAW strikes General Motors

The United Auto Workers organized in 1935 and its leadership decided to go after the largest automaker first.

To obtain union recognition at General Motors, the union struck at what was then GM's heart – Flint.

The sit-down strike begin on Dec. 30, 1936, after a rumor circulated among workers at the Fisher Body Plant No. 1 that production of dies had been shipped to other cities where unions had less influence. When the workers stopped working and sat down at their machines, they began what would become the most important strike in American history.

The strike spread throughout the General Motors' organization and soon plants in 14 states were idle.

The workers staged a sit-down strike instead of a walk-out to ensure that the company could not hire replacement workers during the strike.

The union wanted better pay and working conditions. In the wake of the Great Depression, workers enjoyed popular support from the public, who believed those at the very top of society were enriching themselves at the expense of regular people.

But shutting down the largest manufacturer of cars in the world and essentially taking over one of its factories prompted swift retaliation from General Motors and its president, Arthur P. Sloan Jr. At the outset, the company would not entertain discussions with the union.

Within days, the company had convinced Flint Judge Edward S. Black to issue an injunction that directed the county sheriff to remove the striking workers from the plant.

General Motors may have been on the way to getting what it wanted, but the move proved to be embarrassing – it turned out that Black was a substantial GM shareholder.

The order nonetheless led to a melee between deputies and striking workers when the sheriff attempted to prevent food from being delivered into the plant. The fight left 12 policemen and 16 strikers injured.

General Motors next focused on calling in the National Guard to remove the sit-down strikers from its plant.

Governor Frank Murphy resisted the request, fearing that sending the military into the factory could lead to bloodshed and lead to strife between workers and management that would undermine the state for years to come.

He mobilized the National Guard but ordered them to Flint to preserve peace, refusing to send them into the factory to remove the workers.

The strike was resolved after President Franklin D. Roosevelt insisted that General Motors meet with the union. The company agreed to recognize the UAW at the 17 plants that had been shut down by the strike. Among some of the concessions the workers won were a 5 percent pay hike and the right to speak in the lunchroom. (See Feb. 1)

Dec. 31, 1958
Michigan's first year with no diphtheria deaths

As recently as 1921, Michigan had the highest death rate caused by diphtheria anywhere in the world, with 318.9 cases and 25.2 deaths per 100,000 residents. Diphtheria is an infectious disease of the upper respiratory system that is especially deadly for children.

That year the state legislature approved the distribution of biological products produced by the state health department to fight the disease. After the state health department began to distribute diphtheria toxoid and antitoxin through doctors, the disease became almost nonexistent until 1958, when there were no cases reported.

That year the state health department also reported there had been no deaths from scarlet fever, smallpox or typhoid fever. There was just one fatal case of whooping cough.

Dec. 31, 1862
Seventy-one Michiganders killed in Civil War battle

Toward the end of that year, the Union had suffered a terrible loss in the Battle of Fredericksburg. President Abraham Lincoln wanted a military victory to bolster morale just as the Emancipation Proclamation was to go into effect on the first day of the following year.

The Confederates had hunkered down in Tennessee, where they were positioned to protect Chattanooga and rich farmland that was used to feed the Southern army.

General William Rosecrans led the Union Army in Nashville and General Braxton Bragg commanded the Confederates stationed in Murfreesboro, 30 miles away.

Rosecrans was ordered to attack, and the armies planned their strategies after dark on Dec. 30.

During the cold night, army bands on both sides began to play the evening music. Soldiers on both sides could hear the other army's band between tunes. At some point, one of the bands began to play "Home Sweet Home," and soon the other band played the tune as well. For a time, the armies were united in song.

By dawn on Dec. 31, 1862 any goodwill between the sides was gone. They met on what would become known as the Battle of Stones River, one of the deadliest battles in the Civil War.

The Rebel army struck first and inflicted heavy losses on the Union army, but as the day wore on the Northern forces dug in and used the rocky, forested terrain to their advantage.

Three days of vicious fighting ensued and the Union forces prevailed in a pivotal battle in the Union's victory in the Civil War.

In the end, 71 soldiers from Michigan were dead.

Among them were soldiers from the 21st Michigan Infantry, the 11th Michigan Infantry, the 13th Michigan Infantry, the Fourth Michigan Cavalry, the First Michigan Engineers and Mechanics and the First Michigan Artillery Battery, Company A.

Sources

Much of the information in this almanac has been gleaned from a wide-range of Michigan newspapers, available on microfilm.

Other Selected Sources

The Algiers Motel Incident, John Hersey

All Our Yesterdays: A Narrative History of Traverse City and the Region, Larry Wakefield

Annals of Fort Mackinac, Dwight H. Kelton

Boom Copper: The Story of the First U.S. Mining Boom, Angus Murdoch

City in the Forest: The Story of Lansing, Birt Darling

City of Detroit, Clarence Monroe Burton

The City of Flint Grows Up: The Success of an American Community, Carl Crow

Cradle to Grave: Life, Work and Death in the Lake Superior Copper Mines, Larry D. Lankton

Detroit is my Own Home Town, Malcolm W. Bingay

The Detroit Race Riot: A Study in Violence, Robert Shogand and Tom Craig

A Distant Thunder: Michigan in the Civil War, by Richard Bak

The Early History of Michigan: From First Settlement to 1815, E.M. Sheldon

Ernest Hemingway Fished Here: And Other True North Country Tales, Lawrence Wakefield

From Here, I Shall Finish My Voyage! The Last Days of Father Marquette, by Catherine L. Stebbins

George Armstrong Custer, Frederick Samuel Dellenbaugh

A General History of the State of Michigan, Charles Richard Tuttle

Michigan Every Day

Graveyard of the Lakes, Mark L. Thompson

Great Lakes Ships We Remember, Peter J. Van der Linden and John H. Bascomthe

Great Lakes Shipwrecks and Survivals, William Ratigan

Great Wrecks of the Great Lakes, Frederick Stonehouse

A Hanging in Detroit: Stephen Gifford Simmons and the Last Execution Under Michigan Law, David G. Chardavoyne

Historic Women of Michigan: A Sesquicentennial Celebration, Rosalie Riegle Troester

A History of Ann Arbor, Jonathan Marwil

The History of Detroit and Michigan: Or, the Metropolis Illustrated; A Chronological Cyclopedia of the Past and Present, Including a Full Record of Territorial Days in Michigan, and the Annuls of Wayne County, Silas Farmer

History of Detroit and Wayne County and Early Michigan, Silas Farmer

History of Northern Michigan and Its People, Vol.1, Perry F. Powers

Idlewild: The Black Eden of Michigan, Ronald J. Stephens

The Iron Hunter, Chase M. Osborn

Kalamazoo and How it Grew, by Willis F. Dunbar

Keweenaw Shipwrecks, Frederick Stonehouse

Land of Four Flags, Wilbur M. Cunningham

The Making of Michigan, 1820-1860: A Pioneer Anthology, edited by Justin L. Kestenbaum

The Making of a Mining District: Keweenaw Native Copper 1500-1870, David J. Krause

Michigan: A History, Bruce Catton

Michigan: A History of the Wolverine State, Willis F. Dunbar and George S. May

Michigan in Four Centuries, Frederick Clever Bald

Michigan on Fire, Betty Sodders

A Most Superior Land, Like in the Upper Peninsula of Michigan, David Frimodig

The Muskegon: The Majesty and Tragedy of Michigan's Rarest River, Jeff Alexander

The Old Au Sable, Hazen L. Miller

Outlines of the Political History of Michigan, James Valentine

Personal Memoirs of a Residence of Thirty Years with the Indian Tribes on the American Frontiers: With Brief Notices of Passing Events, Facts, and Opinions, A.D. 1812 to A.D. 1842, Henry Rowe Schoolcraft

Pictorial History of Michigan, George S. May

Potawatomi Tears and Petticoat Pioneers, Larry B. Massie

River of Destiny: The Saint Mary's, by Joseph E. and Estelle L. Bayliss in collaboration with Milo M. Quaife

Romance of Muskegon, Alice Prescott Kyes

The Saga of Beaver Island, Margaret Cronyn, John A. Kenney, and Earl W. De La Vergne

Sixties Sandstorm: The Fight Over Establishment of a Sleeping Bear Dunes National Lakeshore, 1961-1970, Brian C. Kalt

So Cold a Sky: Upper Michigan Weather Stories, Karl Bohnak

The Story of Frankfort, John H. Howard

The Story of Grand Rapids, edited by Z.Z. Lydens

Superior Heartland: A Backwoods History, Fred Rydholm

Supper in the Evening: Pioneer Tales of Michigan, Al Barnes

This is Detroit: 1701-2001, Arthur M. Woodford

This is Our Michigan, William Michael James Baird

This Ontonagon Country, The Story of An American Frontier, James K. Jamison

Michigan Every Day

Ticket to Hell: A Saga of Michigan's Bad Men, Roy L. Dodge

The Town That Wouldn't Die: A Photographic History of Alpena Michigan, Robert E. Haltiner and Ann Taber

Understanding Michigan Black Bear: The Truth about Bears and Bear Huntings, Richard P. Smith

Vinegar Pie and Other Tails of the Grand Traverse Region, Al Barnes

Voyages into Michigan's Past, Larry B. Massie

Wanderings: Sketches of Northern Michigan Yesterday and Today, John T. Nevill

William G. Milliken: Michigan's Passionate Moderate, Dave Dempsey